PLANET LAW SCHOOL

For information, please contact:

The Fine Print Press, Ltd.
350 Ward Avenue - Suite 106
Honolulu, Hawaii 96814-4091
http://www.hits.net/~fpp/
E-mail: fpp@hits.net

Cover artwork by Mark Moreno.

ISBN: 1-888960-02-7

Publisher's Cataloging-in-Publication Data

Falcon, Atticus (pseudonym)

    Planet Law School: What You Need to Know (*Before* You Go)...
    but Didn't Know to Ask
  Includes bibliographical references and index.
    1. Law students—United States—Handbooks, manuals, etc.
2. Law—study and teaching—United States. 3. Law Schools—
United States. I. Title.

379 p. (text)   15.24x22.86 cm.

KF283.F181 1998   340.071173   CIP 97-77865

PRINTED IN THE UNITED STATES OF AMERICA
02 01 00 99   10 9 8 7 6 5 4 3

PLANET LAW SCHOOL:

What You Need to Know
(*Before* You Go)
...but Didn't Know to Ask

by

"ATTICUS FALCON," ESQ.

THE FINE PRINT PRESS, LTD.
Honolulu, Hawaii

Acknowledgments:
Previously Published Material

Planet Law School includes previously published material. Permission to reprint has been granted and is gratefully acknowledged for the following:

Anarchy and Elegance: Confessions of a Journalist at Yale Law School, by Chris Goodrich. Copyright © 1991 by Chris Goodrich. Excerpts used by permission of the author.

Excerpts from BROKEN CONTRACT: A MEMOIR OF HARVARD LAW SCHOOL by Richard D. Kahlenberg. Copyright © 1992 by Richard D. Kahlenberg. Reprinted by permission of Hill & Wang, a division of Farrar, Straus & Giroux, Inc..

Excerpts from ONE L by Scott Turow. Copyright © 1977 by Scott Turow. Reprinted by permission of Farrar, Straus & Giroux, Inc..

Running from the Law: Why Good Lawyers are Getting Out of the Profession, by Deborah L. Arron. Copyright © 1991 by Deborah L. Arron. Excerpts used by permission of the author.

Slaying the Law School Dragon: A Primer on How to Survive and Combat Law School Intimidation (original edition), by George J. Roth. Copyright © 1980 by George J. Roth. Used by permission of John Wiley & Sons, Inc..

The Soul of the Law by Benjamin Sells. Copyright © Benjamin L. Sells 1994. Used by permission of ELEMENT BOOKS, INC.

Table
of
Contents

PLANET

What You Need to Know (*Before*

LAW SCHOOL

You Go)...but Didn't Know to Ask

Planet Law School

Dedicated
to
Mom & Dad

—for Reasons They Know
Only Too Well

Opening Statement

Why *This* Book

*"...I knew I needed help—somebody, something
to show me the way through."*

Scott Turow, *One L*

Most books on law school are for those who are already in it or are about to enter. Those books are short. That's because, by the time students get their hands on them, they have little time to spare for outside reading. As a result, those books leave out most of what you need to know...including things that can make the difference between merely surviving in law school (or, not surviving) and thriving. *Planet Law School* is a lengthy book, because there's a lot you need to know—and you won't find this information anywhere else.

Perhaps you think this work is too much for you to go through. If so, you better forget about law school—now. Once you're in it (if you go), you will read more in three years than the total of what you've read in your entire previous life. If it's just too much trouble for you to read *this* book, you will have trouble in law school. Period. *Planet Law School* is for self-selective, highly motivated, conscientious students, not mere browsers. Nor is it for readers looking for a quick and easy path to success. (There's no such thing in law school.)

In fact, it's primarily for those who have yet to even *apply* to law school. It's for potential legal eagles who are already looking ahead (one of the marks of a good attorney). To shift metaphors: this book is for those who want to carefully look before they leap, and who want to get the highest marks from the judges if and when they execute the dive.

However, what's in here can prove life-saving for those on the verge of entering, or who've already started...as you will see. Regardless of whether you're in law school, or college—or even still in high school—the *earlier* you read this book, the better.*

> As you will discover (if you go to law school),
> *legal education is unlike any academic experience
> you've ever had before.*

Law school is a world unto itself. Its atmosphere and gravity are *vastly* different from those of Earth. Hence the title of this book. And once you've touched down, you can't radio Ground Control for help, saying "Houston, we've got a problem." Not only will *Planet Law School* be your life-support system: it will help you return to Earth safe and sound.

---

* But if you *are* reading it *long* before you go to law school, please re-read it (and try to follow its recommendations—especially those in chapters 5 and 6) before you enroll.

Says Who?

I've been out of law school less than six years. Like you, I tried to look before I leapt. Like Scott Turow, I'd sought help, "somebody, something to show me the way through." In the months between my own acceptance and enrollment, I'd read all the available books on "How to Do Well in Law School." Yet, within a few weeks after matriculating, I realized they'd all been virtually worthless. Nearly half-a-dozen works about law school have been published since the ones I'd used. When deciding whether or not to write *this* book, I read them all. They're mostly the same old stuff, dealing almost entirely in superficialities. If you, too, read those other books and then go to law school, you will end up agreeing with me.*

I'm not sure why they're unrealistic. For some, perhaps it's because they were written by a committee. Committees are notoriously bland, and like to play it safe. A few were written by law school professors. But as you will see in chapters 3 and 4, law school professors are not about to let the cat out of the bag. One book was written by recent law school graduates. It's an anthology. Each contributor wrote on one aspect of the law school experience. Yet, their accounts are trivial. It was like reading a war novel by someone who'd never been in combat. But they'd *been* there. (In fact, one of them had graduated from the same law school I went to.) So I cannot explain why they left out or glossed over so many important things prospective students need to know. (However, were I to play amateur shrink, I'd say they're "in denial"—a behavior pattern in which someone refuses to acknowledge the reality of a situation, past or present. The extreme version of this is the insane delusion.) At any rate, what those other books have in common is that their analysis of what it takes to make it in law school bears scant resemblance to the truth.

---

* A funny thing happened while the manuscript for this book was in progress: the head of the firm that's publishing *this* book (The Fine Print Press, Ltd.), got a call from a high corporate official at a major publishing firm. He'd heard that *Planet Law School* was in the works, and wanted to buy the title—not the manuscript, just the title. He thought that, all by itself, this title would sell a lot of copies of the book.

During the conversation, the man said his firm's name was so well-respected, and its market penetration was so high, that they could "move" several thousand copies of *anything* for law students. It was just a matter of getting the books onto the store shelves. They weren't concerned about the quality of the books in question, just the profits.

Having read some of their works before I began law school—and more prior to starting on the writing of this book—I completely agree that they're only in it for the money. While I obviously hope that this book sells well, and thus proves to have been worth the effort that went into it, *Planet Law School: What You Need to Know* (Before *You* Go)...but *Didn't Know to Ask* was written largely as a rebuke to the mentality of that other firm (and others like it). It fully intends to live up to its title—and I hope that, for once, future law students will get what they pay for when it comes to a book about law school.

Regardless of who wrote them, those other books give prospective law school students only generalities, not the key specifics. Potential future attorneys aren't told what they need to know to comprehend the law and to do well in law school. Instead, they only get clichés ("take notes," "study a lot"). Such platitudes are useless; sometimes they're harmful.

Here's what I think the problem is: Those who did well in law school assume they're just naturally gifted. So, they figure it's impossible to explain the "true" nature of their success. Those who did *not* do well in law school still don't really understand why, usually. But what both groups have in common is that it's no longer in their interest to go to the time and trouble to think things through, or to do the considerable research that's gone into *this* book. After all, why should they? —They're out of law school, have their ticket (the law license), and as far as they're concerned, their law school experience is water under the bridge. And so, if you go by what they wrote, you're likely to get washed away; not washed *out,* necessarily, but certainly swept into a backwater. (In fact, most law students—and new lawyers, too—circle aimlessly in a fog. Either that, or they rush full-steam ahead... onto the rocks.)

Yet, law school isn't brain surgery or rocket science. In fact, *it's actually quite simple.** However, you're not told, beforehand, how the system works....And by the time you've figured it out on your own (if, indeed, you ever do), it's too late.

This is something the other books don't want to admit, apparently. In this way, they contribute to the "macho mystique" of law school—which flatters the authors, of course. Have you ever listened to the brief interviews that athletes and coaches give before and after a game or other sports event? Notice how they all, always, say the same things in any given situation? They're all working from the same scripts, reciting the same formula for any given occasion. Win big, win small, lose big, lose small, you can predict what anyone will say. And it's a safe bet it has nothing to do with what they're *really* thinking, and saying to one another, when there's no reporter around. Same thing's true of TV and movie stars, and politicians. Attorneys are no different. —Nor are the books they write about "what to expect in law the school—and how to succeed." I (and many others) took them at face value before starting law school. Don't you do that.

I attended one of the most reputable law schools in the country. I'm not revealing its name, for the same reason that I've written this book under a pseudonym: there would be Hell to pay. (Arab proverb: "He who would tell the truth must have one foot in the stirrup.") I guess you'll just have to take my word for it that my legal alma mater is ranked within the top dozen of the 200+ law schools in America.

It wasn't Harvard. If you think that the only book worth reading about

---

* But that's not to say it's *easy.*

law school is one written by an HLS alumnus or alumna, reconsider: Roughly 42,000 people start law school each year, but only about 550 of them at Harvard. That's one-and-a-third percent, so *your* chance of enrolling there, all other things being equal (which, granted, they aren't), is approximately one in 76. That's why this book is of more use to you than one written by an HLS grad. (Actually, because nearly all law schools use the same curriculum and methods—copied from the Harvard Law School of more than 125 years ago—it makes almost no difference where I went, or where you'll go, in terms of what it's like.)

My (real) name is not well-known, even in the courthouse of the city where I practice. For that reason, too, you might dismiss this book. If so, then too you would be making a mistake. I assume you will read this book, if you do read it, because you want to avoid mistakes. (As the sage put it, "Mistakes are often stepping stones to failure.") I, not having a great reputation to protect, can easily afford to tell you the truth about law school (and a little about the practice of law). This book will help you to avoid mistakes, both major and minor. "Even a *fool* can learn from his *own* mistakes. A *wise* man learns from the mistakes of *others." Planet Law School* will help you go into law school with the same sort of "inside knowledge" that normally only comes with experience.

This book is not the idiosyncratic commentary of a unique individual, however. On the contrary, it quotes from several books by other lawyers. Unlike this one, theirs were not specifically written for prospective law school students. And unlike the "How to Do Well in Law School" guides, these other writers are often caustic. Yet, they too are graduates of some of the finest law schools in the country, who went on to successful careers.

It's significant that there's a big gap between the reality described by most books for prospective (or current) law students, and the reality described by those writing for other audiences. Both tell the truth. But those written for potential law students tell only a small part of the truth, the least important truths.

This book is different.

Of Good News & Bad News

It's easier to get into law school now than at any time in a long time. As the Baby Boom generation headed for law school in droves, the schools increased the size of their entering classes, and many new law schools opened for business. In 1963, there were 135 ABA-licensed law schools, with just under 21,000 first-year students. Over the next three decades or so, the number of officially approved law schools increased by one-third, and total enrollment more than doubled. And now that the ABA has eased its constraints on law school accreditation, several previously unaccredited law schools will likely soon be "legitimate."

Further, in recent years, while the number of available slots has steadily grown, the number of applicants has steadily *shrunk*. For the 1990-91 academic year, 94,000 would-be lawyers filed a total of 450,500 applications to law schools. Since then, the number of applicants, compared to the previous year, has declined an average of 4.5% *each year*. This is a dramatic reduction. It has almost become what economists call a "buyer's market"—an increasing supply combined with a decreasing demand. The competition to become a lawyer has loosened up.

However, regardless of the size of the graduating class each year, the number of *jobs—good* jobs—for new lawyers has held rather constant. (In the go-go '80s there was an over-expansion. In the early '90s came the correction, a huge contraction. In the late '90s, things are back to normal.) As a general rule, the best offers in the Law are reserved only for those who meet two criteria: 1) they went to the "good" schools—the "national" ones, and preferably just the top dozen or so; and 2) they were in the top 10% of the class.

There are exceptions, of course. Virtually *everyone* who graduates from Harvard, Yale, Stanford, etc., finds a fairly decent job, in terms of salary, prestige, and so forth, regardless of their class standing. And there are those who graduate from "no-name" schools who manage to do quite well, immediately. But in general, the rule holds: If you don't go to a good school, or if you aren't in the top 10% regardless of where you go to law school, the odds are heavily against you.

It behooves you to move to the head of your law school class ASAP—or else have some other way to give yourself an edge. In law school, it's not enough just to endure: you must *prevail*. So, if you don't intend to head for the top, you should seriously consider not heading for law school at all.

However, *intending* to get to the top of the academic heap and actually *getting* there are two different things. It's an intensely competitive game, particularly now, both in law school (especially your first year) and out (especially your first year). *Planet Law School* shows where the traps are set for the unwary.

Even if you already know the score regarding law school and the real world of the Law, this book can help you. There are tricks of the trade, in any trade. And in a sense the role of law school student is itself a trade. It is certainly a full-time job. (That is one of the few things the other books got right.) You're going to have to work hard, no matter what. But hard work by itself doesn't guarantee success—not in law school, and not in life. In fact, for those who think that way, hard work is sometimes counter-productive.

It isn't enough to work hard. Nor is it enough to *be* smart. You have to "work smart," too: acquire a sense of what's important, what's not; set your priorities. This is especially so that all-important first year of law school. You can't know *everything*—but you *can* know what really *counts*...because this book tells you.

Know Thyself

We've all said, from time to time, "If I'd only known then what I know now." Likewise, we've all heard of, or talked with (and *are*) people who muse about "If I'd done this," or "If I hadn't done that," or who tried something because "That's the only way I could find out if it was right for me."

As Omar Khayyam put it in the *Rubaiyat* (F. Scott Fitzgerald's rendering):

> *The Moving Finger writes, and having writ, moves on.*
> *Nor all your wit nor piety shall lure it back to cancel half a line,*
> *Nor all your tears wash out a word of it.*

That's true of life itself, of course. But it's especially true of law school. Life is about options and taking responsibility for our actions (and inactions). Unfortunately, we must always make our decisions based only on imperfect knowledge. Even so, there are different degrees of imperfection. And there are different *kinds* of knowledge; some are more useful, at particular times, than others.

As the man says, "You pays yo' money and you takes yo' choice." This book will help you to avoid buying a (very expensive) pig in a poke. After reading it, you'll have a much better idea of what's inside the poke. Law can be a good way of bringing home the bacon. But this particular porcine investment might not be right for *you*. And even if it is, without this book you'll probably start out feeling as though you're trying to catch a greased pig as you pursue the Law.

It's vital not to get caught up in the madness and the cynicism, recovering your mental balance (if ever) only when it's too late. If, after reading this book, it turns out that—for you—law school should be "the road *not* taken," you won't have to spend the rest of your life second-guessing yourself about it. And if you do choose a life in the Law, you will enter it with the wisdom of foresight. With realistic expectations, you'll avoid (most of) the culture shock of law school. It doesn't have to be a panic-stricken Hell. And if you *do* go, I hope you'll eventually be glad you did. *I* am...although at times as you read this book you might find that *very* hard to believe.

—In fact, you might even end up as one of the few exceptions to the rule: someone who actually *enjoys* law school.

Which Side are You on?

"Knowledge is power," so they say. Law is about power. Law is also the main determinant of who gets (and gets to keep) money, and how much; and money is certainly power. To use a current buzzword, this book will help you to "empower" yourself to outperform the competition. It will show you how to learn what you need to know, procedurally—but more important, substantively—regarding the Law. That, all by itself, will put you ahead of

90% of your classmates, and even of 90% of your fellow attorneys fresh out of law school. And as you will discover, that in turn gives you even more freedom of choice—a form of personal power.

No doubt, some who have read this far are worried that this is a book on how to be a "tough guy," to obliterate one's rivals. If so, please do *not* get the idea that law school and the practice of law are *not* for you. I can get tough, when the occasion calls for it. You can too. It *is* a jungle "out there" (the practice of law) and "in" there (law school). Sometimes it really is "Kill or be killed, eat or be eaten"—especially with a trial, which has only one winner (at least, officially). Even in a "transactions practice," it's often a zero-sum game. It's also dog-eat-dog at exam time in law school, if you're somewhere that uses a forced curve. But even though it's a jungle, that doesn't mean we have to act like vicious beasts when dealing with our fellow law students (or fellow attorneys).

I had hesitated to go into the Law because, given what I'd seen of how attorneys operate, I was afraid of gaining the world only to lose my soul. It hadn't occurred to me that I might lose *both,* which is what nearly happened when I was in law school.

It didn't have to be that way. And it doesn't have to be that way for you... if, indeed, you care about such things. Unfortunately, this book will benefit the future demons of the Law as well as the future angels. That can't be helped. (Don't get me wrong: I'm no angel, and don't even aspire to sainthood. I like to think, though, that I'm closer to that end of the spectrum than the other.) The good guys—and gals—who read this book can use what's in here to (sometimes) beat the bad guys—and gals—without sacrificing your probity.

However, you (probably) can't "beat the system." But you *can* keep the (law school) "system" from beating *you*. That, in itself, is a major victory. With *Planet Law School,* you will win this battle, and thereby position yourself to more easily triumph in your future struggles.

Now I invite you to read on...

"Atticus Falcon"
Member of the Bar
State of Flux

"Law Day,* USA," 1998

---

* May 1 - A date chosen by the American Bar Association (in 1958, when the Cold War was going strong) to coincide with the socialist-communist world's annual May 1 glorification of the"workers," and to contrast the "Rule of Law" with the "dictatorship of the proletariat."

ADDENDUM*
For THOSE WHO WILL *NOT* be
FULL-TIME LAW STUDENTS

This book was written for prospective full-time law school students. However, if you're thinking of going to night school instead, nearly all of what's here is still valid for you. —In fact, whereas for a full-time student this book will "only" mean the difference between surviving and *thriving,* for those who are juggling a full-time *job* and part-time evening classes it could mean the difference between "life" and "death."

Also, there are eight states left—including California and New York—that do not require you to have a law degree to sit for those states' bar exams. (See the addendum to chapter 24.) However, that path is probably even more difficult than night school. *Planet Law School* can't lighten your load, but it *can* make that load a whole lot more manageable. This is especially true when it comes to bar exam preparation (see chapters 17 and 18) when you haven't attended law school.

If you choose either of these alternatives to a full-time program, I wish you well...and good luck: You'll need it, even with this book. The odds are heavily against you. But *Planet Law School* can certainly help you to cut them down.

* "P.S."

Part I:

Landing in a Strange, Little World

Chapter 1 - Courses

The degree that most future attorneys get is the "J.D.". That stands for "Juris Doctor" or "Doctor of Jurisprudence," depending on the school. (Decades ago, the basic law degree was the "LL.B.", "Bachelor of Law.")

Law school isn't like high school or college, where one credit and one year counts as much as another. It's the *first-year* law school grades that determine your future, both within law school and in terms of your job prospects. (You'll see why, later.) First-year is *everything*. Pulling your grades up later is (usually) too little, too late.

First-year courses are of two kinds:

1. The ones that count (now).
2. The ones that don't.

By "the ones that count (now)," I mean the ones that are graded other than pass/fail. (If none of your first-year courses is graded on a pass/fail basis, the ones that count are those used to compute your first-year gpa and class standing. These are what (usually) determine whether or not you Make Law Review after year one, and whether or not you get Prestigious Summer Clerkships. (Chapter 12 discusses both.) These things, in turn, are (almost always) the key determinants of your job options as you approach graduation. Yet, ironically, it's the courses that *don't* count (now) that can make or break your career in the Law.

There is no "Introduction to the Law" course for first-year students, no course in "The Western Legal Tradition." You'll immediately find yourself in the thick of things—with assignments to prepare for your very first day of classes. Ironically, if you want an Introduction to the Law or to the Western Legal Tradition, you better get it before you go to law school (see chapter 23). Otherwise, you'll have to wait until the dust settles from your first year. Even then, such courses are only electives—if they're offered at all—and you might have a schedule conflict with something that, given your hopes for a career, is a must-take.

Virtually all first-year courses are required, and cannot be deferred. Some are year-long, others one semester. Contracts and Civil Procedure last a year. Criminal Law is one semester. Property, Torts, and Constitutional Law can go either way, depending on the school. (Some schools, including Harvard, have recently made Constitutional Law an elective.)

That is the nearly universal first-year curriculum, along with Legal Research and Legal Writing.

Perhaps you are now expecting a survey of each. If you got that, here's what just two of them would cover:

Property: Seisin; Freehold v. Non-Freehold Estates; Absolute v. Qualified (a/k/a Defeasible) Estates—including Fee Simple Determinable, Fee Simple on Condition Subsequent, and Fee Simple on Executory Limitation; Present Possessory v. Future Interests—including Vested Remainders, Vested Remainders Subject to Divestment, Vested Remainders Subject to Open, Contingent Remainders, Springing Executory Interests, Shifting Executory Interests, the Rule Against Perpetuities, the Rule of Convenience, the Rule in Shelly's Case, the Rule in Clobberie's Case, and the Doctrine of Worthier Title; Concurrent Estates—including Joint Tenancy, Tenancy in Common, and Tenancy of the Entirety; Equitable Interests in Land; Rights Incident to Possession—including the Rights of Lateral and Sub-Adjacent Support; Fixtures; Easements—including Appurtenant Easements v. Easements in Gross, Quasi-Easements, and Easements by Prescription, Necessity, and Express Reservation; Profits—including Mesne Profits, *Profit à Prendre,* and the Doctrine of Emblements; Covenants Running with the Land at Law (including Vertical and Horizontal Privity) v. Equitable Servitudes; Present v. Future Covenants of Title; the Doctrine of Shelter, the Equity of Redemption, and the Doctrine of Equitable Conversion; Race v. Notice v. Race/Notice Recording Systems; and Usufructory v. Proprietary Rights...among other things.

Contracts: Offer and Acceptance, Bargained-for Legal Detriment, and Aleatory Contracts; Unilateral v. Bilateral Contracts; Constructive Conditions; the Statute of Frauds; Merger Clauses and Parol Evidence; Reliance v. Restitution v. Expectancy Interest; Rescission, Repudiation, Anticipatory Breach, and Novation; the Uniform Commercial Code—including the Perfect Tender Rule, Cure, and Replevin—

Enough. Now, do you really want a discussion of these things? Let me guess. Besides, in your first-year courses in these subjects it's highly likely that some—and perhaps many—of the topics listed will not be covered, even though every one of them *ought* to be. Unfortunately, you will hear about many of them for the very first time only during your bar review course, after graduation. Also, right now, it really isn't important for you to read about all these things—as though I could even put them in a nutshell for you. This isn't the book for that. (Yet, I strongly recommend that you find out about them *before you start law school,* to give yourself an edge. —And if you can't wait a minute more to find out how to find out, skip to Chapter 5. Otherwise, proceed.)

Here is just a taste of the Big Six, a/k/a the Dirty Half-Dozen...

The Ones That Count (Now)

1. Property

It might surprise you to learn that "property" is—ultimately—only what the courts are willing to recognize as "property."

Perhaps the easiest example of how this works is distinctive characters in the mass media. When the radio—and movies with sound—were first proliferating, the people who'd developed distinctive characters had no property rights in those characters. Anyone could copy either the voice or the appearance for commercial purposes, without permission and without paying a fee—even if the imitation was meant to take business away from the original. A few decades ago, a new trend started, recognizing the property right. Today, for someone living, it's acknowledged in all jurisdictions. But only in the *very* recent past have courts—and legislative bodies—allowed the right to continue after the person's death. So today, when you see a television commercial with someone who looks and sounds like John Wayne, you know the "Duke's" estate signed a contract allowing the portrayal, for a fee. (Either that, or someone's about to get sued for copyright infringement.)

A thousand years ago the English property system regarding real estate was the same as under communism, of all things: the Sovereign owned it all. The only difference was that the King, rather than the State (or "the People") was the Sovereign. He owned it all by right of conquest, as a result of the Battle of Hastings. To the victor go the spoils. And in 1066, William—as in "The Conqueror"—took title to every building and every piece of land in England. More than half a millennium passed before the law developed to where "a man's home is *his* castle."

You probably won't hear about any of these things in your property course—and perhaps not in your entire career as an attorney. But they're two of the very few things that are interesting in Property, so there you are.

2. Contracts

It might surprise you to learn that a "contract" is—ultimately—only what the courts are willing to recognize as a "contract."

Contracts are made regarding property, whether realty or personalty (the latter being legal jargon for "personal property"). Money is a form of property, and most contracts involve the exchange of money.

Granted, historically, some things have "obviously" been contracts—but not necessarily. For example, say a 15-year-old aspiring rock star signs a contract with a recording company. The deal isn't binding on the kid—but it *is* binding on the recording company. Unless the star agrees to the contract anew upon reaching "the age of majority" (18, now, in most states), he or she is free to walk away from the deal and make a better arrangement elsewhere. Bob Dylan was at one time a very big "folk-rock" star. He was discovered and promoted by John Hammond of Columbia Records in the '60s. At the time, the age of majority, everywhere, was 21. Dylan (actually, Robert Zimmerman) was 20. In gratitude to Hammond, personally, Dylan insisted that even though he was a minor, he would honor the contract he'd made with Columbia. So, after Dylan turned 21, Hammond didn't ask him to sign a new agreement. Sure enough, in his 21st year, Dylan repudiated their deal. First Lesson in Contracts: Sometimes the Liar Wins.

—Or rather, Dylan *tried* to repudiate their deal. Unfortunately for him, the lawyer at what he'd intended would be his new record company was not as good as the lawyer at Columbia Records. Columbia's attorney was the young Clive Davis (who went on to fame and considerable fortune by founding a record company of his own). Davis checked to see if Dylan had continued to use Columbia's studios for recording his music after his 21st birthday. Yes. Ergo, Bingo: through his actions, Dylan had made a "constructive ratification" of the otherwise-voidable contract. Second Lesson in Contracts: it helps to know the law.

3. Torts

It might surprise you to learn that a "tort" is—ultimately—only what the courts are willing to recognize as a "tort."

The word is from the Latin, meaning something like "twist." The term became part of the English legal system when the Normans (French) took over after 1066 (see Property, above). Today, it might be better understood as meaning "screw"—because if there's a tort, it's because someone screwed up.

A tort is "an actionable civil wrong." "Civil" means non-criminal. (With few exceptions, litigation has to be either civil or criminal.) "Wrong" means...wrong, as in "She done him wrong." "Actionable" means—whatever the courts decide, which in practice means you can sue someone for it and maybe win. (You can sue anyone for *anything,* by the way. But that doesn't mean your case won't be tossed out immediately; you might even find yourself being fined by the judge for bringing a frivolous suit. And if what you brought suit for isn't a "cause of action" recognized by the courts, you're probably looking for trouble.)

What's a tort today might not have been a tort yesterday, and vice versa.

First example: A century ago, a previously-unmarried female of "marriageable age" in "respectable society" had to be vitally concerned about her reputation for chastity. If she was not a virgin, and this fact was known, she was said to be "ruined." Then she would have to either a) marry *outside* respectable society, or b) resign herself to becoming an "old maid" (and "old" meant over 25).

So, any man who claimed to have what was euphemistically called "carnal knowledge" of that woman could be sued for slander. If a medical examination proved his alleged lover was in fact still a virgin, the man would have to pay her "damages" for the harm he'd done to her by his remarks (and would himself be excluded from respectable society henceforth).

Originally, though, her adult male relatives—one after another—would have just challenged him to a duel until the man was killed. Trial by combat. If and when he died in a duel, the fact of her virginity was thus re-established and her honor—and marriage prospects—(perhaps) restored. After dueling was outlawed, the woman's only recourse regarding the alleged sexual intercourse was to court, for redress of her alleged undress.

Surprisingly, almost all jurisdictions still have such a law on the books, even if it's only in the case law rather than statutory. But it's rarely a basis for a lawsuit, for obvious reasons.

Second example: A century ago, there was no such thing as casualty insurance—at least, not for ordinary people, and maybe not for anyone. If a man held a dangerous job—as a railroad brakeman, a steel-plant operative, or a construction worker, say—and got injured on the job, there was no system of worker's compensation. And if the injury resulted from unsafe working conditions, the injured employee (by then an injured *ex*-employee) could not successfully sue his employer.

The courts, snugly in the pockets of Big Business, gave three reasons for ruling against him:

(a) the employee "assumed the risk" by taking the job in the first place;

(b) while the *ultimate* cause of the injury was (perhaps) unsafe working conditions, the *immediate* cause was usually the action of a fellow employee—who was just doing what he was supposed to be doing, granted, but accidents do happen; and

(c) —this one's my favorite—to *force* Big Business to provide safe working conditions (by allowing workers to sue for on-the-job injuries) would be to interfere with the Freedom of Contract of both the employer and (prospective) employees...which takes us back to (a).

Today, of course, workers are protected by statute *and* by the ability to sue. (But then again, this protection, in practice, usually only extends to the right to recover damages *after the fact*. Workers' safety in all but a very few industries is still woefully underprotected. —And no, I don't handle this type of litigation, so I'm not grinding my own axe here.)

4. Civil Procedure

It might surprise you to learn that a "civil procedure" is—ultimately—only what the courts are willing to recognize as a "civil procedure."

Granted, Congress and the States can enact codes of procedure, criminal as well as civil. But these given procedures can be invalidated by the courts. Because civil procedure regulates the conduct of litigation itself, the courts usually take the lead in this matter: Judicial Conferences (assemblies of judges) often recommend specific rules to the (other) "law-makers," who then adopt these rules—sometimes with changes.

In your first-year Civil Procedure course you'll study this only at the federal level. You will pore over a mere handful of the Federal Rules of Civil Procedure. But they're easy compared to the case law that pre-dated the

FRCP—and you'll definitely be poring over (and maybe crying over) that. For most first-year students, Civ Pro is a nine-month nightmare. (Surely even the worst pregnancy could not be much worse.)

This is not the place to explain *why* it's a nightmare. You'll just have to take me at my word. (However, chapters 5 and 7 will explain how to *cope* with this course, as with your other first-year subjects.) The following is *not* an example of Civ Pro Hell. In fact, it's baby stuff:

You are a lawyer with a firm in New York City. Your firm represents the American interests of a Mexican multinational corporation headquartered in Monterey. One day, you get a call from there. Seems your client has been sued in a state court in Kansas. Come to find out the president of the company, a Mexican, was on a flight from Mexico City to Taipei, Taiwan, Republic of China. The plane had made a brief stop in Los Angeles. While it was on the ground, a process-server handed the legal papers to the executive. The exec sent the documents back to Mexico by overnight courier after he got to Taiwan. You, of course, immediately have them faxed to New York, with originals to follow by overnight delivery.

Your first questions, though, don't concern the nature of the complaint. Instead, you want to see if you can throw a monkey wrench into the works, to mess up the legal machinery your client's opponent has set in motion. Whose airline was the executive on? If it was Aero Mexico, that plane is regarded as Mexican territory, even while it's on the ground in the States. Therefore, service of process is subject to *Mexican* law, or the Hague Convention on same. You need to find out from your Mexican counterpart what the rules are South of the Border. But what if the president stepped off the plane while it was on the ground? If he entered onto American soil, the other side might have him. —But usually, foreign citizens in transit are restricted to the customs area of U.S. airports. They're not regarded as having officially entered onto American soil…you hope. You need to check that out. It just might be that the service of process was invalid. In that case, your client does not have official notice of the suit. And without giving valid, official notice of suit, the opposition is already in trouble: The due process requirement of the fifth Amendment kicks in—as interpreted by the Supremes.

Then you have a second set of questions. All revolve around this one: Why a Kansas state court? Even without knowing what the dispute is about, you will check to see if you can have this case moved elsewhere. For one thing, you—being a New Yorker—absolutely do not want to set foot in the boondocks, and especially not a Godforsaken place like Kansas. Second, you know perfectly well that whoever filed this suit figured they'd have home court advantage. If it's to be a jury trial, they want the edge of having local folks deciding the case against foreigners. So, you have to check out the Kansas law regarding "forum non conveniens." You invoke this to argue that it's really inconvenient for your client to have to go to Kansas to defend this suit, and it would be more appropriate for the Mexican multinational to be sued elsewhere. You also check out the possibility of "removing" the case to federal court—preferably a federal court in, say, Manhattan.

And so on. It's fun, fun, fun.

If you know your Civil Procedure, you can sometimes nip a problem in the bud. This is especially so if the lawyer for the other side isn't a Civ Pro "pro."

5. Criminal Law

It might surprise you to learn that a "crime" is—ultimately—only what the courts are willing to recognize as a "crime."

Granted, some things have always "obviously" been crimes—but not necessarily. For example, "homicide" is the killing of one human being by another. But homicide is just the name of a fact situation; it isn't a crime in and of itself. Given the right circumstances, though, homicide does indeed become a crime—murder, manslaughter, etc..

Homicide occurring as part of an accident is often no crime—although, quite often, it is a tort ("wrongful death"). And as the O.J. Simpson saga demonstrated, the State can prosecute an alleged act as a crime, and private parties can sometimes also file suit, in tort, against the accused.

Years ago, causing the death of a child within the womb was both a crime and a tort. Believe it or not, it often still is—as long as the person who caused the death is someone other than the woman whose womb the child is in. Example: the "life in being" is to be a substantial beneficiary under a will, but another person will inherit if that life is never born, and that other person deliberately contrives the death of the unborn.*

Take it a step farther: What if there is a fertilized egg—but no womb? Here's the scenario:

a) a young married couple
b) the prospective father had suffered an injury rendering him impotent, but
c) his sperm was capable of fertilizing an egg, so
d) he'd had some removed, surgically.

Add to this:
e) the prospective mother, because of a medical condition of her own, would be putting her life at risk to get pregnant and carry a child to term, but
f) her eggs are intact and fertile, so
g) she had had some eggs removed, surgically, and
h) his sperm had been mixed with her egg, in a test tube, and
i) the fertilized egg—now a conceived human being—was about to be implanted in the womb of a woman who'd been hired to be a surrogate mother.

---

* Regardless of your position on the abortion issue, you see why I'm not using the term "fetus."

Now add to *that:*

j) the prospective mother and father had been told by a moneybags relative that if they had a child, Moneybags would leave his entire—and vast—estate to that child, in his will, but

k) if there were no child, Moneybags would leave his estate to Nasty Nephew, and

l) the will has already been drafted accordingly, and

m) prospective mother and father, and Nasty Nephew, are aware of this.

Finale:

n) Nasty Nephew rushes into the medical facility just after the sperm has been united with the egg in the test tube and knocks it to the floor and stomps on it, destroying the fertilized egg.

Has there been a murder?

Would it make any difference if

o) during the attack, Nasty Nephew also destroyed all the rest of the sperm, and all the rest of the eggs, that had been removed, respectively, from the prospective father and mother, and

p) before further surgery could be scheduled to remove additional sperm and eggs, the couple was killed in an automobile accident?

From the perspective of Crim Law, (p) is irrelevant, and (o) is relevant only on the issue of intent. But has there been a *murder?* —Beats me. I don't practice criminal law. (However, I doubt it: there's probably a threshold test of viability of the fetus.)

6. Constitutional Law

By now, you will surely have noticed the pattern: All of the preceding sections started with the words, "It might surprise you to learn that a _____ is—ultimately—only what the courts are willing to recognize as a _____." That's the way law is in America, because our English legal heritage is of the Common Law. Most countries (France and Japan, for examples) have Civil Law systems. (This is not "civil" as in civil vs. criminal proceedings, mentioned above. In a civil law system, the legislators and bureaucrats make *all* the laws and rules, respectively. The courts have almost no power to do so; nor can they invalidate the laws and rules the others make.)

In our system, in contrast, "interpreting" a law is how judges make new law, and this "case law" is every bit as binding as any statute, ordinance, or regulation. (And if the new "case law" is one made by the U.S. Supreme Court, it's even *more* binding than any of the others.) Hence lawyers and courts are vastly more important in the USA and other common law countries than in civil law nations. However, in recent years American law has moved toward more statutes and regulations, both to reduce the courts' dockets and to reduce the disparity in the common law among the states. (For example, a significant part of Contracts now consists of the Uniform Commercial Code—and there are several more Uniform Codes, on other subjects.) Meanwhile, the civil law countries have moved more toward judicial review—the most important part of the (American) common law.

> *"/W/e are under a Constitution, but the Constitution*
> *is what the judges say it is/./"*
>
> Charles Evans Hughes.

Talk about *power*. Note the implication—a reality that Hughes, as Chief Justice of the U.S. Supreme Court, chose to dissemble. As you know, one uppity judge, all by him- or herself, can nullify the action of all 535 members of both houses of Congress *and* the President, for example. And if five members of the committee of lawyers known as the Supreme Court vote to back that judge up, only a Constitutional Amendment (or a change in the Court's membership to produce a new decision, overturning the earlier one) can cancel the judge's nullification. Con Law is all about the history of what the Supreme Court says the Constitution is—and what it should be.

This brings us to the two *most* important courses in law school. Perversely, they're the two courses law schools regard as *least* important: Legal Research, and Legal Writing. (Sometimes they're combined, as "Legal Methods," "Legal Analysis," "Case Analysis," etc..)

The Courses That "Don't Count" (Now)
—But Which Can Make or Break
Your Career in the Law

The discussion of the Big Six first-year courses emphasized that law changes over time. Sometimes the pace is glacial, sometimes almost hectic. Yet, if and when you practice law, it will be very rare that you will have anything whatsoever to do those changes. This is not meant as an insult to you. It's just the way the Law is, for 99.9% of those who are in it. It's safe to say that will include you. It certainly includes me.

In fact, the *weakest* argument you can make to a court is, "The law ought to be *changed.*" That's tantamount to merely making the child's argument, "It's not fair!" In the loftier language employed by the law, this gets translated into "It's against 'Public Policy,' your Honor." This is a favorite argument of law school students—and is *guaranteed* to get you *low* marks, whether from a professor, a supervising attorney, or a judge. If you can't come up with anything better than the nebulous concept of "fairness" (or "justice"), you lose. (This is not to say that fairness and justice aren't important.

Most judges want to "do the right thing"—even though their idea of what's "right" is sometimes bizarre.) You have to come up with something more substantial than that.

The same is true if your message to the judge, on behalf of your client, boils down simply to *"I'm* all right, Jack" (i.e., you're content with things as they are).

1. Legal Research

Legal research has two purposes. The first is to bring yourself up to speed on a new subject. Because many lawyers specialize, that first purpose for doing legal research is infrequent (except in your first few years of practice). The second purpose is to "find authority" for your position. It isn't much of an exaggeration to say the courts don't care what *you* think; courts only care what other *courts* think, especially higher courts.

"Finding authority" means proving that some court (or, at the very least, a mere legislative body) has already made a law that fits your fact situation enough that the judge/s before whom you're appearing should rule in your favor. At minimum, you want something that's similar ("on point"—not to be confused with going "on point" as a ballet *danseuse*...although, come to think of it, litigation is—sometimes—like a ballet). And if you're real lucky, you'll find something that fits perfectly ("on all fours"). Legal Research shows you how to do that.

However, as part of your research, you will—almost always—also find authority that goes *against* you; it might even be *most* of what you find. So you *do* want the law to change. Hence, the art of advocacy.

2. Legal Writing

Advocacy takes two forms: oral and written. In dealing with a court, the written precedes the oral—both in time and importance. Even if you're going into a hearing or trial, you first will have submitted your arguments (which reflect your research) in writing to the court. With respect to "finding authority" for the judge/s, you'll find cases both pro and con. Your writings will argue that the authority favoring your position outweighs the authority that goes against you, and why.

Virtually everything you write as a lawyer will take a position. However, if what you're writing is strictly for use within your law firm, or strictly for your client's use, you want to be less assertive. Instead, here you're present-ing options, and evaluating them. While you can make recommendations, the final decision is for your boss, or your client, to make.

Legal Writing shows you how to handle both situations. However, with the latter type of writing—when you're objectively presenting *both* possible sides of the story—legal writing is probably unlike anything you've ever written before in your entire life. It's a very hard skill to master, and a very important one...in part because it's what's required on every essay exam you'll take in law school, regardless of the subject.

The reasons why legal research and legal writing can make or break your career as an attorney should already be at least somewhat apparent. They're so important that nearly all of Chapter 16 concerns them. (Parts of chapters 16 and 23 concern what you can do to get good in at least some aspects of legal research and legal writing *before* you go to law school.) Chapter 16 explains why these subjects are given the least attention in law school—but after reading chapter 4, you'll probably figure it out yourself.

* * *

Prospective law school students are seldom—if ever—told that the *work* load in year one is far heavier than in years two and three, despite what the official credit load is. And of course, for nearly all beginning law school students, all the material is completely new. First-year is the worst year of law school. For many, it is one of the worst years of their lives.

Part II of *Planet Law School* shows how, in the words of Rudyard Kipling's *If*, you can "Keep your head, while others are losing theirs."
—But first, we need to look at course materials, teaching methods, and professors...

Chapter 2 - Materials

Here are the key materials law students use:

1. Casebooks

Not "textbooks." There are virtually no textbooks in law school. Instead, you'll have "casebooks." There's a required casebook for each course. As the name implies, it's full of cases. Actually, though, it's full of written *opinions*.

For each case, there's a winner and a loser. And unless the court's decision is unanimous, there's also a winning side and a losing side within the court itself. (Most of these are appellate cases. Unlike trial courts, in appellate courts more than one judge hears the case.) The decision is by majority vote. One member of the winning side then writes the "court's" official opinion, stating who won and why. Other members of the majority can write individual opinions; each is a "concurring opinion." Sometimes members of the court who'd voted in favor of the loser then write individual opinions, too. These "dissenting opinions" explain why the loser should have been the winner—and why the majority is wrong.

2. Reporters

The most *common* law books are the books that contain the original written decisions of judges. They aren't called "casebooks," though. Instead, they're "reporters." They got this name because, originally, the *court* reporters (humans) prepared summaries of the arguments the attorneys for each side had presented to the court, and stated which argument the judge/s had agreed with, why, and to what extent. (Back then, the judges themselves didn't put their opinions in writing.) Almost every reporter, whether state or federal, is published by West. (West is the Goliath of legal publishing; the reporters are the main reason it's Goliath.*) Case reporters aren't sold in law school bookstores. You don't buy any: You couldn't afford them, because they're in collections of *hundreds* of volumes. Case reporters are the main purpose of law libraries. (Today the case reporters are also available on CD-ROM.)

---

* In February, 1996, The Thomson Corporation (headquartered in America but officially a Canadian firm) bought West Publishing...for $3.43 *billion*, in *cash*. West's annual sales were reported at $825 million, and its pre-tax profit margin was 25%—which, for any firm, is very good, but for a publishing company, is awesome. West was said to employ *7,000* people. That isn't much compared to General Motors. But for a publishing firm, it's staggering. (Thomson already owned most of the other major legal publishing firms, such as Bancroft-Whitney, and Clark Boardman Callaghan, and Lawyers Co-Op. So now it's like Goliath on *steroids*.)

3. Commercial Outlines

Originally, commercial outlines were to the first year of law school what *Monarch Notes®* and *Cliffs Notes®* are to lower schools. To use an archaic academic term, they were "ponies." They provided canned briefs, summaries of key points. (Regarding "briefs," see chapter 3.) Today, the brief-in-a-can is the least important part of it. Instead, commercial outlines provide what the professors and the casebooks should but don't: knowledge of the law— what it is, and why. They are wonderful. Chapter 5 discusses them in some detail.

4. Other Materials

The most frequent of these are the numerous titles in the paperback Nutshell™ series, published by West. (Sample title: *Secured Transactions in a Nutshell*.) These books vary enormously in quality, as each is written by a different author. West has a "Nutshell" title for each first-year course.

Some other books available are "hornbooks," digests, Shepard's®, and legal encyclopedias.* They're in the library. You'll find out what you need to know about them—which is very little, in law school—once you're in law school (although chapters 5 and 7 discuss hornbooks). You'll *use* them only when you're *out* of law school—unless you do a summer clerkship or legal internship (see chapter 12), or get involved in Moot Court (see chapter 13). The last major set of materials consists of the *Restatements* of the Law. Chapter 5 discusses them.

---

* If you've ever watched re-runs of the old (black-and-white) *Perry Mason* Show, you might have noticed there's a still-shot of a small stack of law books while the credits roll. All are volumes of *Corpus Juris Secundum*. *CJS* is a legal encyclopedia. It looks quite impressive on the TV screen, what with all them thar Latin werds.

Chapter 3 - Methods

Do you know how to play chess? If so, you probably remember how you were taught, regardless of whether by a tutor or a book: You learned the names of all the pieces, their respective home squares, the method of movement unique to each piece, special rules (queen on color, castling, pawn promotion, *en passant* capture) and all the rest. Then you began to play. Gradually, you got better at it.

Even if you don't know how to play chess, imagine what it would be like if you sat down at a chessboard with none of the pieces set up—and you had previously received none of the instruction mentioned above. However, you were still expected to arrange the pieces properly and then play.

You would not be entirely helpless, though. To continue with this chess analogy: perhaps you've noticed "chess problems" in your daily newspaper. *The New York Times*, for example, regularly runs such a column. It presents a diagram showing the situation on a chess board after *x* number of moves by each side. Beneath the diagram is a list of those moves. Perhaps there's even a heading, something like "Nimzo-Indian." The problem then asks what White's (or Black's) next move should be. Or else it says something like "Mate in 3," and the problem consists of figuring out how that happens. There's a brief commentary.

Now, imagine that each day's chess problem is the *only* instruction you got. Yet, you were expected to gradually figure out what all the pieces are, how they move, and everything else discussed above. And you were entered in a chess tournament that began the instant you first sat down at the board.

As you can appreciate, such daily columns really wouldn't be much help at all. In fact, they might just make things more confusing. (For example, the list of moves is written in "chess notation," not English.)

But that's how law is taught, even though it's vastly more complicated than chess. The "teaching" materials are something like a series of these chess problems, from completely different games. And just as in the chess problem, your adversary (here, the professor) says "Your turn."

Welcome to law school.

A. The Case Method—and Briefing

Legal education is built on the Case Method. Hence the casebook (see chapter 2). Casebook opinions have been edited down. Students read several for each class, and should be prepared to discuss them. For this, the student is expected to "brief" each case.

The typical case brief, for a law school class, is a one-page summary, with the following:

1) what I would call "file" information—the "style" of the case (i.e, "X v. Y"), the court from which the opinion came, and—sometimes—the year of the opinion, along with the case reporter citation/s;

2) the *history* of the case (a.k.a. *procedure*), which reports the end result at each step of the way in the lower courts;

3) the *facts* of the case—as reported by the majority opinion, which may have slanted them* to make its decision look more justifiable;

4) the main *issue/s* to be decided (a.k.a. *question/s*);

5) the *holding*—i.e., the one-sentence "rule/s of law" the case announced,

6) the *judgment*—who the court decided for, with its effect on the lower court ruling/s; and

7) the *rationale*—the "why" of the decision.

Sometimes there might also be *dicta*—more correctly known as *obiter dicta* (Latin: loosely, "other talk"), and sometimes called *"dictum"* (the singular form of "dicta"). This is where the opinion says something in passing that's not directly relevant to the holding of the case, but which might have significance all by itself. (Sometimes, it turns out to be the most important part of that case—as with the case that allowed professional baseball's exemption from the Anti-Trust Laws.)

Properly used, case *briefing* is a priceless tool for *mastering* the Law. Unfortunately—as you will see later in this book—it's a tool you will have to learn how to use completely on your own. The way *professors* use the Case Method is counter-productive…by design.

Judicial opinions are written for the benefit of attorneys and for other courts. For that reason, they typically zero in on the narrow issue at hand— the point/s of law on which the case turns. These usually involve issues on the *cutting edge* of the law. Attorneys and other courts already know all the relevant basic legal doctrines. There's no need for the opinion to go into any of that. The court implicitly assumes its readers have such knowledge. If you think of it in terms of Gestalt psychology, everything else is the (back)ground for the "figure" that stands out—the point/s explicitly discussed in the opinion. This approach makes complete sense for attorneys and other courts. It's efficient and concise.

However, even though the opinions in the casebooks involve issues no longer on the cutting edge of the law, the casebook authors do nothing to provide students with the necessary background information to help them put each case in context. Instead, the Case Method takes the inductive approach, i.e., students are supposed to gradually understand the individual trees well enough to eventually understand the nature of the entire forest.

That's the way learning usually occurs in the real world. It's the way, as small children, we go from uttering one or two words to understanding language. It's the way we eventually grasp concepts such as colors, heat and

---

* Or even falsified them. It happens, even in The Highest Court in the Land— as you will discover.

cold, love and hatred, even life and death. But it's the worst possible introduction to the Law.

B. The Socratic Method

The cases are just the starting point for a discussion consisting entirely of
hypotheticals. You have the set of facts presented in the case. The professor
then begins a series of "what if" questions. Then he or she changes the facts.
Should the decision be the same?

For example, under "Criminal Law" in chapter one, there was a long
hypothetical involving the *in vitro* fertilization of a human egg. Change the
facts: Say Nasty Nephew didn't invade the medical lab and destroy everything. Instead, the egg was implanted into the womb of a surrogate mother.
Seven months pass. Everything's proceeding normally. But Nasty Nephew
has heard about what's going on—and he's learned the name and address
of the surrogate mother. One day he accosts her and gives her a *very* hard
punch to the stomach. This causes her to have a miscarriage in a matter of
hours. *Now* has there been a murder?*

This is the so-called Socratic Method. But it isn't. That label was chosen
as an act of vanity, to make it appear that law school profs are the modern
successors of those pre-eminent ancient Greek philosophers, Socrates and
Plato. Because there are those who—understandably—are not familiar with
the genuine, original Socratic Method, an explanation is in order.

Plato wrote a series of books. In them, he supposedly recreated, word for
word, conversations Socrates had with others regarding fundamental philosophical matters. Every time, Socrates and his interlocutors would start out
with opposite opinions. And just as Erle Stanley Gardner made Perry Mason
the perfect questioner who always triumphs in the end despite the steady
resistance of his opponents, so Plato made his Socrates, twenty-four-hundred
years ago. Through skillful questioning, Socrates always brought the others
around to admitting that their assumptions or analysis had been all wrong.

If you believe such things really happen—whether in ancient Athens or a
modern courtroom—you should consider another career besides Law.

Never mind that in all of history, Socrates is the only *real-life* person who
allegedly ever used the Socratic Method successfully. American legal education not only pretends it really happened that way, but tacitly adopts the
even grander pretension that law professors are the equal of Socrates.

Not so. For one thing, Socrates—actually Plato, who was simply putting
his own words into Socrates' mouth—believed that each and every one of us
already understands all the fundamentally important principles of everything: art, science, justice, you name it. For Socrates/Plato, proper educa-

---

*   Once again, beats me. But you'll have to admit it's a much closer call this
    time around.

tion consists merely of clearing away the mental clutter, and allowing us to intuitively realize and acknowledge these fundamental principles. These principles are the Platonic Ideas, which supposedly have an independent, objective, unchanging existence somewhere in the cosmos. And each of us is somehow connected to these Ideas. (Notice the similarity to the belief of the worlds' religions that everyone is somehow connected to that religion's Ultimate Being.)

Law schools insist that, as with Socrates himself, their method is designed to *reveal* principles, to make us aware of what *already* exists. However, the grand principles of the Law are really just *rules of thumb* that have developed through the centuries (or sometimes, within just a few years) to guide courts in resolving disputes.

Disputes ("cases and controversies," in the language of the Constitution) are what the Law is all about. Yet, in general, the Law is supposed to be predictable. People can plan their activities, make their investments, etc., with reasonable assurance that what they're going to do is okay—and will *remain* okay. Over time, the rules of thumb change. But they should be recognizably the same over time—especially regarding the fundamentals. The only guiding principle, however, is a consensus as to what's fair.

There's nothing wrong with this. Indeed, it's hard to imagine any other way of proceeding. But it ain't no set of Platonic Ideas. In fact, from time to time the U.S. Supreme Court has completely upset the applecart of the law in one area or another. (Abortion, affirmative action, and the meaning of the Fourth Amendment being the most recent—and controversial—examples.)

The professor's hypotheticals are the core of the Socratic Method. As just mentioned, legal principles are really just rules of thumb. Students are supposed to figure out those rules of thumb for themselves. The prof gives a hypothetical fact situation. The prof then calls on a student to create a legal rule of thumb, to be used as a basis for deciding the outcome of the case. Every time a student announces what he or she thinks would be a good rule, the professor changes the facts in the hypothetical. Cleverly, the prof changes the facts in such a way that, if the student's proposal were applied to this new situation, the result would be absurd. In other words, the professor gets the student out on a limb…and then chops the limb off. The student falls to the ground—and then the professor pushes him or her back up the tree…and out onto another limb. And so on.

Through trial-and-error, the students eventually begin to formulate legal principles that seem to work well in most situations. No legal principle is complete without exceptions, of course. For some in the class, there comes an "Aha!" moment. The future lawyer has suddenly discovered a combination of rule-and-exceptions that seems to fit almost *every* situation. (No such combination exists, however. That's why judges always have discretion in deciding cases. The most important legal principle of all is…the judge's "fudge factor," more formally known as "judicial discretion.") Eventually, students discover there are exceptions to the *exceptions*.

The irony of the Case/Socratic Method is delicious, for two reasons. first, *even Socrates hadn't worked things through on his own.* He had a teacher, a woman named Diotima. She was a mystic who had been admitted into a realm of knowledge far above our own. He, after spending his youth and early middle age in a fruitless search for enlightenment, went to her. Apparently impressed by Socrates' earnestness and intellect, she tutored him. (Doubters are free to check Plato's *Symposium*—which, as it turns out, is not so much about love as it is about the love of wisdom, and its meaning— i.e., a philosophy of philosophy—"meta-philosophy.")

Defenders of the Socratic Method would say "So what? Socrates simply questioned others the way Diotima had questioned him." But Diotima did not merely *question* Socrates. True, as Socrates subsequently did, she used her questions to make him realize that his understanding was badly flawed. But once he had accepted that he really understood very little after all, she *instructed* him. Further, in an effort to comprehend her teachings, Socrates asked *her* questions. Neither the instruction nor the *counter*-questioning occurs in law school.

To return to the chess analogy: chess is a very complex game, for those who play it well. Yet, the *basics* of chess aren't much more complicated than the basics of poker, and probably less complicated than those of bridge. The basics of chess are taught in a straightforward manner. Law isn't.

C. Cambridge Marx the Spot

The Case Method and the Socratic Method are actually two sides of the same coin. The Case Method provides the body of material with which students work; the Socratic Method is the prod professors use to compel students to do the work. This coin was minted in Cambridge, Massachusetts, by Christopher C. Langdell. Langdell (1826-1905) was the very first Dean of the Harvard Law School. He served for a quarter-century, starting in 1870. He was also a contracts professor there. In 1871, his *Selections of Cases in the Law of Contracts* was published. His fellow Harvard professors quickly followed their new dean's lead, and—as usual—the rest of American education quickly followed Harvard's lead.

At the time of the Socratic/Case Method's creation, the technological breakthroughs of the industrial revolution had led to more than half-a-century's stunning material progress. This gave science enormous prestige. Science was a means not only of understanding the world but of controlling it—and Harvard has always been quite interested in both. Because Law is the chief means, short of war, by which control is effected in this world, Langdell decided to invent a "Scientific Study of the Law." Yes, that's what it was— and is—supposed to be, believe it or not.

Perhaps *Langdell* sincerely believed it so. But if he did, he did not understand the nature of the scientific method *or* the Law. They both use the inductive approach in formulating rules, but the similarity ends there.

Benjamin Sells, in his book *The Soul of the Law: Understanding Lawyers and the Law,* explains:

> Through the case method, objectivity translates visceral human experiences into schemata so they might be more easily compared to other "like cases." In many ways, this process of separating and categorizing facts for the sake of comparison *mimics* the scientific method with its emphasis on analysis and categories. Just think how the law digest system with its headnotes and indices reminds one of a biology text with its families, genera, and species. (Emphasis added.)

This brings us to the second delicious irony of the Case/Socratic Method: the original Socratic Method was anything *but* scientific. It was *Aristotle* who championed the inductive method, which is the essence of science. So he and Plato were almost polar opposites. Thus, Langdell was truly audacious in concocting his so-called "Scientific Study of the Law." (He wanted students to believe—wrongly—that there was "*a* right answer" to any question in the Law...and the professors always knew what it was.)

Who cares? Well, if there's no such thing as a "science" of Law, then perhaps we should reconsider the value of the Case/Socratic Method as a "scientific" study of the Law.

By the early 1920s, Langdell's new method had been in use for more than half-a-century. It had trained generations of highly influential lawyers, jurists, and professors. But it had already failed. Early in the 1920s, the— very prestigious—Committee on the Establishment of a Permanent Organization for the Improvement of the Law issued a report. (Its name alone says much.) The report condemned the "uncertainty" of American law. It said this resulted from "*a lack of agreement among members of the profession on the fundamental principles of the common law.*"

Think about that. If law were really a science, could such pervasive uncertainty have existed? And if law were really a science, would we have, even today, so many ongoing struggles between jurists—as reflected in majority v. dissenting opinions in the courts, including the Supreme Court? The answer is clear. But the Case/Socratic Method blissfully lives on in the ivory towers of the law schools. To this day, the highest earned degree you can get in the law is the J.S.D., "Doctor of Juristic Science."*

It was the same prestige of science—and the same desire for control—that led Karl Marx to call his own brand of communism "*scientific socialism.*" It wasn't until 34 years after his death that his system even began to be implemented. Yet, it's nearly extinct already. But Langdell's triumphed

---

* At some universities, it's the "S.J.D." — "Doctor of Juridical Science." (The LL.D.—Doctor of Laws—by the way, is "just" an honorary degree.)

almost immediately—and is still going strong. It's a toss-up as to which "scientific" system will have done more harm, in the aggregate, by the time the Case/Socratic Method follows communism into the dustbin of history.

D. "Thinking Like a Lawyer"

During the orientation lectures on your very first day of law school, at least one of the speakers will say that you will come out of law school knowing how to "Think Like a Lawyer." Maybe. Most likely, those at the top of the class will—although, based on my experience, even this isn't necessarily so. But no professor will ever tell you *what* "Thinking Like a Lawyer" *means.* — Or rather, no professor will ever give you a *meaningful* definition or explanation, something you can use as a reality-check to measure your own progress. Chapter 6 corrects that deliberate oversight. But first, to explain why you're denied that crucial understanding...

The Case/Socratic Method really amounts to an elaborate game of Hide the Ball, very much like the game adults play with tikes. Unlike the adult-infant relationship, which is designed to provoke the tots' pleasure, the law school method is meant to be torture. At that, it succeeds. "It's for your own good," the professors say, "because you learn how to completely think things through for yourself, on your own—the better for you to understand it." Actually, it's for the *professors'* own good. It ensures they will remain the unchallenged Masters of the Game throughout your first year in law school. Yes, it forces the students to *try* to think things through for themselves. But more important, it allows the *professors* to *avoid* having to think much at *all.* It's like a seasoned professional boxer sparring with a kid who's stepping into the ring for the very first time: No contest. (Worse, sometimes the prof doesn't "pull" any punches—and some poor student gets KO'd.)

However, there's even more to it than making life easy for the professor in the classroom. It also makes life easy when it's time to grade exam papers. The final exam in each course is based entirely on Thinking Like a Lawyer. Unfortunately, by the end of the Basic Six courses, only a small percentage of the students know what that involves. With only a small minority being "smart" enough (or lucky enough—which happens) to provide the answers the professor's looking for, it's very easy to grade papers quickly. (One professor that I know of had his 15-year-old daughter do it for him—after providing her with a "model answer." Another prof allegedly bragged that she never spent more than *five* minutes grading any one student's answers to the exam questions.) It's immediately obvious what's wheat and what's chaff. The professor then has to spend only a relatively small amount of time deciding who among the former will get the one or two A+ grades, the three or four A grades, and the five or six A- grades, etc., in a class of 100 or more.

If professors had to ensure that their students actually *learned* the first-year material, then nearly every student in the class would be expected to score at least 90% on the final. Yet, it would be "unthinkable" for every student in the class to get at least an A-. It would be vastly more difficult for the professor to determine who was in the top 10% of the class and who was in the bottom. A lot more work. Much hair-splitting. No professor wants that.

However, not only are professors *not* required to make sure their students *learn* anything, they're not even required to try to *teach* the students anything.

Based on your own educational experience, you surely find that hard to believe, perhaps impossible. But that's the way it is—as you shall find out for yourself if and when you go to law school.

To elaborate: Normally, in Hide the Ball, the adult eventually presents the heretofore hidden object to the child. Just like Diotima with Socrates. Not so in law school. There is no disclosure, period. Your graded exams are (perhaps) returned to you—and there's only one exam per course, at the end of that course, which may have lasted a full academic year. There is no explanation as to why you got the grades you received; nor can you seek enlightenment from your modern "Socrates."

In *One L,* for example, Scott Turow presents his own experience during his first semester at Harvard Law School:

> As students became more desirous of doing well, they could only grow conscious of the fact that there was now *no sure indication of how much or how well they were learning.* Though we'd all been working like Trojans for a couple of months, none of us could even be sure that we'd *pass* each course…The only end to that fear of failure would come when we were examined in January. There would be no grades until then, and the single test would be the sole basis for determining marks in each course. (Emphasis added.)

For most law students, it would also be the sole basis for determining their future in the Law.

You have to get it on your own—and in time to do well on exams. Most students don't. This led one law professor to write that success in law school "appears to involve a substantial degree of natural talent or 'vision.'" *

Ah, "the 'vision thing.'" Law school tenure-track faculties are drawn exclusively from those who did well in law school. So this particular professor was saying, in effect, that he and his colleagues are just naturally gifted people. This is quite similar to the original John D. Rockefeller's explanation of his vast wealth: "God gave me my money." (He was serious, too, just as the prof was. For those familiar with the history of theology, this is the Calvinist doctrine of Predestination, long since rejected.) The professor's message is thus, "Either you have it, or you don't. And if you don't, that isn't my problem.

---

* Layperson's citation: Kissam, Philip C., "Law School Examinations," *Vanderbilt Law Review,* March, 1989, page 459. Lawyer's form: Philip C. Kissam, *Law School Examinations,* 42 VAND. L. REV. 433, 459 (1989).

In hindsight, you obviously shouldn't have come here in the first place."

In 1991, Chris Goodrich's book, *Anarchy and Elegance: Confessions of a Journalist at Yale Law School,* was published. It is brilliant—perhaps the best book I've ever seen about law school. (It is not, however, a "how to" book such as *Planet Law School* is. Also, unfortunately, it's out of print.) He shared these thoughts on the teaching methods of law school:

> /O/ur professors *wanted* us to get lost in the legal wasteland, apparently, so we would treasure lawyerly skills when mastery finally came. I saw no other explanation: law school was intended to confuse, to intimidate, ultimately to indoctrinate. Students were supposed to endure the same horrors their professors had...and if they couldn't, well, no lawyers they. We were to learn without benefit of the professors' experience—rather ironic, considering the U.S. legal system is based on precedent! (Emphasis and ellipsis in the original.)

Even though I think his book is chock-full of amazingly insightful comments, there is another explanation for the pattern he observed. Goodrich assumed that mastery of lawyerly skills *would* finally come. But for many students, it never happens; nor do the professors care. On the contrary: the professors' teaching methods are designed to *ensure* that only a *handful* of students will *master* lawyerly skills—as opposed to merely doing well enough to get a law degree. (Chapter 21 explores the reasons for this.)

In schools below the rank of "higher" education, the performance measure for teachers is how many students learn the subject matter in question—and how well they learn it. This is especially true if all the students are sincerely—even desperately—trying, and have previously performed quite well in other academic environments. But not in law school, where the professors flatter themselves by sincerely proclaiming that "Many are Called—Few are Chosen." This enables them to keep their consciences clear in the face of the obvious fact that most of their students—all of whom are very bright—haven't "gotten it" by the end of the course.

Another name for this is "Blaming the Victim." It used to be the standard response to rape victims, for example. "What happened is your own fault. Somehow, you brought it on yourself." However, it's still the accepted response to law school students who are certifiably incompetent when they graduate. (The short-term memorization for the bar exam definitely does not provide the knowledge graduates need to practice law.)

Have you had occasion to hire a lawyer yet? Have you ever suspected that a given attorney was actually quite ignorant of the law, and perhaps even dim-witted? Many of them *are*. Warren Burger, at the time Head of the Supremes, gave a speech at Fordham University's law school on November 26,

1973.* In it, he said, in part: "No other profession is as casual or heedless of reality" as is the Law. He particularly condemned the lack of experience and training of attorneys who act as advocates in a courtroom. He condemned their assuming responsibility despite that inexperience and lack of training. Burger should have added that the legal profession is "casual and heedless of reality" with respect to *substantive* matters as well as *procedural.***

A generation has passed since Burger's famous speech. Nothing has changed, really; just a few cosmetic alterations. Unfortunately for you, that isn't the law schools' or law professors' problem...although it certainly should be, for the Case/Socratic Method is pedagogical malpractice.

With apologies to Polonius (in Shakespeare's *Hamlet*) "Though this be method, yet there is madness in't."

The next chapter concerns professors, those Masters of Madness. Then Part II of *Planet Law School* shows how to keep their methodical madness from driving you crazy.

---

* Reproduced, with additional references cited, in 42 Fordham L. Rev. 227 (1974).

** I once sat in on a hearing with no jury present. One attorney was basing his argument, in part, on *force majeure*. *"Force majeure"* is a concept familiar to many laypeople, and should be familiar to all attorneys. But when this judge heard that term, he asked, "Force majeure? What's that?"

Three things make this appalling. First, he'd been on the *bench* for *seven years,* after *ten* in private and public practice. Second, the President of the United States had recently nominated him to a *federal* district judgeship, so he was soon to have *lifetime* tenure as a *federal* judge. Third, this guy went to the same law school *I* did—"one of the most reputable...in the country," as I said in the Opening Statement of this book. So much for what *that* means—which is exactly my point.

Chapter 4 - Professors:

What's in it for *You* v. What's in it for *Them*

Chapter 3 first said it: Law school professors are not there to *teach* you the law.

You, being a perceptive person, are now racing ahead and thinking, "Yeah, yeah, I know: I'm supposed to dig the law out for myself. 'You get out of it what you put in to it,' 'No pain, no gain,' etc., etc.."

Well, before you decide to skip this chapter, it gets worse: The law school faculty is not there even for the purpose of *helping you learn* the law.

And here's the worst news of all: from their point of view, you're a *nuisance.*

If you intend to do well in law school, it's time for you to begin separating the myth of law school from the reality. Right now. To do that, you must look at reality from the faculty's perspective. This chapter spells it out.

The professor at a good law school teaches all of two courses per semester. That's 6-8 hours a week, max. (And I do mean max, because each "hour" of class is actually just 50-55 minutes.) In return, a full professor pulls down somewhere between $50,000 and $100,000 a year...for 34 weeks' employment. At six hours a week, and making $50,000 per academic year, that works out to 245 bucks an hour. If it's eight hours a week, and still "just" $50,000, the rate drops to a mere $184 an hour. But at eight hours a week and $100,000, it jumps to $368 an hour. And at six hours a week for $100,000, it soars to $490. Nice. Very nice.*

This income is *guaranteed.* As you know—or will know—from college, most professors have tenure: That means they're virtually immune from dismissal. They can do almost anything, as long as they don't a) shoot up heroin—in class, b) throw daggers at or fire guns at their students, c) expose their

---

* The range and upper limit stated here are conservative. According to a survey by the American Bar Association, for the 1994-95 academic year, a full professor at Duke got $122,000 a year; at the University of Texas, $118,000. For Harvard, the figure was $137,000. (Yale and the University of Chicago refused to respond to the ABA's request for information.) Full profs at schools much lower than the top 20 also were doing quite well: for Touro College, the figure was nearly $110,000; at Thomas M. Cooley, full professors were getting just over $100,000. (Prior to reading the ABA's survey, I'd never even heard of these last two institutions—though for all I know, they're fine.) In fact, the highest sum of all, nearly $143,000, was at Fordham University, a mid-ranked school. The survey showed more than half of all full professors made in excess of $90,000 a year. Further, these salaries—including those quoted at the six schools mentioned by name—are for "base pay." Thus, it excludes such things as "research grants," which can be substantial. As I said: Nice. Very nice. (And I doubt there's been any *decline* in the professoriate's compensation since 1994-95.)

"private parts" to their students—in front of witnesses, or d) otherwise indicate that they're a menace to society. Barring that, they can't be fired.

A professor's office is rent-free. Secretarial services are free, too: the school pays the secretary's salary. The phone, lights, copier, etc., are also free.

No lawyer makes as much money with such little effort—and such a low performance standard. Most judges do have such a low overhead; but while most judges also have "tenure," *no* judge gets by with working so little in return for such a high income. Granted, most professors are expected to keep "office hours." However, no one (other than students, if they're foolish) will take them to task if they don't honor that obligation. And yes, there are faculty meetings, schmoozing with the powers-that-be, etc., all of which is virtually mandatory. (Those are part of most other lines of work, too.) But it's not exactly a stressful way to make a living. In fact, it's cushy.

For the typical *college* or *grad school* professor, salary is maybe 90% of his or her annual income. Sure, some professors have investment income, maybe even a trust fund. They can teach summer school, too, and pick up some extra money from that. And there are those who get royalties from published writings, and so forth. But for most collegiate and grad school professors, what they're selling is something for which there is virtually no demand outside the ivory tower.

For law school professors, it's different. Very different.

In America, we proudly say we have "a government of laws, not men." But the laws have to be written, and administered, and interpreted by men—and women. We do indeed have a government of laws: we are heavily regulated by statutes, treaties, administrative regulations, ordinances, and case law. Lawyers handle all of that.

This means there's a big demand for legal experts. They serve as consultants when legislation or rules are being drafted and when arguments are being prepared for presentation to a court. They're hired to advise corporations on the meaning of new statutes and rules—and sometimes on the meaning of old ones.

A law school professorship gives one a chance to become a recognized expert in some area of the law. That faculty appointment is a magnificent credential, a drawing card for outside income. The more prestigious the law school, the more valuable the credential.

It doesn't take a genius to figure out the result. It's a matter of incentives. But just in case you're resisting the analysis, here it is, step by step:

You have a job where all you have to do is show up in a specified location at specified times, a total of 6-8 hours a week. (And if you have something better to do with your time, you can always cancel a class—or even a week's worth of classes—and make them up later.) You don't have to really "teach," in the substantive sense, which is a matter of subjective interpretation anyway. All you have to do is be there and conduct yourself in such a way as to appear to "teach," in a merely procedural sense (the Case/Socratic Method). Outside class, your time is your own. And it gets even better, as the professor sees it.

Your faculty salary is just your *starting* point: one of a number of potential income streams that are tributaries to your financial well-being. Or, to look at it differently, the law school professorship is just the hub of a wheel with many potentially lucrative spokes.

Now, what are you going to spend the rest of your time on? Here are your choices:

> A. Preparing diligently for class—reading law review articles on the first-year subject/s you teach, discussing your intended approach with others, thinking of new examples to use, new questions to ask, etc..

> B. Further developing a good reputation in some eso-teric or fast-growing area of the law, so that *you* can become the hired consultant, the hired expert witness, etc.—and make bunches more money from these out-side activities...without jeopardizing the income you get from supposedly teaching your students.

If you picked "A," you are not cut out to deal with the real world of the Law—or the real world of *anything*. "B" is the path to profit and glory. And that's (supposedly) what life's all about.

Hypothetical example: You're a law professor, tenured. There are, for real, an appalling number of systematic atrocities underway around the world. And there is now an effort underway to establish a permanent interna-tional tribunal for war crimes. You figure there will soon be some war crimes trials, in various international tribunals. You have no experience as a trial lawyer. But you know that a lot of trials turn on interpretations of the law rather than interpretations of facts—and interpretations of the law are argued to judges, on paper, not to a jury. So let's say you want to become a consultant in the area of war crimes.

You take on a research assistant or two, selected from your students. You don't have to pay them. They're in it as willing slaves, trying to bask in what they hope is—or will be—your reflected glory. (The *school* might be paying them, though, under a work-study program. Even then, it's minimum-wage.) You decide to submit a law review article for publication. The students do all the research, and maybe even all the writing. The article gets published, preferably in a prestigious law journal. (You mention your student helpers in the acknowledgments, with a quickie expression of gratitude. But the by-line on the article is yours alone.) You then start to work on another article—a variation on the theme. Maybe you even do a casebook on the subject. These things get you noticed by the lawyers who'll handle the war crimes trials.

But you want the politicians to become aware of your existence and expertise, too. So you also try to get some op-ed pieces into the *New York Times, Washington Post, Wall Street Journal,* or a newspaper chain via syndication. An interview on ABC's *Nightline,* an appearance on PBS's *Frontline.*

Meanwhile, you teach a class in the subject. Or maybe you just teach a seminar. (Seminars are easier to do, because you don't need to use notes. And they involve far fewer students, so there are fewer potential demands on your time during office hours.)

Many people work a full-time day job, and also "moonlight" part-time. However, for most law school professors, the "full time" law school job *is* the moonlighting. Unfortunately, law school profs are not required to disclose how much time they spend each week on "outside" work. And (other than the income tax return, which is confidential) they're not required to report how much money they make from outside work. Based on my own observations, and those of former fellow students, it is reasonable to assert that an ambitious law school professor easily spends four times as many hours on outside activities as he or she does in class—and makes easily four times as much money from it.

But without that law professorship, each would be just another lawyer.

According to *The American Lawyer* Magazine, Lawrence Tribe—the very prominent Harvard Law professor—bills his time for outside work at $1,200 an hour. (That's one thousand, two hundred.) The magazine estimates his annual income at 3-4 million dollars. Professor Tribe, of course, is at the very capstone of the American law school pyramid; no doubt, faculty at lower schools make less from their "moonlighting." And were he to devote *all* his "free time" to private practice, he might make even more. For all I know, he is a very good teacher, and devotes a great deal of time outside class to his students and to class preparation. Regardless, you see how the system works.

Why is American legal education so bad? And why is it the same throughout the land? Old saying: "If it ain't broke, don't fix it." —For the 5000+ full-time faculty at America's law schools, the American system of legal education *works,* quite well indeed.

When a law school professor points out that his or her job involves all that time spent on research, it's true—but not the whole truth. In fact, it's quite misleading. Only a handful of law school professors in America do research in the subjects that comprise the *first-year* curriculum—the foundation of future attorneys' skills.

Now here's the real kicker: the *law school's* reputation is based on how many nationally (or internationally) recognized experts it has on its faculty. (So, they would argue, the "outside activities" are actually integral.) In this, it's no different from the reputation of universities' science departments, which depend on the number of Nobel prize-winners they have. But there's a difference: the typical Nobel-winner actually teaches—and only a handful of students, whom he or she *rigorously* trains, as assistants. Sometimes these students are so well trained that they eventually win Nobel prizes in their own right. Such is not the case with law school professors. First, law school profs often have large classes. Second, unlike science, the realm of untapped potential *meaningful* research in the law is relatively small.

The law school concurs in the faculty's desire to give first-year courses bottom priority. (And because law school casebook publishers provide a free teacher's manual, the professor need only consult that for any new developments in the subject.)

Maybe you're in (or went to, or will go to) an undergraduate school big enough to employ "teaching assistants" (TAs). Actually, the teaching "assistants" do *all* the teaching. The professor's name is listed as the person conducting the course, but the professor is nowhere to be found come class time. Teaching the freshman undergraduates is the last thing that 99.9% of the professoriate wants to do. Their interest is in the advanced classes, preferably seminars with seniors or graduate students—who serve as their (unpaid) research assistants.

Law school also has TAs. However, they only teach the two courses thought to be beneath the dignity of professors: legal research and legal writing. In all your other courses, throughout your three years of law school, you will be taught by a genuine professor. So, at least on paper, there's a big difference. Sounds good—but wait: the problem with the first-year courses is that, nine times out of ten, the law school professor feels the same way as the college professor who teaches freshman English (if, indeed, your freshman English course had, has, or will have a professor actually presiding in the classroom): He or she really does not want to be there. And it shows. Often, the professor takes it out on the students. Especially in law school.

Exceptions That Prove the Rule

Granted, there are exceptions to this rule. The biggest is the newly-hired (and sometimes naïve) assistant professor. (An assistant prof does not yet have tenure.) The new kid on the block is the one who gets stuck with teaching the first-year courses. (But because new tenure-track hires are rare, nearly all first-year courses are taught by tenured—associate or full—professors.) Some of these assistant profs are idealistic and take their teaching duties seriously. If you're—*very*—lucky, they might actually be good at it.

However, as you perhaps know by now, good teaching is frowned on in American higher education, in general. Law school is no exception. The "publish or perish" rule controls promotions in law school, as elsewhere. And because one's reputation in the academic community is based on publications, teachers without tenure know the road to tenure is based on something other than good teaching. In fact, they're advised to tone down their enthusiasm, not get the students so interested in the subject matter. The good teacher makes the mediocre teacher look bad in comparison—and you don't get tenure by making the members of the Tenure Committee look bad. (At one prominent law school, the same faculty member constantly won the "Teacher of the Year" award. But he didn't publish. So, he languished as an assistant professor. When he still had not published, the faculty removed him from the tenure track. He is now listed in the catalogue as an "assistant 'adjunct' *instructor*," and gets paid accordingly. They wouldn't even permit him the title of "lecturer," which would have allowed him to preserve some dignity. Only a T.A. is lower. He chooses to stay only because of the school's high ranking. —And the school permits him to stay only because he agrees to teach at least one first-year course every semester.)

There's a further problem with assistant law school professors. Here's the path to a tenure-track teaching job with a reputable law school: Great grades in law school, followed by a judicial clerkship—preferably with a U.S. Supreme Court justice, or at least with a federal appellate judge.

Notice what's missing? —Proven ability to teach. The performance standard is "drudgeship"—the ability to grind away for grades in law school, and ability to grind away as slave labor for a federal judge. (It's the same criterion big law firms have when hiring new associates, by the way.) Drudgeship is hardly conducive to creativity and spontaneity, which good teaching often involves. At least a future Ph.D. starts out as a T.A. (for what little that's usually worth). Future law profs don't start out as TAs. Instead, they Make Law Review. (See chapter 12.)

And notice what else is missing? —Experience in the *practice* of law. In fact, at the very top schools, those who have more than a year or two as attorneys in the real world are regarded as "tainted," and are unwelcome as tenure-track faculty.

Perhaps you think I exaggerate. Well, in 1980 a former deputy attorney general of the state of California, George J. Roth, wrote a book called *Slaying the Law School Dragon*. (It's still in print, in a 1991 revised edition.) Roth was a graduate of New York University's Law School—another of the "most reputable schools in the country." He wrote the book when he was 60 years old. So, he was no Young Turk such as I am. (In fact, he'd been out of law school for 38 years.) One gets the feeling that he was finally expressing a lifetime of repressed rage when he wrote these words:

> A large part of the problem is caused by the professors. Most of them are not good teachers. In most cases, they are people who have been top students themselves and who have gone into teaching law right out of law school...These professors are only interested in the theory of the law; the teaching of it is merely an incidental way of earning a living while affording them the time to delve deeply into the exotic mystiques of their specialty muses.
>
> Oh sure, there usually are some professors on every campus who really love to teach; who thrive on development of the intellectual maturity of their students; who year after year can make the abstract turn into the concrete. But these beloved magicians are rare. They're grossly counterbalanced by the intellectual snobs and academaciated clones who make up the bulk of the American law school faculty army. (Ellipsis supplied.)

I take issue with Roth on just two minor points: 1) "right out of law school," most (future) law school professors became law clerks in federal courts (see chapter 19), *then* went into teaching; and 2) delving into "the exotic mystiques of their specialty muses" is the way professors make a *magnificent* living—compared to which their faculty salary, ample enough in its own right, is secondary.

Roth is now in his late 70s, and retired. Unfortunately, in his revised edition, he omitted the paragraphs above. Instead, in his preface to the revised edition, he made some statements about how things had changed somewhat since his day. Having been a law school student during and after the year in which he revised his original edition, I disagree. Instead, I would say that with respect to law school, the more things change, the more they stay the same. (If and when you go, you can see how it is at your school.)

Teaching is the least important thing to the typical law school professor. But even for the entry-level prof who desires to teach well, it's a matter of trial and error—mostly error. Having one's heart in the right place is no guarantee of ability to follow one's heart's desire. If you've ever had an instructor who's never taught before, yet who's trying desperately to teach well, you know how painful it can be for all concerned.

The other major exception regarding desire to teach is the adjunct professor. The adjunct professor did not come up the assistant-associate-full prof route, and is ineligible for tenure. Rather, he or she is typically a full-time practicing attorney, usually in some specialty. Adjunct professors do not teach first-year courses. They teach second-and third-year courses in their specialty, usually just one class per semester, one semester a year.

However, even adjunct profs often have no desire to teach. Instead, they too, often, just want the credential of being a faculty member at a reputable law school. This is especially so with lawyers who serve as expert witnesses or as consulting attorneys. (For example, most jurors have only a high school diploma, if that. They don't know the meaning of the word "adjunct." But if my legal expert witness identifies herself as an "adjunct professor on the faculty of the Stanford University School of Law," and your legal expert witness identifies herself as "an attorney with 20 years' experience," guess who has the edge with the jury?)

The third exception is a minor one—and, as Roth points out, rarely seen: the tenured professor who is *skilled* at teaching. Granted, in law school recruitment literature, you can read about professors who've won an "excellence in teaching" award from the students. But in truth, they're insignificant from the law school's point of view. Even when they're showcased, they mean little.

Here's the analogy: We've all been brought up on television, so we've seen millions of commercials. These include commercials touting insurance. They often consist of testimonials from policy-holders who suffered a major loss (auto accident, fire, tornado, flood, etc.). The friendly insurance company's claims adjuster *immediately* came out, evaluated the damage—and, lo and behold—almost *immediately* got the devastated victim a check for the *full amount* of the loss. From agony to (near-) ecstasy, in 48 hours flat.

Now, if you believe that's the way insurance companies operate when it comes to paying *out* money—as opposed to taking it in—Have I got a bridge for you! Sure, at least some insurance adjusters are decent. And I don't doubt but what at least one policy-holder, somewhere, received prompt service and payment in full for his or her loss. But in the real world, any claims adjuster who does this more than once gets a reprimand. Those examples are carefully *contrived*—for use in future television commercials. Like the shill who helps the con artist fleece the sucker, these (unwitting) shills are the very rare exceptions that prove the almost-universal rule. (If you don't believe me, wait 'til you start reading cases in the law books…and I will not even go into cases from my own experience against insurance companies defending those my clients have sued.)

Yes, there are some genuinely good teachers in law school. But they are very few and very far between. The law school professor who's a good teacher is similar to the aged law professor who was once a star legal scholar but has long passed his prime—and retirement age. He or she is kept on because it's good to be able to trot that prof out as an example of the school's illustrious faculty. Otherwise, he or she is ignored. (The same thing happens with famous over-the-hill partners at certain big-name law firms.)

Of Soap Boxes and Snow Jobs

Further, just because a prof likes to teach, that doesn't necessarily mean that he or she is any good at it. In fact, it is often quite the contrary. Sometimes, the ineptness is almost deliberate.

Two examples by way of explanation—both from my first-year classes: Two ideologues, one a leftist, the other a right-winger. Both just loved to "teach"—but only because each wanted to use his or her respective subject matter as an opportunity to grind an axe. And so, week after week, we first-year students would go from the flaming reactionary's harangue at 9 a.m. on one subject to the flaming radical's harangue at 11 a.m. on another. Anyone looking at the syllabus would note that the assigned reading covered everything a first-year course in the subject was supposed to cover. And indeed, at least one of the assigned cases was usually discussed in class. The professor in each subject used the required Socratic Method. But the cases were just the springboard to a series of mini-lectures within each class session, during which the professor in question would try to win converts to his or her political persuasion. Students soon realized they should at least use the "politically correct" terminology (liberal or conservative) when asking or answering a question. If they didn't, the professor would launch into another mini-lecture in an attempt to apprise the future lawyer of the error of his or her ways.

I'm sure you've had—or will have—at least one prof or T.A. like that in college. Just be advised that you'll find them in law school, too. The difference is the professor calls on you whether you like it or not—and the questions aren't easy.

Another exception regarding professors who like to teach involves the faculty member who has become an expert in his or her subject area, and the area happens to be something that fits within a first-year course. Then, the professor decides to pretend that the class is actually a third-year seminar, or a meeting of those who are fellow scholars. Daily discussion consists of the very fine points of narrow areas of the law…but without any previous grounding in the basics. (You're thinking the assigned reading provides the basics? Wrong—as chapter 3 showed.)

With either the ideologues or the aloof experts, the same thing happens: When you get into advanced courses, or take the bar exam, you'll suddenly realize how much you should have been taught about the basics that wasn't even *mentioned* in your first-year courses in these subjects.

I shall relate one other exception regarding teachers who like to teach: a very rare exception, but quite memorable. One of my first-year professors was zealous in proving that he was our friend, that he really cared about us, about teaching, about the Law, etc.. He even threw a big "get acquainted" party for us at his house early in the first semester so we'd feel more at ease with him in class. Many of us loved him, because—unlike the other professors— he was clearly on *our* side in the struggle to master the Law.

However, for some strange reason, try as he might, he could never make the Law clear to us. The more questions we asked, the more confused we became on hearing his answers. He was generous with his time outside of class. He'd recommend materials for "further reading." However, these were always abstruse, sometimes downright opaque. We just thought that's the way the Law is. Gee, it was hard. We felt very humble, even humiliated, in the face of this body of learning—and the professor's seeming familiarity with it all. If only we could penetrate the mysteries, join the ranks of the initiates. Someday. But when? It seemed as though we'd never find the key to unlock the door to the Hall of Understanding.

Because we were convinced that the professor was trying so hard to help us, we didn't want to let him down. We were sure he felt badly because we just weren't getting it—although he didn't let it show. And so, most of us probably put more time in on that course than any other…to no avail. We felt so much sympathy for him, because we were obviously so stupid and unworthy of his sincere exertions on our behalf.

Too late, the pattern became clear. Grading had been on the curve, so it was guaranteed that at least some students would score well even if they didn't understand the subject matter. A few of them later went to this professor for letters of recommendation. One of them, a friend of mine, seemed to have been one of the professor's chosen few in class. Both my friend and I were shocked when he received—in a "rejection packet"—a copy of the letter of "recommendation" the prof had sent to the firm in question. You've heard of "damning with faint praise"? That's what happened. After reading that letter, even I would not have hired my friend.

The prof habitually led people on, then let them down—or let them tear themselves apart, as we did in his first-year class. This was his routine practice; many unsuspecting students fell for it, and suffered for it. It was far, far too late before most of us realized that he'd started the course by using cases that represented the *exceptions* to the main rules. Naturally, we'd assumed the cases *were* the rules. Further, he deliberately chose cases not normally covered by the commercial outlines, and cases that weren't highlighted in the legal treatises. We were lost—and that's the way he liked it. Unfortunately, he wanted us to *stay* lost…even beyond the last day of class, apparently. (His "seduce and abandon" method continued in the advanced courses.)

I later learned that—after doing very well when he was in law school— he'd spent one year working for a federal appellate judge. Then he'd spent one year as an entry-level associate at a nationally prestigious law firm. But he himself had never handled a case in the subject matter he regularly taught to first-year law students—or any of his other courses, for that matter. He probably couldn't've made things clear to us even if he'd wanted to: he really didn't know what he was talking about, period.

(Much later, he told me that he had been in psychoanalysis one hour a day, five days a week, for three years—with no end in sight. It was bad enough that he was screwed up, as indeed he was. But it was much worse that one of his problems was his deliberate betrayal of those who'd trusted him. The worst enemy you can have is the one you think is your good friend— until he or she stabs you in the back. This holds true in the practice of law, also, but I was surprised to have found it in law school…or rather, in a law school professor—especially such a seemingly-likable one.)

Because the in-class method of that teacher involved deliberately confusing students, this is the place to mention another professor who did the same thing—but for a different reason. This example comes from my third year of law school, not the first, but it's relevant here.

I took a course in the law of defamation (libel and slander). The professor was a recognized expert in the subject. Numerous publishers and broadcasters had him on retainer. Yet, he bluntly told us in class, several times, that "this area of the law is so complicated, and so confusing, that it's really impossible to teach it." And so, he didn't. But that hadn't stopped him from repeatedly offering the course, to enhance his credentials. Granted, he assigned cases, and we discussed them in class. But he told us it was "impossible" to provide even a simple definition of basic concepts such as slander *per se* and libel *per quod*.

After graduation, I naturally saw former classmates from time to time. Once in awhile, one of them would have a case—or know of a case—that involved defamation. Without exception, if the case was complicated, his or her first reaction was to recommend good old Professor X as a consultant. A major purpose of Professor X's class was to drum up future business for himself. His hourly rate was staggering, as was his retainer. That is not uncommon.

And I should also mention one other prof. He was a lousy teacher, but that's not why I'm telling you about him. Instead, he was the source of one of my class's oddest experiences in first-year.

He failed to show up for class one day during the second semester. Nor was he there for the next class session, or the next, and the next. Calls from the school to his home went unanswered, we were told. No one had heard from him. He'd vanished into thin air. Naturally, we suspected something terrible had happened to him.

The tip-off that should have allayed our concerns came from the man's secretary, who was not particularly anxious. She said she shared our worries, but she believed everything would be all right. Nearly two weeks after his disappearance, a notice was posted that his classes would meet again as of the following day. When we showed up, he was there.

"I really can't go into why I was gone and what that was all about," he said, airily. "All I can say is that I had a case of 'the vapors,' I suppose we can call it."

Weeks later, one of his research assistants let slip the truth. The man had been in Las Vegas on an extended gambling junket—something he did at least once a year. The professor had had a serious falling-out with the deans a few years before. He had tenure, so he was immune to dismissal. To thumb his nose at the administration, he annually disappeared for several days, without notice—and always during the semester, rather than during breaks.

The two weeks he was gone made life easier for us. But instead of promptly making up the lost classes, he waited until the last two weeks before finals. That made life much more difficult for us. (It wasn't just the administration he was thumbing his nose at.) We wanted to "vaporize" him.

Forewarned is Forearmed

All these experiences I've related were clearly bad ones. I'm omitting bad experiences other students had. (One quick exception: Normally, a law school final lasts three or four hours. One professor gave his first-year contracts class an *eight-hour* final, all day Saturday. He was a truly sadistic bastard, even in class.)

I'm also omitting my good experiences. Why? For one thing, I had very few. Interestingly, they usually involved adjunct professors. Either that, or visiting professors who were on their best behavior because they were hoping to get an offer to become part of the permanent faculty at my school. For another reason—well, I'll refer you to the motto I use when going into trial:

> *Hope for the Best,*
> *Expect the Worst*
> *—And Try to Be*
> *Ready for Anything.*

This book is meant to acquaint you with the reality of law school and—to a far lesser extent—the practice of law. Your experiences may well be better than mine. If so, I will be happy for you...In fact, the main purpose of this book is to try to ensure that your experiences *will* be better than mine.

I'm concentrating on the bad, for reasons that should be obvious: It's easy to be ready for the "best," because smooth sailing is easy when conditions are ideal. It's when you encounter stormy seas that you're tempted to turn back, or even to abandon ship. But maybe you should never have signed up for that voyage in the first place. —Or maybe you would've been better able to ride out the storm out if you'd anticipated what might go wrong and had prepared for it: have the bilge pumps in good working order, for example, in case you take on water. If you haven't even thought about what could go wrong, it's more difficult to deal with it if it does. That's why this chapter has given you the "downside." Once *you're* in law school, you'll have nowhere to go but "up" (I hope).

You have now why seen law school professors are not in your corner. For most of them, the classroom experience is a necessary "evil," a chore to be endured much as they endured performing household chores when they were kids. For most members of the professoriate, students are a nuisance—unless the students can be recruited as research assistants or used as a source of future income. Law school professors want to spend their time feathering their own nests—which is understandable. Students aren't even fledglings yet, let alone legal eagles; your professors do not want to attend to the needs of insistent hatchlings, all of whom have gaping, chirping beaks and wildly flapping wings. Would *you?**

Richard D. Kahlenberg is a 1989 graduate of Harvard's law school. In 1992, his book, *Broken Contract: A Memoir of Harvard Law School,* was published. At one point in it, he discusses a bull session with other students. All were unhappy.

> The main complaint was that we students were ignored. "Sometimes I feel as though the law school grinds on and the students are just extras," one student said. "As if the real purpose of the university was to allow professors to do their thing, and that the students were just here to make it seem like a university."

---

* At some law schools, the faculty has its own law library, off-limits to students. Officially, this is because they'll never have to worry about being able to find a book they're looking for. However, law professors are even worse than students when it comes to replacing books on the shelves. —And because the profs can take the books from the faculty library without checking them out, those books often disappear forever. The real reason for the faculty law library is so that professors won't encounter students. Students, by definition, are pesky.

Yup, that's it—not by accident, but by *design*. It's true of America's universities in general, but particularly true of America's law schools.

So here is the most important thing to get from *this* chapter:

> You're going to have to rely on yourself,
> *to a greater extent than you thought possible.*

Part II tells you how.

Part II:

The Secrets of First-Year Success

Chapter 5 - Getting the Jump on
Your Adversary

If you've ever studied a foreign language, you know the teacher and the textbook try to make it as easy as possible for you—because no matter how much help you get, it's still hard to master a foreign tongue. As a beginning student, you're immediately hit with a new vocabulary. However, the new words are presented merely as a different way of communicating something you already know how to communicate in English. You just start using the foreign words instead of the English. If the new language has a different way of organizing a sentence than English does, you're shown what it is and how it works. Gradually, you expand your vocabulary and your comprehension of the syntax. You create more complicated sentences, using more new words.

In law school, the material is made as *difficult* as possible for you, on *purpose*. In first-year, you aren't even necessarily *told* the new words. And you certainly aren't told the concepts that the words apply to. The words, and especially the *concepts,* are totally new. Learning to Think Like a Lawyer is not the same as learning how to "think in a foreign language." It's more like going from a lifetime spent in a world based on Newtonian physics, to one based on quantum mechanics.

In quantum mechanics, the distinction between time and space is a source of confusion rather than clarification. You must take your choice between knowing something's location and knowing its speed, because you cannot determine both at the same time. And you get hit with a bizarre new vocabulary: mesons, mu-mesons, particles, quarks, "spooky action at a distance," etc..

Yet, any good physics teacher tries to help the students make sense of this radical new method of understanding. Not so in law school. To put it differently, going to law school isn't really like going to another planet, despite the title of this book. That would be too easy. Instead, it's more like stepping into the Twilight Zone®—truly another dimension.

Chapter 3 quoted Chris Goodrich's book, *Anarchy and Elegance,* about how (at Yale) "our professors *wanted* us to get lost in the legal wasteland, apparently," and about the horrors of law school. Chapter 4 quoted Richard Kahlenberg's book, *Broken Contract*, about how students were the least important of the academy's considerations. Here's another one from Kahlenberg: *"/M/y hatred for Harvard Law only grew as I realized that this school didn't have to put people through this hell, that there were other, more effective teaching methods."* (Emphasis added.) These two authors were writing about schools at the pinnacle of the Law's academic hierarchy. However, what they say is true of every law school in the country.

Professors could easily start each first-year course by teaching the language of the law in a straightforward manner. They could simultaneously make sure that the students learn the concepts the legal jargon refers to. *Then* the professor could go into the Socratic Method, to test the students' understanding of the material. But as it is, the students literally don't know what the professor is talking about. By the time they begin to catch on, the course is almost over. And that's the way the professors like it, for reasons discussed in chapters 3 and 4.

To again quote Kahlenberg's fellow HLS alumnus Scott Turow (in *One L*):

> It's obvious, in looking back, that one of the things which made me feel most at sea initially was the fact that I barely understood much of what I was reading or hearing...What we were going through seemed like a kind of Berlitz assault in "Legal," a language I didn't speak and in which I was being forced to read and think sixteen hours a day.

So, it's obvious, in looking ahead, that there's no better way to get the jump on your adversary than by learning the jargon and the concepts on your *own*...before you *start* law school.

Take another look at the listing of topics covered under Property and Contracts at the very beginning of chapter 1—and see how you feel. Lost, right? Now, imagine how much better you'd feel if you already had at least *some* idea of what many of those terms meant.

Most law school students learn too little, too late. They have no chance at reaching the top 10%. They aren't contenders. They end their first-year as also-rans. (This is especially true in schools that use a *forced* curve—as most do. There, the number of students getting any given grade is fixed in advance, regardless of what the grade distribution would be on a normal curve.)

Goodrich saw the heart of the problem: "The students were *already* supposed to understand, apparently, what I thought we were here to *learn*." (Emphasis added.) He's right. Go figure.*

Your mission, if you choose to accept it, is to be far, far ahead of your professor before the very first day of class. By that, I don't (necessarily) mean that you've already read all the topics the course will cover. Rather, I mean you will already *understand* a given topic before it's reached in class. —If you're presently in law school, or are about to enroll, you still have time between now and finals to get the jump on the prof: your adversary. Either way, that's what this chapter is for: to give you a shot at the top. "Well begun is half-done."

Chapter 4 ended by saying you're going to have to rely on yourself, to a

---

* Actually, much of chapter 21 consists of the figuring-out.

greater extent than you thought possible. I'll amend that, now: *you're going to have to rely on outside materials your professors will never tell you about.* This chapter is all about those materials.

Unless you're already in law school, take advantage of these materials *before* you go. Once you've started law school—as you know if you *are* in law school now— your professors will *bury* you under mountains of *make-work.* To shift the metaphor: you'll be on a treadmill, with little time to spare even for *necessities* such as these. (Chapter 7 concerns what to do to follow through on these materials *after* you've started law school.)

Scouting the Terrain - Phase One: *"Primers"*

Start with what I'm calling legal "primers."* (Remember grade school? "See Spot run.") However, they are quite thorough and do not talk down to the reader. These are definitely not casebooks. And even though they are text-books, of a sort, they're intended for independent study. They're excellent.

Aspen Law & Business, a division of Aspen Publishing, has very good primers for most first-year courses. They're in its "Examples & Explanations" series, all in paperback. Each takes it one step at a time, point-by-point. They're written for the total beginner. After each section, there's a series of narrow questions, with answers and a discussion of each answer. That way, you can make sure that you've gotten each new subject "down pat" before moving on.

The first is *The Law of Torts,* by Joseph W. Glannon. It came out in 1995 and costs about $26.

You will also be required to take civil procedure in first-year. As chapter 1 mentioned, Civ Pro is a year-long nightmare. Professor Glannon has done a book on that, too, for Aspen: the third edition of *Civil Procedure.* This 1997 work is roughly $29.

As chapter 1 said, you will likely also be required to take a first-year course in Constitutional Law. Aspen has two complementary volumes on this. Both are by Christopher N. May and Allan Ides, and both have *Constitutional Law* as the main title. The first is subtitled *National Power and Federalism;* the second, *Individual Rights.* (The authors' names are in reverse order for the second volume.) If your Con Law course is just one

---

* And by the way, *this* "primer"—unlike the one that involves paint—is pronounced as though it were spelled "primmer."

semester, chances are you'll just need the first volume; if two semesters, both. Both volumes came out in 1998. Each costs $31.

Aspen also does two complementary volumes for Crim Law, but they're by different authors. The first is *Criminal Procedure,* a 1996 paperback for $27, by Robert M. Bloom and Mark S. Brodin. The second is *Criminal Law,* a 1997 work by Richard G. Singer and John Q. LaFond, also $27. The difference between them is that the first book, as its title implies, covers criminal procedures. This is where Constitutional rights become especially important. The second covers substantive criminal law. It deals with questions such as "How do we define a crime?" and "What is criminal 'intent'?" The first-year Crim Law course at your school might emphasize either the procedural or the substantive aspect. But you won't know in advance. So get both books and read them. That way you'll be prepared, regardless.

Aspen has a book entitled *Contracts,* too, by Brian A. Blum, in its Examples and Explanations series. Published in 1998, it costs $32. And Aspen has a second book, *Rules of Contract Law,* by Charles L. Knapp and Nathan M. Crystal. This is not part of the "Examples & Explanations" series. Most of it is just what the title says, the rules of contract law— a sampler of key items from various statutes and treatises. However, at the end of the book, the authors present sample exam questions, and then discuss the answers in detail. This 1993 paperback sells for $16.50.

Property is the only first-year subject for which Aspen does not (yet) have a primer. Fortunately, though, West Publishing has a great book out on this. It's Cornelius Moynihan's *Introduction to the Law of Real Property: An Historical Background of the Common Law of Real Property and Its Modern Applications, 2d. ed.*. It's a classic. The book is hardcover, but just $28. Further, it's a slim volume and written in a surprisingly lively style. Moynihan discusses the reasons how and why property law got to be the way it is. Even though he doesn't include questions and answers the way Aspen's Examples & Explanations series does, after reading his book, the subject will *make sense*.

A very important part of property is "Estates and Future Interests." Moynihan's book covers it. If you don't master this, you're taking a big chance. Estates and Future Interests is the foundation for other areas of the law, such as wills and trusts. Even if you have no desire to ever deal with these, you will still have to understand these subjects, as the bar exam in *all* states tests them.

Only one of these books existed when I was in first-year, even though that was just a few years ago. I wish to God they'd *all* been around then, and that I'd been able to find them and use them. That's how good they are. They provide an opportunity for *you*—an opportunity that I and hundreds of thousands of others never had. As you will see (if and when you go to law school) they're worth their weight in gold.

(West Publishing does a voluminous Nutshell™ series, first mentioned in chapter 2. There's a "Nutshell" for every first-year course. Matthew Bender does an "Understanding the Law" series, but it doesn't cover all first-year subjects. However, all these books, from both firms, are much longer and more detailed than Aspen's "Examples & Explanations." Their level of difficulty, particularly for the novice, is much higher. None include questions and answers. If you have a *lot* of time between now and your first year of law school, and at some point want to get into a lot of detail, go ahead and get one of the "Nutshells" or "Understanding the Law" books. But you really should learn how to crawl before you decide to walk—and especially before you try long-distance running.)

Scouting the Terrain - Phase Two: Legal Reasoning

As chapter 3 showed, law school tries to force you to "dig the law out for yourself." Professors explain that students "learn better that way." Nonsense (for reasons discussed in chapter 3). To return to the analogy at the outset of this chapter: Rudimentary knowledge of a foreign language consists of minimal conversational or reading and writing skills. ("Pleased to meet you." "How are you?" "What does it cost?" *"How* much?" "Where is the bathroom?") *Fluency* is entirely different. It's the ability to read (or better yet, to translate well) a newspaper, or the ability to carry on a sophisticated conversation about art, politics, or history. However, law professors perversely try to thwart students' acquisition of even the merely rudimentary skills. It's as though teaching baby-talk to an infant runs the "risk" that the child will outshine the parent by suddenly reciting Hamlet's soliloquy.

To express it another way, the first year of law school puts the cart before the horse...and doesn't provide you with the horse. (In fact, you aren't even told how to *find* the horse—and the harness.) It's up to *you* to acquire the animal and hitch it to the wagon you're going to ride through finals.

The primers discussed above are, for your purposes at this point, the horse. Now for a cart...

After you have read at least the Glannon primer on torts and the Blum primer on contracts, there's a book that will show you how to Think Like a Lawyer with respect to case briefing. Its title is *Learning Legal Reasoning: Briefing, Analysis, and Theory.* The author is John Delaney. The revised edition was done in 1987. Like Moynihan's book, it's a classic. Unlike Moynihan's book, it's in paperback, and costs just $14. It's available from the author's own firm, John Delaney Publications.

Learning Legal Reasoning is *brilliant,* but without being flashy. It's one of the very best books I've ever seen on the law. Delaney shows how the Case Method *ought* to be used—and how case *briefing* can be an *invaluable* approach to *mastery* of the law—*once you've learned the basics.* (This is why you should read at least the Glannon book on torts and the Blum book on contracts before you read *Learning Legal Reasoning.*) Unfortunately, as chapter 3 showed, you won't get the basics in law school. Instead, you'll go straight into the cases. Worse, though, for most law students, case briefing is a perfunctory exercise that few, if any, professors properly exploit. However, it's so important that chapter 16, "Critical Skills," takes it up again.

To switch back to the language analogy: with *Learning Legal Reasoning,* you'll be ready to move on from "See Spot Run" to studying the works of Shakespeare. Then, on your final exams, you might indeed be ready to recite Hamlet's soliloquy—to the astonishment of your professors.

* * *

If, as you read *Planet Law School,* you are unsure whether or not you want to go to law school or even to apply, you should get at least some of these books anyway. They teach law the way it *should* be taught—i.e., they actually *teach* the law, and are intended to help you *understand* the law. Amazing. It doesn't get any better than this. Law school itself will probably be much, much worse. So try the primers, one at a time. Save *Learning Legal Reasoning* 'til the end.

If you just can't get the *slightest* bit interested in *any* subject, then you should admit that law school most likely is not for you. Better to then cut your losses, and be sadder but wiser. For about $260 (and even that only if you've bought *all* of these before making your decision), you'll have realized you should avoid the waste of tens of thousands more—and of three years of your life.

(You can always resell these to another prospective law school student, or to someone who's already in law school—the latter being the intended market for these materials in the first place. If and when you decide not to go to law school after reading these, and you haven't taken the LSAT—Law School Aptitude Test—yet, you'll also have saved yourself the cost, and stress, of *that* lovely experience.)

* * *

If you're already sure that you're going to go to law school, *soon,* try to get these early enough to read them in the first month of summer vacation. (This assumes you are graduating from college at the end of the spring semester, and starting law school with the upcoming fall semester.)

These are not "kiddie books," to be read only by those not yet in law school. *Quite the contrary.* But I carefully selected them from among the dozens of self-help books for beginning law students. —And, after all, *beginning* law students know nothing more than *you* do about the law (and perhaps less), even if you're still in high school. Because you've read *this* book to *this* point, I am sure they're not over your head.

If you can't find these works in a law school bookstore, and can't or don't want to order them through a bookstore, you can order them direct. Have your credit card ready. If you prefer, when you call you can get information for ordering by mail, prepaid. The phone numbers that follow are repeated in the appendix:

Aspen Law & Business · (800) 234-1660
Delaney Publications*   (201) 836-2543
West   (800) 328-9352

Settling In - Phase One:
Commercial Outlines

Any law school professor who's asked—and some who aren't—will warn you against buying a commercial outline. But as chapter 3 showed, the profs are not in your corner. Commercial outlines are absolute necessities. (In fact, many of them are written by law school professors.)

Note: Commercial Outlines are not to be confused with your personal *outline, discussed in chapter 7. Even though* both *are absolute necessities, the difference is crucial.*

Many publishers do commercial outlines. In alphabetical order, the ones I'm aware of are Black Letter Law (published by West), Blond's® (an imprint of Sulzburger & Graham), Casenote, Emanuel, the Finals Law School Exam Series, Finkelstein, Gilbert (a Harcourt Brace division), Legalines (another Harcourt Brace division), Siegel's (an Emanuel imprint), Smith's Review (another Emanuel imprint), Spectra, and Sum & Substance (a division of West). Few law school bookstores carry them all, however. They're nearly always in an 8½" x 11" format, and run about $11-$23, even new. (See below on how to get used copies at half-price.)

There are two kinds of commercial outlines. The first consists mostly of canned briefs. The same publisher does, say, three different outlines for Contracts. Each is meant to accompany a specific casebook or two. The commercial outline also includes—as the name implies—a short outline of the law in that subject. Usually, this is interspersed with the canned briefs. With these, you can easily follow along in the course.

The second type is more like a *textbook* of first-year law for the course in question. It concerns Black Letter Law. This consists of the basic legal concepts and their definitions. Black Letter Law outlines dispense with the briefs. Instead, they just give a one-sentence summary of key cases, in passing.

Casenote, for example, has *two* series of outlines now. One, the "Legal Brief" series, contains—as its name implies—just the briefs. Apparently, it contains briefs for *all* the cases used in *all* the first-year casebooks. The other, "Law Outlines," concerns Black Letter Law, with only passing mention of the cases. Another publisher that does two kinds of commercial outlines is Harcourt Brace. Its Legalines series contains briefs. The Gilbert series contains Black Letter Law.

I recommend the second type.

---

* For Delaney Publications, just leave your order and your address. They enclose a bill with the shipment—and trust you to pay it.

> Your (Black Letter Law)* commercial outline will be
> your single most important information source—other
> than the personal outline you prepare yourself.

Even though Black Letter Law commercial outlines are absolute necessities, it probably doesn't make any difference whose you buy. And there's really little difference among all the products for either type of outline. I like material that contains questions, and then gives answers and explanations as to why the right answer was right and the wrong answers were wrong. It's a good way to test your knowledge. (Gilbert and Siegel's are especially useful for this.) But there are other ways to do it—as you'll see in the addendum to chapter 7. Try to get those whose content seems better for *you.*

If you live near several law schools, check out the selection of commercial outlines in each of their bookstores, so you can survey as many choices as possible. Take some time to browse, and try to get the one you like most for each course—even if you have to buy it new.

On the other hand, once you've pulled out the Black Letter Law on a topic, you won't need to refer to that section of the outline any more. So, it isn't like a reference manual where you're constantly going over the same material in it again and again. (However, you'll be doing that with your *personal* outline.) Therefore, unless you have a strong preference, any used copy in clean condition is probably your best choice in any given subject.

Unlike the situation with the canned briefs outlines, Black Letter Law outlines stay virtually the same from year to year. And because they aren't assigned reading (quite the contrary!), you don't have to wait to find out what casebooks you'll be using. Definitely don't wait until you get to law school before you buy them, because by then all the used copies will be gone. Instead, a couple of weeks after the end of the fall and spring semester before you start law school, go to the bookstore/s at whatever law schools are nearby. By then, the stores will have finished buying back materials and will have priced them and put them back out on the shelf. You'll probably find several in very good condition.

You should have read the primers before you look at the corresponding Black Letter Law commercial outlines. (This is because if you don't have at least some grounding in the subject matter, you'll have a much harder time deciding which outline is good.)

---

* My use of "Black Letter Law" does not specifically refer to West Publishing's "Black Letter Law" commercial outline series. Chapter 6 discusses Black Letter Law in the usual, generic sense.

Settling In - Phase Two:
The Restatements

If you're pretty sure you want to go to law school, or have already been accepted (or have already started), here are some more self-help books that are extremely useful...

It's possible that when you've read the primers, *Learning Legal Reasoning,* and the commercial outlines, you'll find that you really *like* Law. If so, you might want to get ahold of some *real* law books. And there's nothing better than the *Restatements.*

These are multi-volume works, prepared by the American Law Institute (ALI). Chapter 3 mentioned how, in the early 1920s, the Committee on the Establishment of a Permanent Organization for the Improvement of the Law had criticized the "lack of agreement among members of the profession on the fundamental principles of the common law." The permanent organization that resulted from its report, in 1923, is the American Law Institute. It's a *very* prestigious outfit. Each *Restatement* is the work of some of the best legal minds in the U.S., who put in *years* on it. They get a thorough critique of each draft, from hundreds of law professors, judges, and practitioners. It has been said that the *Restatements* have authority second only to U.S. Supreme Court case law. Often, that's no exaggeration.

As their name implies, they state general legal principles in an updated form. The first set of *Restatements* was done between 1923 and the end of WWII. A second one followed, starting in 1952. It's always referred to as *The Restatement (Second) of...*Whatever. In 1987, ALI began its Third *Restatements* project.

For Torts, Property, and Contracts, among others, the Second series is the current one. Reference to these works is abbreviated "R2T," R2P," and "R2K" for torts, property, and contracts, respectively.* A *Restatement (Third) of Property* is in the works, but it might not be available until you're out of law school. In contrast, the *original* series of volumes on Restitution is *still* used, because there's been no need to overhaul the subject.

The American Law Institute sells them. Law libraries get them in hardcover. However, ALI also has a student edition. It's in paperback. The volumes in the student edition are sold as a set, not individually. They do not include the case citations the cloth edition has. Big deal. No loss, given your needs at this point.

The Contracts set is in three volumes, for $46 (plus $4 postage). The Torts set is in two volumes, for $37, including postage. (As mentioned, property is

---

* In sports, "K" is a baseball term, meaning a "strike." But in law, "K" stands for "contract." The course, Contracts, is abbreviated "Ks." Although at first glance it appears that the logical abbreviation for Contract is "Con," "Con" is the designated abbreviation for "Constitutional," as in "Con Law."

now being updated, and the *Restatements* that you could use for the other first-year subjects aren't as directly related to your needs.)

You do not have to consider a purchase just on the basis of my comments, though. Visit a law library and see the (hardcover) sets for yourself. If you wish, call ALI, at (800) 253-6397. They'll send you a catalogue with a detailed description of the contents of everything they publish, along with a history of the ALI. (Oddly, though, the catalogue they sent me didn't list the student editions of the *Restatements*. So be sure to specifically ask them to include this.)

Settling In - Phase Three: First-Year on Tape

You should get one more set of materials besides the primers, *Learning Legal Reasoning,* and the Black Letter Law commercial outlines: audio cassette tapes. Several vendors offer these (for advanced as well as first-year courses). Their approach is quite straightforward. No Socratic Method,* just lectures. They *de-mystify* first-year law. The vendors have gone to a lot of trouble to make these *interesting*.

If you get the primers and the commercial outlines, you might wonder why you should get the tapes, too. —After all, if you've already learned the jargon and the concepts from the primers and the commercial outlines, why bother? The primers don't try to cover everything—just key concepts, especially the concepts students have the most trouble with. So you should start with them. The commercial outlines do cover everything, but they're very cut-and-dried. The tapes combine many of the best features of these other materials—and pull each course together in a way that the other two can't. The Law can be difficult. It's certainly extensive. It will take some effort to master it. Yet, you don't want to keep going over exactly the same teaching materials again and again. That gets boring: the eyes glaze over, the ears stop hearing. But using *all* these materials gives you a variety of approaches. Something you didn't "get" when it was presented one way might make sense when presented another way. And going over something again, but from a different perspective, might give you some insights you would otherwise have missed.

Even if you prepare early for law school, the material is completely new to you. It takes awhile to let it sink in. There are many points of law that I simply did not comprehend the first time around—or maybe it was the second, or third. And even when I began to catch on, it took a while to fully grasp the ins and outs of it, so that I could do more than just parrot what I'd read. True understanding takes time—and true understanding saves you a

---

* Amen. —And by the way, these tapes prove that at least *some* law professors *can* teach…when they want to.

lot of time (and anxiety) during your final exams (and in law practice). But once you're in law school, you don't *have* time to let something sink in...unless you've had a head start.

So now you're probably wondering, why bother with the *other* materials? Why not just get the tapes? Well, for one thing, all you get are the tapes; no written materials (usually). For another, they're intended to be used to *review* a course, before the final. They assume you're already familiar with the material. The pace on the ones I listened to was brisk. So, if you do get any or all of them, you will need to have read the appropriate primer, and preferably the commercial outline that covers the Black Letter Law for the course.

Unlike the primers, some of these tapes were on the market when I was in law school. But I was not aware of them. The bookstores at my law school didn't carry them. I (again) wish to God I'd known they existed, and that I'd discovered them before *starting* law school. Although I've only heard a few of the following, my hunch is that the others are every bit as good as the ones I sampled. (Their toll-free numbers follow after all the descriptions.)

<u>Aspen Law & Business</u>

As mentioned, Aspen does primers. As of this writing, they're testing the tapes market with just one subject, Civil Procedure. It's the first install-ment of what's apparently going to be called the "Fireside" series.

You get six cassettes, total running time about nine hours, for roughly $50. Joseph W. Glannon—who's a professor at Boston's Suffolk University—is the lecturer. I've heard the entire set, and can vouch for it. (Glannon isn't as good a lecturer as he is a writer, in part because he's just reading a script into a microphone rather than lecturing to a live audience. But despite the less than stellar style, the substance of his tapes is very good.) With the tapes, you get a booklet of questions he poses on the cassettes—to which he then gives the answers on the cassettes. You can look the questions over ahead of time, work out your answers, and then listen to find out how well you did. (If Aspen succeeds with this, perhaps they'll put Glannon on tape for torts, too.)

<u>Blond's®</u>

As mentioned above, Blond's does commercial outlines. Niel Blond, a University of Akron law school graduate, started the company more than a decade ago. He still runs it—though it's now a division of Sulzburger & Graham, the publishing firm. So far, Blond's does tapes on three first-year subjects: Civ Pro, Con Law, and Torts. Each subject has six hours' worth of cassettes, and costs $50. The Civ Pro lecturer is Lisa Ann Kloppenberg, of the University of Oregon. The Con Law and Torts lecturer is Glenn Harlan Reynolds, of the University of Tennessee.

<u>Emanuel</u>

Emanuel is another commercial outline company that's getting into the audio cassette business. As of this writing, they have one subject on the market: Constitutional Law. The series has 11 tapes. Running time is 16- hours. Cost is $38. The instructor is Mr. Emanuel himself. I've not heard any of his cassettes. But assuming Emanuel is a good lecturer, his tapes are clearly the best generic buy in Constitutional Law. (By the time you're reading this book, his company should have additional courses on cassette.)

<u>Fleming's Fundamentals of Law (FFL)</u>

FFL's founder and sole instructor is Jeff A. Fleming, who teaches at the West Los Angeles School of Law. I have heard some demo tapes of Fleming's lectures, and was impressed.

He does cassettes for all six first-year courses. Each is split in half, "I" and "II." For each half, you get two tapes (though for Prop I, you get three). Each set of two (or three) tapes costs about $60. So, for most subjects, the total cost is roughly $120—for four or five tapes, total.* That's more than anyone else charges, but apparently there are some good reasons for that:

First, these tapes include more than the substantive material. Each part of each subject is four hours long. The first 3½ hours are the substantive material. The final half-hour has examsmanship tips (see next chapter).

Second, unlike the other vendors, Fleming provides written materials. These include a course outline, twice-a-year updates on changes in the law, and some suggestions for tricks to help you remember things about the substantive law for each course. In truth, these outlines are not important. Nor are the updates, because first-year material hardly changes at all, let alone quickly. However, the memory-retention devices could be helpful.

Third, the FFL materials include three sample exam questions, with a sample "model answer" for each one.

Fourth—and perhaps most important of all—Fleming asks you to answer a mock-exam question and then send in your answer. An attorney on the Fleming staff will critique your answer, orally, on a cassette tape—and will mail the tape back to you. Unfortunately, you only get one time around for this, per course. (And obviously, you shouldn't do it until you've studied the material.) Even so, no one else offers it.

---

* Fleming also does a bar review course, but it's just for California, unlike many of the others'. (See chapter 18 re. bar review courses.) And as with many of the other bar-prep companies, FFL wants students to sign up in first-year, even though they won't take it until more than two years hence. If you're in California, and sign up for the FFL California bar review course, you pay a $150 deposit. That deposit entitles you to a 20% discount on any FFL materials you purchase. (Fleming's first-year tapes are good for non-Californians, too. But only those taking the California bar prep course from FFL get the discounts.) By putting the $150 down, you get each tape for approximately $47—a total of $94 per subject.

Unlike nearly all the other vendors, the FFL materials and tapes are available only through mail-order (or at an on-site course). They aren't sold in stores, except in northern California and a handful of cities in other states.

Gilbert "Legal Legends" / "First Year Program"

Gilbert (a division of Harcourt Brace). was listed above as another commercial outline vendor. Its audio cassette series is called "Legal Legends." Here are the selections for first-year...

Civ Pro: 5 tapes, 7½ hours, $60.
   Richard D. Freer, Emory U. (I've listened to them. They're very good.)
Con Law: 4 tapes, about 6 hours, $46.
   John E. Nowak, Univ. of Illinois.
Contracts: same.
   Michael I. Spak, Chicago-Kent College of Law,
   Illinois Institute of Technology.
Crim: 4 tapes, also about 6 hours, $40 (not $46).
   Charles H. Whitebread, U. of Southern California.
Prop: 4 tapes, 6 hours, $46.
   Paula A. Franzese, Seton Hall Univ. Law School.
Torts: same.
   Richard J. Conviser, Chicago-Kent.

If you buy these Gilbert tapes separately, the total cost is just under $285. However, in a neat competitive move, Gilbert packages five of these six (all but Con Law) as its "First Year Program." It sells for $195—which saves you $45 compared to buying its five subjects (Civ Pro, Contracts, Crim, Prop, and Torts) separately. Plus, they throw in a couple of cassettes on Law School Exam Writing ($20 if purchased separately). I've heard the Law School Exam Writing tapes, and don't think much of them. But the price on the First Year Program looks right, anyway. (If you do get the FYP, and will be taking Con Law in year one, be sure to get Con Law tapes, too, from any of these vendors.)

PMBR

PMBR is a bar-review company. (Chapter 18 discusses these.) It's also evidently the parent company of Multistate Legal Press, Inc., which does the Finals commercial outline series. PMBR has put its material on audio. However, recently they've been marketing this as first-year tapes as well, killing two birds with one stone. No harm in that. Just keep in mind that because these tapes are for those who have long since finished first-year, they're light on explanations, and heavy on quickly covering *everything*. If you're only planning to get one set of tapes, though, don't get these. Instead, use some other vendor's as your audio primer. Use PMBR's, if at all, only at the very end of the course, as a true review.
   (Note: The tapes I heard started out by saying that the majority of first-

year law school exams today are multiple choice. Although I have not conducted a survey of all the law schools in America, I have yet to hear of even one law school that uses anything other than essay exams for the Big Six first-year courses. There's nothing wrong with using bar-review tapes to study for first-year finals. But PMBR is flat-out wrong when they say essay exams are vanishing from first-year finals.)

The lecturers are PMBR staff members. The lectures are recorded from live bar exam prep sessions. For Civ Pro, Prop, and Torts, the tapes run six hours. For Crim Law, they run three hours. And for Contracts, nine. Each subject costs $50.

Sum & Substance "Outstanding Professor" Series

Sum & Substance was mentioned above as a vendor of commercial outlines (and a division of West Publishing). Its audio cassettes are as follows...

Civ Pro: Your choice of two—
   1) a 4-tape set, running 5 hours, about $60, presented by
      Arthur R. Miller of Harvard Law School, or
   2) a 5-tape set, running time 6 hours, about $50, presented by
      Doug Blaze of the University of Tennessee.
   (Note the premium for the Harvard prof.)
Con Law: 6 tapes, 8 hours, 50 bucks.
   Mary Cheh, George Washington U.. (I've heard her. She's good.)
Contracts: 4 tapes, 6- hours, $50.
   Douglas Whaley, Ohio State U.
Crim: 5 tapes, "7.2" hours, $50.
   Joshua Dressler, McGeorge School of Law - Univ. of the Pacific.
Prop: 5 tapes, 7 hours, $50.
   Julian C. Juergensmeyer, Univ. of Florida.
Torts: 4 tapes, 6- hours, $50.
   Steven R. Finz, author, legal expert, and practicing attorney.

Depending on which Civ Pro set you get, total cost is about $310 - $320.

TextTour™

Tiger Publishing Group does two types of audio cassettes. The first is their "TextTour"™ series. For each first-year course, they do a set of tapes tailored to *specific casebooks.* So, you shouldn't consider getting any until you know what casebook is assigned for each class. That's the first difference between TextTour™ and the other products mentioned above. The second is that Tiger Publishing didn't hire law professors to give these lectures. They use a professional narrator. (The scripts, however, are prepared using material supplied by law professors—supposedly.) Third, you get more tapes. Whereas the other vendors provide 4-6 cassettes per subject, TextTour™ gives you 12-18: each subject in TextTour™ has two sets of tapes, and each set has 6-9 cassettes in it. Fourth, each set costs $35. So, to get all the tapes for a specific casebook and course, the price is $70. (I'm not mentioning the running time, because these are casebook-specific. You can check this out for yourself.)

I listened to a demo tape that included material from the series on Civ Pro. To me, there seemed no loss in quality just because the lecturer was a professional narrator and not a "Law School Legend" or "Outstanding Professor." The style was good, and the contents were comparable to those I've heard from other vendors.

Tiger Publishing does a second type of cassette tape series: "Incredibly Easy" Black Letter Law. These are generic, not casebook-specific. Each tape lasts about an hour and a half. For Civ Pro and Property, you get nine cassettes; for Con Law, six. (As of this writing, there's a set on Contracts in the works.) And, not surprisingly, the price is lower for the generic tapes: $45 per subject.

(Be advised: When I called Tiger Publishing, I spoke with a manager. He informed me that each year a national magazine for law school students rates the various books, tapes, and computer programs available to law school students, and that TextTour's tapes were annually rated better than anyone else's. Curious, I then called the magazine in question and spoke with its editor. Contrary to what the guy at Tiger Publishing had told me, she said that her magazine just *listed,* every year, the books, tapes, and computer programs available. They did not rate them. I don't know if the manager's statement was an honest mistake. But if you call and someone tells you the same thing, it simply ain't so.)

Black's Law Publishing - The Marino System

This vendor is listed out of its alphabetical order because my research assistant and I, for reasons we cannot fathom, could not get them to provide any information other than what's in their ads. Each of us called and got an "orders only" answering service. They said they couldn't send us any sales materials. However, the order-takers promised to contact Black's Law Publishing to have them send product literature. Nothing happened, despite further calls. Eventually, we got the number of the company itself, and phoned there. Again we were promised brochures, etc., but nothing happened—despite a final, fruitless, call.

It made no difference whether we identified ourselves as potential customers or as researchers gathering information for a book. With regard to the latter, it had been explained that this book intended to list the company, its toll-free number, and its product. Regardless of why we said we wanted the material, we got nothing, despite a month's worth of phone calls.

Apparently, The Marino System expects law school students to spend hundreds of dollars on tapes with nothing more to go on than the ads it runs in various magazines. Yet, most vendors of cassette tapes do not allow you to return their product for a refund if you're not satisfied with it. So, you're expected to buy a pig in a poke. I assume they've had success with this approach, or else they wouldn't keep running the ads. However, I don't do business that way—and I hope you don't either.

* * *

Some law school bookstores carry one or more of these vendors' tape series. However, you can also order them by phone, or call to make arrangements to order them by mail. Be sure to ask for product literature.

Toll-free numbers (repeated in the appendix):

Aspen Law & Business	(800) 234-1660
Blond's® (Sulzburger & Graham)	(800) 436-2348
Emanuel	(800) 362-6835
Fleming's Fundamentals of Law	
California Only	(800) 529-3926
Calls from Elsewhere	(714) 770-3040
Gilbert "Law School Legends"	
(Harcourt Brace)	(800) 787-8717
PMBR	(800) 523-0777
Sum & Substance "Outstanding	
Professor" (West)	(800) 876-4457
TextTour™ & "Incredibly Easy"	
(Tiger Publishing)	(800) 428-0456

Of Cost-Sharing and Confidentiality

If you have time, get a set of tapes for each subject and listen to them before you even set foot in law school—provided you've read the appropriate primer and commercial outline first. And if you do listen before you start law school, listen again just before the course ends. It's great review—which is what it's meant to be.

The problem, of course, is deciding whose product to buy. Do you choose on the basis of price? Number of tapes? Cost per minute of running time? Reputation of the law school where the lecturer is a professor? Sorry, but I can be no help here. —Besides, more important than *which* one you choose is that you *do* choose one...and then conscientiously absorb what's in it.

Whatever you decide, maybe you can find another prospective law school student to share the cost with you. Regardless of whether you purchase them alone or with others, you can always sell these tapes, later, to one or more fellow students and recoup part of your expense. (However, it might be a very good idea for you to save them until after you've passed your bar exam. This is because at least five of the subjects on virtually every state's bar exam are first-year subjects. Chapters 17 and 18 discuss all this. —And even if you decide to save your tapes, you can always rent them out in the meantime.)

But whatever you do, I urge you *not* to make these tapes available to your fellow students while *you're* still in first-year. If you do as this chapter advises, you'll be far ahead of others. You don't want to give up that edge just for a few dollars in the short run. That's why you should get these tapes during the summer, splitting the cost with one or more other people—who, preferably, are going to a different law school from the one you'll be attending. If you do end up selling the tapes or renting them out during first-year, at least make sure your customers aren't fellow students at *your* school. And, I am sorry to say, you should not tell anyone else at your law school about it—until after your first year, that is.*

The only possible exception to this concerns your study group. (Chapter 7 discusses what a study group is and how it should work.) If you have not bought tapes for all your subjects before you start law school, and want to share the cost with others, the members of your study group are the logical candidates.

Dollars & Sense

Whether or not you get any of the materials recommended in this chapter is more a matter of time than money. Especially if you have the time between now and law school, these things are a *very* worthwhile investment. Law school will still be difficult even if you show up with a knowledge of all the basic terms and concepts. Getting the jump on the professor doesn't mean you'll land on easy street and be able to coast through first-year. It does mean you'll have a very good chance to do very well.

You're probably thinking that it's easy for me to urge you to buy things, because it doesn't take any money out of *my* pocket. Actually, though, it did: I've acquired and "tested" much of what's recommended here, because that was the only way to see if it was worthwhile. The total cost for all these recommended items is just over $500, as of this writing.

It may be that you're not interested in getting a starting salary of close to $100,000 a year, in which case you don't have to care whether or not you do well in law school. Good for you. (If you take out loans to pay for it, though, your pre-law indifference to the "green" will turn into the post-graduate "blues" with amazing speed.) But whatever you plan to do with your law degree, you should at least *learn the law*. If you're an idealist who eschews the big firms and the in-house corporate counsel route, it will be all the more important for you to know the law when you go your own way: Those who don't play it safe by joining a large organization (law firm, corporation, government) will suddenly realize that they'd *better* know the law, when going up against people from large organizations. Often, there's no time to look it up before you need to make decisions. And when you're on your own, there's virtually no one to turn to. Even with a large organization, you might soon be *out in* the cold if you don't *know* the law, cold. And as I hope is clear by now, law school itself is of little help in this regard.

---

* And although it goes against my own commercial interest, I advise you not to tell anyone else at your law school about *Planet Law School*—until you've finished first-year, that is (with the possible exception of those in your study group.)

As mentioned regarding the primers, if you get these materials before you go to law school, and then decide not to go after all, you can resell them; even those who *are* in law school will buy them—for in fact, that's really whom they were created for.

Please note that I am not recommending that you buy just anything and everything simply because it concerns the law or law school. Quite the contrary...as you will see by the end of this chapter. To again turn to Turow's *One L*: Here's what happened to him in his first semester, when he realized he was in trouble— "I grabbed at anything which could make the law surer, more clear. I became a kind of instant sucker." And later: "For me, the anxieties showed in a spending spree on hornbooks, outlines, prepared briefs...but I could not resist my insecurities...I was convinced that if I skipped the purchase of any one item it would prove to be crucial." But by then it was too late. He no longer had time to effectively study them.

The same thing happened to me—and it happens to almost every law student.* Don't let it happen to you. Remember the fable of the tortoise and the hare? Be a tortoise. And get a head start. Otherwise, you'll either be leaping in every direction (as Turow and I did)—or you'll be frozen in terror, caught in the glare of the headlights of the final exams bearing down on you at accelerating speed.

There are "study aids," and there are study *aids*. Don't go the sucker route simply because you've hit the panic button as finals approach. Although I can't promise you'll be delighted with these materials, I can guarantee that you'll find them a lot more useful than your casebooks or class sessions. So spend the bucks and buy the books (and the commercial outlines—and the tapes). By investing your money (and your time) wisely now, you'll avoid wasting time and money later—when you can no longer afford to. Those who heed this advice will be very glad you did. Those who don't will realize, too late, that I was right.

Law school is costly. You'll be paying tens of thousands of dollars for tuition, etc.—and giving up tens of thousands of dollars you could have earned in the three years you'll be spending in law school. In light of that, now is not the time to pinch pennies on things that can give you an edge. The financial return you can get on your investment in the aforementioned materials will truly astound you...if you follow through with them.

---

* Perhaps that's why some of the vendors mentioned in this book would not send product literature—by definition, a panic-stricken consumer does not take time to make an informed choice.

Now, having exhorted you to spend money, here are some more tips on how to *save* it...

<u>Casebooks</u>

The simple truth is: You don't need to buy any of the assigned casebooks. Repeat: *You don't need to buy any of the assigned casebooks.*

No, that doesn't mean you should steal them, or mooch other students' copies. Just think it through: No matter how efficient your professors are, they'll never cover more than a *small* fraction of the material in those books. Once you finish your courses, you'll never again have any use for any of their casebooks: they're worthless as reference materials. So you're paying a lot for very little.

—The casebooks are *expensive.* Sure, you might be able to sell them back to the bookstore at the end of the courses in question. (Maybe, but only if they aren't about to be replaced by newer editions. And even if they're still state-of-the-art, when you sell them back you only get, at most, a fourth of what you paid for them new.)

They're *heavy.* If you feel that you just aren't a proper law student unless you're lugging around 20 pounds of nearly useless material, you have an unfortunate psychological condition that this book cannot cure.

If you buy your casebooks as software (see the addendum to this chapter), you avoid the weight problem. You can print out the cases, and your case briefs, as you go along. Then take them to class with you. However, you clearly can't sell your materials back to the bookstore—or to another student, for that matter. And you still have the problem of having paid a lot for relatively little.

For those of you who are practical—and, dare I say, wise?— your law school's library will have at least one copy of the edition of each casebook that each of your professors has assigned. Look at the cases there, for free. If you want to have the casebook material with you when you go into class, you can make a photocopy. If your law school library doesn't have the relevant casebook, you might make a deal with a fellow student to photocopy the assigned material. (Of course, you're not supposed to photocopy copyrighted material. As an attorney, therefore, I cannot advise you to engage in a no-no. However, I have no control over your actions, so...) No matter what you spend on this, it will be far less than what you spend if you buy the casebook itself.

If the professor calls on you, it's unlikely he or she will even notice whether or not you have a casebook. It would be astonishing if the professor criticized you for having "mere" photocopies or print-outs. And you will probably be called on only once, if at all, from the first through the last day of the course—unless you volunteer (which you shouldn't; see chapter 8). You will not be penalized on your final grade even if you get "caught" without the casebook. (But you *might* be penalized if you bring a *commercial outline* into the classroom.)

Don't buy the casebooks. Use those funds, instead, for the materials discussed above—and below.*

However, because most of you will ignore the preceding advice, here's a tip on how to save money even while spending it: You will be assigned to a "section" (although your school might use another term for it). Professors have also been assigned to each of your section's courses. Those profs were required to notify the law school bookstore of what casebooks they will use. The bookstore has (presumably) ordered them. After you have notified your law school that you will enroll there, call it sometime in the summer. Find out what section you've been assigned to. Then find out the name and phone number of the law school bookstore. Call and get the list of required books for your section's courses. Be sure to find out which *edition* will be used: Most casebooks have more lives than the *Friday the 13th* movie series. You particularly want to know if a required casebook is a *new* edition. As mentioned above, many bookstores buy back students' books at the end of each semester. If a given book is still the current edition, and can be used again, this is likely. The bookstore pays (at most) 25% of what it sold them for as new. Then it re-sells them as used books. (The mark-up is 100%—five times the mark-up when it sells the book new. But the price to you is still just 50% of what it would otherwise be.) You want to get your hands on *used* copies of old casebooks that have not been superseded. You thereby cut your expenses for required books in half. (Just wait 'til you see what they cost *new*.) Wherever you are, there's probably a law school nearby. Call its bookstore and see if they stock the titles you need. However, even if they do, they might not tell you on the phone if they have used copies. Regardless, if it's not too far away, go to the store and try to find what you need, used.

That's the way I did it. I got nearly all my required casebooks as used copies—and some of them were in such good condition you couldn't even tell they weren't new. (Yes, I bought the damned casebooks—and eventually realized that I'd still wasted my money, despite having bought them used.) Even if the only used casebook you can find is full of highlighting and ink underlinings, don't worry: you shouldn't pay full price just to get a pristine copy of something that's a waste of money in the first place. It's the least important book you will use in law school, and you will be disposing of it after the course. This is no time to splurge just to satisfy a misplaced sense of duty. (Remember: Be sure to get the right edition.)

You can probably get a used law dictionary and used commercial outlines while you're in the bookstore, too. And you don't have to rely solely on law

---

* Then again, if you have money to burn: Leather-bound copies of *Planet Law School* are available in a limited edition for $400 apiece. Each copy is numbered and signed by the author. For an additional $100, the author will inscribe a personal message of your choosing, up to 25 words. —And for a *thousand* dollars, the author will record this entire book on audio cassettes for you. Contact the publisher.

school bookstores. In many cities, there are stores that carry only used books. Some of these have a section on law. Several of the law books I own came from these stores.

Dictionaries

What follows is (more) heresy.

1) Once you're in law school, you do not *need* to buy a law dictionary. When you encounter a term the meaning of which is unknown to you, you can go to the law library and consult a dictionary there.

However, if you choose to follow the recommendations in Chapter 23 regarding pre-law-school activities, you definitely *should* buy a law dictionary. (If you don't follow those recommendations, don't bother to get a law dictionary at all...until you graduate.)

2) And you *don't* have to buy *Black's*. Yes, it's the standard legal dictionary (and is yet another West publication). It's the one the courts nearly always rely on, in their opinions, to state the meanings of terms. But it's of very little use to a first-year law student (or any law student, for that matter). It's even of little use to a practitioner. (For example, as a student, I came across the term "extrinsic evidence," and tried to look it up in my copy of *Black's*. No entry, whether under "evidence" or "extrinsic." —And upon asking several trial lawyers what extrinsic evidence was, I discovered *they* didn't know, either...but they certainly should have. As a second example: there's a basic principle of law known as "contra proferentum." It means that where there's a writing that's ambiguous, and one interpretation favors the side that wrote the document, and the other interpretation goes against that side, a court will choose the second interpretation. After all, the writer had a chance to make it clear, and blew it. So why give the writer a break? But *Black's* doesn't list "contra proferentum." —And of the few dictionaries that do, they usually misspell it as "contra preferentum.")

Courts cite *Black's* because *Black's* has acquired a prestige from the long-standing usage: courts expect to see definitions only from *Black's*. Fine. When you're writing something for a court, and need to quote a definition (which will almost *never* happen), quote *Black's*—after looking the word up in someone else's copy. And if you're the sort of person who just has to own the most expensive, prestigious, impressive something (be it a fountain pen, a car, luggage, what have you), then go ahead and get your own (hardbound) copy. But if you want to understand the meaning of a legal term, get some other publisher's legal dictionary, too; you'll be glad you did. They're better for your needs and cheaper than *Black's*. Examples: *Ballantine's Law Dictionary,* $25 in hardcover; *Barron's Law Dictionary,* prepared by Steven H. Gifis, about $13 in paperback; *Dictionary of Legal Terms,* compiled by the Gilbert-Harcourt Brace staff, approximately $15, paperback, with a pocket-sized version for less than $8; and *A Dictionary of Modern Legal Usage,* compiled by Bryan A. Garner, roughly $17, paperback. (Garner's book includes both "extrinsic evidence" and "contra proferentum.")

One dictionary deserves special mention. It's *Latin for Lawyers,* put out by Emanuel. Most law dictionaries have entries for all the standard Latin phrases the Law uses, so you really don't need this. However, for those who are *already* students of Latin, it could be fun. And it costs less than five bucks.

"Hornbooks"

I hope you will not be the only person in your first-year classes who's read *Planet Law School* (although if you are, then you'll really have an edge). But whether or not you even go to law school, you'll be one of the few people who knows the origin of the term "hornbook," because you're about to find out. (This information is useless academically. But I was always curious about it, and you might be too.)

First, though, a false claim: There are those who say the hornbook got its name during the old circuit-riding days, when lawyers and judges rode horseback from courthouse to courthouse. Supposedly, the hornbook was a reference work that was slung around the horn of the lawyer's saddle. Nonsense. Any books went into saddlebags. (Anyone who's ridden a horse can explain why.) Further, even back then most lawyers and judges rode in buggies. (Lawyers—and courts—are found only where there's enough of an economic surplus to support them—and only after the initial surplus has gone into the infrastructure, such as roads, however primitive.) Also, the only book lawyers and judges usually had in those days was *Blackstone's Commentaries* in an abridged one-volume edition. It concerned only English law, anyway. It was called "Blackstone's," not "the hornbook."

The original hornbook was the generic term of a primer for children in England. (See the *Encyclopedia Britannica's Micropedia,* under "hornbook.") It was not even a book, in the modern sense, for originally it had no pages and no paper in it. It had one small sheet to it, of vellum. This was what people were using until rag paper became the norm (as it still is). On the vellum was printed the alphabet, some diphthongs, and the first ten numerals. The vellum was then stretched onto a wooden rack. The rack had a handle. The vellum was delicate and easily soiled, especially by children. So, it was covered with a layer of cowhorn, pounded so thin as to be nearly transparent.

Thus, the origin of the word "hornbook" is not such as to flatter future attorneys.

If you buy a hornbook for law school, you're wasting your money. They're tempting—after all, they're written by the same authors who did the casebooks: you hope that by reading the hornbook you'll have everything in the corresponding casebook all laid out for you. No way. When you see how thick a hornbook is, you'll see that you won't have time to read it during your first year. (However, I did read most of *Prosser & Keeton on Torts,* before *starting* law school. Alas, it proved to be an inefficient use of my time, because it provided far, far more than I needed to know as a beginning law student. —I was studying hard, but not *smart.*) There are better ways of getting comfortable with the subject matter, as this chapter has shown. Chapter 7 discusses the limited conditions under which you'll want to consult a hornbook.

Save your money. If you feel you really must read a hornbook to be a dutiful first-year student, go to your law school's library and peruse it there, for free. (The sole *possible* exception to this is when the professor who's teaching your course is the author of the hornbook in question. This, of course, is extremely rare. And even then, think twice about opening your wallet.)

Usually a hornbook is just called a hornbook. But occasionally someone refers to it as a "textbook." (Normally, the term "hornbook" is exclusively associated with West publishing.)

* * *

The law is an ocean, and in law school, it's either sink or swim. By the end of each first-year course, most students have learned only how to tread water, at best. The "primers" recommended in this chapter let you splash around with no danger of drowning. The commercial outlines then teach you how to swim, at your own rate, and in water that's shallow enough for you to stand up on the bottom if you need to. With the first-year cassette tapes, you venture into the depths. —But since you will already have learned how to swim, you'll have nothing to fear.

If and when you take the *plunge* into law school, you'll be prepared for that highly competitive on-going event. You'll never be in danger of drowning. And if you follow through on the rest of the advice in this book—especially in the next two chapters—you'll be able to go for the gold on finals.

ADDENDUM to CHAPTER 5:
SOFTWARE for LAW STUDENTS

Emanuel

All of Emanuel's first-year commercial outlines are available as software. The firm has a demo CD-ROM that includes a sampling of all of them (along with some second- and third-year outlines). Many law school bookstores carry this CD-ROM, or you can get it directly from Emanuel by calling. (The number was given in the main body of this chapter, and is repeated in the appendix.) After viewing the demo, you can "unlock" the rest of the material on it via modem or telephone, using your credit card number. Each subject costs $20.

Gilbert

Gilbert Law Summaries, with the Black Letter Law, are available on disk for $28 apiece. The company now also sells, separately, "Casebriefs Interactive Software," which—as the name implies—contains canned case briefs. These are also $28 per subject. If you can't find them in your law school's bookstore, you can call Gilbert at the number given in the main body of this chapter (and repeated in the appendix).

Numina

Numina is a company started in 1989 by two guys who were law school students at the time. It has two software products for Windows®. Each is available for WordPerfect®, MS/Word®, and perhaps others.

The first is the Numina CaseBriefs™. As the name implies, it contains canned briefs, just like the first type of commercial outline discussed in the main body of this chapter. Each software package is geared to a specific casebook. —So, don't consider getting any until you know what casebook you'll be using for each course. The Numina CaseBriefs™ allows you to customize a brief, or to create your own from scratch. You can print out a hard copy for class.

The firm's second product is called the Numina Socratutor™. It's a Black Letter Law program, like the second type of commercial outline. The Emanuel and Smith's Review commercial outlines are available on the Numina Socratutor™; your choice. The Emanuel material is a "capsule outline." The Smith's Review material is more complete. As with the Numina CaseBriefs™, you can customize it to suit your own needs.

The price for each set of Numina's software, whether CaseBriefs™ or Socratutor™, is about $23. Some law school bookstores now carry Numina's products. The toll-free number (repeated in the appendix) is (800) 529-1065.

Athena IntelliSystems

This company does software called Top 10™. It's available for Contracts, Torts, Property, and Constitutional Law, among others, but no Civil Procedure (as of this writing). The first-year material is generic, rather than case-book-specific. Contracts, Torts, and Property are sold together as a "First Year Power Pack" for $50, which is $25 less than if you bought them separately.

My research assistant placed several calls to their toll-free number during a three-week period. Each time, he only got an answering machine. Each time, he left a message giving my name and address and requesting product literature. I never received any. However, at one point—after I left an angry message complaining about not getting anything—someone from the company called, apologized, and promised to send product literature to me immediately. I had explained I was trying to gather material for this book. I never did get anything, despite leaving another angry message two weeks later on their answering machine. If you can't find their software in a law school bookstore, you'd probably do best to forget it. I figure if they're so sloppy about dealing with someone who's trying to give them a little bit of free publicity, they'll be very sloppy indeed in dealing with their customers.

West

West Publishing's Black Letter Law commercial outlines now include a software disk along with the paperback book. Because West's materials are available in virtually all law school bookstores, I won't go into detail about them. However, if you can't find them, call West's toll-free number, given in the main body of this chapter.

The Lexis "Student Office"

Lexis* is the legal half of Lexis-Nexis. The Lexis "half" is for lawyers. The Nexis "half" is for everyone else. Both have huge databases. I've listed Lexis last, instead of in alphabetical order, because it requires some explaining.

Lexis is a major on-line database service, used extensively by lawyers. (The other major vendor is Westlaw, part of the West legal publishing empire...And I'm just waiting for a person or corporation named Kohls to start something called "Kohlslaw.") Law schools sign up with Lexis (or Westlaw), to give all their students access to the on-line database. As part of the deal, Lexis (and Westlaw) provide (rudimentary) training in how to use

---

* "Lexis" is a made-up word, based on the Latin, "lex." "Lex" means both "the word" (as in "lexicography") and "the law." "Lex" is the nominative singular. Our words "legal" and "legislate" come from the genitive singular, "legis." (Very few lawyers—these days—know this...or care. Nor should they, necessarily. However, as with the origin of the term "hornbook," discussed in the main body of this chapter, it's a nice tidbit of legal trivia. —No, I can't explain "Lexus" for a car...and I'm told that Lexis once *sued* Lexus for trade-mark infringement.)

the service efficiently.

Recently, though, Lexis has gone a step farther, with its "Student Office." Under the normal situation, a student has to go into the law school and use one of the computers there in order to access the Lexis database. With the Student Office, you can access Lexis directly from your home, on your own computer. You do this by purchasing the Lexis "Folio VIEWS®," which enables your computer to interface with Lexis and import and process the database material.*

The price depends on what school you attend. Some schools have a "full partnership" with Lexis, whereby the school itself picks up almost the entire tab. Others have only a "limited partnership," to one extent or another. At those schools, the student has to pay something directly to Lexis. As of this writing, the most a student has to pay for Folio VIEWS® is $90. However, it's a sure thing this price will go up: the people at Lexis told me so.

Lexis also has an arrangement with Steven L. Emanuel, the commercial outline entrepreneur (and Harvard Law grad). You can acquire Emanuel outlines—through Lexis—on disk, in a format compatible with Folio VIEWS®. There's a separate charge for each outline you get. Also, Lexis is a subsidiary of Reed-Elsevier, Inc.. Another Reed-Elsevier sub is The Michie Company. ("Michie" is pronounced "Mickey.") It's a casebook/textbook vendor. (The Butterworth Company, another Reed-Elsevier subsidiary that's a legal publisher, recently was merged into Michie.) Michie casebooks and textbooks are also available on disk now, through Lexis, at a separate price per book.

The Lexis representatives make much of the fact that the Student Office will enable you to join a Lexis e-mail system with other law students. They also tout the fact that Steven Emanuel hosts on-line conferences in which law students can participate. And it's true that Westlaw, the Lexis competitor, offers nothing like this (as of this writing), other than its own Westlaw database.

If you're a real computer whiz, and don't already have some sort of e-mail arrangement, the Student Office could be very nice. Likewise, if you want to use Emanuel commercial outlines, and prefer printing out the text on an as-needed basis. As for the "conferences" hosted by Emanuel himself, I have my doubts. And regarding the Michie casebooks and textbooks, this has value only if one or more of those books are assigned. The fact is, you don't *need* this in first-year, and perhaps not at all in law school.

—On the other hand, if you're planning to do some heavy-duty legal writing, the database import feature can save you an *enormous* amount of

---

* Computer people—of which I am definitely not one—know that Folio VIEWS® is used on tens of millions of desktop computers, in the form of Novell Netware® Help, as the delivery system for more than a thousand commercial publishers on CD-ROM and diskette.

time. It will be worth the $90 (or more). Then too, skill at Computer-Assisted Legal Research is becoming an absolute necessity. You can practice using a computer at your law school, but you may well prefer to do it from home. If you've already invested a bundle in a computer and a modem, I'd say put the extra 90 bucks or so into the Lexis Student Office, even if you end up doing without the Emanuel outlines and Michie books.

If you want to check all this out, here's the toll-free number (repeated in the appendix): (800) 528-1891. Lexis will send you a free demo disk and product literature.

* * *

For those who are really into computers and the Information Super-Highway, the American Bar Association has a book by G. Burgess Allison, *The Lawyer's Guide to the Internet.* It's a 1995 paperback, $30. The ABA's toll-free number is (800) 285-2221. Nolo Publishing has a better one, a 1996 paperback for $40, *Law on the Net,* by James Evans. It's also available via subscription on CD-ROM for $90 a year, and through America Online. For these last two, it's updated quarterly. Nolo Publishing's number (repeated in the appendix) is (800) 992-6656.

Chapter 6 - Examsmanship*

The pedagogy of law school brings to mind a famous slip of the tongue by Richard J. Daley, Sr., for decades the notorious Mayor of Chicago. (The current mayor is Richard *M.* Daley, one of his sons.) The Vietnam War was at its peak in 1968, and the Democratic National Convention was being held in the Windy City. Large numbers of Chicago's Finest went berserk and repeatedly attacked peace demonstrators who'd gathered at some distance from the convention site. Upon receiving reports that his "thin blue line" had rioted, Hizzoner stated, "The policeman is not there to *create* disorder. The policeman is there to *preserve* disorder." (Obviously, he'd meant to say "prevent" rather than "preserve.") Every time I think of law school professors, I remember that statement of Richard Daley's. The professor deliberately both *creates* disorder *and* seeks to preserve it. It's *your* job to bring *order* to it—especially to the mess presented to you as the essay questions of your law school finals. (And by the way, it's similar to the practice of law.)

Scott Turow had this to say, in *One L,* about the experience:

> Finals were regarded with an institutional earnestness which had left my classmates and me believing for months that the tests would offer some consummate *evaluation,* not simply of how well we'd *learned,* but— almost mystically—of the depths of our *capacity* in the law. Exams were something to point to, a proving ground for all the hard and sincere labor. And instead they had been intellectual quick-draw contests, frantic exercises that seemed to place no premium on the sustained insight and imagination which I most admired in others, and when they occurred, felt proudest of in myself. (Emphasis added.)

As you will see in chapter 9, Turow got it wrong—or rather, what seemed to be so at the time was based on misperception. For him, the finals may indeed have been "intellectual quick-draw contents, frantic frantic exercises." But that is not what they *should* have been...not for him, and especially not for you. Exams are indeed "something to point to." But if you don't know *what* it is they're supposed to measure, it's pretty hard to understand what it is they really do "place /a/ premium on." In this chapter, you'll find out.

As mentioned in chapter 3, first-year law school exams are based *entirely* on Thinking Like a Lawyer—as is the practice of law itself, allegedly.

---

* I know, I know: In these days of gender-neutral language, it should be "Examspersonship." But I just can't bring myself to write that.

It's what you (supposedly) learn to do in law school. But what is it?

Here's an analogy: If a cook wants to prepare a meal, he or she asks some questions re. each course—

      1. What are the required ingredients?
      2. Do we have these ingredients on hand
        —or are some of them missing?
      3. What's the procedure for combining these
        ingredients—the order and amounts?
      4. What can cause this to turn out wrong?

Typically, a cook starts with a recipe (written or memorized), and then assembles the required ingredients and combines them in the right way. But in the law, instead of starting with the recipe, you start with a table covered with ingredients—the legal equivalent of eggs, flour, sugar, milk, and baking soda, say. Then you have to ask yourself, "What can I make out of this stuff?" Your analysis is based on 1) several recipes that you have *memorized*, and 2) your ability to recognize the ingredients for what they are (for many of them are not labeled).

As you look at what's on the table, you notice things: There aren't enough eggs to make an omelet for two, but there are enough to make a cake. But when you check out what appears to be the flour, you discover it isn't made from wheat, which is what a cake requires. Instead, it's corn meal, best used for cornbread. If there's no sugar on the table, but there is molasses, perhaps you can substitute that for the sugar. And so on.

When baking, say, a cake, everything can go fine—and then someone slams a door, and the vibrations reach the oven and cause the cake to "fall," ruining it. The same thing can happen when cooking up something in the Law.

Virtually all the other exams you've ever taken in your life have involved simply repeating what you learned from the textbook or class lectures. But in law school, there are *no* textbooks, *no* lectures. Yet, for your exams, it's *assumed* you know *everything, cold*. In your answer, you must demonstrate that you do indeed know it—because, of course, you might *not* know it. However, even after you've proved you know it, that, by itself, will only get you a *passing* grade—barely.

To return to the cooking analogy for a minute: Any time you begin talking with someone else about cooking, your interlocutor won't start out by making sure you know the difference between baking soda and yeast. That's assumed, a given. But he or she will speedily notice if you *don't* know the difference, and will soon terminate the conversation. —Now you see why it's so easy to quickly grade so many of the law students' exams, giving them low marks. (Because my own knowledge of cooking is limited to how long to keep something in the microwave, I have to drop the analogy at this point. But I hope you got the idea. —And if you don't like the analogy of cooking, use auto mechanics, cosmetics, whatever.)

Most professors—and books on succeeding in law school—will tell you only that doing well on a law school exam requires "issue spotting." But they never define it in a useful way. Sometimes, they'll tell you to use the "IRAC model."—State the **I**ssue, state the **R**ule that applies, **A**pply the rule to the facts, and state your **C**onclusion. Sounds fine, but in practice it's no help; nor is the perfunctory explanation that usually accompanies it. Even when professors provide copies of exams they've given in previous years, along with "model answers," that doesn't explain what's involved at *arriving* at the model answer.

There is a *system* for handling the law school essay exam well. It's the single most important key to law school success. And I dearly wish that I'd been the one to invent it.

Disclaimer

This chapter provides only an *introduction* to this system, with some merely cursory examples. (The end of this chapter tells how you can get further instruction.) In Chapter 7, you learn how to *practice* it, long *before* the final exam.

—And don't kid yourself that this method is a "gimmick," a "magic wand" you can wave at the midnight hour to instantly make everything easy for you on the next day's final.

Goodrich, in *Anarchy and Elegance,* said: "Once we learned law's philosophical framework, law school seemed largely an exercise in placing facts and arguments in the right places." Once again, he went to the heart of the matter. Law school *exams* are *entirely* about "placing facts and arguments in the right places." (So is the essay portion of the bar exam. And for that matter, so is trial and appellate litigation.)

Most law school finals—and *all* first-year finals—are essay. They're every bit as confused and contradictory as what happens in the real world. Learning How to Think Like a Lawyer means learning how to organize what at first appears to be near-chaos. You learn to see who has a problem, why, and what's relevant to their problem/s. You rank the relevant information, and decide what additional information you need. You look at the possibilities of the situation, and also try to figure out what the *other* side of the story is. It's actually a very simple process. But the process assumes you can spot which facts are relevant and important—because those facts give rise to arguments and counter-arguments you can use.

There you have it: the essence (and the "secret") of "Thinking Like a Lawyer."

Here's how it works in practice...

The Step-by-Step Approach

The following example is based on torts. (If you don't remember the definitions of the terms used here, look back at chapter 1.)

Your professor provides you with a lot of facts. Let's start with this: X got into a fistfight. B was involved. C and A were there too, and were also involved somehow.

Step 1: Identify the parties. Who's involved here—and who's *potentially* involved here? (Sometimes you can go after parties who aren't obvious at first…and sometimes parties that aren't obvious at first suddenly appear out of nowhere and file claims against your client. Don't leave them out.)

Where did the fistfight occur? It may have been at *D's* house. D might be the father of B, a minor. D might have been present when the fight occurred, even though he wasn't involved.

Step 2: Establish *"conflict pairings."* Pick out two parties who seem to have a problem between them. It may be that X has problems with A, B, and C (and don't forget D). But start with just X v. B. Let the others go, for now. Take this one step at a time.

Step 3: Spot each gripe that one party in the conflict pairing has against the other, *in layman's terms.*

What gripes does X have against B, based on the facts? Well, B slugged X, causing X to lose some teeth. X wants B to pay the dental bill, and to pay something in addition. (Save any and all of B's gripes against X for later. Remember, *one step at a time.*)

Step 4: Begin to apply the *law—in light of the facts.*

Here, does X have a potential *legal* claim against B because of it? This is where you start filtering facts through a legal screen, and labeling what comes through. No matter what the gripe is, X probably can't go to court about it unless it's a recognized cause of action. (And in a first-year law course, you're dealing *only* with recognized causes of action.) Each cause of action has a name. Here's one: "battery." ("Assault and battery" is a criminal offense. On the civil side, in tort, there's a difference between "assault" and "battery.") The allegation of battery becomes the potential legal ground for (maybe) getting a judgment against B to pay X. This is X's "legal basis of entitlement."

Step 5: Proceed to the *elements* of the relevant cause of action.

Here, immediately go to the *definition* of battery—a continuation of the process of applying the law to the facts (and of the assumption that you know the law, cold). Like all definitions, this one has parts that are put together to make the whole. These parts, in the law, are called elements.

(Lawyers don't speak of the "definition" of a cause of action, just of the "elements.")

Battery is 1) an act of the alleged wrongdoer, 2) involving intentional physical contact with the plaintiff, or the threat of it, 3) without the plaintiff's consent, 4) where contact does occur, and 5) such contact was harmful or offensive.

Step 6: Taking each element in turn, look to see if the facts of the matter fit it. If they don't, see if the facts flat out contradict it. Maybe you don't know enough at the present time to be able to tell one way or the other. State the situation: fit, don't fit, don't know; *element-by-element*. You're trying to use the real-world facts as lines, to connect up the dots (the legal elements), to see if they form a completed figure visible for all to see.

Step 7: Look for possible *defenses*, "the other side of the story."

Here's a quick look at one for B's action: B was sitting in a darkened room with A and C, watching a horror film on the VCR, when suddenly X rushed into the room. B may have struck X thinking he, B, was acting in self-defense against Freddy Krueger.

In steps 1-7, don't *fight* the facts. But don't read into them anything more than appears at face value. Don't immediately jump to legal jargon. Take it one step at a time, from facts to law. You can *speculate* about other possible facts implied by the facts you have, but leave it for last, say *explicitly* that you're speculating—and *don't spend much time on it*. Also, be sure to explicitly state what facts are missing.

Step 8: *Reverse* the approach, with the current conflict-pairing.

In this example, see if *B* has any "colorable" claims against *X*. (A colorable claim is, in effect, one you can make with a straight face, because there's at least one shred of authority or doctrine to back you up.) Here are some possibilities:

1) Slander—maybe X had made a highly unfavorable remark about B's paternity, prompting B's punch to X's mouth.* The slanderous remark does not negate X's potential claim for battery, but it does perhaps give B his own cause of action against X, independent of X's cause of action against B. Check the facts.

2) Trespass—if D did not in fact invite X into D's house, and B had not done so either, B might have something here. Check the facts.

3) Assault—assault is a deliberate act intended to cause apprehension of an imminent battery. If B and C and A were indeed watching a horror film on the VCR, and X knew that, X may have been trying to play a practical joke on B & Company, scaring the hell out of them. If so, X might have a good argument there, too. Check the facts.

---

* Note the precision of that last clause: you must learn to think in *precise* "who's doing what to whom" language.

Steps 9 - ?: Repeat steps 1-8, with other conflict pairings (X v. D, for example).

It's not your place to decide who wins and who loses on each point in controversy. It *is* your job to *present* both *sides and to* weigh *them.* This is exactly what you should do for a client (or your supervising attorney) when you get out in the real world. The final decision is always the client's (or your supervisor's), not yours. *Who* wins or loses isn't as important as *why.* Granted, you discuss the *strength* of each argument and counter-argument, based on the facts. But what counts is your *analysis*—not your *decision* (as though you were playing judge). It would be an exaggeration to say the process is more important than the product. However, it's no exaggeration to say the product *is* the *process.*

As part of proving your ability, you must *identify and define*—but only in *passing*—what it is you're talking about. Yet, you're not just regurgitating things from memory—or rather, you're not *just* regurgitating things from memory. In fact, you are indeed regurgitating—as much as you can, as fast as you can. But that's just to get your foot in the door (to mix metaphors in an appalling way). You still have to make the sale. The professor doesn't want bare statements of the law. He or she wants you to analyze the facts in light of the law. Still, you have to formally state the elements of the relevant law so the prof can be sure you know what you're talking about. That formal statement is just your *starting* point.

The above example involved torts. Here's an example of strutting your stuff, almost as a mere *aside,* on a contracts exam: "Do Alpha and Omega have a valid bilateral contract? The elements are: 1) legal capacity to contract —i.e., no minority, insanity, or intoxication to render their contracting void or voidable, 2) a lawful purpose to the agreement and the means of achieving it, 3) genuine agreement—i.e., offer and acceptance, no mutual mistake, no unilateral mistake such as would make it unconscionable to enforce certain terms in the contract, no fraud in the factum; and 4) consideration provided by both parties—i.e., mutually bargained-for legal detriment. Looking at each, in light of the facts:…" Etc.

Sometimes, the professor plays dirty: the facts will present an outrageous situation where a bad guy is really hurting a good guy. Idealistic students pounce on everything that helps the good guy and hurts the bad guy. They deliberately downplay all the things that help the bad guy and hurt the good guy. The answers of such students are easy to grade, and their scores are low. (Remember, regarding contracts: Sometimes the Liar Wins.)*

---

* And by the way, every *client* you will ever have will definitely present only a one-sided version of the facts. It's up to you to be on the alert for the other side of the story—because if there were no dispute as to what the facts are, your client wouldn't need to be telling you his or her side of the story in the first place. —But it's still dirty for the prof not to have warned you about this with regard to your final exam, rather than letting you learn it the hard way.

"ATTICUS FALCON," ESQ.

Another sneaky thing professors—and sometimes bar examiners, too—like to do is to *tell* you there's a valid contract, or a valid will, etc.. Every time, several poor schmucks suspect a trick, and decide to cover their anatomy. So they waste valuable minutes explaining *why* the contract or the will or whatever is valid. There is indeed a trick: the trick is to do the students a favor, knowing some of them will reject it and thereby shoot themselves in the foot.

Because I'm not going to use the cooking analogy any more, I'll switch to the trial lawyers' favorite, the jigsaw puzzle. The professor has designed a puzzle. He or she knows what it looks like as a complete picture. *You don't.* The prof gives you this puzzle, after cutting it up into dozens of tiny pieces. The pieces the professor *provides* consist almost exclusively of *facts.* And for good measure, the prof also throws in some other pieces that don't even *belong* in that puzzle, but which are intended to confuse and mislead the unwary. These are pieces from other, *irrelevant* puzzles.

But most important of all, the professor *leaves out* dozens of other pieces that *do* belong in the puzzle: i.e., the basic legal concepts and their elements. These you should have acquired on your own (with the "help" of the Case/Socratic Method).

You then have three or four hours to re-create the omitted pieces (the relevant legal elements), and to combine them with the provided pieces that concern the (relevant) facts—in other words, to correctly reproduce the original design…and only the professor knows for sure what it looks like.

If you've done a jigsaw puzzle for real, you know how it goes: You group things together that seem to belong together. Then you go into the nitty-gritty of trying to fit individual pieces into one another. So it is with law school essay exams. You start with the more significant, and work down to the less important. However, because of the time constraint, and because you have to supply all of the law pieces yourself, it's unlikely you'll be able to reproduce the complete picture…especially because—of course—you don't know, beforehand, what it's supposed to look like when done.

There are major issues, and there are minor issues—just as, in a jigsaw puzzle, there are major patterns and minor ones. The *key* issues in a law school exam are the ones where *both* sides of the story seem pretty strong. The minor issues are where the facts are either so weak, or maybe so few, that there really doesn't seem to be much of an argument. In your exam answer, you want to do a *thorough* job of discussing the *key* issues. You don't spend as much time on the minor ones. —Naturally, this presumes you know the law so well that you don't have to spend much time trying to *figure out* which are the major issues and which are the minor. For each, the argument usually centers on just one element of the cause of action in question.

This is what "issue-spotting" is all about. It's fun, fun, fun.

But you don't have to take my word for it. Here's Scott Turow's description, in *One L*:

Invariably, the narrative has been constructed in such a way that its facts straddle the boundaries of dozens of legal categories...For the student, the job is to sort quickly through the situation to try to name the endless skein of applicable rules and also to describe the implications of one rule rather than another. Like a good lawyer, the student is expected to be able to argue both sides of each choice.

Black Letter Law—Again

Black Letter Law is the basic nuts and bolts—or maybe the "toolkit"—of the law. The essence of Thinking Like a Lawyer is the ability to pick out the right legal principles to apply to a given set of facts, and to weigh the pros and cons of the situation. And it's all grounded in Black Letter Law: the basic legal concepts and their elements. Black Letter Law is what's tested in first-year exams, regardless of how philosophical and abstract the class discussions were. That's also what's tested on the bar exam. You'd better know it. But it isn't tested on the basis of rote memorization (fill in the blank, etc.). It's tested on the basis of analytical skill—ability to *choose* and *use* the correct Black Letter Law.

So it's a shame the law schools seldom even bother to teach Black Letter Law—let alone the relationship between Black Letter Law and Thinking Like a Lawyer.

But you now see at least part of the reason why they don't: first, if first-year law students knew, coming in, how relatively simple it all is, then nearly everyone would do very well...which is unthinkable, for reasons discussed in chapter 3. Second, if laypeople ever got wind of how relatively easy it is to Think Like a Lawyer, the mystique and prestige of the Law would nearly evaporate...which is unthinkable. Heaven forbid that anyone would ever believe that those at the top of the class (from whom the ranks of law school professors are filled) are anything other than brilliant scholars. And heaven forbid that non-lawyers (from whom the bank accounts of lawyers are filled) would ever believe that attorneys are anything other than Masters of the Occult Arcana of the Law. (Chapter 21 gives additional reasons.)

The Relevance of Legal Writing

As chapter 1 mentioned, Legal Writing is one of the two courses (the other being Legal Research) that don't count "now" (i.e., in law school), but which can make or break your legal career. However, while Legal Writing doesn't *officially* count "now" (i.e., in law school), in a sense it counts more than any other course, even though it's (usually) pass-fail. This is because law school exams are almost entirely *essay* exams, not multiple-choice, fill-in-the-blank, short answer, etc.. An essay, by definition, means writing. For a *law* school essay exam, that means *legal* writing. —And as chapter 1 also mentioned, one type of legal writing involves objectively telling *both* (probable) sides of the story…and it is different from any other writing you've ever done.

As in all good writing, you need to make it simple and direct: the "KISS" Rule—"Keep It Simple, Smarty." But you also have to make it complete: you have to cover a *lot* of ground, *fast,* spotting and discussing—*simply*—each of *many* issues. That's *hard.*

To further complicate matters, *issues* arise from *facts.* That is why, in the foregoing, the initial steps had nothing to do with legal concepts. One of the biggest mistakes you can make is to hastily proceed to a *legal* analysis *without seeing the facts for what they are, in and of themselves.* This ability to start with "Just the facts, Ma'am," and to subsequently evaluate them in terms of what's *relevant*, legally, and what's *important,* legally, is the major part of Thinking Like a Lawyer. And what makes all this especially difficult is that a law school exam puts you under extreme time pressure. Your ability to *Think* Like a Lawyer is just part of it. Your ability to *write* like a *good* lawyer—and quickly—is what separates the winners from the losers.

A law school essay exam places a premium on your ability to *analyze* the facts, to *organize* your thoughts, and to *allocate* your time and energy so you "cover all the bases" before time is called. So, in a sense, your *procedural* skills are just as vital as your knowledge of the *substantive* law. Hence the importance of examsmanship.

Examsmanship Training

Wentworth Miller's LEEWS

This chapter has given an *introduction* to a systematic approach to Thinking Like a Lawyer. Its creator is Wentworth E. Miller. A Yale Law grad, he is the founder of "Wentworth Miller's LEEWS." LEEWS stands for the "Legal Essay Exam Writing System." It is probably the best-kept secret on Planet Law School.

When I was in third-year, a friend who'd Made Law Review told me he'd discovered that every one of his fellow editors had taken the LEEWS in their first semester of law school, as had he. It was too much of a coincidence to be a coincidence.

I then took it because I was curious. But it was far too late to make a difference in my prospects after graduation. Don't you make that mistake. Those who took it in their first semester of law school had kept the information all to themselves—and did not recommend the program to others. That gave them a huge advantage over their fellow students. Indeed, even though I am praising it highly, I advise *you* to keep it to yourself, too—just as the future Law Review editors did during their first-year. As sadly Machiavellian as it is, you need any edge you can get in law school. Other than *this* book, Wentworth Miller's LEEWS—or something like it—is the best thing you could possibly have going for you.

If you think you can get by merely on this chapter's introduction to Miller's method, you are being penny wise and pound foolish. The LEEWS manual is over 80 pages long, single-spaced. It covers far more potential situations than this chapter did—including situations where you need to modify the approach laid out in the example. What's here is a quite watered-down and revised version of what's in the LEEWS manual—which is not available through bookstores. (And what's here does not fit Con Law or Property, at all.)

Miller himself, or his associate, JoAnne Page—another Yale Law grad— gives one-day workshops on his method, all around the country. If you are not now in law school, you should take it before you even *start.* LEEWS is more than just an exam-taking system. It's also a system for studying. (Other material in this book, including much of the next chapter, is also based on Miller's system.) And it's designed for those who've been in law school only a few weeks. Other than some jargon and concepts, *beginning* law students don't know much more than *you* do. Further, if you read just the Glannon primer on torts, the Blum primer on contracts (and perhaps also *Rules of Contract Law),* and Delaney's *Learning Legal Reasoning* (all recommended in chapter 5), you'll have enough knowledge to easily understand all the LEEWS material.

The program itself is seven hours long, and there's an hour for lunch. It's intense—and Miller is no Milquetoast. If you cannot attend a live presentation, you can purchase the program on cassette tapes. In fact, if you are not in law school yet, and it's almost summertime, that would be the wiser move. This is because the LEEWS workshops are offered only during the *academic* year.

Whether live or on tape, the program costs less than $100. Depending on the option you choose, the price for the on-site presentation can be as low as $65. Wentworth Miller's LEEWS is a steal for what he charges. For information as to workshop itinerary and costs, or to get the tapes and manual, call (800) 765-8246.

Ace Seminars

For years, Miller had the market all to himself. Now there's competition: Ace Seminars, for one. Their on-site program lasts four hours. The instructor at each presentation is either David R. Simon or Cheryl A. Holland. Both are USC law alumni. You get Ace's examsmanship manual, *Conquering Legal Exams,* and a workbook that includes many practice exams with examples. You also get a copy of the *American Standard Law Dictionary,* compiled by Ace. (So, if you plan to take the Ace Seminar, don't buy a law dictionary beforehand.)

For those who enroll at least a week before the on-site program, the price is $70 - $100, depending on whether you sign up alone or as part of a group. The program is also available on tape (2 cassettes) for $100, including all the printed materials. Ace's number is (800) 748-6953.

Note: Both Wentworth Miller's LEEWS and Ace Seminars offer a money-back guarantee to those who attend an on-site program. If you don't achieve a certain gpa, or don't achieve a certain level of improvement over your previous gpa, you get about 75% of your money back. Even though you don't get this offer if you acquire the program on tape, I still believe the tapes are the better way to go; but it's your call.

Excel — "The Skillman Method"

There's one in every crowd, and apparently one in every category of vendor: My research assistant and I could get no information from this company. In its advertising, "Excel — The Skillman Method" lists various numbers to call. We called them all, repeatedly. Each time, no matter which number it was, we only got an answering machine. Each time, we left a message requesting program literature and providing my name and address. No response, ever. Although I don't know for sure what it is this company is selling, it does appear to be some sort of examsmanship course, so I'm mentioning it in this section. You are free to draw your own conclusions as to whether or not you should do business with this outfit.*

Fleming's LEWW

Chapter 5 introduced Jeff Fleming and his Fleming's Fundamentals of Law (FFL), regarding audio cassette tapes. He also does an examsmanship program: the Legal Examination Writing Workshop. (LEWW, not LEEWS. It gets confusing, which is why what used to be called just LEEWS is now called "Wentworth Miller's LEEWS." —Easier to remember these as Miller's v. Fleming's.) Based on what I've heard, Fleming's is the only one that might be even better than Miller's—but it's much costlier.

The on-site program lasts two afternoons, Saturday and Sunday, six hours each day. You can repeat it as often as you want, at no extra charge. However, the in-person program is offered only in California. —If you're already signed up for FFL's California bar review course, the live *examsmanship* program is just under $140. Otherwise, it's just over $170. By registering with others as a group, you can bring the price down to $125. You can also get the workshop on audio cassette tapes, for the $170+ price.

Either way, you also get a 100-page manual. And you get access to their telephone tutoring service: You can call and get live instruction. (I don't know how much total time you're allowed.) This feature is unique to LEWW.

As with Fleming's first-year tapes, you get a personal critique of your written answer to a practice exam question. This is done orally, on an audio cassette tape that's mailed to you after the workshop. (In the on-site course, you also go over one answer in class.) This too is unique to Fleming's.

---

* More than *six months after* I'd given up, Excel sent me two pages of photocopied material about what is indeed its examsmanship course. What a way to run a railroad.

For those who do not want to take the full examsmanship workshop, Fleming's also sells manuals for various law school courses. Each manual is about $22. (However, if you've signed up to take FFL's bar review, the price drops to just over 17 bucks each.) Each manual covers three subjects. Apparently these manuals do double-duty as bar exam preparation, because some of the manuals include advanced topics in with first-year. The material on each subject includes five model questions and answers. (As chapter 5 mentioned, the FFL first-year tapes include sample essay questions, with model answers. That's another alternative.

Chapter 5 gave Fleming's phone numbers (repeated in the appendix) for those in California and for those living outside the Golden State.

Strictly Store-Bought or Mail-Order Items

John Delaney

Delaney is a professor at the Law School of the City University of New York - Queens College. Chapter 5 discussed his book, *Learning Legal Reasoning.*. He does not teach an on-site examsmanship course (at least, not that I know of). However, he has another self-help book, called *How to do Your Best on Law School Exams, rev. ed.*. It's $15. Even assuming that you take one of the examsmanship courses discussed above, I strongly recommend this book in *addition* to that course.

As with other "how to" books, Delaney's provides sample questions and a model answer to each one. But he provides more than *one* model answer to each one: what might be called "high honors" answers, and others that are just "honors" answers. For most questions, he also provides a *lousy* answer. And he *analyzes* each one.

You already know, from experience, the difference between a fine athletic performance and a poor one, even if you're not an athlete yourself. You also know, from experience, the difference between a fine musical performance and a poor one, even if you have no musical talent yourself. Your experience of the poor performance helps you understand what makes a good performance good.

But you have *no* experience of law school exams. Therefore, if all you see are the model answers—which are always *good* ones—you might fail to fully grasp the *essence* of a good answer. Then, without meaning to, the answer *you* give on an exam might fall short of your professor's standards. If you really want to understand—beyond any doubts—the difference between a good answer and a lousy answer, look at *How to Do Your Best on Law School Exams.* (In fact, if you start on chapter 5's recommendations far enough in advance of law school, you can even answer some questions in Delaney's book. Then see which category *your* answer is in.)

Delaney also has an audiocassette version of his book: three tapes that run just under $3\frac{1}{2}$ hours, total. They cost $25. I do not recommend them. They were recorded in a classroom; the miking is poor, and street noises—

among others—distract. (Miller's, in contrast, were professionally recorded, in a sound studio.) They add very little to what's in the book. (But don't let the comparatively low value of the tapes dissuade you from getting the book. —You don't get the book with the tapes, and there's no "package deal" if your order the tapes and the books at the same time.) The phone number was listed in chapter 5, and is repeated in the appendix.

Emanuel

Emanuel has a series of *First Year Questions & Answers*. These are *short-answer*, and the number varies by topics. (Crim Pro is the lowest, with 131; Civ Pro the highest, with 253.) The book for each subject is $19. The Emanuel number was given in chapter 5, and is repeated in the appendix.

Gilbert

This division of Harcourt Brace does a book called *The Eight Secrets of Top Exam Performance*, by Prof. Charles Whitebread of the University of Southern California School of Law. It costs $10. I haven't seen it. However, as chapter 5 said, I did listen to the Gilbert tapes on "Law School Exam Writing" (which cost $20). They're part of its "Legal Legends" tape series discussed in chapter 5. Whitebread does them...and, as mentioned in chapter 5, I was disappointed in them. Because I assume the book has the same material as the tapes, I don't recommend it—even though I haven't even seen it. (Whitebread also does the Gilbert "Legal Legends" tapes on Criminal Law. I have not heard these, but I've been told that they're the best tapes on the subject. Win some, lose some.)

Also, the Gilbert Law Summaries (commercial outlines) include sample essay questions, with model answers.

Siegel

As noted elsewhere, Siegel's, a commercial outline series, is owned by Emanuel. They do a series of books called "Answers to Essay and Multiple Choice Questions" for each subject. Each one contains 20-25 essay questions, and 85-100 multiple-choice questions. Brian Siegel himself wrote the model answers. The books are available for all of the Big Six of first-year. Each costs $16. The Siegel's number is the same as that for Emanuel.

Sum & Substance

This West subsidiary has a set of cassettes called the "Intensive Exam Writing (Essay) Seminar" (IEWES). No on-site presentations. The four tapes in the series total six hours' running time. The package includes a 210-page workbook. The Sum & Substance people have assured me that their tapes "blow away" Wentworth Miller's LEEWS, Ace Seminars, Jeff Fleming's LEWW, etc.. However, not having heard these cassettes, I can't say anything about the quality of this product. The lectures cover case briefing and personal outline preparation as well as examsmanship. The set sells for $95.

For those who don't want to spend $95, S&S also has a two-tape set called "Exam Essay Writing." It runs for 2 hours, 45 minutes. The price is $25. (The Sum & Substance toll-free number was presented in chapter 5, and is repeated in the appendix.)

* * *

Whichever examsmanship course you choose, you should get it on *tape,* before you *start* law school. That way, you can listen to it at your leisure— and stop when you want, replay a portion of the tape if you wish, etc.. Plus, the tapes are yours to *keep,* so you can review them again in law school. However, the written materials that come with the course should be your top priority—especially for reviewing.

Even with all the preparation chapter 5 advocates, you're still going to be faced with a lot of new stuff in law school. If you've already become familiar with any of these systems for dealing with your finals, it will free up some time once you're there. You will be amazed at how important that can be. — And an examsmanship course will certainly improve the focus (and effectiveness) of your *studying.*

Perhaps you can find another future law school student to share the cost with you. You still get the written materials if you buy the tapes, of course— and Miller's LEEWS, for example, is willing to sell extra copies of its manual. (Whoever pays the lion's share of the cost is the one who gets to keep the tapes.)

You can sell them to someone else later—after you finish first-year. Can't do *that* if you attend a live presentation.

Go for it. You'll be glad you did.

Chapter 7 - From Mystery to Mastery

> Final exams play on a law student's world like some
> weirdly orbiting moon. They are always in sight; but
> while they're at a distance, they serve merely to create
> the tensions which swell like daily tides—to read, to keep
> pace, to understand. As exams draw close, however, in
> December and May, their gravitational force starts to
> shake the whole place to pieces.
>
> Scott Turow, *One L*

As chapters 3 and 4 indicated, the purpose of first-year is to leave you mystified. To cope with that, chapter 5, and an examsmanship course such as discussed in chapter 6, presented things you should do before you even start law school (if you're reading this book before you go; otherwise, get on them *now*). *This* chapter presents things you can best do—and in some cases, can *only* do—once you're *in* law school. Here is where you leave the mystery behind, once and for all, and *master* first-year.

* * *

Educators have long known that the best way for students to learn is through feedback mechanisms built into the learning process itself. Exams, of course, are a feedback mechanism. But by then it's too late to correct one's errors. That's why students have homework assignments, "exercise questions," and quizzes before the final. These are good reality-checks, to use a current buzzword (which itself is a buzzword, come to think of it).

As you've seen by now, you get none of this in law school…unless you do it yourself.

Granted, sometimes, the professor in a year-long first-year course will give a midterm. Usually, your score on that exam either doesn't count or else just barely counts as part of your grade for the course. (However, it can be crucial to your effort to get a summer *clerkship* after *first*-year. See chapter 12.) The test is just a dry run for the real thing. But you still get no feedback other than your score. Besides, it's one hell of a shock to bomb on a midterm—and suddenly realize you now have exactly one semester in which to a) find out why you never "got it" in first semester, so you don't repeat the mistake in your second semester; b) go back and learn everything you should have learned in the first semester—which is still fair game for the final; all the while c) learning everything you need to learn in the second semester. It's likely that if you blew one midterm you blew others, because Thinking Like a Lawyer—or failing to do so—cuts across the curriculum.

So, suddenly, you're cramming your entire first year of law school into just one semester. And what makes it a real kick in the head is that without the midterm, you wouldn't even have known how much trouble you were in. At least with a midterm you still have a chance to avoid a total disaster on your finals. (However, if your course is only one semester long, you don't even have a midterm.)

—But *you* have *this* book, and you have read this far. If you're willing to put some effort into it, this book will enable you to walk into your finals totally prepared, totally in control. Instead of thinking of your finals with dread, and fearing to look at your grades, you'll be eager for the opportunity to stand out from the crowd in a way that will mark you as Someone On the Way to the Top.

You must know the law, *cold*—as you saw in chapter 6. But you must also be able to bring order out of a nearly chaotic set of facts, so that you can analyze the situation in light of the law. To do that, you have to play around with hypos.

Hypotheticals

Hypotheticals ("hypos") were discussed in chapter 3, under the section on the Socratic Method. However, telling you what they are and how the professor uses them does not help you to play with them yourself.

First, it's important to understand that *any* question that asks you to analyze a situation is, at least technically, a hypothetical. This includes the question/s on your final exam in law school. (The big difference is that a law school final exam question is many questions rolled into one. *Part* of the test is figuring out *how many,* and *what they are.*) But such questions are static.

A true hypothetical, in the law school sense, is *dynamic,* i.e., when you think you've applied relevant legal principles to the facts, change the facts. See if the same legal principles apply—and if so, whether or not they apply in the same way. Recall that chapter 3 said all legal principles are really just rules of thumb, and that no legal principle is without its exceptions. Changing the facts can change the outcome. It's almost like a kaleidoscope, really. Give it one twist and a whole new pattern is formed. Circumstances alter cases. However, in the Law, that doesn't necessarily mean you have to apply a whole new set of legal principles. It just means you have to keep Thinking Like a Lawyer.

The Return of Black Letter Law

From chapter 6, you know that Thinking Like a Lawyer involves applying Black Letter Law to a set of facts. So, you start your exam preparation with Black Letter Law.

Chapter 5 introduced you to primers, to commercial outlines, and to audio cassette series. Those enable you to "hit the deck running" when you get to law school. (And if you only get them after you've already started law school, at least you have a way of gradually eliminating first-year chaos.) Chapter 6 introduced you to exam preparation courses and materials. It spoke of the importance of spotting the key element of a legal basis of entitlement in a given fact situation, and then analyzing that situation in light of that element.

So, from Day One—and even before, if you follow the recommendations of chapter 5—you want to *memorize the elements of each legal basis of entitlement in every course.*

This doesn't necessarily mean you have to be working 'way ahead of the class, especially if you don't start on this before law school—although that helps, a lot. It does mean, at the very least, that you should be working at far more profound levels, at any given point, than the rest of the class is. Your torts professor, for example, will probably start with the intentional torts. The tort of battery was used to illustrate examsmanship in chapter 6. You should have all the elements of battery memorized before battery is discussed in class.

You find the elements in the commercial outline or a primer. You also get examples of fact situations. They show you which element is key in that situation, why, and to what effect—a static hypothetical. But you can begin constructing your own *dynamic* hypotheticals before the professor even opens his or her mouth.

Still Thinking Like a Lawyer

You don't have to memorize all the elements of each legal basis of entitlement before you start playing with dynamic hypos, though. In fact, working the hypotheticals helps you memorize the elements. By definition, Thinking Like a Lawyer involves the elements. So, even if you have to look them up in your commercial outline again as you work a hypo, you will gradually be committing the elements to memory. One hand washes the other.

Restatements
The best introduction to actually playing with hypotheticals is one of the *Restatements of the Law.* (Chapter 5 tells what they are and how they came to be.) After summarizing the law, the *Restatement* gives a hypo. It's a dynamic one. It starts with one set of facts, and gives the legal outcome. Then it changes the facts—and tells you how those changes affect the legal outcome, if at all.

Start with the *Restatement (Second) of Torts.* Read the summary of a point of law. (These summaries are *excellent,* by the way.) Then look at the first set of facts given. Try to predict the answer, and check and see how well you did. Next, read the fact changes, and try to predict the change in the legal outcome.

Note: The *Restatements'* text is usually set up in such a way that you see the statement of the effect of the changes almost at the same time as you see the changes. Photocopy this material. Make two copies of each page. In the first, black out the part that states the legal effect of the changes. Use that as your practice question, and try to work the answer out on your own. Leave the second as is. Then use the second to check your answer. (If you copy enough of these with the answers blacked out, by the time you start to try to work them, you'll have long since forgotten what those answers were even if you noticed them when you were first doing the copying.) You can always go over the copied material again, to see if you've lost anything, mentally, since the first time you went through it. Do all this by yourself.

Study Groups:
Your Devil's Advocates

The *Restatement*'s hypotheticals are just for starters. Playing with some-one else is usually better than playing with yourself. This is especially true when you're playing with hypos.

With study partners, it is almost certain that you will sometimes have differences of opinion. Others will see things that you completely missed, and vice-versa. That is very important. Perhaps their insights came from reading something you didn't—a law journal article, a leading case, part of a treatise, etc. Regardless of who's right and who's wrong, these differences of opinion will cause your vision to keep expanding, to increase the range of your thinking. Come exam time *you* will need to be able to think of *everything*, *quickly*, all by yourself.

In a sense, you will *internalize* your group's diversity. It's almost as though (while you quickly sketch your answer elsewhere before writing it out for the professor during the exam) you're asking yourself, "Now, what would so-and-so say about this?" This might cause you to stumble onto something important. Or maybe you'll just throw in a little bit extra that you'd other-wise have left out—something that gets you some extra points. (If you've covered the bases well, your professor will be pleasantly surprised to discover that *you've* thought of something he or she *hadn't*—as long as your originality isn't off-the-wall.)

This does not mean you should refuse to work with someone just because that person seems to think too much like you do. Sometimes it's easier to comprehend and accept someone else's insight if that other person seems to think the way you do. Nor does it mean you should get together with a *large* group of people just to maximize the potential diversity of input. Some-times it's difficult just to find a mutually convenient time for *two* people to meet. Even though all your fellow first-year students will have exactly the same class schedule as you (or almost the same), schedules outside class can vary widely.

Most important, your study partner/s have to be serious students. You cannot afford to waste much time when you're together. This means, to some extent, that your study partners need to have already done enough homework to at least have a feel for the elements of the causes of action you'll be discussing. Better one good partner than three mediocre ones. You don't want to spend much time going over the basics. And even though it's a great ego-trip, you don't want to constantly play tutor to the others.

Keep the small-talk, jokes, and gossip to a minimum. *You* have better things to do with your time, even if they don't. Last, do not conduct your group study sessions over a pitcher of beer. Better for you to get a reputation as a hard-ass who aced the finals, than to be known as a Good-Time Charlie who finished as an also-ran. —Unless, of course, you go to law school only because you can't think of anything better to do, and you really don't care. (Then too, you might have a ten-million dollar trust fund you're living off of—in which case, your future is set, regardless. Congratulations.)

Another advantage of a study group is in seeking out new sources of insights. For any given course, there are many leading cases, law review articles, legal encyclopedia sections, treatises, and so forth. For your purposes, most of this is just potential icing on the cake you're trying to bake. However, sometimes you find something that enables you to *decorate* the cake—to the surprised delight of your professor. (But remember: you still have to *bake* the cake, first. If you haven't, spreading all the icing in the world will do you no good.)

Once you've reached a certain point, you'll be ready for this. (And you'll know whether or not you've reached that point.) You go on scouting forays, legal research missions. You're searching for those leading cases, law review articles, treatises, and so forth. They'll certainly help you to deepen and broaden your understanding, which might come in handy at exam time. So, one member of your group scans the digests for relevant cases, reads them, and then photocopies the ones that seem worthwhile—with a copy for each member of the group. Another does the same thing for portions of relevant treatises. A third handles law review articles. The fourth searches out any relevant writings by your professor for that course. Each member of the group then takes these materials and does with them what he or she will. However, you don't memorize cases, authors, excerpts, etc.. And you certainly won't cite any of these on your finals. (Except in Con Law, and perhaps Civ Pro, you don't even cite casebook material.) Instead, you're using these as a way to broaden and deepen your understanding of the law. However, do *not* give these scouting forays high priority. If you have time for them, fine. Otherwise, let them go.

How often to get together? That's up to your group. —Once at week, at *least,* for several hours each time.

How do you select study partners? —See chapter 8.

Hornbooks

Chapter 5 advised against *buying* any hornbooks. However, there are times when it's worthwhile to *consult* one. If you have a problem—a disagreement with a fellow student—about a finer point of law, a hornbook on that subject might settle the issue. (Matthew Bender's "Understanding the Law" and West's "Nutshell" series are good, too. Both publishers have a volume on each major subject. Also, unlike the hornbooks, these are in paperback.)

Hornbooks are best when you want to know all the aspects of a point of law. (Despite its authority, you can't take a *Restatement* as the last word on a subject. There are situations where the *Restatement* is in conflict with statutory law, or where there's a strong minority view not reflected in the *Restatement.* —And once in a great while, the *Restatement* itself is the minority view. A hornbook gives all viewpoints worth considering…although the hornbook author/s sometimes grind an axe, subtly.)

Hornbooks also include a history of the development of a particular legal doctrine. Knowing this history can be helpful. You might be recommending something that would turn back the clock, usually a no-no. More important, a critic in class or your study group might *accuse* you of trying to turn back the clock. The hornbook shows you *where* "the clock was set," way back-when. You can see if your critic is right; if he or she is not, you can then explain the difference, and thus refute your accuser. Most important of all, the hornbook tells you the philosophy behind the development of the doctrine in a particular direction. So, you will be in a much stronger position to argue that your analysis is consistent with that philosophy. This is especially true if you are recommending a change in the law, or an adoption of a new rule where there has been *no* previous rule. (By the way, lawyers never speak of "philosophy." Instead, they speak of the "policy" behind something.)

However, to repeat: despite the appeal of a hornbook, you should not buy one. Law school exams are just a matter of nuts and bolts, not the finer points of the law (history, trends, policy, etc.) discussed in hornbooks. (That's another reason to give the scouting forays *bottom* priority.) If you have your heart set on getting a hornbook, wait until you graduate. For one thing, that's when the finer points might become relevant (not likely at trial, but perhaps on appeal). For another, a new edition might be out by then— and your old edition would be obsolete.

As you can see, a hornbook is not the place to *start* learning the law. As chapter 5 said, you get too much, too soon. You won't be able to keep it all straight, and you'll be overwhelmed. (McLuhan: "Information overload causes breakdown.") That's why you should start with the primers, the commercial outlines, and the tapes.

Making Your Own *Outlines*

One of the few times professors are nearly *honest* with students is when they tell them to create their own outlines instead of relying on the commercial ones. But, as usual, they really don't explain *why*. Students get the impression that an outline is something that they're supposed to use in the final weeks of the course, to prepare for finals. You are indeed supposed to use it to prepare for finals. But you should be using it almost from *Day One*. The outline *you* create enables you to *synthesize* everything you've learned, from all sources—with the *commercial* outline being just *one* of those sources.

The commercial outline tells you most of what you need to know. Working the hypotheticals helps you to memorize it. The *Restatements,* hornbooks, law review articles, etc., help you to understand it. However, you must *systematize* your understanding, in a way that works best for *you*. That's why it's vital to do your *own* outline. Your study group should *never* split up the work of doing course outlines. If the other members of your group want to do a collective work, fight it. If you're outvoted, you should still do your *own* outline for *every* course, in addition to your assigned part. This is too important to screw it up because of ill-considered demands from others.

The crucial part of mastering the material is *putting it in your* own *words*. It's when you try to do this that you'll realize what you don't understand. (As Confucius said, "Great Man is aware of what he knows—and of what he *doesn't* know.") If all you're doing is copying phrases from a commercial outline, or trying to memorize phrases someone *else* prepared for a personal outline, you'll never realize what it is you don't know. If all you can do is repeat things from memory, you won't do well on finals. But when you try to condense it into your *own* words, you'll become keenly aware of the gaps in your knowledge, and you'll try to fill in those gaps.

Reworking Your Outlines

But here's the most important part of all: Each week, you *rework* your personal outline for each course. (There goes the weekend.) You'll be learning new material, learning more things about old material, etc.. (You should be finding new things in your scouting forays, for example.) Just as a *hypothetical* has to be dynamic to be any good, so does the process of making your personal *outline*. That's why you should not rely solely on a commercial product, nor on a *collective* effort.

When you first learn something—anything—you have to commit many details to memory before mastering it. Remember when you first learned to drive? There was so much to keep in mind. Yet, within a very short time, driving became second nature to you.

If you now had to teach someone else to drive, how would you do it? —It would take you a good while to think it through, right? You could even try to write a manual. But you wouldn't need to write a manual for *yourself*.

You already *know* how to drive—so well, in fact, that you don't even have to think about it. You just *do* it.

—And that's the key. You must *use* the law *regularly*: playing with hypos, reworking your outline. The more you work with it, the faster it'll become second nature. Then you won't need a *big* outline. You'll know most of it so well that it would take more time than it's worth to read it through.

Again, think of writing and then reading a "How to Drive a Car" manual for *yourself,* versus just getting in the vehicle and taking off in it. If you were about to drive someone *else's* car, the only mental notes you might want for yourself would be those concerning that car's idiosyncrasies. Perhaps you have to shift gears yourself—and it's a five- instead of a four-speed. Maybe the brakes tend to grab, or you have to push really hard on the horn, or the engine tends to stall, etc.. Obviously, such mental notes would be minimal. That's the goal of your outline.

As you start on each new topic for a course, you'll have a lot of notes—material from commercial outlines, especially. Because you want to make sure you get everything right the first time, you'll spell it all out. You'll thoroughly cover each point. So, each section will be a long one. And then, as you search out the written materials discussed above, you'll have new things to insert. (You'll have a folder for each course, containing your outline and other written materials. Even if you use a computer and have your outline on disk, you should still make—and study—a hard copy of the revised version for every subject, each week.) As you integrate those things into your outline, the relevant section will get bigger still.

But then a funny thing will happen: You'll notice, each week as you rework your outline, that you don't need to cover everything so thoroughly as before: some of it has started to become second nature. So you condense it. Even though you're adding new material to the *old* parts of your outline, those parts will start *shrinking*. Meanwhile, the *newest* topics in your outline will be *growing*.

Your outline in each subject will be like a conquering army: At first, there's a huge commitment, because the struggle is still underway. Enormous resources are concentrated in one place. But assuming the army wins the battle, it then moves on. The front constantly changes. Only a garrison is left behind to occupy each conquered territory and to mop up any lingering resistance. But even in a pacified area, the occupying force remains on the alert: It conducts exercises and practices its skills. That's what you should be doing too, as your study group works new hypos on old subjects —and concocts hypos that cut across several areas within each course. (For those who dislike a military analogy, I invite you to create your own.)

In the alternative: Picture your outline as a thin wedge. As you do a new draft of each outline every week, the older material gets narrowed down some more. Of course, there will be bulges here and there—more difficult material, new finds to integrate into old material. But the overall shape should be a lot like a golf tee.

Note: Reworking your outline each week is vastly different from rewriting (or typing up) your class notes each day. The latter is a waste of time. For one thing, you should be taking very few notes in class. (See chapter 8.) For another, anything that's worthwhile in your class notes should be worked into that course's outline at the end of the week. Then you *throw the class notes away*. By the end of the semester, you want to have a minimum of written material to review for the final. In part, this is because by then most of what you need to know should be solidly lodged in your mind. You won't even have to look over the original text of *Restatement* material or law review articles, etc., that are in your course folder. Their key points should already be in your outline.

Likewise, do not look up the cases listed in the casebook footnotes. It's a dead-end. The return on your investment in such activity will be zero. (Remember: casebooks are written by professors, and professors are not on your side. There are no secrets hidden in the note cases, awaiting only the diligence of students willing to put in the extra work on the casebook material. There is no pot of gold at the end of this rainbow, so don't chase after it. — Come to think of it, there are no rainbows in law school…just an endless downpour.)

Don't kid yourself as to what you're doing, and what you're accomplishing. You have more important things to do than counter-productive make-work such as typing up your class notes and looking up the note cases.

Briefing as though it Matters
—because it Does

There's one more thing you should do on your own: case briefing. Chapter 3 spoke of what briefing a case involves, and Delaney's *Learning Legal Reasoning* (discussed in chapter 5) deals exclusively with case briefing. However, as for what will probably happen in your law school classes, what's in the casebook is trivially important, at best. (Exceptions: Con Law, and —sometimes—Civ Pro.) Regardless, come exam time, all that counts is Black Letter Law and Thinking Like a Lawyer. (After the first few weeks of year one, most professors don't ask students to recite a case briefing in class. In fact, you might not have to brief a case ever again in law school.) However, even though, in practice, they really give it only "lip service," professors pretend the Case Method is important. So you have to play along. Brief the cases for class.

It might be that, after reading *Learning Legal Reasoning* and doing the briefing in it, you still lack confidence in your ability. Then check the briefs you do for your course against the canned briefs in the first type of commercial outline. (Don't buy one, though—just consult someone else's.) I'm sure you'll quickly see that your own work is at least adequate. After awhile, your briefs will probably be superior to the commercial ones. And they'll almost certainly be *far* better than the level required for class discussion.

Even so, go the extra mile, no matter what, for your *own* sake in the *long* run, by briefing—the way Delaney shows you. (Yet, to repeat: you need to have *already* learned the basics, *before* briefing the case. Put the cart before the horse—instead of doing it bass-ackwards the way law professors deviously insist you should.) Even if you've read Delaney's *Learning Legal Reasoning* before law school, you should *study* it once you're *in* law school. But you don't take each case in isolation. Don't just brief the cases assigned for class. Instead, brief at least one or two of the cases discussed within each assigned opinion. Using Delaney's method, you learn to "parse the cases," to see the similarities and the differences regarding fact patterns and applicable law. *Excellence* in briefing is important to you, even if it's only "Mickey Mouse" in class: *By understanding the fine distinctions and nuances of fact and law in your case briefing, you learn to spot the key facts in a case—which in turn give rise to the key legal bases for entitlement on your final exams (and in the practice of law).* And those are the key to your success on finals (and maybe even in your career).

Note: Even if the prof didn't go over an assigned case in class, the legal point/s the omitted cases dealt with are still fair game on the final. (As the end of the course nears, the prof might tell you he or she is not going to get beyond a certain point in the syllabus. But you're still responsible for every-thing up to that point, whether or not the professor discussed all the assigned cases in class.) To repeat what was said earlier, you won't cite specific cases in your answers—except in Con Law and perhaps Civ Pro. However, briefing *all* the cases, and comparing and contrasting them with other cases on the same topic will improve your ability to analyze things in a lawyerlike manner—which is what finals are all about.

The Summary Outline

Your personal outline for each course, referred to above, is actually your *Master* Outline. (I call it this in part because it helps you *master* the material.) But as finals approach, you want to create a *new* personal outline for each course. This one, however, is not just another draft of the old Master. (And you do *not* stop working on your Master Outline.) This one is radically different. In fact, it's only two pages, at most, for each course—because it's almost just a checklist.

In the last few weeks of the semester, *drill, drill, drill, on being able to reproduce that Summary Outline word-for-word in a* very *short time.*

There's a good reason to do this: most law school exams are "closed-book." (You can't bring anything into the exam room, other than a pen.) And even if the prof has announced it's "open-book" (you can bring materials such as your Master Outline), he or she is always free to break the promise. More important, when you're in the exam, the adrenaline (and caffeine, nicotine, or perhaps other substances) will be pumping through your body. No matter how well-prepared you are, there will be at least a little bit of tension.

It's easy to "blank out." So, as soon as you're permitted to begin work on the exam, you want to use some scratch paper to quickly reproduce your Summary Outline in its entirety. The process of setting this down on paper should take only a few minutes. *You do this even before you read the exam questions.* Then, after you've outlined (on other scratch paper) your *answer* to a question, you take a few moments to look over your Summary Outline, to see if there's anything you missed and should include in the answer you're about to set down for the professor's eyes.

That's another reason for reworking the Master Outlines: as the name implies, the Summary Outlines are just a further, *drastic* reduction of material that should already be quite familiar to you. Granted, your Summary Outline should include the elements of each legal basis of entitlement. But everything else should instantly trigger almost everything else in the corresponding section of the Master Outline.

(A fellow student used a truly unique approach to her outlines. I don't know whether what she did could be called a Master Outline for each subject, or a series of Summary Outlines. She was musically gifted. So, she took various rock-and-roll songs and changed the lyrics. She had a song about Bilateral Contracts, one about Unilateral Contracts, one about Capacity to Contract, etc.. For each new topic in each course, she created new lyrics for another song. It was amazing. She did *very* well on her finals; but because I typed mine, instead of writing them in bluebooks by hand as she did, I don't know if she *hummed* her way through the exams. —You could also try rewording some of those poems you had to memorize in grade school and have never forgotten: "I think that I shall never see / A tort that's lovelier than battery...")

Warning: West Publishing does a Sum & Substance Quick Review series; and Harcourt Brace publishes a new "mini-outline" series, Ryan's Course Capsules. Please do not rely on either of these. If you want to spend the money, get one just to compare it with your own outline, if you must. But your personal outline should contain far more than the corresponding Sum & Substance Quick Review or Ryan's Course Capsule, in the same number of pages—because your outline is your *own* work, and is merely the external manifestation of things you've already completely internalized. Most important of all, your *personal* outlines are *specific* to what *your* professors are holding you responsible for.

A Fun Way to Learn

This brings me to an entertaining form of reviewing the law: board games. Just as a change of pace, something you and the other members of your study group can do together, you might want to try it. I know of three. The first is called "Sue You!" The second is "Attorney Power," and the third is "Blind Justice: The Game of Lawsuits." They certainly don't require anywhere near the level of knowledge that a law school exam does, but at least you're still thinking about the subject matter, and in appropriate ways.

Just don't overdo it.

If you're interested, call For Counsel, a mail-order firm for products and gifts for lawyers. They'll send you a catalogue that includes a description of each game. For Counsel's toll-free number is (800) 637-0098.

Working Old Exams

Obviously, you can't start working old exams until the end of the course approaches. You won't have mastered all the material until then—unless everyone in your study group has read *Planet Law School* and followed its recommendations.

Most first-year profs make at least one or two old exams available to their students. Sometimes they even provide a "model answer" to one of them.* Get all the available first-year exams (and model answers) for each of your courses from *all* the first-year profs. They'll be issue-spotters, probably. Usually they're on reserve in the library. (If not, you might need to ask the professor if they're available, and where. If your professor won't tell you, ask your legal research & writing T.A.—or any other second- or third-year student.) You can photocopy them.

Do not look them over—except to see whether or not they have model answers. But if they do, don't look *at the model answers.*

Start with the first-year exams from profs *other* than your own. And start with the old exams that *don't* have model answers. If you have several old exams for a given course, try one as a take-home, despite the fact that it was given as an in-class exam. Everyone in your study group should start with the same exam at the same time. Set a deadline for completion, at the end of an upcoming weekend. As you work out your answer, consult your Master Outline, and everything else—except each other—as needed.

Each member of your group should give everyone else a copy of his or her answer to each question. Then you compare and contrast. Because you're starting with exams that don't have model answers, you won't know what the best answer is. However, it will be obvious who's spotting issues, and who's not. Yet, this isn't a one-upmanship situation (although it unavoidably will have some of that to it). This is a continuation of your quest to cover all the bases. Just because someone does well on the take-home, or

---

* Once in a great while, some professor gives *exactly* the *same* exam as was given in a previous year. (It's so much trouble to have to actually practice what you preach, to Think Like a Lawyer, and *answer* questions—for once—instead of just always asking them.) On rare occasions, this exam is one
  * where the prof has also provided a model answer. Either way, by having worked that exam in practice, you're *really* prepared. —But if the old exam did include a model answer, you'll need to come up with something even better than what the prof himself or herself did: it's a sure bet you won't be the only one who's prepared...and the competition for the very top scores will be that much stiffer.

does poorly, that does not mean he or she will perform similarly on an in-class, timed, high-pressure final.

Different professors teaching the same subject will cover different topics within it. But there's a lot of overlap. And the typical essay exam covers many topics. Even if the old exams from other professors do include some topics your prof's course has not covered, so what? There will still be plenty of topics which your own professor did cover. Hit those. Let the others go.

You should, of course, have learned the examsmanship approach discussed in chapter 6—preferably from tapes or an on-site presentation.

And you should definitely have studied John Delaney's *How to Do Your Best on Law School Exams*.

Next, as a *group,* and taking your time, work through an exam or two that has no model answer. But again, do not look at the old exam before working on it. Then "brainstorm it." You want to think of anything and everything. Most law school exams are intended to last three or four hours. But your group should take longer than that—all day, if necessary.

(If you took the Fleming's examsmanship workshop, or purchased any of its subject-review books, you can get one or more of your practice exam answers critiqued by Fleming's. Assuming you took its course on *tape,* mail your essay answer in—just as you do with your answer to the review-book questions. You could send in your *group* answer, if you wish; just put it under the name of the member who officially purchased the materials, of course.)

Practicing exams under time pressure comes next. After you've done all the exams that don't have model answers, you start on those that do. If you have model answers from your own profs, and model answers from others, begin with those from the other profs. Work them as a *group.* But this time, limit yourselves to the time allotted for your final. See how it goes. One person will have to act as secretary for each question, as you compose your collective answer. (Rotate the secretarial duty.)

The last old exams you work should be those from your own prof that have model answers. If none exist, then the last old exams you work should be those from the other profs, if they have model answers. As always, you should not have looked at either the exam or the model answer beforehand.

Turow, in *One L,* disclosed a sickening revelation that came too late—i.e., during his first final:

> What had never quite struck home with me about a law exam was the importance of *time.* I had realized that we would be tested over a few hours on knowledge which had taken months to acquire. And I'd looked at past exams. But I'd never really tried to write out an answer. (Emphasis added.)

So, the last exams you work should be done as *timed* exams—under *real-world* conditions. If possible, your entire study group should do this together; if not everyone, then as many as possible. Find a room at the law school, on a Saturday or Sunday. Meet at the same time your exam in that subject is scheduled for. Use bluebooks (or typewriters and typing paper, if that's the way you'll be doing the real exam). Then take the test as though it were for real. No collective effort. No talking, period. No outside materials. Reproduce your Summary Outline as soon as you start the clock. Sketch out each answer on scratch paper, before going to your first bluebook.*

When time is up, take a break. Then, as before, compare, contrast, and *discuss* your answers.

* * *

Whether or not you get the first-year tapes (discussed in chapter 5) and listen to them before you even start law school, you should listen to them before working your dry-run finals. If you hear anything that doesn't sound completely familiar to you, fill in the gap, quickly. Also, the professors on these tapes often give tips as to what the most "testable" topics are, what the typical law school prof is looking for in the answer. Sometimes, they also discuss typical mistakes first-year students make on finals.

* * *

Here's yet another quotation from *One L*—another of the many sad insights Turow had. This one came after he'd finished his finals: "It was not that I felt that I'd done *poorly*. I just realized that I'd *missed the chance* to do very *well*." (Emphasis added.)**

To close on a happier note, here's a quotation from Mark Twain (in *Letter to the Golden Era*). The way you want to end up, both going into final exams and while waiting for the results, is to have "the serene confidence a Christian feels—in four aces."

---

* You really should *type* your answers, though, if you can get your hands on a typewriter. (Laptop computers are not allowed, because they have memory— nor are typewriters with programmable memory.) My hunch is professors will be less impatient with those whose words are legible—i.e., typed— rather than a frantic scrawl.

** I am not trying to make Turow out to be an idiot by quoting so extensively with respect to his mistakes. On the contrary, I admire his guts for sharing such embarrassing and painful truths. By now, you no doubt have perceived that my confusion and even terror in first-year were at least as bad as his.

ADDENDUM to CHAPTER 7:
MORE RESOURCES for FIRST-YEAR

Property: The Killer Material

Property and Civil Procedure are the two most difficult first-year courses. However, one area of Property is the hardest topic of all: Estates and Future Interests. Chapter 5 briefly mentioned this, and told why it's important. (And if you master it in first-year, it will be much less difficult to refresh your memory in later courses and when reviewing for the bar exam.)

The following books will help you enormously—far more than anything else that's available:

Laurence, Robert, and Minzer, Pamela, *A Student's Guide to Estates in Land and Future Interests, 2d ed.,* 1995, about $25 in paperback, from Matthew Bender.

Makdisi, John, *Estates in Land & Future Interests: Problems & Answers,* a 1995 paperback for roughly $20, from Aspen.

(For learning the *bare bones* of Estates and Future Interests, the Laurence & Minzer book is by far the better of these two. However, to flesh it out and test yourself on it, the Makdisi book is by far the better. I strongly recommend *both* of them. Start with Laurence & Minzer. Then check your understanding by means of Makdisi. Go back to L&M to re-learn what you missed on Makdisi's tests. —And don't forget the Moynihan book, discussed in chapter 5, for background.)

Schwartz, Frederic S., *A Student's Guide to the Rule Against Perpetuities,* 1988, from Matthew Bender, in paperback, about $25. It is not quite as good as the ones above, but is still worthwhile.

(As you will discover, if you don't understand the Rule Against Perpetuities, "the RAP," you're likely to get ZAPPED. And you'll have trouble with Wills, and with Trusts, regardless of whether you take these subjects in law school. —Sometimes students refer to the RAP as the "CRAP." The "C" stands for "Confounded.")

Siegel, Stephen A., *A Student's Guide to Easements, Real Covenants, and Equitable Servitudes,* 1988, approximately $25, in paperback from Matthew Bender. This one is not so good as a primer. However, I can't find anything else on this area, and his book is better than going without.

If you can't find the Matthew Bender books at your law school bookstore, you can order them direct by calling (800) 223-1940. Aspen's number was given in chapter 5. But to repeat, it's (800) 234-1660.

Chapter 5 listed audio cassette tapes for first-year subjects, including Property. However, two vendors have material specifically for Future Interests. The Gilbert "Legal Legends" set consists of two tapes, running about three hours, for $25. Catherine L. Carpenter, the dean of Southwestern U. Law School, is the lecturer. The Sum & Substance "Outstanding Professor" set consists of one tape, running time about 90 minutes, for $16. Julian C. Juergensmeyer of the University of Florida is the lecturer. (He's the same person who does the S&S first-year property tape.)

The phone numbers for both these vendors were given in chapter 5. But to repeat: the Gilbert (actually, Harcourt Brace) number is (800) 787-8717; the Sum & Substance (actually, West) number is (800) 876-4457.

If you have to choose between the books and the tapes, definitely get the books. But if you can afford it, consider getting the books *and* the tapes.

Don't get any of these books or tapes on Estates and Future Interests until you're *sure* you'll be going to law school—or you're already in it. Then the books are a *must*.

Civ Pro

One of the things that amazed me about law school is that you don't get a general overview of the litigation process unless you take an advanced course in civil procedure. Seems to me such an overview ought to be included as part of first-year Civ Pro. Oh well.

In 1996 a book was first published that takes you step-by-step through *"everything"* in a lawsuit, from both the plaintiff's and defendant's point of view: moves, countermoves, you name it. You see how all the pieces fit together, from start to finish. The title of this godsend is *O'Connor's Federal Rules — Civil Trials*. Its (chief) author is Michol M. O'Connor. (Michol is a she, but she pronounces "Michol" at though it were spelled "Michael." Argh.)

Virtually all courts, state or federal, are more or less alike when it comes to civil procedure. That's because all the procedures grew out of the same common law tradition. Further, most state courts model their specific rules on those of the federal courts. So, if you read *O'Connor's Federal Rules,* you will have a thorough grasp of the way things work, in general, in the courts of whatever state you're in (or will be in). And this book is a *priceless* volume for future trial lawyers.

Granted, it has far, far more than you would ever need to know as a student. (In fact, it's intended for real-world lawyers, practitioners in federal courts.) But so far as I have been able to determine, no other publisher offers anything like it. You can skip over the more intricate stuff.

I recommend this work only if you have managed to get a head start on first-year. However, even if you do not get a head start, it can still be a wonderful book to have—for the reasons mentioned above. Also, it's possible that *your* civ pro professor will emphasize the *individual rules* of the federal code of civil procedure. In that case, *O'Connor's Federal Rules* is a *must,* period. There's a new edition each year, incorporating changes in the case law, etc..

The publisher is Jones McClure. They discount the price for law school students: $35. (You might have to fax them a copy of your student I.D. to get the book at that lower price.) It'll probably be difficult to find it or order it through a bookstore (although a few law school stores have started to carry it). Jones McClure's toll-free number is (800) OCONNOR (clever). That's (800) 626-6667.

Chapters 3 and 4 said your law professors make things as difficult as possible for you, on purpose. When the first edition of *O'Connor's Federal Rules* was first published, the students at one law school heard about it through word-of-mouth. The school's bookstore was owned by the law school itself. The faculty *ordered* the store not to stock the book and to refuse to order it for any student who asked. They said it would make first-year Civ Pro "too easy." (The students got the book anyway, directly from the publisher. The next year, the faculty reluctantly lifted the ban.) This is a *typical* example of law professors' mentality...and of their efforts to *prevent* students' learning the subject—*any* subject. (As mentioned, chapter 21 discusses why.)

Case Briefing, Revisited

Chapter 5 discussed John Delaney's book, *Learning Legal Reasoning.* The reasoning process is what gives the Common Law its legitimacy—and predictability (within limits). That's what makes it possible for the holding of a case to "make sense" to others, instead of being a merely arbitrary statement by individual judges who ruled on that case.

The very soul of reasoning is *logic.* There are two kinds: deductive and inductive. Lawyers—and especially judges—use both. (New "rules of thumb" result from inductive reasoning—as does the destruction of old ones. Deductive reasoning applies the still-respected rules of thumb to the case at hand.)

Good as Delaney's book is, in the long run it's not enough by itself. His concerns the case-by-case *inductive* approach. But there's a second one you need to read, which emphasizes the *deductive* approach. As you might expect, there's a lot of material in it that's not in Delaney's (and vice-versa). This second book is *Logic for Lawyers: A Guide to Clear Legal Thinking,* by Ruggero J. Aldisert. (He's a senior judge on the Third Circuit, one of the federal appellate courts.)

His is the *only* book I know of that—as its title says—discusses "logic for *lawyers.*" By looking at the rules of logic in connection with specific court opinions, he shows how important it is to know those rules. By working with his material, you'll begin to *consciously* think logically—so well that it becomes second nature to you. That can help you avoid making a bonehead analysis—in class or on an exam...and later, in the real world.

Further, as Aldisert points out, the overall *value* that a court chooses as its starting point will often determine the outcome of that case. That may sound obvious. But in the Law, quite often there are several ways of looking at a given case. Sometimes, one relevant principle is as good as another. A case that at first appears to turn on one legal principle might actually end up turning on quite another—if that's the way the court wants it.

Why the court chose the controlling value it did can be enlightening. And usually, the court pretends that the relevant principle it chose is the only *possible* one. In that instance, you will get no explicit guidance from the court as to why it framed "the terms of the debate" the way it did. You have to figure it out on your own. But once you've done that, your awareness can be of enormous help to you in analyzing and comparing other cases that, on the surface, seem quite similar—or dissimilar—to the case at hand. And along the way as you read Aldisert's book, you'll absorb some *profound* insights about the Law.

You should *study* both *Learning Legal Reasoning* AND *Logic for Lawyers*. Start with Delaney's, though, because it's the easier of the two. But don't stop there. Go on to Aldisert's.

The third edition of *Logic for Lawyers* was published in 1997. It costs $28 in paperback, from the National Institute for Trial Advocacy ("NITA"). You can order it by calling (800) 225-6482.

Other Subjects

Testing yourself, and getting instruction in the areas where you goofed, is a very good way to master material.

Blond's®, the commercial outline publisher, has two books available so far with first-year essay questions and answers in them, 25 per book. The two subjects to date are torts and contracts. Each book is $20. Blond's® toll-free number was presented in chapter 5.

As chapter 6 said, Emanuel has a series of *First Year Questions & Answers*. These are short-answer questions, and the number varies by topics. (Crim Pro is the lowest, with 131; Civ Pro the highest, with 253.) The book for each subject is $19. The Emanuel number was given in chapter 5.

As noted, Emanuel owns Siegel's, another commercial outline series. As chapter 6 stated, it has a series of books called "Answers to Essay and Multiple Choice Questions" for each subject: 20-25 essay questions, and 85-100 multiple-choice questions, per book; $16 apiece. Again, the Siegel's number is the same as that for Emanuel.

The Gilbert Law Summaries (a Harcourt Brace division), contain sample essay questions and model answers—as noted previously. But they also contain multiple-choice questions and answers for the same subject.

Legalines—which, as mentioned, is another division of Harcourt Brace—publishes *Criminal Law Questions & Answers* and *Torts Questions & Answers*. Each is about $13. If your law school bookstore doesn't have these, you can special order them. The Legalines number is the Harcourt Brace number.

Survival Series Publishing Company has a book called *First Year Law School Survival Kit,* by Jeff Adachi, a California attorney. It covers case briefing, outline preparation, and how to answer essay exam questions. Throughout, it takes what the author calls "a problem-solving approach." *The First Year Law School Survival Kit* is a good one-volume review of all the Big Six courses—and, like Delaney's examsmanship book, it's a good supplement to a formal examsmanship course. Adachi's book costs $40, and is available through Legal Books Distributing: (800) 200-7110.

Flash Cards

Remember flash cards? If you studied a foreign language, you probably used them. You might've used them in other courses, too. As Turow pointed out, legalese is a foreign language. And just as you have to drill in the vocabulary of a foreign language, so you have to drill in the vocabulary (and the concepts) of the Law.

Emanuel, a commercial outline publisher, has a product line called Law-in-a-Flash®. It sells sets of flash cards for each course. A set costs less than $20, per subject. I recommend them—but not at the *start* of the course. The sets are meant for review, just before finals. But you need to be doing that from the very beginning. So, *make your own,* using index cards, as you go along. You can test yourself with them, even before you find someone to study with.

Then why get a vendor's flash cards? —Because you want to make sure you've covered all the bases. Granted, the commercial flash cards include topics your professor omitted from the course. Just set those presently-irrelevant cards aside. (They'll come in handy less than two years later, when you're studying for the bar exam.) What's left might include something you'd never thought of.

And there's another advantage. By the time you've been working with your own flash cards for a semester, or an entire year, you begin to play a bad game with yourself: You memorize the question as well as the answer. As soon as you see the question, you know the answer—but you know the answer only as an extension of that specific question. So, if the question's phrased differently, it can throw you completely off. A law school exam is *intended* to throw you completely off. (So is the Multistate portion of the bar exam, discussed in chapter 17.) Therefore, it's worthwhile to test yourself with a set of questions that might approach the subject matter in a way that's different from yours.

The toll-free number for Emanuel / Law-in-a-Flash® is (800) 362-6835.

* * *

(The names and phone numbers of all these vendors are repeated in the appendix.)

Chapter 8 - Classes: "DOs & DON'Ts"

First thing: Do not even *think* about trying to hold a job during first-year. You simply cannot balance employment and full-time law school. Law school itself is full-time work. (I am told that in the movie *Love Story,* the hero held *three* jobs in first-year, and still placed third in his class…at Harvard Law School. Sure. —The novel on which the movie was based was written by someone who'd never spent a day of his life as a law school student, anywhere…Then again, the author was a Yalie. So perhaps that was his very sly way of knocking Harvard.)

Second-year employment is okay, but even then it should be something directly related to the law. (See chapter 12 regarding internships and research assistantships.) If you believe you can handle full-time first-year and even *one* part-time job, you're headed for a fall in the fall.

Now, with that out of the way, the rest of this chapter concerns only classes…

* * *

In courses you took before law school, the purpose of class sessions was to understand the material. Having (supposedly) read the assignment, you showed up in class expecting to get any confusion cleared up. The professor lectured, then called for questions. If the professor asked questions, they were merely rhetorical: the prof would always end up answering them (or confirming the right answers from students).

Not so in law school. *Things will not be explained to you in class.*

As chapter 5 showed, your goal should be to know the jargon and to understand the concepts before you even start law school. Ironically, if you don't understand them *before* you go to class, class will be almost a complete waste of time.

What happens in class has almost nothing to do with what's on the final. Therefore, *what happens in class has almost nothing to do with your grade.*

You probably find that hard to believe. But you'll see. Meantime, here's another quotation from Scott Turow's *One L:*

> /A/s the semester went on, more and more *class discussion* had focused on the philosophical, political, economic, and other pragmatic concerns which justify the rules and usually pass under the name of "policy." Issue spotters, then, do not seem to *test* what was *learned.* (Emphasis added.)

—That's because classes, especially in first-year, are just *something to fill the time until finals.* What the professors were pretending that the students were supposed to be learning was merely a *sideshow,* a diversion from the real learning that was supposed to be going on, on your own.

A law school professor is similar to a magician. The magician distracts the attention of the audience from the machinations of the trick's performance. And then, suddenly, *voilà,* the surprise. Of course, to the magician's audience, it's delightful. Not so for law school students—because the professor's surprise takes the form of a final exam that has little to do with what the professor appeared to be stressing in class. Unlike Turow—and I—at the time, you know better, now, *before* the magic show begins.

A national TV show a few years ago exposed how a magician does the trick of "sawing a woman in half." I wish it hadn't. Part of the fun of seeing magic tricks is trying to figure out, on your own, how they're done. (And if they're done right, you *can't.*) But the law school professors' tricks are *dirty.* —And they're far more important than mere entertainment (except, perhaps, to the professors). It is vital for you to know what's going on, and to not be taken in by machinations that can hurt you very badly, for life. Then, by the time *you* get to the final exams, you'll have correctly anticipated, in rough form, what's actually coming—and you'll be ready for *anything.*

You should be taking *very* few notes in class—because you've already mastered the material.

So why go to class at all? Well, in some schools it's mandatory; points are deducted from your final grade if you miss too many sessions. (This is becoming more common, as more students realize that class is almost a complete waste of time. If the rule exists at your school, you'll know.) Regardless, there is a very good reason to attend: It's another way to *test* your mastery of the material.

Nothing should happen in the classroom that leaves you feeling worried. The main reason you go is to pick up the occasional insight about Black Letter Law, here and there. ("Blow off" anything that *doesn't* concern Black Letter Law—for reasons the quotation from *One L* makes clear.) If someone says something useful (which is unlikely), and it's something you hadn't thought of on your own, make a note of it. Then revise your personal-outline-in-progress in light of it. As chapter 7 indicated, the key to doing well in law school is constant review of the material, updating it and applying it to new hypotheticals. You should be grateful anytime someone gives you a hint as to a new way of looking at something, because it enables you to expand your repertory of analysis. Or, something said in class might pique your curiosity about a point of law, or cause you to think of new questions and hypos on your own. The more angles you can expose, the fewer are left hidden. That, in turn, means whatever is on the final exam is unlikely to take you by surprise.

(Speaking of being taken by surprise: Assignments for your section's very first day of class in each course will be posted together, someplace. Find out where that place is, and then do all the assignments in time. —And by the way: Most law schools now use the continuous-surface desktop rows arranged in concentric semi-circles. At most schools, each student is assigned a specific seat. But those who come to class unprepared sit in the back row, which is normally empty. The professor doesn't call on a student until confirming that the student is in the assigned seat. So the "back bench" is a sanctuary…However, some professors regularly violate this alleged sanctuary.)

Another good reason to go to class—the "final" one, though not the last one: Your professors might explicitly state (or strongly hint) what will be on their final exams. This is particularly likely as your courses near their end. (But sometimes the professors don't keep their word.)

Your performance in class is irrelevant, as far as your grade is concerned— although some profs make a big show of promising to add a point or two to the final grade of students who do exceptionally well in class. That's B.S.. But it's harmless B.S..

However, just because class doesn't count, that doesn't mean you can get cute, or be the class clown, or get sarcastic, or defiantly fold your arms and say "I don't know" when called on. Those things can get you marked for punishment, such as being repeatedly called on—and ridiculed. (Also, see "blind" grading, in chapter 10.)

On the other hand, don't try to show off in class. If you follow the recommendations of chapters 5 and 7, you'll know far more than the average law student. *Don't let it show.* Your fellow students will probably resent it if you do. Your professor will feel threatened by it—and will make it a point to put you back in your place ASAP. And no matter how much you know about the law, the professor—perhaps—knows more…or at least, can do a better job of faking it. (This also applies to discussions of non-law topics on which you may well be a bona fide expert. The prof does not want to hear your "useful information.") You are not even there to engage in a true *dialogue* with the professor, let alone a *contest*. Trying to out-shine the prof is a no-win situation. You'd do better to leave law school altogether if you can't resist this one-upmanship urge, because it is suicidal.

Resisting the one-upmanship urge especially applies in your very first class on the very first day. Typically, the professor will ask each student to briefly introduce himself or herself. This is no time to brag. If one of your ancestors once sat on the U.S. Supreme Court, do not inform your fellow students of it. (The professor already knows: the admissions committee will have passed around any tidbits concerning various members of the entering class. Count on it.) If you won six Gold Medals at the most recent Olympics, keep a lid on it. (The professor already knows.) On the other hand, don't be timid, self-deprecating, and so forth. Also, avoid the *false* modesty routine; the smugness always shows through the facade. Don't be a comedian. If you're a direct descendant of Jesse James, don't make a joke about it—at least, not in class…unless it's criminal law. And above all, make no observations about how the legal profession is held in such low esteem by the public. Let the prof do that.

You don't get a second chance to make a first impression. From Day One, you want to come across as a mature, well-prepared, articulate professional. But don't overdo it, acting like a pompous ass. (Save it for your clients and the media—after you get your license.)

The key word here is "crispness." It's a buzzword, but "crispness" expresses that air of calm self-confidence that you want to have. (Herman Hesse, in *Magister Ludi*—Latin for "Master of the Game"—describing the hero: "Although humble, he was completely at ease." That's the way you want to be in class.) Of course, if that's not you, so be it. You have to be true to yourself—but at least try to be true to your *better* self.

Do not ask the professor a question in class—even if the professor invites it (rare). Join the after-class crowd at the lectern, or wait until office hours (if the prof has them). Better yet, take the matter up with your study group. In class, you want to keep a low profile. Do an adequate job when called on, but no more—even though you could. And don't play "teacher's pet" and raise your hand to answer a question someone else has struggled with. That's something to have outgrown by the end of grade school.

If you've been brilliant in class, and bomb on the final, your in-class brilliance will come back to haunt you. The word *will* get around to your fellow students, even if you try to keep it secret, that hot-shot you didn't do so well come crunch-time. (They'll know when they see you didn't Make Law Review.) *Save the in-class brilliance for years 2 and 3…if then.*

However, whether or not you live up to your image when the grades come in, you'll have *another* problem in the meantime: Your fellow students will call upon you outside of class to answer *their* questions. Answering others' questions is indeed a good way to test your own knowledge. And unlike the process of answering practice questions in a book, it's a real ego trip. But it gets old, fast. You'll soon find you can't handle all these people's demands on your time. If you then start turning them away, they'll not forgive you for it; nor will they forget it—*ever*. They'll make you the scapegoat for their poor performance. Playing know-it-all tutor is what economists call a "diminishing returns" situation. Better to hide your enlightenment under a basket and let others continue to curse their own dimness instead of cursing *you*. (Exception: your study group—but they shouldn't have to ask anyway; they should already know.)

Here's another reason to go to class: to scout out your fellow students. True, after the self-introductions in your very first class, each student will be called on perhaps only once in the entire academic year, in each course. But you'll take all (or nearly all) your first-year courses with this same group of people. By attending class regularly, the odds are you'll hear many of them speak at least once in class during the first few weeks of law school. Also, as mentioned, during those self-introductions, you'll get to observe the pose everyone strikes during this opening tableau. That's important.

These first few days are when first impressions are made—and first impressions are hard to dislodge. (That's another reason for you to always be prepared for class. I can still remember a few of those who gave particularly incompetent answers in first-year classes. And I *very* clearly remember the time *I* gave a totally wrong answer, in torts.)

There will be contact outside of class, yes. (But spare your fellow students the bragging—and any false modesty—even then.) However, what happens in-class has a special weight. Assuming you and your classmates don't scatter to the winds after graduation, your paths will cross. (Three-fourths of all attorneys practice within 200 miles of where they went to law school.) You'll have these people as allies, opponents, and consultants from case to case. You need to learn who's reliable, who's a quick thinker, who's lazy, who's foolhardy, who's timid, who's belligerent, etc.. Class is a good place to start doing that, to see what their standard operating procedure is— and how they perform under pressure.

Above all, in the short run, you need to find worthy partner/s to study with, as you bounce hypotheticals back and forth—discussed in chapter 7. True, the show-off might be brilliant. And maybe that person won't regard you as a worthy study partner unless you too have displayed brilliance in the classroom. However, hold off until you're in a 1:1 or small-group encounter *outside* class. Then the "genius" will be properly impressed. And if this star is *truly* brilliant, he or she will fully understand and appreciate your in-class discretion.

But if you still aren't accepted, don't worry about it. My experience with the genius show-offs is that they're a pain in the neck. In trial law, the key to success is "preparedness—plus fighting spirit." It's no different with law school finals. High intelligence and a brain that works fast are important. However, regardless of their mental endowment, *the study partners you want are the solid types, even the plodders, who stick with the material until they have it all down.* It doesn't take brilliance to do this. And it doesn't take brilliance to concoct hypotheticals. *It does take mastery of Black Letter Law and knowing how to Think Like a Lawyer.* Although many lawyers—and nearly all law professors—like to pretend otherwise, the life of the law is not the life of the mind. (More on this in chapters 16 and the addendum to 21.) It certainly is neither rocket science nor brain surgery. (One attorney aptly described lawyers as "mechanics with words.") The more you work at it, the better you'll get. You might even discover that you've become "brilliant" yourself by the time the exam questions are handed out.

Very few of your section mates will have read *Planet Law School.* So, if you have a study group composed only of those who *have,* it will be a real powerhouse. Then, it will just be a question of which person in your group is #1, #2, etc., in each of your courses when the grades come in. You want to find those people. Even though they're your natural rivals, you want them on *your* side. You've heard of "synergy"? —"The whole is greater than the sum of its parts." This is especially so when everyone in your study group is first-class. The rich get richer, etc.; and the rich (usually) know when to stick together regarding their common interest. By forming a study group of "gifted" students, the members will gain more from each other, by working *together,* than they would by each joining various other study groups composed of those who haven't taken advantage of *Planet Law School.*

—But then again, you don't want to let the cat out of the bag, either, regarding what this book can do for those not already in the know. Here's a suggestion: Before the very first meeting of your very first class, everyone will look at the posted chart to find their assigned seats. Post your own notice right next to it. Word it cryptically: "Section ____ PLS Study Group to Form." Then put your phone number, no name. Those who've read *PLS* will know what you're talking about—and (presumably) will call. Then all you have to do is make sure that they've done more than just *read* this book.

If you get no response, here's an alternative method: The ones who impressed you as being sharp during the opening tableau, but who then did not speak up in class (unless called upon), are the ones you want to check out...the strong, silent types.

Chapter 9 - Caught Up in the Madness:

The Paper Chase and *One L*

Anyone who's considering law school is often told to see one movie and to read one book, to "find out what it's really like." The movie is *The Paper Chase;* the book, *One L.* Both concern a student's first year at Harvard Law School.

The Paper Chase came out in 1973. It was based on a 1971 novel by John Jay Osborn, Jr.. (I am told that, at the time, Osborn had never attended law school—but that he subsequently got a law degree from Yale.) The novel is now out of print, but the film still shows up on TV from time to time, and is available in video rental stores. Timothy Bottoms had the lead, playing a character whose surname is Hart (get it?). John Houseman was the main supporting actor, in his classic role as Professor Charles W. Kingsfield.

One L was the first book by Scott Turow, the lawyer-novelist. (I don't know how good he is as a lawyer, but he's definitely a *very* good novelist.) The book was originally published in 1977. Unlike Turow's subsequent works, this one is non-fiction. "One L" is shorthand for a first-year student at HLS, and as a 1L, Turow kept a diary. The following summer, he turned it into a book; published while he was still in law school. I suspect he did it as a "post mortem," a sort of self-help psychotherapy. —In writing *One L,* he was perhaps trying to come to terms with what he'd just been through. Maybe he wanted to put his first year of law school behind him once and for all, before moving on to second-year. (One might suspect that much of *Planet Law School*, and Kahlenberg's *Broken Contract,* are also post-mortems, a sort of delayed self-help psychotherapy to try to come to terms with *all* of law school. And in *Anarchy and Elegance,* Goodrich was explicit that he'd started work on his own book as self-help psychotherapy during first-year at Yale.) Turow changed the names, descriptions, and backgrounds of the people involved, to protect the innocent (and the guilty). *One L* is still in print, a solid backlist title. (As you've seen, *Planet Law School* quotes it several times, with Turow's—paid-for—permission.)

If you have not yet exposed yourself to *The Paper Chase* or *One L,* approach them with caution. The problem is not that they give a false impression. Quite the contrary. What they present is the truth. But it should not be true for *you.* By that I mean the reality depicted in those works should not become *your* reality. They're "What it really should *not* be like."

You've heard of the so-called "self-fulfilling prophecy"? Well, regarding lawyers-to-be, *The Paper Chase* and *One L* both set you up for a bad time. The reality they present is actually a bizarre "unreality." Together, they're the single biggest trap for the unwary with regard to law school. That's why this entire chapter is devoted to showing what's wrong with the model they present.*

The Kingsfield Syndrome

From a future law student's perspective, the key figure in *The Paper Chase* was Professor Kingsfield, who teaches contracts. He is brilliant and aloof. He is also merciless in his pedagogy. But *The Paper Chase* would have us believe that this was the academic equivalent of what's now being called "tough love." Kingsfield's seeming hostility supposedly masked a concern for his students' intellectual progress that ran very, very deep. "Hart" had quickly concluded that Kingsfield's disdain and ruthlessness were for the students' own good. The awe he felt toward Kingsfield from the very beginning had grown even stronger by film's end. Hart had supposedly gained a mature understanding of the true nature of the Great Scholar, and of the Law's Majesty. Hence the mystical bullshit about "Having a true Socratic experience."

One L was published six years after *The Paper Chase* was, and four years after the Osborn novel had been made into a movie. Surely, as a teacher of creative writing at the time the novel came out, Turow had read Osborn's work at some point. And even more surely, he would have seen the film before going to Harvard Law. Yet, he mentions neither in *One L; The Paper Chase* is conspicuous by its absence. However, Turow's commentary on it screams from between the lines.

Turow also reported *his* experiences in a contracts course, with a Professor "Perini." I have not attempted to learn from the author of either book if the contracts professor was modeled on a specific HLS prof. However, I have spoken with several people at Harvard Law School, some of whom were employees there prior to the publication of either book. They reported much speculation as to who the "real" Kingsfield or Perini was, but no agreement. Therefore, I believe it is too much of a coincidence to be a coincidence that Turow, in *One L,* has Perini teaching the same subject as Kingsfield.

(In the alternative, it's possible that both Osborn and Turow had their professor teaching Contracts because, as mentioned in chapter 3, the Case/Socratic Method was *started*—in 1870—by a Contracts professor at Harvard Law: Christopher C. Langdell, who also happened to be the dean there.)

As with "Hart," Turow began the academic year in awe of his contracts prof. However, unlike the movie's constantly increasing adulation, Turow's

---

* Certainly Turow was not deliberately setting a trap. He obviously didn't cherish his experience. I have not read the novel on which *The Paper Chase* is based, so I can say nothing regarding that author's intentions. However, the movie takes a real "macho" attitude toward surviving the tortures and terrors of first-year…similar to the Marine Corps' explicit statement that "boot camp will make a *man* of you." (And even Turow fell into this, somewhat.)

opinion moves in the opposite direction. (I can't help but wonder if Osborn's novel would have been more like *One L* if Osborn had waited until *after* he'd gone to law school before he wrote it. As Goodrich makes clear in *Anarchy and Elegance,* Yale Law had no shortage of professors who were pompous assholes and bullies *à la* Kingsfield.)

Perini, too, was a pompous asshole and a bully. However, in the movie, Kingsfield spoke with an upper-class British accent. This makes his academic brutality easier to overlook, because of course all Americans have been conditioned to genuflect at the sound of an upper-class British accent. To make Perini's obnoxiousness more apparent, Turow went to the other extreme, and has Perini speak with a distinctively Southern accent. — Americans have also been conditioned to believe that anyone who speaks with a strong Southern accent is either a fool, an ignoramus, a bigot, a brutal sadist, or some combination thereof. Perini fit the brutal sadist stereotype. To make him even more clearly objectionable, Turow goes out of his way to mention that Perini's law degree was from the University of Texas...and we all know how obnoxious anyone from Texas is, right?

But the movie's image of Kingsfield in *The Paper Chase* naturally overwhelms *One L's* written image of Perini. In fact, it has led to what I call the Kingsfield Syndrome: Many law school professors have—subconsciously or deliberately—imitated it. (This life-imitating-art is similar to the way the world's mobsters have quite consciously imitated the dress, choice of automobiles, and methods of speaking and acting portrayed by American gangster films.) Unfortunately, the many professors who imitate Kingsfield are able to copy only the aloofness and the harshness, not the brilliance. They mistake sarcasm and sadism for education. They self-indulgently abuse their authority in the name of pedagogy.

Students are conditioned to respond with fawning adulation to this display of arrogance and cruelty. It is no exaggeration to compare this to the "battered wife syndrome." The victimized spouse decides to stay in the relationship because—however oddly by objective standards—she thinks, "If he didn't care so much about me, he wouldn't be so abusive."

(By the way, the scene in *The Paper Chase* when Kingsfield starts to expel Hart from class is based on a true incident at HLS. The real-life professor's name was Edward Henry Warren, who taught Corporations Law and Property Law at Harvard from 1904-43. His nickname was "The Bull."* In the movie, Hart gives a smart-ass response to an inquiry from Kingsfield. In real-life, the student's response was merely inept. In the movie, Kingsfield summons Hart to the lectern, hands him a dime—the cost of a payphone call in 1973—and orders him to call his mother to tell her that he does not have the makings of a lawyer. In real life, "Bull" roared at the student,

---

* "Bull" Warren is not to be confused with *Earl* Warren, the former Governor of California who served as Chief Justice of the U.S. Supreme Court from 1953-69.

"You will never make a lawyer! You might just as well pack up your books now and leave the school!" The student, shocked, stood and gathered up his belongings. In both the film and real-life, he then moved toward the door—but then turned and faced the professor. In the movie, Hart loudly says, "You are a son-of-a-bitch, Kingsfield!" Thereupon, Kingsfield replies, "Mr. Hart, that is the most intelligent thing you have said today." The class bursts out laughing…which distracts us from the truth of Hart's statement. Then Kingsfield says, "You may take your seat." In real life, the student had declaimed to Professor Warren, "I accept your suggestion, Sir. But I do not propose to leave without giving myself the pleasure of telling you to go plumb straight to Hell." Immediately, the Bull replied: "Sit down, Sir. Sit down. Your response makes it clear that my judgment was too hasty." —Don't know about you, but I prefer the true version.)

Mistakes in Common

Although *The Paper Chase* and *One L* finished with opposite views of their respective contracts professors, the students in both works made the same major mistakes. As with lemmings jumping off the cliff, they mindlessly followed what others were doing. Neither Osborn nor Turow understood (at the time) how students could avoid the trauma these authors described.

In hindsight, Turow would surely have done it all quite differently if he had the chance. And I hope that when Osborn did finally go to law school himself that he didn't have the same attitude or methods his fictional hero did. However, any future law student, turning to either of these works, would naturally and naively assume this is the way law school is, unavoidably. And so, like the fatalistic cavalry in Tennyson's "The Charge of the Light Brigade," they vigorously attack. ("Theirs not to reason why, / Theirs but to do and die.")

Don't you be that way. In law school, there is no safety in numbers (exception: your study group—which is a very *small* number). Don't follow the herd—because the herd is unwittingly headed for the slaughterhouse. Be a maverick. You're thinking about going to law school because you have a good brain. *Use it.*

Here's how the students of *The Paper Chase* and *One L* screwed up:

Burning the Midnight Oil—and the 11th-Hour Panic
If you're burning the midnight oil, you're doing something seriously wrong. As the Opening Statement of *this* book put it,

> You're going to have to work hard, no matter what.
> But hard work by itself doesn't guarantee success—not
> in law school, and not in life. In fact, for those who think
> that way, hard work is sometimes counter-productive…
> It isn't enough to *work* hard. Nor is it enough to *be*
> smart. You have to "work smart," too.

And there's even more to it than that. You need to take good care of your health and to build up reserves of energy. As you begin your final exams in first-year, you want to be fully rested, yet completely alert. Constantly burning the midnight oil, playing some kind of macho game to see how few hours' sleep you can get by on each night, is academically suicidal. I assume you do not have a death-wish. So don't work yourself to death. You've heard the saying, "If it's worth doing at all, it's worth doing well"? Nonsense. In law school, there's too much to do—and much of it isn't worth doing at all...And if it's just barely worth doing in the first place, it certainly isn't worth doing well. To again quote the Opening Statement: "You have to acquire a sense for what's important, what's not. Set your priorities. This is especially so that all-important first year of law school. You can't know *everything*—but you *can* know what really *counts*...."

Neither Hart, nor Turow (nor anyone else) had the foggiest idea of what it took to do well on final exams. True, *The Paper Chase* leaves the audience with the impression that Hart did well. But we never find out—for good reason: The odds were that he was destined for a Hart-breaking discovery, given the way he'd approached his courses. Turow, after *his* finals (and before the grades were issued) said he and his fellow students *still* didn't know whether or not they'd done well.

That's how it goes, for all students at all law schools. —And it tells you something about what's wrong with law school pedagogy: Success is virtually haphazard, even among "the best and the brightest" who've worked so hard to master the material. (Long ago, Wall Street discovered that a randomly-selected stock portfolio, chosen simply by throwing darts at a list of securities, would perform about as well as one chosen by professional investors. However, because that didn't require managers or any of the other big-ticket costs, any investor would do better to buy a dartboard and dispense with hired advice. Naturally, that has never happened. Everyone, especially those who *succeed,* wants to *believe* in the system—and that they beat it through more than sheer luck.) I'll bet that if Harvard Law School had chosen *x* number of students at random, and had declared *them* to be at the top of the class—regardless of their performance on finals—their subsequent careers would have fared the same as those who won the finals lottery, as long as their secret didn't get out. Of course, no law school would dare conduct such a longitudinal comparison test, because then the myth would be shattered, the mystique would be gone. (However, with *Planet Law School*, it will not be a matter of chance for *you.*)

Both Hart and Turow crammed for finals. But there's a difference between cramming and intensive studying. It's more than semantic. Cramming is the hare's approach, and hare-brained. Intensive study, at less than the frantic level of cramming, is the tortoise approach. (A determined tortoise can cover a lot of ground.) It's more practical, determined, and thorough. Just before finals, Hart and a fellow student spent a few days together in a hideaway. They tried to quickly memorize all the material for each course, in one marathon session. That's cramming—and foolish.

There is absolutely no reason to spend the final days before an exam working yourself into a frenzy, burning yourself out at the very time you most need to be in top condition, both physically and mentally. And there is absolutely no excuse, now that you're reading *Planet Law School,* for running around like a chicken with your head cut off, the way students in *The Paper Chase* and *One L* did…which is the way it still is, even today.

(You might, perversely, be looking forward to such a traumatic experience—thinking that, years hence, you'll look back on it and laugh. If so, the joke will be on you. And it won't be funny, even then.)

Granted, Hart had been doing intensive study throughout the semester. So had Turow. But neither of them knew how to "work *smart.*" So they both just worked *hard*—very hard. Too hard. Yes, *too* hard. *Good* work is all that counts, and it's indicated by the *results.* In law school, there's no such thing as "An 'A' for effort."

Classes, Study Groups, and Outlines

In both *The Paper Chase* and *One L,* many students tried to play teacher's pet in class. They raised their hands, sure they had the right answer. They desperately wanted to outperform some unfortunate fellow student who had just failed to shine. As Turow discerned, students "tended to see classroom performance as an index of standing" —i.e., of how good they were. Further, in *The Paper Chase,* there were several scenes where students made cutting remarks in class about answers another student had just given. They pumped themselves up by putting others down. Professor Kingsfield encouraged this dog-eat-dog approach. That is sick. (Unfortunately, it's also the norm for our species.) Yet, as Turow also noted, when the grades came out, often those who seemed smartest in class had been washed away, somehow.

(From your point of view, though, what's most important about class is that all of this is irrelevant. That's why all of chapter 8 dealt with how to play the in-class game correctly.)

In both portrayals of law school, study groups formed early in the year. However, after the initial meeting, they did not begin work as a *group* until several weeks before the exams. *Big* mistake. As chapter 7 showed, your study group should be working *together* on *hypotheticals,* starting with the first week of law school.

In *One L,* Turow said it was a problem that the members of his study group couldn't agree on how to approach each subject. They wanted all to be on the same wavelength. But the best way for a study group to cover all the bases is by having intellectual diversity—discussed in chapter 7.

Neither work made the distinction between Master and Summary Outlines that *this* book makes. What their students did were Master Outlines. In *The Paper Chase* and *One L,* the study group members divided up the task. In the former, each person outlined only one course. Then they exchanged outlines just before finals—or were supposed to. In the latter, each worked on some material in every course, so the outline for each course was a collective work.

You can't very well internalize someone else's outline, or someone else's part of a collective outline. All you can do is memorize it—and even that is unlikely, given the short time remaining before exams. As chapter 7 explained, to internalize your own outline, you have to write the material in your *own* words and to *constantly re-work* it. Your outline should contain what's useful to *you*.

And as both works showed, sometimes others proved unreliable: they either provided a very poor outline, or none at all. One of the best things about doing your own outlines is you don't have to worry about someone leaving you in the lurch at the last minute.

The resulting outlines were far too long. In *One L,* one "outline" was more than 400 pages. In *The Paper Chase,* there was an *800*-page outline. Even during an open-book exam, it would be impossible to make use of one of those monstrosities. If the students had been reworking their outlines, as discussed in chapter 7, they could have pared each Master Outline down to 50 pages at the most.

But as chapter 7 also mentioned, if the exam is closed-book (which it nearly always is) you want to take the first few minutes to *reproduce* your *Summary* Outline in its entirety—where everything in it automatically triggers something else in your mind. This is another reason why you should supplement your work on the Master Outline with flash cards on the elements of each legal basis of entitlement—to gain practice at instant recall.

Odd as it may sound, the outline itself is not what's most important. It's the *process* of *making* your own personal outline, and of *constantly reworking* it, that's paramount. *That's* how—along with working hypotheticals—you *absorb* the material, and master it.

The most important purpose of a study group is to practice hypotheticals, not to split up the work of making outlines. Do the one, not the other.

Cheating

Unlike Turow, Hart cheated. *The Paper Chase* finessed it, but he cheated. He committed a breaking-and-entering of the law school library in the wee hours. He sought, and got, the notes Professor Kingsfield had taken when *he'd* been a first-year law student in contracts (at Harvard). Hart wanted to make sure he'd completely "psyched out" Kingsfield, the better to anticipate what he, Hart, should say in answer to the final exam questions in contracts. What better answer to give than the professor's? Hart could easily have mined Kingsfield's own thoughts by consulting other sources. In fact, he did—Kingsfield's published articles, for example. But that clearly wasn't enough. He wanted to give himself that extra, *unethical* edge.

Thus, *The Paper Chase* gave the false impression that, as a result, Hart *did* have an extra edge. (Maybe that's why he wasn't worried about his grades at film's end—or, at least, his contracts grade.) But *success in law school is a very simple matter:* Black Letter Law; Thinking Like a Lawyer.

There's no magic to it, no Secret Writings such as the Red Set, hidden in a locked room the way they were in the movie. Yet, this is the message the film conveyed. Even if Kingsfield had freely given all his students copies of his first-year notes, the effect would have been minimal. (And his notes certainly didn't include the questions he would be asking on finals he'd be giving to his own students in years to come.)

There is simply no need to even *try* to give yourself an extra edge by doing something unethical. —And if the penalty for getting caught is "death," doing something unethical borders on sheer lunacy. It simply isn't worth it, given that the additional benefit is trivial, at best—and probably nonexistent. It could even be counter-productive: you take it easy, counting on the easy score, instead of preparing yourself to meet the real challenge.

Another message from this episode in the movie was that it's okay to cheat if you're a "good guy." But what "bad guy" *doesn't* think of himself as a "good guy" who deserves a break—even if it involves break-and-enter?

* * *

You might think it odd of me to go off on such a tangent about a movie. But I practice trial law. And trial lawyers know that a jury remembers only a small fraction of what it hears, and an even smaller fraction of what it reads in documents. However, a jury remembers a very large percentage of what it *sees*—especially if what it sees has been chosen for visual impact. Most of all, a jury remembers what it sees and *simultaneously* hears, if it's something dramatic. A movie, as a form of drama, is by definition dramatic. That's why Kingsfield will be remembered and revered, even though Perini is truer to real-life. Unfortunately, that's also why errors *The Paper Chase* students made will stay in your mind much better than the lessons of *Planet Law School*. You might even forget that the students' mistakes in that film *were* mistakes. (Another thing any trial lawyer can vouch for is that people's minds play tricks on them. Memories are amazingly faulty, and open to suggestion.) You should not watch that movie.

* * *

According to *One L,* Scott Turow's LSAT score was in the *99th* percentile. If you recall its full name is Law School *Aptitude* Test, Turow should have aced first-year. He didn't. The very lack of a correlation between his LSAT result and his initial HLS performance is a good indication that something is terribly wrong with the system. The correlation—or rather, the lack thereof—between LSAT scores and first-year law school grades is, no doubt, yet another well-kept secret that enables the academic emperor to claim he is fully dressed as he struts about the classroom. (Then again, I shudder at the thought of Professor Kingsfield buck naked.)

Actually, like the Emperor's New "Clothes," it's a "secret" that's out in the open. *Law Services Report* is a newsletter of the Law School Admissions Services—LSAS, the folks who do the LSAT. In its March, 1988 issue, there was an interesting statement from the then-director of services and programs for LSAS. She reported that there was a *very disappointing correlation* between LSAT scores and "early" law school performance. Because "early" performance (i.e., first-year) is the only one that really counts, her statement was fraught with enormity. —But never mind, it's still business-as-usual regarding the LSAT and its crucial importance as a basis for the law school admissions decision.

More and more, it appears the LSAT does not test aptitude for law *school*. However, perhaps it *does* accurately test it for *law*—or rather, for one's *potential* to Think Like a Lawyer. There's a difference between the one and the other.

Students with natural athletic, musical, or artistic talent still need to be guided in the nature of the skill in question. They aren't expected to learn it on their own. Yet, law school *itself* is *sabotaging,* for its own selfish and cynical reasons, the very people entrusted to its charge. (More on this in chapter 21.)

Near the start of *The Paper Chase,* Professor Kingsfield gives a little speech. In it, he says something about how his questions probe the students' brains and reshape the students' cerebral mush into something that enables them to Think Like a Lawyer.

I beg to differ. True, you don't go into law school already knowing how to Think Like a Lawyer. But I've seen plenty of attorneys who came *out* of law school *still* not knowing how to Think Like a Lawyer. What the Case/Socratic Method does is to turn your layperson's brain *into* cerebral mush. It's up to *you* to reshape that mental mess into a fine instrument capable of good legal analysis. Most law school students never get good at it. They just get by.

Given Turow's intelligence and humanity, what he experienced was tragic.* Perhaps the same could be said of Osborn. It can certainly be said of Chris Goodrich, Richard Kahlenberg, and George J. Roth, whose works have also been quoted in this book. The fault lay not with the students, but with the Case/Socratic method, and the deliberate pedagogical malpractice of law schools. Someday, perhaps decades from now, *One L* will have only historical interest, in the same way that we read about how, once upon a time, all surgery was done by *barbers*—without anesthetic.

Sorry to say, the only reason for you to read *One L*—or to see *The Paper Chase*—is to learn how *not* to go about being a first-year law student.

---

* However, Turow did well enough in years two and three to graduate *cum laude.*

Better to avoid these altogether. Turow, Hart, and their fellow 1Ls made almost every mistake possible. (So did I—and then some.) If you have already seen the movie or read the book, keep it in mind as a cautionary tale. And if you find yourself feeling or acting the way Turow, Hart, and their fellow students did, the tocsin should sound in your brain, for you are doing something terribly wrong. Use *Planet Law School* to avoid such travail.*

One L tells how it was for Turow. (Its subtitle is *The Turbulent True Story of a First Year at Harvard Law School.*) Kahlenberg's *Broken Contract* referred to his own experience at the same law school as "hell." Goodrich told how first-year at Yale was filled with "horrors." The original edition of Roth's *Slaying the Law School Dragon* was graphic in its depiction of what happens. That's how it was for me, too. It's that way for nearly everyone else who attends law school without having been clued-in to what it's really all about.

But 1, 2, or 3, thanks to *Planet Law School* it shouldn't be 'ell for you.

---

* Yet, Hart did manage to get *laid* fairly regularly. More power to him. Turow, in contrast, had the far more typical experience: Even though he was married, he had no sex life; he had neither the time nor the energy. (Then again, Hart was a purely fictional character, invented by someone with no experience of law school. Turow was in-the-flesh.)

Don't burn the midnight oil. Get your own fire lit instead. Often. It's the better way to work yourself into an 11th-hour frenzy. And the emotional and physical release will improve your academic performance. Seriously. —On the other hand, beware involvements that can lead to emotional upheavals...especially before finals.

—And regardless of whether or not you have a sex life, you should get some vigorous physical exercise on a regular basis through sports, calisthenics, jogging, etc.. It will improve your *mental* vitality and resilience.

Last, law students (and lawyers) often have stooped shoulders, and back problems. This comes from lugging around all those law books. The advice in chapter 5 (regarding casebooks) should help you avoid that. But just to be safe, your exercise program should include things that will keep your back in good shape.

One other thing you might consider is learning how to do something like Transcendental Meditation®. As with a good dose of laughter or a good physical workout, it's a healthful way to relieve stress.

Chapter 10 - Let the Student Beware

1. "Blind" Grading

Virtually every law school says it uses blind grading on written exams. It's similar to the SAT or LSAT that way. (Those, of course, are multiple-choice. Nearly all law school exams are essay.) You're assigned a number. You write that number on each "bluebook" you use during the exam ("0103— 1st of 42," etc.). All the professor sees are the bluebooks with the code numbers. There's a receipt, of sorts. It's in two parts. The first part you turn in to the exam proctor. Your name and code number are on it. When the professor turns in the grades, the grade sheet shows the score each student got, but only by the student's code number, not name. So the registrar's office then refers to its own list, which has students' names *and* code numbers. Next, it enters the score each student got, onto that student's record. The grades are posted, with scores listed by code number, just as on the professor's gradesheet. Each student has kept the other half of the exam code number receipt, and uses that to look up his or her own score on the posted gradesheet. (At some schools, however, the recorder's office gives the grades directly to the student, in person or by mail.)

Because the professor doesn't know whose bluebooks he or she is grading, personal bias can't enter into the final score. True. However, *afterwards,* a *tenured* professor can find out the grade he or she gave to a particular student, by name—*before it's recorded.* The professor can then raise or lower that score before it's entered on the student's transcript. (He or she will then change the score in the student's bluebooks, too, before returning them, of course—if, indeed, the bluebooks are returned at all.) It happens. Your law school will deny it, but it happens. Rarely; but it happens. (We'll get to another practice that belies the preaching—one that's far more common— in chapter 12.)

The moral is: Don't think you can get on a professor's bad side just because you're sure you'll ace the final. True, a professor can't change your grade and flunk you if you did well. But a half-dozen points can make a *big* difference in your class standing—so even if you do ace the final, you still lose. (And please don't dream that just because the prof seems to like you so much, you don't have to worry about your final grade—as though your friendly faculty member will change it to something better if you don't do well. That happens only in the movies…and not in movies about law school. Although theoretically it can work in both directions, in practice it's usually just one way: down.)

You better get used to it right now, if you haven't already: Lawyers sometimes lie. (Gasp!) And nearly all law school professors are lawyers (at least, on paper). Don't let the pretense of the academic "above it all" attitude fool you. Behind the facade, these people can be just as petty and vindictive as you or I…and you're on *their* turf, playing by *their* rules.

2. Dealing with the "Character and Fitness" Committee

Part of the P.R. the legal profession persists in spouting is that all future lawyers are screened to determine their "character" and "fitness" to see if they're "worthy" of entering this noble profession. When you start law school, if you intend to practice law in the state where your law school is located, you must file a "Statement of Intent to Study Law" with that state's supreme court, bar association, or other agency authorized to license attorneys. Then the Character and Fitness (C&F) Committee decides whether or not you're entitled, on moral grounds, to join the ranks of those engaged in the virtuous calling of the Law.

You will be scrutinized. But the bar is too cheap to conduct more than a perfunctory investigation on its own. Instead, it relies on *you* to tell it the truth and the whole truth, first on your Statement of Intent, and then on your Application for a law license. If at any time the powers-that-be discover you lied, *you* will discover just how much power they have—and the clever tortures they can inflict effortlessly. So, if you were put on probation for a semester in college because you didn't turn in 20 long-overdue library books, you'd better report it.

Once you *have* a law license, you can seduce clients, perjure yourself, bill for work never done, rip off the trust fund you set up to provide for a rich client's heirs, etc.. Almost *anything* goes—as long as you don't *flaunt* your turpitude *and* you're well-connected with the powers-that-be in your state's regulatory agency. (I am not exaggerating…as you will see for yourself once you're admitted to the guild. And no, I have not engaged in unethical behavior myself—well, not *seriously* unethical behavior. But I know of several lawyers— and judges—who have engaged in *heinous* behavior, again and again, yet have never received so much as a token slap on the wrist for it, despite strenuous efforts by their victims.) However, until you *get* that union card, you'd better at least *pretend* to be a sanctimonious pinhead.

The C&F committee is often more concerned with dishonesty *vis-à-vis* the C&F Committee than with the transgression itself. Let's say you have 90 unpaid parking tickets. That's bad. It means you're a scofflaw. But if you "come clean," and confess, then at least you've shown you're an honest scofflaw. And if you can concoct a convincing story as to *why* you didn't pay those 90 tickets, you might get off the hook. (Sample: "I sold that car to my sister, but we never got around to having the registration changed regarding the license plates. *She's* the one who accumulated all those tickets. I even have correspondence to that effect, between the two of us and between the city and me." Good luck. You'll probably need a written confession from your sister, which you're unlikely to get. —Then again, maybe someday she'll want the free services of her lawyer sibling. Hmm…)

Here's the one that really gets to me most of all: If you go through any type of psychological therapy or counseling, you have to report it to the C&F people. *You might also have to sign a waiver giving them access to your file.* In the state where I went to law school, it was a Catch-22 situation:

The strain of law school was enormous, but students were explicitly advised *not* to seek counseling—because it might jeopardize getting a law license in that state! —We could go to a counselor, but anything we said about having doubts regarding the Law, or lawyers, could be used against us. It could also be used against us if we ever felt like committing suicide in law school (which feelings were not so rare, actually), or felt like murdering a professor (which feelings were *definitely* not so rare).

Even if a therapist-patient privilege exists in your state, you will be asked to waive that privilege. Refusal to do so will count heavily against you. We're not talking Constitutional Rights here. We're talking about the Character & Fitness Committee. As far as they're concerned, you have no rights. And the U.S. Supreme Court, for the most part, has backed them up.

The other thing that can jeopardize your future license is lack of gravity. I am not joking when I say you have to appear to be a sanctimonious pinhead. The C&F people have absolutely no sense of humor—and very little sense of humanity.

I am not making up the following: A student (at a law school that shall remain nameless) filled out the Statement of Intent to Study Law form. There was a question on it as to whether or not he would "uphold" the Constitution of the United States. It was—and still is—a ridiculous question to ask. So he gave a flippant answer: "Of course: I'm a 'constitutional' kind of guy." His state's Board of Bar Examiners decided, on the basis of that one answer, that the student in question was unfit to practice law. It refused to allow him to sit for the bar exam. He sued. *Years* later, his state's Supreme Court ruled in his favor. By then, of course, his prospects for a career with a reputable firm were gone, as was his bank account. (However, I don't know if he ever passed the bar exam: It was—and is—based on "blind" grading—and guess who, in that state, gets to grade 60% of it?)

Another example, also involving loyalty to the Constitution: A black student was at another, anonymous, law school during a time when a number of "racial incidents" were going on around the country. One day in class, she said she was uncertain of her loyalty to the U.S. Constitution because it was the basic document of a system that was so oppressive to blacks. A fellow student (white) reported her to that state's C&F committee. The Committee conducted a full investigation. In my opinion, she was cleared only because she was black. There was a danger of adverse publicity—perhaps even "racial incidents"—if she was barred from the bar. (I have no quarrel with letting her off the hook because of her race, if indeed that's why she got off. My quarrel is with a regulatory agency that comes down hard on a student who makes such a thoughtful comment*—and then looks the other way while licensed attorneys routinely and deliberately subvert the Constitution,

---

* I disagree with her, by the way. But that's beside the point: at least she was thinking and refusing to take things at face value...and after all, that's part of what a good lawyer is supposed to do.

the rule of law, the "justice" system, and so forth.)

Never, never, *never* raise your voice to anyone who's on or connected with the C&F committee—whether on the phone or (metaphorically) in writing. They have even been known to make extensive notes of any conversations, whether on the phone or in person. These people have all the power. They know it. They often act it.*

Actually, the experience is good training for dealing with superiors in your law firm, or with judges: No matter what they say, no matter what they do, they're right. Remember that dictum from the Middle Ages? —"The King can do no wrong." Well, the Character & Fitness Committee can do no wrong—while you're under their authority. (Nor can a judge—while you're in that judge's court. Nor can a superior at your law firm—while you're an employee of that law firm.) No matter what they do, you grin and bear it—although there are ways to politely and discreetly take issue with them. Above all, be humble and respectful, even to the point of humiliation. No matter how petty, ridiculous, or stupid these people seem (and, often, *are),* they have the power over your future.

Granted, for the vast majority of law school students and graduates, the process of getting vetted goes smoothly. It's a routine procedure. Don't be the exception that proves the rule.

3. Sexual Harassment

There are rules against it, but it happens. Welcome to the real world of law school. Remember, the professors have tenure. They're immune. (And if an assistant professor, without tenure yet, is stupid enough to harass others about sex, that person doesn't have what it takes to play the faculty's games anyway.) The rules are only for P.R. purposes—just as the "rules of ethics" that supposedly guide practicing attorneys are only for P.R. purposes. You file a complaint, see what happens to it. And see what happens to you.

Sure, there are exceptions. If you're the editor-in-chief of your school's law review, and the daughter of an attorney who's a prominent member of the state bar, you can get some action—maybe even something as drastic as a *private reprimand.* (*That'll* show'm.) Otherwise, you'll be subjected to a very stressful round of interrogations, meetings, hearings, etc.. Just what you need when you're trying to get good grades in law school.

There is the retaliation factor, too. (See "blind" grading, and the "character and fitness" committee, above. —There's more than *one* way to screw a student.)

---

* I speak from (second-hand) experience, having counseled a law school graduate who ran afoul of my state's C&F committee because he'd run afoul of a department chairman at a grad school he'd attended. The professor had set out to ruin the student's life—and nearly succeeded.

So what to do? I'm sorry, but I am going to dodge the question. I am not a trained counselor, have never handled a sexual harassment case of any kind, and am male. There are people far better qualified than I to give you advice. All I will say is it's better to head it off at the pass (as it were). If you can attend any presentations, or read any material, that helps you to protect yourself, I urge you to do so—*before* you go to law school (or even college, as the case may be). An ounce of prevention, etc.. Planet Law School is like nothing you've experienced before. Don't let it turn into *Invasion of the Body-Snatchers.*

Here are two incidents of sexual harassment I observed, personally, in law school. Obviously, since I was present—and not a participant—these weren't in 1:1 settings. In fact, all my section-mates were fellow witnesses.

The first was directed to the female students in general. A—male— professor launched a discussion of "social utility" as a concept for imputing liability in tort. He steered the social utility concept into the realm of criminal acts, within the context of civil liability for same. He chose rape as his example.

He then said that *civil* liability for rape should be based on a "balancing test." In the one scale was the social "disutility" with respect to the rape victim. However, in his opinion, this "disutility" was only potential, and might be minimal. "And she might *enjoy* it." (Yes, he said that.) On the other hand, the rapist obviously derived pleasure from committing the rape. So there was the definite "social *utility*" to weigh against any disutility. Theoretically, then, given a certain fact pattern, an act of rape could be a benefit to society. (I am not making this up. More than 100 people can confirm this. — And I graduated from law school in the early *'90s,* not the '50s.)

The second example was directed to an individual. As one of its main cases, my first-year civ pro casebook discussed *Owen Equipment and Erection Company v. Kroger.** The civil procedure professor, male, thought it would be cute to embarrass a female student by asking her about it. He called on the most attractive woman in the class—one of the most beautiful women I have ever seen, in fact.

"Tell me about *Owen,*" he said.

She started to brief the case. He interrupted her.

"I see this company's full name is 'Owen Equipment and Erection Company.' Which would you prefer: 'Equipment,' or 'Erection'?"

She politely said either one would do. He wouldn't stop.

"I'm surprised. I would think *you'd* want 'Erection'—although I suppose an erection is impossible without the equipment for it. Could you tell me why you might *prefer* 'Erection'?" She did not become flustered, nor did she respond, other that to say (in a neutral tone), "No, I can't." Good for her. Having failed to unnerve her, the prof let it go.

---

* 437 U.S. 365, 98 S.Ct. 2398, 57 L.Ed.2d 274 (1978)

Granted, these incidents were minor forms of sexual harassment. But they *were* sexual harassment, in my book (and this *is* my book, after all). In neither of these instances did anyone voice a complaint in class (or afterwards, to my knowledge). Why? —Because we were all in our very first semester of law school, and living in fear and trembling...which is the way the professors liked it. I think it's more than coincidental that no similar incident occurred *after* first-year.

4. Racial Harassment

I am not referring to racial harassment by fellow students, but to racial harassment by professors. Yes, that too happens, even today. It's rare, at least in its overt form, but it still happens. I never witnessed any such incidents while I was in law school. However, I heard of one. It involved yet another of my first-year professors, and quickly made the rounds of the entire school.

This particular professor was the "flaming reactionary" mentioned in chapter 4. He hated anything that he regarded as reverse discrimination, and had written extensively in opposition to it. My school had several students from minority groups in it. One of these students, black, was in the professor's course. One day in class, the prof called on the guy, who gave an inept answer. The professor glared at him silently for awhile, then said, "You're the best argument I've ever seen against affirmative action."

Never mind that white students had often given inept answers. Never mind that even good students sometimes have bad days. All the prof cared about was that this student was black—and as far as the prof was concerned, the only way a black could get into this particular law school was as the result of reverse discrimination. In short, the professor was a racist. His remark was as savage as it was uncalled-for.*

Because I was not an eyewitness, I cannot swear it happened this way, or that it happened at all. But I had occasion, later, to discuss it with another faculty member, who confirmed it. He said the professor who'd made the remark was privately urged not to be so indiscreet again...and that was the end of the matter.

Once again, I shall duck the question of how to cope—in part because I'm a WASP. But once again, if you're a member of a minority group, I urge you

---

* This is not to say that *all* whites who oppose affirmative action are racists. (As a logical proposition: "All 'A' are 'B'" does not mean "All 'B' are 'A'.") However, all who are racists do use their opposition to affirmative action as a stalking horse for their bigotry. This professor's own bigotry was ironic, as he was descended from late-19th-century immigrants whom WASPs had heavily discriminated against because of their religion and national origin. This group eventually won acceptance in "polite society" only through the power of the ballot box, by voting as a block in big-city elections.

to attend presentations and read relevant material before you even enroll in law school. (However, I will note that if the student hadn't been so stunned, he might have shot back:"And you're the best argument I've ever seen against tenure.")

5. Difficulties for the Disabled

This section concerns only those in wheelchairs. I apologize for leaving out those with other physical disabilities. My only excuse is that, if you're deaf, etc., it's very easy to determine whether your prospective law school is considerate in this regard. Such is not the case regarding promises of wheelchair accessibility. (And as for other disabilities, I apologize for my ignorance as to your needs.)*

If you're in a wheelchair, you already know that the symbol indicating "access for the disabled" is sometmes fraudulent. The "wheelchair ramp" turns out to be at a 35-degree angle, accessible only to a motor-driven chair with *very* high power; the interior doors (especially to the restrooms) aren't wide enough to accommodate passage of a wheelchair; or the sole elevator turns out to be the freight elevator by the loading dock—and you have to find a janitor with a key to make use of it.

At my law school—a wealthy one—accommodations were minimal. To the best of my knowledge, while I was there no one in a wheelchair was ever on the premises—perhaps for good reason: I could easily see attending classes would have been very difficult for such a person. Despite this, the school's promotional materials proclaimed that it was fully wheelchair-accessible.

If the buildings of your proposed law school are relatively new (say, within the last decade), they were probably designed and built to be truly barrier-free. Regardless, if a given law school accepts you, it might have a videotape it can send you, showing that it's wheelchair-accessible. But don't trust the self-serving proclamation in the promotional literature, and not even a videotape. And don't even take the word of a disabled person on the *faculty or staff*. It might be worth the expense of a visit before you decide to enroll there. Check out the auditoriums, classrooms, elevators, cafeteria and snack bar, the lounges—everything. This includes living quarters and transportation arrangements. If you can't afford the visit—or maybe even if you can— ask if there's a *student* there who's disabled, or a recent graduate who's disabled. Get that person's name and phone number from the school. Call that person up (or, if you visit, meet that person face-to-face if you can). Insist on it. (Of course, as was the case at my school, there might be no such

---

* However, I shall briefly mention one situation, involving a law school that shall remain nameless. It had built a good reputation for itself for accommodating the disabled. This included providing help for students with dyslexia—such as providing assistants for taking notes in class and extra time when taking exams. Then the administration abruptly reversed its policy, without notice. A class action suit against the school was successful.

person. You either make the visit, or you take your chances.)

At a previous school I attended, the administration deliberately lured disabled students by promising to create a "barrier-free environment" in a special dormitory for them. In the years I was there—which was more than three years after the promises were made—nothing was done to honor the commitment. (My hunch is the school was getting federal funds for the project, then diverting them. To this day, I am told, there is no barrier-free dorm.) The disabled students I spoke with were very bitter; rightfully so.

You don't need such an additional burden anywhere—but especially not in law school.

> An ounce of prevention is worth a pound of cure, no matter what the subject. (This applies when counseling your future clients, too.)

Chapter 11 - Of Gravity—and Levity

It's easy—*very* easy—to get caught up in the madness discussed in chapter 9. And you do need to be wary of the dangers discussed in chapter 10. You need to take law school seriously. But if you take it *too* seriously, it will probably interfere with your ability to learn. It will certainly interfere with your humanity.

The ancient Greeks had an ideal as to how a person should be. They sought to avoid the two extremes of personality. At the one end was the "funny man," always cutting up and horsing around. Their word for him was "bomolokos." You won't find many of that sort, if any, in law school. The other end of the continuum was the "agroikos," who seldom even smiled. "Pinheads" is a good modern word for them—and a lot of them are lawyers. The Golden Mean was the "eutrapelos," a paradoxical combination and balance of gravity and levity. My favorite description of it is "one who kicks the world away, with the airy grace of a dancer—yet, at the same time, presses it to his or her heart." I am sure this is something like what Herman Hesse had in mind when he wrote the statement in *Magister Ludi,* quoted in chapter 8: "Although humble, he was completely at ease." To narrow the idea down to just one word, it's "grace"—not in the religious sense, but as in "grace under pressure." And boy are you ever under pressure in law school.

A naturally-gifted dancer has grace. However, natural talent is seldom enough to make a living. Even if you have a natural gift for the Law, it will take a lot of effort to acquire mastery of it. Don't let it get to you.

I'm sure you've seen the 1939 movie, *The Wizard of Oz,* starring Judy Garland. When Dorothy & Company first arrive in the Emerald City, they soon enter a great hall. The similarities between the Great Hall and Law School, and between the "Wizard" and law professors, are profound.

For example, when Dorothy and the others first enter the room, a curtain opens at the far end, revealing a huge screen surrounded by upward-shooting flames. Remember? Then there appears on the screen a frightening, awesome image: the disembodied head of the great Wizard himself.

"I AM *OZ*—THE GREAT AND POWERFUL!" his voice booms. He then arrogantly demands, "WHO ARE *YOU?*"

Dorothy identifies herself and her friends, then says, "We've come to ask—."

But the Wizard cuts her off: "*I'LL* ASK. THE GREAT AND POWERFUL WIZARD *KNOWS* WHY YOU'VE COME." He then insults the Scarecrow, the Tin Man, and the Lion. His visitors were terrified, and nearly lost their nerve—which is exactly what he wanted.

That is the ambiance of the Socratic/Case Method. If you really want to understand the Kingsfield Syndrome, discussed in chapter 9, but without exposing yourself to the psychological virus of *The Paper Chase,* catch these scenes in *The Wizard of Oz* instead. (Okay, I'm exaggerating—but not by all that much, really.)

The band of heroes then leaves, as ordered. They eventually return with the broom of the Wicked Witch of the West. Again they appear before that awesome image. Recall that the Wiz then tries to renege on his pledge to grant their wishes if they brought him this trophy.

When Dorothy dares to take him to task for trying to break his promise, the Wizard warns her: "DO NOT AROUSE THE WRATH OF THE GREAT AND POWERFUL OZ!" "DO YOU PRESUME TO *CRITICIZE* THE GREAT OZ?!" And when she again chastises him by saying, "You ought to be *ashamed* of yourself, when we came to you for *help*," he peremptorily bellows, "*SILENCE*, WHIPPERSNAPPER!" Finally, the Wizard tries to dismiss her and the others by announcing, "THE GREAT OZ HAS SPOKEN!"

However, Toto, Dorothy's mutt, pulls back a second curtain, on the side of the room, near where Dorothy and the others are standing. Turns out that the awesome image was just a projected picture of the altered face of a little old man who'd been a sideshow mountebank in the same world Dorothy came from. Exposed as a charlatan, he comes clean, and offers to do what little he can as a mere mortal to help the heroine get home.

Unfortunately, in real life, unlike the Wizard, the great and powerful law professors routinely are able to get away with breaking their promise to educate students in the law. They feel no contrition. Instead, as chapter 3 showed, they blame their *students*. (In law as in war, the best defense is a good offense.)

—And if you really want to understand *attorneys* (especially most trial attorneys), you can do no better than to contemplate those scenes near the end, when the "Wizard's" charlatanry has been exposed. He does not apologize for having sent Dorothy and the others to what he had hoped would be their *deaths,* just so *he* would not have to *admit* his inability to honor his worthless commitment. Instead, the consummate con artist, he then persuades his "clients"—the Scarecrow, the Tin Man, and the Lion—to believe that he *has* done something for them, something *wonderful,* by giving them mere trinkets instead of fulfilling their needs as he'd promised. Then he takes his leave of the situation—appropriately enough, by means of a *hot air* balloon. *Unlike* attorneys, however, he did not collect a fee.

Like Toto, I've been yapping—and pulling back the curtain.*

---

  * And as long as I'm grousing, I have a bone to pick with Glinda, the Good Witch of the North, too: She held herself out as a real know-it-all (that bit about how Dorothy could have used the ruby slippers to go home any time she wanted, for example). But if she was such a smartypants, how come she didn't know the guy she referred to as "The great and wonderful Wizard of Oz" was a *fraud?* Huh? That broad floating around in the bubble was a real bubble-head, as far as I can tell.

    Seems to me, Dorothy had a cause of action in tort against Glinda: for the malpractice of witchcraft. *Dorothy Gale, et al., v. Glinda, Good Witch of the North.* She'd need to file it in Kansas, however, to get the "home court" advantage—although Glinda would probably file for "forum non conveniens,"

/Footnote continued on next page./

Unfortunately, my bark is much worse than my bite…so far. And even if you are someday inclined to agree with me that law school is mostly smoke and mirrors, the *poseurs* who run the show will never admit their grand fraud. In short, unlike Dorothy when confronting the merely human "wizard," you will never be able to "call a spade a spade" in law school. You will have to play along. But at least, in your own mind, learn to see it for what it is, and to laugh at it…and at yourself.

Do not be in awe of the Law. And *especially* do not be in awe of your law *professors.*

As you can tell from this book, I am no *eutrapelos*—and I hope *you* prove better able than I to practice what I can only preach. *Planet Law School* has been a relentless jeremiad up to this point. In its own way, this book has taken law school too seriously.

So, heeding my own advice, I hereby present some tidbits to lighten the mood. They're taken from a newsletter called *The Court Jester* (which is now, unfortunately, defunct), and are excerpts from transcripts of real-life Depositions, Hearings, and Trials, repeated verbatim.

* * *

to have it dismissed in Kansas so it could be refiled in Oz, if at all.

There might also be a good cause of action here against the "Wizard," for fraud, breach of contract, and intentional infliction of emotional distress.

—And there's more: granted, the Wicked Witch of the West was dead by movie's end; even so, Dorothy, the Scarecrow, the Tin Man, and the Lion all had a cause of action against the Wicked Witch's estate for assault, battery, and intentional infliction of emotional distress—just for starters. Then there's the matter of the decedent's estate: the Wicked Witch had probably accumulated considerable assets (just look at that castle!), and I'll bet she died intestate (i.e., without a will). A probate attorney could get rich just from distributing the estate to her heirs—and could certainly run up a nice bill *looking* for those heirs, what with the sister of the Wicked Witch of West (i.e., the Wicked Witch of the East) having predeceased her.

—Come to think of it, there's even more legal work that needs doing in Oz: The Lollipop Guild probably could use a good labor lawyer—as long as they pay in cash rather than suckers. And the Lullaby League might need counsel, too. The Emerald City probably lacks a City Attorney, and the County of Oz probably has been doing without a County Attorney.

Then there's the matter of the Munchkins. Notice that *everyone* in Munchkin-Land is, well…a Munchkin? Birth defects on that scale must have a cause—groundwater contamination, perhaps. I can see it now: a class action on behalf of all the Munchkins for what is obviously some polluter's toxic tort.

Why, County Oz is a gold mine! "Yellow brick road," indeed: *paved* with gold for an enterprising lawyer!

However, as has been truly said, "If a town has only *one* lawyer, he or she will *starve;* but *two* will make their *fortune.*" Anyone care to sign up? (Now you see what "Thinking Like a Lawyer" *really* means.)

The Truth, the Whole Truth, and Nothing but the Truth

Love That Jury Duty

During jury selection, the following exchange occurred between the presiding judge and a prospective juror:

Female Panelist: Yes, your Honor. We were taken to a hotel while we were deliberating, and we were all seduced in the hotel.
Court: You were *what?*
Panelist: We were seduced in the hotel.
Court: Do you mean *"sequestered"?*
Panelist: That's the word.

You Asked — Part I
Attorney: What were you convicted of?
Witness: Miscellaneous receiving.
Attorney: What did you receive?
Witness: I received one to five years.

Go Figure
Attorney: Do you have a middle name?
Witness: P.
Attorney: And what does it stand for?
Witness: For "Latimer," on my mother's side.

Of Sages and Wages
Attorney: Were you paid by the hour?
Witness: No, on Saturdays.

You Asked — Part II
Attorney: What did he do after that?
Witness: Well, he walked down the deck, as far as I remember.
Attorney: How did he walk?
Witness: With his two feet.

So *That's* How the Name Originated
Attorney: After the anesthesia, when you came out of it, what did you observe with respect to your scalp?
Witness: I didn't see my scalp the whole time I was in the hospital.
Attorney: It was covered?
Witness: Yes, bandaged.
Attorney: Then later on, when you first observed it, what did you see?
Witness: I had a skin graft. My whole buttocks and my leg were removed and put on top of my head.

From the Books

Judicial Notice
"In protecting women, courts and juries should be careful to protect men, too, for men are not only useful to general society, but to women especially."

—Bleckley, J., *Humphrey v. Copeland,*
54 Ga. 543, 544 (1875)

Another One from the Immortal Bleckley:
"/T/he venereal disease was not a partnership malady. That was individual property."

—Bleckley, J., *Gilbert v. Crystal Fountain Lodge,*
80 Ga. 284, 286, 4 S.E. 905, 906 (1887)

The Case Name Says It All
Swindle v. Poore, 59 Ga. 336 (1877)

They Call It "Thinking Like a Lawyer"

Actual Questions that Real Lawyers Asked at Depositions, Hearings, and Trials..../And for those who wish to become *trial* lawyers, these are at least as *instructive* as they arc entertaining./

The Things They Don't Teach You in Law School — Part I
Attorney: Mr. Josephson, you went on an extended honeymoon?
Witness: Yes, touring Europe.
Attorney: You took your wife with you?

Well, He *Did* Like to "Growl" at Suspects
Attorney: And how did you know the policeman wasn't a dog?

Logic 101
Attorney: What happened then?
Witness: He told me, he says, "I have to kill you because you can identify me."
Attorney: Did he kill you?

The Things They Don't Teach in Law School — Part II
Attorney: Mr. Edwards, are you the father of Robert Edwards?
Witness: No.
Attorney: Do you know who the father is?
Witness: Yes. Bill Daniels is the father.
Attorney: Tell us how Bill Daniels happens to be the father of that child.

The Private Life of a Proper English Gentlewoman

In a British case, a woman sued a municipal bus company for personal injury. She said that as she exited from the back of the bus, the driver started to drive on, causing her to be thrown down, and her face struck the pavement. During his final argument, her lawyer made this statement:

"Through this most unfortunate accident, caused by the gross negligence of the servant of defendant Company, my unfortunate client suffered this most grievous injury to her jaw, with the dire result that she could not—for quite a long time after—bite her bottom with her top teeth."

Doctor's Revenge - Part I

Attorney: Dr. Browning, you conducted the autopsy on Mark Samuels?
Witness: I did.
Attorney: And he was dead at the time?
/Here's the richly-deserved answer—/
Witness: No, you stupid asshole. He was sitting up on the table, asking me what the hell I was doing.

Such As?

Attorney: Do you have any children or anything of that kind?

Doctor's Revenge - Part II

Attorney: Dr. Gold, you say you're here to testify about the cause of Mr. Blake's death, correct?
Witness: That's right.
Attorney: But Dr. Gold, you did not, yourself, conduct the autopsy on Mr. Blake, did you?
Witness: That's right.
Attorney: Dr. Jeffries conducted the autopsy on Mr. Blake, didn't he?
Witness: That's right.
Attorney: You weren't present when Dr. Jeffries conducted the autopsy on Mr. Blake, were you?
Witness (Sighing): That's right.
Attorney: In fact, you never even saw the body of Mr. Blake, did you?
Witness (Patience Growing Thin): That's right.
Attorney: And all you have are Dr. Jeffries's notes from that alleged autopsy, correct?
Witness (Annoyed): That's right.
Attorney (Triumphant): Then you cannot *even* say for *certain* that Mr. Blake is *dead,* can you?
Witness: That's right, counselor. I *do* have his *brain* sitting in a jar on a shelf in my office. But for all I know, the *rest* of him could be out practicing *law* somewhere.

Lawyer Jokes We <u>Like</u>

The trial lawyer returned to court after lunch with the strong odor of an alcoholic beverage on his breath. As he approached the bench for a conference, the judge—a teetotaler—angrily said, "Counselor! You reek of whiskey!"

Proving that his potation had not impaired his powers of cerebration, the quick-thinking attorney replied, "If your Honor's sense of *justice* is as good as his sense of *smell,* my client will *prevail* in this case!"

Newspaper Reporter to Bragging Lawyer: How many court cases have you lost?
Lawyer: None.
Reporter: None?!
Lawyer: None. *I* have *never* lost a case in court...but some of my *clients* have.

Of Laughter and Lawyers

/The following is an excerpt from an article in *The Court Jester...*/

According to Dr. William Fry, of Stanford University Medical School, there is a close relationship between laughter and mental and physical well-being. "We have a lot of evidence that shows that mirth and laughter affect most of the major physical systems of the body. You can get a really good workout from it."

Dr. Fry is an authority on the physiology of laughter. He was interviewed at the sixth International Humor Conference, held at Arizona State University, where the topic was the subject of much—serious, scientific—discussion. He continued: "Laughter is an activity that has both physiological and psychological energy—like sex and exercise."

According to him, in less than 20 seconds, intense laughter can cause the rate of heartbeat to double, for three to five minutes. In contrast, strenuous exercise (such as rowing) must continue for three minutes before the change occurs. As for sex, the time it takes for the heartbeat to change, the rate achieved, and its duration all depend on psychological factors as much as physiological. For some encounters, the rate can nearly triple—and stay that way for a long time. However, whereas the fatality rate during or shortly after these other activities is often remarked, people who've literally died laughing are virtually unheard of.

During intense laughter, the primary muscles involved are those in the abdomen, neck, face, scalp, shoulders, and chest. Fry also noted that the muscles not directly involved in laughter are more *relaxed* than usual during the paroxysm occurring elsewhere within the body.

And laughter clearly benefits the respiratory system. During normal breathing, much "tidal air"— a residuum of carbon dioxide-laden vapors—remains in the lungs. Fry says that laughing "makes you evacuate more of that 'tidal air,' so that you have an enlargement of 'air exchange.'" —More air is expelled with the next breath. But the new intake is oxygen-rich and interfaces with the lung tissue at sites where the carbon dioxide residuum had been. The improved "air exchange" can replace sluggishness with renewed mental snap.

What's more, says Fry, "During laughter, there is an increase in rapid /brain-/ wave behavior which is indicative of greater alertness and greater cerebral functioning, such as occurs when a person is working on a mathematical problem...

It isn't just the oxygen-for-carbon dioxide switch that does this, though. Laughter also stimulates the production of catecholamines. There are three, the best-known of which is adrenaline. These stimulate the nervous system and mental alertness.

Laughter has another benefit, for those whose days in the law are filled with clients and cases that are a pain in the neck (if not elsewhere). Laughing, says Fry, also stimulates the secretion of endorphins—the body's natural anesthetics. If an external problem is starting to have internal effects (such as a headache), a dose of humor is the prescription.

So, give your funny bone a regular workout, especially in first-year. (However, be careful about showing your sense of humor in class—at least until late in your first semester.) Although you certainly shouldn't spend much time watching television, do tune in your favorite comedy show—or, if you have a VCR, rent a funny movie every so often. Go out to a comedy nightclub, read a Dave Barry book, whatever works. Assuming Dr. Fry is correct, you might even "seriously" consider doing at least one of these just before you go to take each final. —Get that rapid brain-wave pattern goin'. (But *never* display any humor in your answer to a final exam, even if the prof likes to have some jollies in class.)

Here's how that article from *The Court Jester* ended:

"Atticus Falcon," Esq.

As Samuel Richardson, the 18th-century English writer, put it: "I struggle and struggle, and try to buffet down my cruel reflections as they arise; and when I cannot, I am forced to try to make myself laugh that I may not cry; for one or other I must do; and is it not philosophy carried to the highest pitch for a man to conquer such tumults of soul as I am sometimes agitated by, and in the very height of the storm to quaver out a horse-laugh?"

Enough said. Now, having made an excursus in the direction of the *eutrapelos,* I return in Part III to my *agroikos* ways...

Part III:

One Down, Two to Go

Chapter 12 - Honing Your Skills I:

Law Review "Drudgeships," Summer Clerkships, Internships, and Research Assistantships

Hard to believe, but by the end of your first year of law school, you will have acquired some skills. However, they will be minimal. They will consist mostly of how to Think Like a Lawyer—if you've followed the advice of this book. At least you'll already be far ahead of the typical layperson.

"Honing Your Skills" refers to making the transition from having abstract knowledge to building on that foundation in practical ways.

Law Review

Law Review is the Holy Grail of Law School, as you will fast discover. (At a few schools, it's called Law Journal. You'll quickly be told what it is at your school.) Those who Make Law Review see themselves—and are seen as—an elite. Those who end up in the top positions on their school's Law Review regard themselves—and are regarded as—minor divinities. There is a mystique about it. Law Review imparts a cachet that never diminishes.*

Many schools publish more than one academic legal periodical. These are unique in that they are the only academic journals edited solely by students. Mere students choose which proposed articles to accept and reject. Yet, the submitted manuscripts come mostly from law school professors. Often, they're from assistant professors trying to get tenure. (Tenure requires publications—preferably in prestigious journals.) However, the prestigious journals also get submissions from professors who've long had tenure. These hope to use the journal as a forum for influencing the law itself or the legal profession—or, more often, to get a job at a more prominent school. Manuscripts also come in from attorneys, judges, and an occasional public official in the legislative or executive branches. And there are submissions from fellow editors. (But a student's published article is only called a "note," or a "commentary.")

The editors do more than accept and reject articles, though. They also edit them. A 23-year-old kid can slash passages, or rewrite them, in a manuscript prepared by someone two or even three times his or her age. There's

---

* Because Making Law Review means high grades, this is a good place to mention the Order of the Coif. Coif is to Law School what Phi Beta Kappa is to college. As with PBK, it's nationwide, and you don't get in until you're about to graduate. Most law schools also have their own individual honor society, and there are some legal fraternities that require high grades to get in. However, as with Phi Beta Kappa, Coif is in a class by itself.

give-and-take when the writer objects (and *all* writers object to *any* changes by an editor). But the student editor has the final say-so…unless the author is a legal superstar. As you can see, the student editors of a prestigious Law Review have an awful lot of power. It's heady stuff.

Those who have a sufficient gpa after first-year are automatically invited to join the Law Review. They spend all of their second year working as "volunteer slave labor" for third-year students who occupy the top slots. It involves an enormous amount of work, all of it boring. This is because, for the second-year slave labor, *all* they do is Check Citations and find Authority.

Everything in a Law Review article must contain a citation to authority, via footnotes. The second-year slave's job is to check each of these citations for accuracy. The process is called "cite-checking," for short.

Example: On page 34 in chapter 3, there's a reference in a footnote. If this were a Law Review article, a staff member would check that citation for accuracy, to ensure 1) the author's name was correctly stated—and correctly spelled, 2) the title of the article was correctly stated, 3) the quotation is accurately stated, word for word, 4) the article appeared in a Vanderbilt academic legal periodical, 5) the academic legal periodical is called Law Review, not Law Journal, 6) the correct abbreviation for "Vanderbilt" is "Vand." 7) it was in the 42nd volume of the Review, 8) the article started on page 433, 9) the quotation presented appears on page 459, and 10) the article was published in 1989.

Second example: On page 135 in chapter 10, there's a case citation. Were this in a Law Review article, a staff member would check to make sure 1) the "style" of the case was as given—and would find that it is more accurately written as *Owen Equip. & Erection Co. v. Kroger,* 2) the case is reported in the official U.S. Supreme Court reporter starting on page 365 of volume 437, 3) the case is reported in West Publishing's Supreme Court Reporter—the one most people use—starting on page 2398 of volume 98, 4) the case is reported in Lawyers Co-Operative Publishing's case reporter starting on page 274 of volume 57, and 5) the decision was issued in 1978.

Are we having *fun* yet? Sometimes one sentence will have references to as many as half-a-dozen footnotes, or more. These are so extensive that sometimes they take up half the article's space. (To the best of my knowledge, the record for most footnotes is 4,824—in one article. The record for the longest footnote is said to be five complete pages, of *tiny* print.)

But that's not all. If the article says "The sky is blue," there has to be a footnote to some Authority regarding that alleged fact. Often, the manuscript includes an assertion without any such reference. Or worse, the reference is incorrect. Shame, shame, shame. Then the Law Review slave has to find Authority. —That is, the staff member must do what the author (or the author's assistant/s) should have done: "prove it." (This doesn't actually mean "proving" it, though. It just means there's some authoritative evidence to support the assertion.)

If there's an error, whether in cite-checking or finding authority, it's the legal journal's reputation, not the author's, that suffers. A volunteer slave who goofs too often (such as more than once) will not be promoted to an editorship in third-year. As you can appreciate, second-year Law Review involves dozens of hours a week in the law school library (or on-line). There's no academic credit for this, so it comes on top of studying for classes. But if you impress your superiors, and make enough of the right friends, you can become an editor in your third year. (The outgoing editors choose their successors just before graduation, by voting on who gets the top slot, the #2 position, etc. The current third-year editors also started out as second-year apprentices, doing the slave labor.) Those who don't become editors are generously allowed to remain as staff members in year three…as slave labor.

However, the very *highest* positions usually go only to those who *automatically* Made Law Review because of their first-year grades.

The other way to Make Law Review is through the "Write-On." Early in second-year, the Law Review announces the topic of a legal essay. Each Law Review wanna-be then researches the topic and writes a legal essay on it. The editors pick the winners, and the student authors get to join the ranks of the slaves. (At some schools, grades count even in the write-on. Your law school gpa is combined with your write-on score to produce a final score. Different schools weight the grades and the write-on score in different ways.) Automatic admittance is better than write-on, but the latter is vastly better than not Making Law Review at all.*

As a second-year slave, you will be required to fulfill a commitment of x hours per semester to Law Review. The hours are flexible, as long as you meet your quota. As a third-year editor, you will have to make a *full*-time "voluntary" commitment. You will have neither time nor energy for anything else. (Recall how chapter 4 said that, for law professors, time spent in class was really just "moonlighting" to them. The same is true of third-year Law Review editors—who, unlike the professors, don't get *paid* for showing up for class.) Quite often, the top editors appear only for the final exam. (You will shortly see how they can do this and still ace their courses.)

If you Make Law Review at a reputable school, and end up as one of its editors, your future is all but assured. But even if you're still just slave labor in year three, you will still have received an invaluable—albeit dismal—training, for you will have learned how to do legal research *very* well.

The reason why your future is almost "in the bag" is twofold. first, most law firm partners and important judges Made Law Review themselves. They know about the second-year slave labor. They know how much work it is, how boring it is, how hard it is to keep on with the "drudgeship" month after month. And they know that such people are the perfect employees: robots-

---

* If you have to go the write-on route, be sure to take a "safe" approach. If you say anything controversial, it's certain that you will offend *someone's* sensibilities. Insights are fine, but stick with the conventional wisdom.

at-law, disguised as human beings. But the second reason is also very important, even though it's related to the first. As you will see in chapter 16, finding Authority is crucial to legal advocacy. Those who've Made Law Review know how to find Authority—*boy,* do they know how to find Authority. And if someone goes on to an editorship in third-year, then the future employer knows that person must have performed satisfactorily in second-year. Thus, it's really the *second*-year participation in Law Review, not your eventual third-year title, that's crucial.

Your third-year is still important, of course, because one's rank in the final standings is determined by interpersonal skills as well as drudgeship, and interpersonal skills are very important to a legal career. (However, second-year grades also play a large role in the choice of third-year editors. Even so, second-year grades, unlike interpersonal skills, are objectively verifiable.) Most firms hire only a handful of new associates each year. The more prestigious the firm, the more likely it will hire only from the most prestigious schools, and only from the very *top* of the Law Review staff. These people are supposedly the "best and the brightest." (Yet, as David Halberstam's book of that title showed, it was the "best and the brightest" who got us into the war in Vietnam. Many law firms have had similar debâcles.)

As mentioned, most schools have academic legal periodicals besides Law Review. These, too, are student-edited. But they don't carry the prestige of the flagship publication. Often, *their* second-year slaves were admitted because of their performance in just one particular first-year course, rather than because of their overall first-year gpa. And sometimes, the journal in question is so highly specialized that future employers shun those who work on it, unless they're looking to hire people for that specialized area of the law. (Law Review, in contrast, has a general editorial content.) Sometimes these *secondary* journals at the *top* schools count more, however, with future employers than even Law Review at lesser schools. (And lower positions with the Law Review count more than the highest positions on other journals, at all schools.)

Besides the post-graduate benefits described above, Making Law Review confers advantages even while still in law school. The first benefit concerns registering for the next semester's classes. Normally, there's a deadline for students to submit their "dreamsheet" as to what they want to be enrolled in for the next semester. They usually have to list alternative choices, as well. Supposedly, the recorder's office then fills each course's slots in the order in which the staff goes through the dreamsheets—and that order is random. At larger schools, it's all done by computer, supposedly. But funny thing, the students who Made Law Review always seem to get whatever they wanted. Could it be that their dreamsheets are pulled out, set aside, and processed before the others'? No, impossible.

The second reason concerns making life somewhat easier for you. Chapter 7 stressed the importance of creating your own outline, and not relying on the work of others. In first-year, that's absolutely true; but not in years two and three. In first-year, it's true because your personal outline is the *sine qua non* ("without which /there is/ nothing"). But once you understand your first-year subjects extremely well, it's no longer vital that you do all the work yourself: the advanced courses, for the most part, are just narrow variations on the themes you learned in year one.

Even though Law Review is an enormous amount of work, on top of classes, you don't have to run yourself ragged. This is because the third-year editors have a collection of *excellent* outlines for virtually *every* second- and third-year course, specific to *each* professor. When a prof teaches an advanced course, he or she uses the same casebook, same notes, same points tested on the final exam, year after year. The Law Review outline collection reflects this. One of the best perquisites of Making Law Review is that you get access to a very good outline for almost any course you take—although sometimes only the third-year staff, or perhaps just the very top editors, get this. Because class itself is a waste of time (just as in first-year), being able to study a *good* off-the-shelf outline as finals approach can make all the difference in the world.

So now you know the secret of how it's possible to work nearly full-time on Law Review while carrying a full credit load...and still ace your courses. (Assuming they're available even to second-years, once you Make Law Review, you want to choose your advanced courses based on the availability of a Law Review outline for the course and professor in question.)

—And just in case the outlines aren't enough to get you to the top, there's a third possible reason. Recall chapter 10's discussion of "blind" grading, and surreptitious revisions to grades before they're recorded. Unlike most other revisions, for those who Made Law Review the change can *add* points. It isn't automatic, and in fact it's rare, but it does happen—especially for the top editors...and especially if one of the editor's parents is a VIP in the legal community, who channels big bucks to the alumni fund.

Rank Hath Its Privileges.

If you don't Make Law Review, it isn't the end of your life. But it will seem that way at the time. This is partly so because law school (and the legal profession) is *very* status conscious. If you thought *high* school was bad, just you wait.

Summer Clerkships

"Summer clerkship" does not mean just a summer job in a law office. Instead, the term refers to a structured experience. Only the prestigious firms—which are usually larger—have them. Typically, students interview for them in the first semester of their second year. First-year grades are the major criterion. However, many firms even interview students in the second semester of their *first* year. In that case, mid-term scores in full-year courses, and final grades in one-semester courses from the previous fall, are the criteria—along with your *college* transcript, and the prestige of that college. Either way, the clerkship then occurs the following summer. Today, at most firms, these student employees are now called "summer associates."

The typical summer clerkship lasts six weeks. The firms run two sets of them, one in the first half of the summer, one in the second. So, during the two summers you're in law school, you can have four clerkships, tops. At some firms, though, the clerkship lasts the entire summer, not just six weeks.* If you're a summer associate following your first-year, you might be asked to return to the same firm after second-year, of course.

You get paid the same rate as an entry-level associate attorney. So, if the going rate is $90,000 per annum for a new hire, you get roughly $1,750 a week: More than $10,000 for your month-and-a-half. Not bad. (However, first-year summer associates might not make as much as a second-year does. Life can be cruel.)

The summer clerk gets rotated through the major departments. The workload is moderate, and stress is almost non-existent. (Once you're a *real* associate, though, the workload and stress will be *crushing*—and commensurate with your starting salary.)

There's a lot of socializing with members of the firm. There's a reason for this. The firm is not really looking to discover your ability as a future lawyer. It assumes you already have that ability, because you did so well in first-year. Instead, the people there are evaluating your character and personality. They want to see how well you fit in to the firm's culture. Each person is asking him- or herself, "Do I want to deal with this guy, or gal, day-in and day-out? Do I really want to have this person around for *years?*" (Employers in other summer jobs in the law are thinking the same thing. But the difference is that they will evaluate you much more on the quality of your work than on your social skills.)

At the end of the summer after a second-year clerkship, you will probably be told whether or not there's a permanent job waiting for you when you graduate the following spring. Those who interviewed you for the summer position will have already decided you are at least worthy of being considered by their peers. That's why you got the summer job. However, in the fall of their third year, many a summer associate is anxiously searching for post-graduate employment, just like everyone else.

For this reason, it's extremely important that you carefully choose where you seek a position as a summer associate. It is *vital* that you try to get with firms where you and the firm will be a good "fit." And yes, there are differences,

---

* However, some firms are quite possessive: they don't want you clerking any-where else, ever, especially if you clerk for that firm after first-year and they ask you to return the following summer. They say this tests the sincerity of your desire to work for *them,* your loyalty, etc.. B.S.. What it means is that you've put all your eggs in one basket—so now you have no place else to go. But if you Make Law Review, they'll probably want you, regardless.

one law firm from another—despite my sardonic comments about pinheads, drudgeships, robots-at-law, and so forth. (Chapter 20 concerns finding a permanent job, but is just as relevant to finding a summer clerkship.)

Internships

Unlike summer clerkships, internships are possible during the school year—and they often carry academic credit. I did an internship, of sorts, for my state's bar association while in law school. The pay was great, and I made some good connections, but I got no academic credit. (Which suited me fine: to get academic credit, you have to pay tuition for it, even though the law school provides nothing other than the credit itself. The fee charged is pure profit.) Other students I knew worked as interns for state judges. They got paid *and* got academic credit for it. Some universities have one of their own attorneys just for the students' needs. Sometimes law students can work as interns for that person. The pay is low or nonexistent, but usually there's academic credit. And you get real-life cases with real-life clients, especially regarding disputes with landlords and merchants.

It might be that your internship is something new. Hence, no provision was previously made for giving academic credit for it. Talk with the dean's office and see if you can at least get "independent study" credit for what you'll be doing. You might have to obtain an official supervising faculty member, and you might have to write a paper on your experience. Big deal. Find a friendly—and lazy—prof who will let you get by with a short report.

For future litigators, working as a *court* intern is a terrific introduction to how—and, more important, how *not*—to practice trial law. You will be disgusted at what some attorneys submit for a judge to read…and you will hear what the judge thinks of it. You will get to sit in on hearings and trials, from which you can learn a great deal (especially if the judge later offers a critique, privately).

In some states, the appellate courts have internships. An appellate court internship can be extremely valuable even for someone who plans to be a trial attorney and to leave the appellate work to others. This is because it isn't enough to win a case at trial. You have to "protect the record" for the appeal. Unfortunately, many brilliant trial lawyers, who are consistently able to wrap entire juries around their little fingers, are woefully inadequate at protecting the case for the appeal. Many a large jury award has been knocked down, or knocked *out,* on appeal. Sometimes, the victory itself is reversed. If you learn to see a trial the way an *appellate* court sees it, it will stand you in good stead. This is true no matter which litigation path (trial, appellate) you pursue. —And even if you decide not to go the litigation route, it still Looks Good on the Résumé.

Don't go for an internship with a trial court, and probably not an appellate court, until and unless you understand trial law. This includes your state's rules of civil (or criminal) procedure, the rules of evidence, etc..

(See the addendum to chapter 13 for self-help study materials.) You better be good at legal research, too, because your major responsibility will be looking up cases, statutes, etc., to see if they say what the attorneys say they do. —And to understand what the law actually says, you must also understand it…or be able to find out, fast.

Another important area of conflict resolution is mediation and arbitration. If you don't want to do trials *or* appeals, but *do* want to get involved in disputes and help resolve them, try to get an internship with a mediator or arbitrator. You will get to sit in on the sessions, just as with a court internship, and you can learn a lot from them. —But you'll still be spending at least *some* time looking up the law. (See the addendum to chapter 13 for books on mediation and arbitration.)

Research Assistantships

Working as a research assistant for a professor is similar to working as second-year slave labor for the Law Review. However, while the nature of the work is similar, there's less work (usually). Recall the discussion in chapter 4 of how professors try to enhance their reputations and their outside income, and how publication is the main way they do this. And the student assistants are the ones who find Authority to provide the proper footnotes for the article. Sometimes the student assistants are the ones who *draft** the article.

Research assistants, unlike Law Review slaves, often get paid—by the school, as part of a work-study program. But they don't get paid much. And as with Law Review, there's no academic credit for it. The only reason to become a research assistant is to attach yourself to a Big Gun in the Law. This means you have to scout the faculty.

The easiest (and most reliable) way to find out is to start with a list of all the tenured professors at your school. Then check a database that lists all the times their work (law review articles and books) is cited by other authors of law review articles and law books. With few exceptions, those with a high count are the VIPs.

If you're interested in a particular subject area, go to the secretary of the professor who teaches that subject. Get the name of that professor's student assistant/s. Contact the assistant/s and explain that you're interested in the subject. They'll let you know if they're working for a VIP. The assistant you talk with might be a second-year who's planning to keep the job in third-year, in which case you have a problem. Or, he or she might be planning to move on, in which case there will be an opening for you. Of course, if the professor is *not* a Big Gun in the area you're interested in, and merely teaches the course for the hell of it, there's no point becoming that prof's assistant anyway.

---

* Legalese for "write."

Then again, you can always do it the way I did. In both cases, I was extremely lucky, so I don't recommend this; but here it is. In the first, I signed up for a seminar in an artsy-fartsy subject I dearly loved. Then I went to the professor and asked him if he needed a research assistant in the subject. I hit paydirt. Not only did he need a research assistant but, unbeknownst to me, he was one of the Biggest Guns in the field—as I soon discovered from working for him.

In the second case, I was taking a course in a subject unrelated to the one I ended up working on as a research assistant. The professor had office hours, and welcomed visitors. I sometimes dropped by to ask him about this and that. Apparently he took a liking to me (or else he was scraping the bottom of the barrel): One day, he casually mentioned his old research assistant was graduating and he needed someone new. I casually asked what it involved. It was exactly the area I wanted to practice in upon graduation. Better still, it turned out this guy was the heir apparent to one of the Biggest Guns in *that* field, who was long past retirement age and was about to hang it up. My guy was the one who'd be doing the next edition of the VIP's hornbook—and would get his name added as co-author. Dropping the pretense of nonchalance, I leapt at the chance.

Note: If a professor at your school is also a big-name litigator (whether trial or appellate), being a research assistant for that professor is like being a first-year associate at a law firm where that lawyer is a senior partner. But unlike what would happen at a law firm, you get to work *directly* for and with that lawyer, rather than for and with some intermediary who's senior to you. This is a *fantastic* opportunity to learn from a Master—perhaps once-in-a-lifetime.

Usually, to have a shot at this, you had to have taken a course with that professor, and had to have done very well. As a general rule, you also have to know the relevant rules of procedure and evidence—which usually means you need to have taken courses in those subjects, too. (But see the addendum to chapter 13 regarding do-it-yourself materials.)

Chapter 13 - Honing Your Skills II:

Clinics & Extra-Curricular Activities

Clinics

A clinic is a real-world program, under the auspices of your school, for which you get academic credit. It has a lot in common with an internship, discussed in the previous chapter. However, the more reputable the law school, the more likely its clinics will be of low quality. Prestigious schools tend to think that anything having to do with the real world, as part of the curriculum, is beneath that school's dignity. Go figure. But even if the quality is low, it can still be quite valuable…as a real eye-opener.

Such was true of the clinic I was in, criminal defense. In the "CDC," you get to be a lawyer for real, handling cases of real-life clients accused of misdemeanors. You're under the supervision of a practicing criminal defense attorney, of course. And the lawyer, in turn, is—supposedly—under the supervision of a faculty member. However—as I belatedly discovered— what you do is just a "motion practice" (filing pre-trial motions to quash the prosecutor's evidence, for example). There's also a lot of plea-bargaining with various assistant district attorneys. Actual trial experience is rare. I was assigned five cases: criminal trespass, public intoxication (on appeal from a municipal court), DUI, shoplifting, and vandalism. (No point in going into details, except to say I did well by my clients…with one exception that I *definitely* won't go in to.)

Other common clinics are those helping old people to get Medicare or Social Security benefits, protecting children's rights *vis-à-vis* the state's foster care bureaucrats, and helping poor people resolve problems with creditors, merchants, landlords, or spouses (or ex-spouses, as with child support).

Before you decide whether to sign up for a clinic, sound out the students already in it. Hang out around the clinic office, pick some students at random and quiz them about it—in private, one at a time. Get a good sample before you make your decision. And if possible, sit in on some of the clinic meetings where the students report on their work and get comments and instructions. These things will give you a good feel for the program's quality. But even though my criminal defense clinic's quality was low, if I had it to do over again, I would, just for the experience. (I'd also do it again just to get away from the typical law school class—which is boring, boring, boring.)

Extra-Curricular Activities

By "extra-curricular activities," I mean those related to academics.* This excludes activities solely for entertainment purposes or for relieving stress. So, no discussion of intramural sports, parties, talent shows, sex, etc..

However, student associations do merit brief discussion. Your law school will have lots of clubs, along with student "government." Many of those who join try to become high officers in them because they think it will Look Good on the Résumé. Forget that. Sometimes these groups bring in guest speakers— and then everyone hits the speaker up for a job. Forget that too (which is one reason it's real hard to get guest speakers for student organizations in law school).

But there are good reasons for joining a student association. You have more opportunity to meet and talk with other students in that setting than you do anywhere else. And, by definition, you already have an interest in common (whatever the association's for) other than studying law. Also, you can learn a lot from guest speakers. (For members of minority groups, chapter 20 discusses the best reason of all.)

The extra-curricular activities that follow are competitive events. All are intramural. Many times they're interscholastic, too. They're organized as tournaments, with elimination rounds.

1. Mock Trial: "Mock" means fake, pretend, as in the Mock Turtle Soup in *Alice in Wonderland*. (There's probably also a connection with the verb "to mock," as in "to ridicule"—but I'll let that go.) Except in the final rounds, there is no jury present, but you pretend there is. (This is important in terms of what you can say. Certain things cannot be uttered—or rather, aren't *supposed* to be uttered—in the presence of the jury. Part of the competition is knowing the rules about this, and following them.) Normally, you don't dare sign up for mock trial until you've completed a course in the rules of evidence, at least. (That's the other major basis for scoring points in the competition.) Each side has two "attorneys," and you split up the work. As you quickly find out, very little of what you've ever seen on TV or in a movie, or read about in a novel, is allowed in a real courtroom—or even a Mock Trial.

To do it right, you must make a very heavy time commitment. (The addendum to this chapter lists some materials to help you get a head start.)

However, be advised: litigators prefer to hire those who've Made Law Review, not those who've starred at Mock Trial. In part, this is because Mock Trial usually rewards behavior the real-world *penalizes*.

For example, in Mock Trial, you score points by making a valid objection. But in the real world of a *jury* trial, you *lose* points—with the jurors—every

---

* The most important extra-curricular activity by far, of course, is Law Review. Chapter 12 discussed it.

time you make an objection. (Jurors resent it when they think some lawyer is trying to hide something from them.) So, in actual practice, trial lawyers make objections only when they absolutely have to. —Further, there are some types of objections that a trial lawyer would *never* make, period. (These are objections that alert the other side to something you'd rather your opponent not be aware of—such as when he or she is inappropriately asking leading questions during direct examination.) But in Mock Trial, you *have* to make them to score—even though you run the risk of building a very bad habit. Also, in the real world, if the trial is to a jury, the most important part of the trial is quite often the so-called "jury selection" phase. Mock Trial doesn't include this.

2. Moot Court: The term "moot" means "having no significance," or "irrelevant," as in "The point is moot." So, Moot Court could just as easily be called "Mock Court." But that would obviously cause confusion with Mock Trial, so "Moot Court" it is. Moot Court concerns *appellate* court. No jury, real or pretend. No "Objection, Your Honor!" No direct examination, no cross. No exhibits or testimony. Instead, you're arguing a fake case on appeal. However, unlike Mock Trial, a key part of Moot Court is your written brief.* The judges will have read it before you make your oral presentation. Skilled legal writing counts. And here's the one time legal *research* becomes (brief-ly, as it were) relevant in law school (other than for Law Review slave-labor).

Then you get grilled by a panel of "appellate judges" (usually practicing attorneys). They'll interrupt your presentation, deliberately try to throw you off balance with hypotheticals. (It's a lot like your classroom experience with the Socratic Method.)

As with Mock Trial, each side has two participants. Again you split up the work—the research and writing, and the oral argument to the judges. During your first year, participation in Moot Court might be required. After that, it's optional.

And again as with Mock Trial, Moot Court requires a very heavy time commitment to do it right. (And again, see the addendum to this chapter for materials.)

A Digression, FYI...

In civil trials, juries only decide what the facts (supposedly) really are. They then also decide, given those facts, whether or not one side is to pay money to the other, and how much. However, these jury decisions are merely *advisory*. The judge can *overrule* the jury, both as to what the facts are and

---

* Not to be confused with a "case" brief such as is used for class recitation. For some courts, this "brief" can be 50 pages long or more.

as to how much money is to be paid, or indeed if any money is to be paid at all. (Of course, an appellate court can always say that the trial court judge was wrong to overrule the jury—or that the trial court judge was wrong to accept the jury's findings.) In the language of the law, juries are merely "finders of fact." (In a non-jury trial, it's the judge who's the "fact-finder.") Once the facts have been determined, the judge "applies the law" in light of those facts—and it's the *judge* who renders the decision.

So, in a nutshell, trial law involves arguing the facts, usually to a jury— although the pre-trial phase involves arguing the law (to the judge), *in light of* the facts. Appellate work involves arguing just the law (but the law *in light of the facts*). This is because, as just mentioned, the facts have already been decided at the trial level. The appellate court usually only decides whether or not, given those findings of fact, the trial court judge correctly applied the law to them. Therefore, to oversimplify, appellate work is more cerebral; trial work, more emotional.

And I'll take it a step farther: Despite the myth, trial is not a truth-seeking process. Rather, each side is trying to get an *opinion* as to which side's story is more *likely* the truth. Trial law is actually a *storytelling contest*.

It's said that "there are two sides to every story." However, juries don't hear out both sides and then compose their *own* story that takes something from each. They can't. Before the jurors go into their deliberations, the attorneys for each side have met with the judge and have drawn up "jury questions" as to what the facts are. These questions are put in terms of "yes / no," "either /or." There's no middle ground. The jurors have to go one way or the other with each one. (However, if they're not happy about deciding facts that clearly favor the plaintiff, they can always make the victory a bittersweet one by voting very small "damages" to the plaintiff. So, then, there is a middle ground of sorts, sometimes.)

That's why trial work tends to be more emotional—or, as non-trial law attorneys say (among themselves), good trial attorneys are good bullshit artists. They're right: all good story-tellers are. Further, juries—like voters—have an unfortunate tendency to decide in favor of whom they find more *likable*. Usually, they focus on the attorneys. However, a particularly likable or unlikable party or witness is sometimes the main determinant of credibility.

If this disillusions you, you have my sympathy. But better for you to know the reality now rather than learning it the hard way later. Bad as it may seem, given human nature it's far preferable to any alternative—including dispensing with the jury altogether and letting some supposedly-objective judge decide the case alone. There is no such thing as an objective judge, because judges are human too—even though they often like to pretend otherwise. However, judges are supposed to *try* to be objective—as are juries, for that matter. So, the fact that true objectivity is impossible does not justify dispensing with making any effort whatsoever to be impartial.

As a general rule the only cases that make it all the way to a jury are cases "deep in the gray" regarding the facts. (If it were a clear-cut situation, there either never would have been a suit in the first place, or else it would have long since settled.) Juries are vital, because they bring together something approaching a cross-section of the community, with a wide range of experience and a lot of common sense.* And even though I admit that good trial lawyers are good bullshit artists, juries tend to have very good built-in bullshit-detectors. They *tend* to have a good feel for which side "rings true" compared to the other. So the trial lawyer who relies *solely* on bullshit to win his or her case is (usually) asking for trouble. If the facts aren't on your side, and you haven't *thoroughly* prepared your case, all the smoke and mirrors in the world probably won't save you and your client.

End of digression. —But keep it in mind if you're interested in a career in litigation.

* * *

3. Negotiations Exercise: In the real world, even trial lawyers spend far more time in negotiations than they ever do in court. *Very* few cases ever go to trial, so most litigators have just a "motion practice." Because most cases settle before trial, negotiating skill is very important. Yet, in law school, Negotiations Exercises are much less common than Mock Trial and Moot Court. Perhaps this is because it's harder for an academic exercise to successfully emulate the real-world.

As its name implies, you and a partner negotiate as a team against another team. Each side is given a set of materials, but neither side gets exactly the same material as the other. This introduces uncertainty, just as in the real world. Although my law school experience with this was limited, I had the strong impression that if the negotiations had "fallen through," both sides would have been penalized heavily. In a sense, this is like the real world. But it's also unfair, because in the real world the threat of "walking" —and going to trial—is a very useful negotiating tool. (This is especially true if you have a reputation as a decent trial attorney and the lawyer on the other side does not.) So, the Negotiations Exercise is not as valuable as Mock Trial and Moot Court.

4. Client Counseling Competition: This is a session with a new "client" who has a problem. As always, you work with a partner. Through questioning the client, you have to find out what the problem is and try to understand all its facets. Then you have to lay out some alternatives for the client's consideration. It seems the original purpose of the Client Counseling Competition was to demonstrate good "people skills," similar to a physician's need to have a good "bedside manner." But in practice, at least at my school, it was just an oral version of a final exam. It may be different at your school.

---

* Yet, as one wag said, "Common sense is the *least* common of the senses."

In the real world, client counseling is one of the most important skills of all. Word-of-mouth advertising is the best kind you can have, and word-of-mouth advertising depends largely on good client counseling skills. Further, if things go wrong, one of the best ways to avoid getting sued for legal malpractice is to have had good relations with your clients; effective counseling is a big part of that. Unfortunately, it's almost impossible to practice this within the constraints of a law school. So, Client Counseling Competition is not common.

* * *

For any of these activities, try sitting in during your first year, especially during the championship rounds—quarterfinals and up. (This is particularly useful with Client Counseling Competition, to find out which approach is used: oral final exam or genuine counseling.) But think twice about signing up for any of these if your school doesn't take it seriously. Often, these activities are strictly "Mickey Mouse." Given the amount of time you have to put in, you need to ensure that it will be worthwhile—that you will *learn* a *lot*—because you'll get no academic credit for it. Here's a good way to find out: If your school gets involved in interscholastic competitions, and does well, then you know it takes the activity in question seriously. (But you'll still have to find out how seriously your prospective *employers* take it.)

Regardless, if your school has an intramural tournament whose winner/s get their names on a plaque or entered in the yearbook or something impressive, that can be worth pursuing: If you have your sights set on being hired as a trial or appellate lawyer of any kind, this accomplishment does indeed Look Good on the Résumé.

Many students participate just to get a feel for what it's like, simply to satisfy their curiosity. Nothing wrong with that, either.

Finally, if you're honestly eager to get involved in an activity, regardless of the school's commitment to ensuring its quality, then better something than nothing.

However, no matter whether your school takes Mock Trial and Moot Court seriously, you should attempt to get at least some experience in a court internship, discussed in chapter 12. And in truth, unless you are *very* good at Mock Trial or Moot Court, you'll learn more from working for a judge (whether at the trial court or appellate level), than you will from the competitions.* And it will mean more to your prospective employers—especially if the judge you worked for is well-respected.

---

* The same thing is true regarding Negotiations Competitions. But instead of going to work for a sitting judge and a court, you go to work for a Mediator or Arbitrator. You might also learn more from working as a "research assistant" to a professor who's a top-notch litigator, in a real-live case (as discussed in chapter 12.) But even there, you might not learn as much as from a court internship.

ADDENDUM to CHAPTER 13:
RESOURCES for LITIGATORS

Evidence

Those who intend to go into trial law—or at least who enter the Mock Trial competition—feel obliged to take a course in evidence. However, most are quite disappointed. Apparently, professors make evidence every bit as complicated and as confusing as they do their first-year courses. (For one thing, they use the Case Method.) Whaddaya know. And as with everything else in law school, it shouldn't be that way. It certainly doesn't have to be that way for you, because you can learn it on your own. In fact, to learn it *well,* you *must* do it yourself.

The following items meet two criteria: 1) they're the best, and 2) they're easily accessible and affordable to law school students.

The pattern recommended before continues with respect to trial advocacy: Start with the written materials. Then, when you're familiar with the jargon and the concepts, consider moving on to the audio—and perhaps video—tapes. The vendors' toll-free numbers are at the end of this addendum, and are repeated in the appendix.

<u>Understanding the Rules</u>

Best, Arthur, *Evidence: Examples & Explanations, 2d ed.,* 1997, Aspen Law & Business, paperback, roughly $28. —Another of the excellent works in the Aspen "Examples & Explanations" series, introduced in chapter 5. Best really does live up to his name.

Fishman, Clifford S., *A Student's Guide to Hearsay,* 1990, Matthew Bender, paperback, about $25. —Another of the excellent works in the Matthew Bender "Student's Guide" series, first mentioned in chapter 7's addendum.

These two are wonderful, whether for a law school course in evidence, Mock Trial, or the evidence portion of the bar exam. They're so good that I regularly re-read them and re-work the problems in them, just to keep from getting rusty in areas where there's been no need to stay up to speed for specific cases.

Surveys of trial lawyers regularly disclose that the rules of evidence are the most difficult part of their practice—and hearsay is the most difficult of all. (In my own first outing, my client and I got slaughtered—largely because I was not sufficiently conversant with the rules of evidence. And I did not get a firm grasp on hearsay until I'd read the Fishman book and worked its exercises.) If you have mastered the rules of evidence in general, and hearsay in particular, you'll "wow" your Mock Trial judge. You'll also win the respect and confidence of many a real-world judge. (You'd be surprised at how many *trial judges* have never mastered evidence.)

Aspen Law & Business, in addition to its "Examples and Explanations" series, has an "Essential Terms & Concepts" series. *Evidence: Essential Terms*

& Concepts, by Mark Reutlinger, is a 1996 book, in paperback, for $26. What I especially like about it is the way Reutlinger puts the rules of evidence into context. He provides background as to how the rules came to be as they are, historically. You don't have to just memorize a seemingly-arbitrary rule. Instead, he gives you a grasp of what the alternatives were and why they were rejected. That "big picture" understanding can be very helpful—especially when you're trying to deal with a particularly strange situation for which there is no clearly applicable rule.

Mueller, Christopher B., & Kirkpatrick, Laird C., *Federal Rules of Evidence, with Advisory Committee Notes, Legislative History, and Cases,* 1995, another Aspen Law & Business book, is in paperback, for approximately $26. Most states' rules of evidence are modeled on the federal rules. Many states, by law, expressly look to rulings in federal courts on the federal rules of evidence to guide them. The federal courts, in turn, usually look to the Advisory Committee Notes and the legislative history of the federal rules of evidence to guide *them*. Yet, for some strange reason, few books on evidence—and few law school courses—go into this material. It will impress the trial judge if you can produce a "bench memo," based on this material, as to why the judge should rule in your favor on an evidentiary point. (In law school, though, you won't be doing bench memos for Mock Trial.) Even without a bench memo, if you've mastered this material, you will be in the right when you make your objections—or respond to the other side's objections. (In the real world, this will help you on appeal.) And the Mueller & Kirkpatrick book is excellent material for bar exam review. Sometimes, you have to go with your gut feel when answering a question on the bar exam. The M&K work helps you to digest evidence quite well.

Practice Makes Perfect

No discussion of becoming skilled in the courtroom is complete without mention of NITA (the National Institute for Trial Advocacy, first mentioned in chapter 7.) It trains aspiring barristers around the country. In Mock Trial or a class on "trial ad," your law school will likely use one of many fictitious case files developed for a jurisdiction called "The State of NITA."

The Institute has a 1993 book by Anthony J. Bocchino and David A. Sonenshein, *A Practical Guide to Federal Evidence: Objections, Responses, Rules, and Practice Commentary, 3d ed.,* a $29 paperback. (NITA also has state-specific volumes for California, Iowa, Oregon, Texas, and Wisconsin. Bocchino and Sonenshein are co-authors for each of them, and bring in an expert from the state in question as a third co-author.) For both Mock Trial and real trials, the *Practical Guide* is awesome. It tells you what to do, when to do it, how to do it—whether it's on your own or in response to what opposing counsel has done.

Bocchino and Sonenshein are joined by a third author—JoAnne A. Epps—for something else that's wonderful. This is *Trial Evidence—Making and Meeting Objections.* The book presents several dozen situations that are very real-world sounding. (Most involve civil trials.) If the question or answer presented is improper, you have to explain why. If an objection is made, your job is to explain whether it should be sustained or overruled, and why. The book is $22. However, you have to get the *Instructor's Manual* to get the answers, and that costs another $9. (The material in the situations book is also available on cassette tape, as mentioned below. I recommend you get that instead of the hard copy.) The *Instructor's Manual* mentions things about the rules of evidence that I've never seen elsewhere—yet they're things every barrister* needs to know.

Just knowing the rules of evidence isn't enough. In fact, even just knowing what to object to, or how to respond to groundless objections, isn't enough. You must also know the step-by-step "mechanics" of getting things *admitted into evidence* by the court. For that, Edward J. Imwinkelreid's *Evidentiary Foundations, 3d. ed.,* is an absolute necessity. This 1995 book is a $26 paperback from the Michie (to repeat: it's pronounced "Mickey") Company. If you're planning to do Mock Trial, and especially if you intend to become a trial lawyer, you must get this book. (This is the generic edition. Imwinkelreid, with co-authors, also does specialized editions for California, Florida, Illinois, New York, and Texas.)

Audio Cassettes

As mentioned in chapter 5's discussion of audio cassettes, the vendors do tapes for advanced courses, too. The Gilbert "Law School Legends" series on Evidence is a set of five, almost 7 hours' running time, for $46. The Sum & Substance series on Evidence is also a set of five, "7.8" hours' running time, for $50. PMBR sells its bar review tape on evidence: six hours, $50. By the time this book is published, Tiger Publishing's "Incredibly Easy" series will have a set on evidence, too—but as of this writing, neither the length nor the price has been set. As with all the other materials on evidence, it will concern the federal rules.

Use tapes only to *check* your understanding: The rules of evidence are so demanding that you need to study lots of written materials, over and over, to master them.

---

* Strictly speaking, a "barrister" is not the same as thing as a trial lawyer. The term "barrister" is from England. They make a distinction between trial lawyers and "transactions" lawyers, who draft contracts, wills, deeds, etc.. They call these people "solicitors." However, in America, the trial lawyer (supposedly) prepares his or her case from Day One, including all the pre-trial. In the United Kingdom, the solicitor does this, based on instructions from the barrister. (In the U.K., barristers have much more social status than solicitors. That's because, historically, *aristocrats* who deigned to become lawyers only became trial attorneys, not solicitors.) I think the American system is much better. —And by the way: in the U.K., law is an *undergraduate* degree...as it was in the USA until about the 20th century.

Trial "Ad"

Books

It appears that everyone in law school trial advocacy classes or mock trial programs is told to read two works: Thomas A. Mauet's *Fundamentals of Trial Techniques,* now in its fourth edition; and James W. Jeans, Sr.'s *Trial Advocacy,* currently in its second edition. With all due respect to these scholars (and a lot of respect *is* due), I do not recommend their books. They're text-books. Instead, here are what in my opinion are the four best books for aspiring trial attorneys:

In no particular order...the first two are West Nutshell™ paperbacks: Paul Bergman's *Trial Advocacy in a Nutshell, 2d ed.,* 1989, $16; and Kenney F. Hegland's *Trial and Practice Skills in a Nutshell, 2d ed.,* 1994, also $16. The third is also from West: Keith Evans's *The Common Sense Rules of Trial Advocacy,* 1994, paperback, $28.

The fourth is not from West. It's *Theater Tips and Strategies for Jury Trials, rev. ed.,* by David Ball; a 1997 work from NITA, $29 in paperback. Ball is a trial consultant, not a practicing attorney. His background is in theater. Yet, he understands trial law better than the vast majority of trial attorneys. The title of his book is unfortunate. It sounds like it's full of simple tricks to use "here and there" along the way. On the contrary: there's stuff in here you'll find nowhere else. *Jury Trials as Theater* would have been a more accurate title, and even that wouldn't do it justice.

I could rave about how great these are, but you can see for yourself, if you wish. Almost any law school bookstore should have all of them. For a "first book" on trial ad, go with either Bergman's or Evans's; ideally, both. But if and when you read those two, be sure to then get Ball's. (All trial attorneys should have Ball's, don't you think?—Even if only in the metaphorical sense for the distaff.) In the interest of full disclosure, though, I need to say that Hegland's book isn't *quite* as useful for law *students* as the other three are. However, it's still so good that I have to list it as one of the best on the market. Also, he touches on things that the other three "best works" mentioned here do not. So I still strongly recommend it. Just save it for last.

Actually, there's a third author whose works all law school students in trial advocacy classes or mock trial programs are told to read: James W. McElhaney. McElhaney's books are good. However, you shouldn't get them until you've become at least somewhat familiar with the federal rules of evidence and the federal rules of civil procedure, and have read the Bergman and Evans books. They're pricey—because they're published by the American Bar Association, which always charges too much. *McElhaney's Trial Note-book, 3d ed.,* is about $40 in paperback. *McElhaney's Litigation, 2d. ed.,* is roughly $35, paperback.

NITA has more materials—but these aren't in the same class as Ball, Bergman, Evans, and Hegland: *Modern Trial Advocacy: Analysis and Practice,* by Steven Lubet, is okay. But it's more of a textbook, really. It's a 1993 work, for $31.

And there's *Closing Argument,* by Jim Seckinger, a $12 booklet published in 1992. It's very good, and well worth the twelve bucks.

Audio Cassettes

The only material I know that's available *only* on audio is NITA's *Opening Statements: A Modern Approach.* It's one cassette, 69 minutes long, by Judge Sanford M. Brook, for $50. You get hard-copy material with it. However, the hard-copy material presents 95% of what's on tape. And the printed material is just a 7" x 3⅝" pocket-sized brochure. Worst of all, Judge Brook is clearly just *reading* from *that* text, in a boring manner. NITA has needlessly packaged this in an exorbitantly expensive format. (It's also available on video.) I felt as though I'd been "had"—"taken" for a $50. Don't spend your money on this.*

The American Bar Association does two sets of tapes by Terry McCarthy. The first is *Less Boring Direct Examination;* the second, *The Science of Cross Examination.* Each runs about four hours. For once, the ABA hasn't charged too much: they're about $40 per subject. Unfortunately, they're not very good—although *The Science of Cross Examination* is *very* entertaining.

More Expensive Items

Books

Deanne C. Seamer's *Tangible Evidence: How to Use Exhibits at Depositions and Trials, 3d ed.,* is a 1996 paperback from NITA. It costs $50. However, it's worth a lot more than that. When you're ready to go from apprentice to journey-person status, this is the very best book there is.

The ABA publishes a *Litigation Manual, 2d ed.,* at $85. (That's not a misprint. It's eighty-five dollars—for a paperback.) And it sells a decent book by Michael Tigar, a very prominent trial lawyer (and law professor), called *Examining Witnesses,* for *110 (!)* bucks. It's in hardcover. (For that price, it ought to be.) But save your money...at least, for now.

Audio & Video: Evidence & Trial Ad

As mentioned above, NITA's *Trial Evidence—Making and Meeting Objections* is available on cassette. The situations are presented using many different actors, in mock trial. After each situation where something occurs that's improper—or which is alleged to be improper—there's a pause. You

---

* Despite this outburst, I am deeply grateful to NITA for what it does. In fact, the National Institute for Trial Advocacy's programs and materials have played such a large role in my family's financial well-being that my wife and I gave our first-born daughter the middle name of "Nita." (Our *second* daughter's *first* name is "Sue." Not "Susan" or "Suzanne." Just "Sue." —And as long as I'm listing all the kiddies: our son's name is, of course, "Bill.")

have about 1-2 seconds to make an objection or to respond to an objection, stating your reasons. (Actually, though, you just hit the "pause" button on the tape player to give yourself more time.) When you get the situations tape (available in audio or video), NITA includes the *Instructor's Manual* with the answers in it.

Because I got this on cassette, I can't say for sure the tapes exactly duplicate what's in the textbook. But on the tapes, there are 62 "vignettes." No more than two or three are drawn from the same mock trial. However, you then get 23 more vignettes taken from one criminal trial, followed by 50 vignettes taken from a civil trial. The running time of the tapes is two hours, 40 minutes. But it actually takes many more hours than that to go through them, because you'll be pausing to consider your responses and then checking your responses against what's in the *Instructor's Manual*.

On audio cassette, *Trial Evidence—Making and Meeting Objections* costs $150. That's a lot. But it's worth it. There's something about *voices*, as opposed to just reading text, that makes a *big* difference. The cassettes are a much closer approximation of the real world. So they're much better as a practice tool. Because there are so many situations on the tape, there's no danger that you'll memorize them and the appropriate responses. That means you can work through them all again, from time to time.

When I was in law school, Court TV was just starting. So, we students had to make do with *mock* trial videotape presentations by local trial lawyers. It was pretty bad stuff, but it was that or nothing. Now, however, Court TV has a Video Library Service. This includes tapes from real trials. And Court TV has also established "The Art and Science of Litigation" series: video cassettes on basic skills, using excerpts from real trials; a moderator and a panel of attorneys then critique the performances. There's one each on Opening Statement, Direct Examination, Cross Examination, Examination of Expert Witnesses, and Closing Argument. Each tape lasts about an hour, and costs about $100. Pricey. Better to forgo these, for what you get. But if you can find some other students to split the cost with you, and then share the tapes, that's a different matter. If you don't get any Court TV video-tapes, you can still learn a lot from watching Court TV itself.

Irving Younger was a legend in his own time, as a teacher of the law. He had a gift for presenting detailed subjects in a way that was both memo-rable and entertaining. He's the star of two sets of NITA materials.

The first is *Basic Concepts in the Law of Evidence with Irving Younger,* a solo performance by the *maestro*. These 15 tapes run just over 12 hours. On audio, they're $100. With the tapes, you get an outline of the subject.

The second is *Mastering the Art of Cross-Examination with Irving Younger.* This includes his famous "Ten Commandments of Cross-Examination." You get 11 tapes—running time nearly 8 hours—and a *lot* of supporting materials, for $195 (audio). It includes several other attorneys besides Younger, and presents a number of "problem situations." The lawyers then attempt to deal with each problem. Afterwards, Younger discusses the attempted solutions—why they did what they did, and what others thought of it. The set is apparently meant to be used as a teaching exercise to a group.

However, be advised: Younger's "Ten Commandments" have been criticized in recent years.

(The NITA catalogue has detailed information on both sets of tapes.)

The Complete Advocate: Courtroom Speaking Skills is available only on video. Brian Johnson is the presenter. The tape lasts one hour, 15 minutes, and costs $130. I haven't seen it, but I did see Brian Johnson give a (live) lecture on the subject. He was fantastic. I later spoke with him about the tape. He said it presents the same material as his lecture. That being so, it's well worth getting…but not necessarily right away, because of the high price.

NITA has many more programs on video, but they tend to be *very* expensive, intended for purchase only by (big) law firms. You can call, and get NITA to send you a catalogue.

Note: *No returns allowed,* but NITA has "preview tapes" for some of its videos. (These previews do double-duty for the corresponding audio.)

Trial Advocacy Software

In a real trial, it isn't enough to make an objection. You must also state the grounds for the objection, unless those grounds are obvious. You also have to state your objection and the grounds for it very quickly—such as before the witness answers. Otherwise, at least in a jury trial, the damage is done, even if the judge grants your request to have the question and answer stricken from the record. ("You can't 'un-ring' a bell once the jury's heard it.")

A company called TransMedia has developed four sets of software for trial advocacy. Its original program was called "Objection!" As the name implies, it tests your knowledge of the appropriate grounds for objecting to a question by opposing counsel. The original program was for a criminal trial, with a complete cast of characters and a little bit of animation. (It is now sold as version 3.0, called "Objection!!"—with *two* exclamation points.)

TransMedia then created "Civil Objection!!" Instead of defending someone accused of murder, as in the original program, you'll be plaintiff's counsel in a personal injury suit that arose from a car crash. So, instead of seeking an acquittal, you're seeking a jury verdict awarding lots of money to your client (and, of course, indirectly, to you).

The third program concerns expert witnesses, and the fourth is a "slip and fall" personal injury case.

Three of these (all but the expert witness program) present an entire trial, with both direct and cross examination of witnesses, and the presentation of documents. The expert witness software only has direct and cross-ex (of an expert witness). There's some limited animation of the characters. The also include limited sound—though all the questions and answers appear in text on the screen.

When opposing counsel is cross-examining your witness, or is doing a direct examination of its own witness, the program tells you what question was just asked. You must very quickly decide whether that question was proper; if not, you must object—pronto. If *you're* doing the examination, and the witness on the stand is *yours,* the program gives you a proposed question to ask. You must quickly decide whether or not it's proper. If it isn't, you must quickly say so. If you quickly make the correct objection, or quickly approve a proposed question that's proper, you score points. But if you make your response slowly, or on the wrong grounds, or fail to object at all to an improper question, you don't score as well. (The lowest score is a zero.)

There are different stopping points along the way. If you don't have enough points to advance farther, the program stops the trial and you have to "bone up" on the rules and start over.

I got the criminal program, and then the civil one, too, when it came out, but have yet to get the expert witness program or the new "slip & fall" one. I have four criticisms. First, the clock starts running as soon as the text of the proposed question appears on the screen. But it always takes time to read that text—and you're rapidly losing points even as you read. Second, a few of the questions posed are just plain stupid. I cannot imagine an attorney asking some of these—even though, as chapter 11 proved, sometimes lawyers do ask *amazingly* stupid questions. However, at least the stupid questions are few and far between. Third, as with Mock Trial, the program rewards objections that are penalized in the real world. Fourth and most serious, some of what TransMedia cites as the law in my jurisdiction is just plain wrong.

However, I am glad I got the original program, and am delighted with the "Civil Objection!" program. They're obviously similar to NITA's *Trial Evidence—Making and Meeting Objections.* However, while the nature of the questions, and the appropriate objections, are the same from one run to the next, the exact questions, and the order in which they occur, are not. So, you can't memorize the script and then score points based just on your memory rather than on your ability to think fast. (I assume TransMedia is eventually going to bring out a version that *only* uses sound, so you don't lose time reading the text. If and when they do, this will be a better buy than NITA's material. However, they'll have a very hard time coming up with anything near as good as the *Instructor's Manual.* And, so far the situations NITA poses are a better test than those on TransMedia's computer program.)

Each program is about 100 bucks. There's also a manual stating the most common rules of evidence. It can be used with either the civil, criminal, or expert witness software. To get any version *and* the manual, the price is about $160. However, you don't need the manual: instructions about making objections come with the disk. Good as this stuff is, though, don't get *any* of them while you're in law school unless you're serious about doing

Mock Trial. (And remember: in the real world, you want to make only those objections that are absolutely necessary. Even so, you always need to *think fast*—which is what these programs force you to do.)*

Organizations for Litigators

So far, I can find only two organizations that allow law students to join.

The first is the Law Students Division of the American Bar Association, known as the ABA/LSD. (Love it.) You can join the Litigation Section, which gets you subscriptions to useful publications and invitations to ABA gatherings for litigators. (You also get a discount on ABA books and tapes. But since most of them are far too costly, and usually not very good regardless of the price, the discount is not much of a benefit.) Dues are $15 a year.

The second organization is the Association of Trial Lawyers of America, headquartered in Washington, D.C.. ATLA (pronounced as though it were a word) is a plaintiffs' attorneys' group, most of whom do "P.I." (personal injury) cases. (Defense lawyers refer to the organization as "ATiLA"—as in "The Hun.") Like NITA, ATLA does books, tapes, and workshops. Student dues are $10 a year, and entitle you to a discount. (However, amazingly, ATLA's stuff is even more expensive than the ABA's.)

Defense attorneys who handle civil cases have their own organization, The Defense Research Institute and Trial Lawyers Association, headquartered in Chicago. Their materials and programs are for "defense, insurance, and corporate counsel." However, it's open only to licensed attorneys.

Associations of criminal defense attorneys exist, too. But I'm not listing them: 98% of all litigators only do civil work, and whatever you learn for civil litigation will stand you in good stead for criminal litigation; besides, most future criminal defense counsel cut their teeth as prosecutors.

Resources for Activities Other than Mock Trial

Moot Court

NITA has two books for appellate advocacy. Both are intended for use in the real world, not law school. However, they're useful even within the ivory tower.

The first is by Josephine R. Potuto, *Winning Appeals: Persuasive Argument and the Appellate Process*. This 1992 book is $23.

The second is *Winning on Appeal: Better Briefs and Oral Argument,* by Ruggero J. Aldisert. (He also wrote *Logic for Lawyers,* first discussed in the addendum to chapter 7.) It's a 1996 paperback, for $35.

Sum & Substance has a set of two tapes, *Winning at Moot Court.* They run for three hours, and cost $40.

---

* And I hereby confess that I have a crush on Lisa Lamborghini, the key witness in most of TransMedia's software. This is the first time I've fallen in love with a cartoon character since…Pocahontas. Oh, well.

Mediation & Arbitration

NITA has a 1996 book, *The Art of Mediation,* by Mark Bennett and Michele Hermann. This is a $35 paperback. It's meant to be "a workbook for individuals undertaking basic mediation training." NITA has another book, *A Practical Guide to Mediation and Arbitration Advocacy,* by John Cooley. He's a former U.S. Magistrate (see chapter 19), and is now a law professor at Loyola University of Chicago. This 1996 book costs $30, paperback.

Another one is *How to Mediate Your Dispute,* by Peter Lovenheim. It's a 1996 paperback from Nolo Press, for $19. As you can tell from the title, it's for laypeople who are looking for an alternative to litigation. However, if you're still not sure about law school, but are interested in becoming a mediator if and when you do decide to go to law school, this would be a good book for you. Then, if you decide not to become an attorney, *How to Mediate Your Dispute* might come in handy anyway, someday. (It might come in handy even if you do go to law school and then have an internship with a mediator.) The book should be available in bookstores, or you can special order it.

Negotiating

General bookstores have many books on negotiating. However, I'll mention one that's meant for lawyers: *A Practical Guide to Negotiation,* by Thomas F. Guernsey. It's a 1996 title from NITA; $22 in paperback. (And by the time you read these words, Guernsey should have assumed the job of dean of Southern Illinois U's law school.)

Toll-Free Numbers

American Bar Association	(800) 285-2221
Aspen Law & Business	(800) 234-1660
ATLA	(800) 424-2727
Court TV - not toll-free	(212) 973-2882
Gilbert (Harcourt Brace)	(800) 787-8717
Matthew Bender	(800) 331-9352
The Michie Company	(800) 446-3410
NITA	(800) 225-6482
Nolo Press	(800) 955-4775
PMBR	(800) 523-0777
Sum & Substance	(800) 876-4457
Tiger Publishing	(800) 428-0456
TransMedia	(800) 832-4980
West	(800) 328-9352

Chapter 14 - What to Take in Years 2 and 3

It's no accident that the two chapters on honing your skills preceded this one. Just as *attending* class is the *least* important part of your first-year courses, so the very courses *themselves* are the least important part of years two and three. Law school could teach everything you need to know in just three semesters. Instead, it takes three years to teach far *less* than you need to know.*

Chapter 3 quoted a famous 1973 speech of then-Chief Justice Warren Burger. In that same speech, he said law school should be reduced to *two* years. Beyond that, law should somewhat imitate the medical profession. But instead of having an internship for all graduates, as medicine does, he said law should go directly to the equivalent of the medical residency: training in a specialty. Whether or not you agree with his proposal, the point here is that Burger was saying the "core curriculum" common to all future attorneys need last only two years, not three. This will not happen, of course. The reason for this is the prestige factor—and money.

Law traditionally has been close to medicine in prestige.** Medical school lasts four years. Apparently med students need all four of those years to master the necessary skills. But if law school ran even one year less than it does, it would be difficult for lawyers to claim status comparable to doctors'. Instead, they'd be "down there" with mere MBAs. So, the curriculum gets padded with make-work courses, to ensure that a lawyer's formal education is comparable to that of doctors, if only in terms of duration.

Ironically, more than a generation after Burger's Fordham speech, his proposal has been revived—in a perverted form. Astoundingly, there is a serious effort underway to make law school *four* years. Law would indeed imitate medicine, by adding a year of mandatory clinical experience as part of the *law school* curriculum, rather than as an internship or residency.

However, most law schools already do an abysmal job with the clinics they provide, because they aren't willing to put enough resources into these

---

* You perhaps think I'm engaging in rhetorical excess. Well, in Britain, roughly a third of all non-trial lawyers there do not get a law degree (and as mentioned earlier, in Britain it's an undergraduate degree). Instead, they get a year's intensive training in the law after finishing college. (And regardless of whether they have a law degree, future attorneys then take a year of courses in "lawyering.") So, law "school" there can last as little as two years.

** Maybe that's because clients sometimes put their livelihoods—and perhaps even their lives—into a lawyer's hands, as patients occasionally put their very lives into a doctor's hands. That is power. Although you can make more money on Wall Street, Wall Street doesn't have the prestige. Bankers do—because bankers have power…though not nearly as much as they used to, in any given community.

programs to make them worthwhile. Med school clinics are vastly different. They're far more intensive. Students get more hands-on experience (figuratively as well as literally). There are fewer students per supervisor, and students work much more closely with each. It's more like an apprenticeship. And it's a *key* part of their training, not a mere sop to alumni demands for *practical* courses. If law schools were serious about meaningful clinics, they'd vastly improve the ones they have now, before adding a fourth year to legal education. As it is, they're (in effect) asking to be financially *rewarded* for their failure.

And this brings us to the major reason why law school lasts three years: money. Law school is a "cash cow." (It yields cash-flow the way a cow gives milk: at minimal cost.) In contrast, most graduate schools have a small student enrollment, and few students per professor. Not much profit there. —And grad schools in the *sciences* have hugely expensive laboratories, big budgets for supplies, etc.. Those places run at a loss. But a law school? — Put 100 students in a room with one professor wasting a year of their time with the Case/Socratic Method, and charge them as much as $600 a *credit* for it. It doesn't take a crook of Michael Milken's caliber to spot the enormous profit *there*. Hence the proliferation of law schools—including for-profit ones—despite the steady decline in the number of job openings for lawyers. (For the same reason, there's been a proliferation of graduate business schools—and the usual MBA program lasts two years, not one, unlike most master's programs.) A university typically rakes off 20% of the law students' tuition, and uses those funds elsewhere.*

Under Burger's "residency" proposal, the specialist training would *not* be part of law *school*. Presumably, like medical residents, these law school graduates would be getting paid—albeit poorly—during their training. Bad enough from the law schools' perspective that *they* would *not* be receiving any tuition money during that year of specialist training. Much worse that, because Burger recommended cutting law school itself from three years to two, the schools would have *lost* a year's tuition they were *already* receiving.

---

* I once attended an institution that was having difficulty raising funds for its graduate departments. So the school started an MBA program. When it failed to generate the expected revenues, the administration proposed starting a law school—explicitly for the purpose of subsidizing the other graduate programs. The faculty and students threatened mayhem. The administration quietly dropped the proposal.

Further, when I was in law school the Dean appointed a consulting committee to find ways to improve the institution. At the time, the market was becoming glutted with lawyers. One of the committee's private recommendations was to cut the size of the next entering class by almost a fourth. The university immediately vetoed the suggestion. Not only was its veto made public, so was the reason: it wanted the extra tuition revenue...even though it knew many students would be wasting their money because there would be no jobs for them when they graduated.

Easy to see why Burger's proposal never went anywhere...until its recent transmogrified revival.

In your second and third year of law school, you have two priorities: 1) extra-curricular activities related to getting a job, and 2) getting a job. As you plan your schedule, keep that in mind. (All of chapter 20 concerns finding a job.) The first semester of your second and third year are the prime times for job-hunting. (And in the second semester of year three you should already be preparing for the bar exam.)

If you do well in first year—and you will, if you conscientiously follow the recommendations in this book—you'll Make Law Review. Law Review will be your main concern for the rest of your days in school. You won't have to worry much about finding *a* job—just finding the *right* job.

If you don't Make Law Review, and instead enter the Mock Trial or Moot Court competitions, *those* might be your main concern for the rest of your days in law school. If you do extremely well, you won't find work as easily as the Law Review people do, but your stellar performance should set you up with a good litigation firm. —However, as chapter 13 mentioned, even *trial* lawyers prefer to hire those who Made Law Review over those who were "stars" in Mock Trial and Moot Court. (Another reason why is that, in their first few years of practice, most apprentice litigators get *no* litigation experience. Instead, they endure a lot of office drudgery—and Law Review is the acme of drudgery.)

Regardless, in terms of classes, you're looking for the maximum number of *credits*—and easy *high grades*—with the *minimum amount of effort*. You have better—more important—things to spend your time on than make-work academic bullshit, to put it bluntly.

There are exceptions to this, of course. (In the Law, there is at least one exception to *anything*.) They are 1) courses in a specialized area of law that requires an in-depth background, 2) courses that Look Good on the Résumé, 3) courses with a Big Gun professor whom you want to impress, 4) courses that prepare you for the bar examination, and 5) Legal Research and Legal Writing. (Nearly all of chapter 16 is devoted to the last of these. Chapters 17 and 18 deal with the bar exam and preparing for it.)

> *Note: If you want to have a career in corporate law (which includes a career with a prestigious law firm), there's a list of courses that are virtually mandatory. It will be easy to find out what they are at your school.*
>
> *(To a lesser extent, the situation is similar for future litigators as well.)*

After first-year, no course lasts more than one semester. However, some, in effect, actually *are* year-long. But unlike first-year, there's a grade for each semester's work. Better still, you don't have to take the second semester of the course immediately after the first—or ever, for that matter. Sometimes there's a different professor for part two than for part one. If the prof in part one was a dud, you can delay taking part two, in hope someone better comes along.

Other than in first-year, there are almost no mandatory courses in law school. If you had to take a one-semester course in Constitutional Law during first-year, there's a good chance you'll have to take Con Law II sometime later. (Con Law covers the Constitution itself, usually skips over the Bill of Rights and jumps to the Reconstruction Amendments. Con Law II usually focuses on a particular Amendment within the Bill of Rights. At some schools, first-year Con Law lasts all year: one semester each for what would otherwise be called Con Law I and II.) Most schools also require a "Professional Responsibility" course. Chapter 17 discusses this.

Your Best Source of Information

Throughout your first year, you want to meet as many second- and third-year students as you can. Learn from their experience. They can tell you what to take, when to take it, what's easy, what's hard, who's good, who's boring, and who's a jerk. But keep in mind that just because several students have the same opinion, that doesn't mean they're right. If someone tells you Professor X is a great (or lousy), ask *why*. The more students you talk with, the better. You'll certainly have a better chance of getting a feel for what's right for *you*.

Do not rely on student surveys—unless they've very thorough. At some schools, they consist merely of polls whereby professors are rated on a scale of 1-10 in various categories. Those don't tell you what you need to know.

If you actually want to learn something from your courses, look for the professors who can *teach*. They're few and far between. There's an old jazz saying, "The singer, not the song." This means that a good jazz singer can take even a mediocre song and make it sound like something special—whereas a mediocre singer can take a wonderful song and turn it into musical mush. In law school, all other things being equal, go with the prof, not the course. The Law can be wonderful, but that's seldom so—especially in law school. The basic concepts stay the same. Choose the prof who has a reputation for helping students understand the ins and outs of those concepts—if you can find one. A lousy professor can ruin an otherwise-interesting subject. He or she can also reduce your drive to try to ace the course: you have to force yourself to do the work, and thus spend much more time and energy on it than you should. A professor who makes the subject interesting makes it easier for you to do the work on it. Your attitude toward a course makes a big difference in how much energy you have left over when you've finished the homework for it and have to move on. So, it indirectly affects your work on *other* tasks.

During your first year, the last thing on your mind will be what to take in years two and three—until the next fall's schedule is posted, that is. But *try to sit in on upper-level courses during your first year, even during your first semester.* Be sure to go to the professor beforehand to get his or her permission. Explain that you're a first-year, and the course is something that sounds interesting to you. Ask if you can sit in on it *once.*

If you follow the advice of chapters 5 and 7, there's a greater likelihood you'll be able to comprehend what's being talked about in a second- or third-year class you're auditing in first-year. But even if you don't, by sitting in you get to see for yourself what kind of teacher this professor is.

Afterwards, ask if the professor will be offering that class in the next year's schedule, or the year after. (Of course, you will have started by expressing your appreciation for the opportunity to audit, and complimenting him or her for providing such a meaningful experience. Just don't overdo it.) If the class is already listed in the projected schedule, confirm it. If not, maybe some other professor teaches a similar course, and so it will still be available to you. Ask the professor what other courses he or she will be offering. And it never hurts to ask what you should take and in what order. This is particularly true if you—supposedly—might specialize in that professor's area of expertise. (Be sure to find out, beforehand, what it is.)

Do not make your after-class approach by going to the lectern immediately after the class. Instead, stand out from the crowd: catch the prof in his or her office later that day—certainly no more than a few days later. Handle all this carefully. As long as you don't act like a suck-up, the prof might be pleased. He or she will also be impressed by your thinking ahead (but don't expect a compliment). It always helps if a member of the faculty has a favorable opinion of you, especially if the prof in question is a Big Gun in some field. (Profs do talk among themselves about their students.)

Also, sometimes one of next semester's courses fills and "closes." Then the only way to get in is by special permission from the prof, waiving the class limit. (Just like college.) If *you're* the one who expressed interest while still in first-year, and move fast, guess who gets the waiver?

Getting "In Synch"

You have no official "major" in law school. But, as mentioned for corporate or trial law, there are prescribed courses. Sometimes, you must take at least some of these courses in a prescribed sequence. However, often the law school catalogue will not tell you what the sequence is, or else the courses it lists are no longer being offered under those names. In some cases, only one professor teaches a given subject, and only once a year—or once every two years. So, you have to take it at the right time, or you don't get to take it at all. (Usually, though, other professors offer comparable courses. One of them might even be better at it.) No matter what, though, don't trust the printed projection of future courses. Confirm everything you're seriously interested in, as to who, what, and when. And watch out for prerequisites. If your school has a club devoted to the area of the law you want to concentrate in, its members should be able to tell you what you need to know.

You can only carry three or four courses a semester. Thus, in your final four semesters, you get to take maybe 12 to 15, total. That doesn't leave a lot of room for error. Further, at many law schools, after the semester has started you can't drop and add courses with anywhere near the freedom most colleges allow. If you're trying to pursue a specific program of study, fill those slots carefully.

Some that Glitters isn't Gold

Most first-year law students get their ideas of "growth" areas of the law from the general media. However, by the time the general media have learned of these, such areas have probably neared the saturation point. Worse, from your point of view, probably every other student looking for a job will tell the interviewer that he or she wants to go into one of those growth areas. The interviewer no doubt then thinks, "Another one who confuses the hype for the reality—and who's looking for the easy way to the top. Next!" So, be chary of what's "hot." (Chapter 20 tells how to find where the *truly* hot areas are.)

Then there's what's *cool*—courses such as "Entertainment and Sports Law," or "Art Law." These might sound wonderful, but only a handful of lawyers in this country can make their living at it. If you don't have the right connections for it, and are just hoping that a miracle will somehow happen to let you practice in that area, reconsider. Any serious firm looking at your résumé or transcript might conclude you're some kind of flake with stars in his or her eyes, unwilling to put nose-to-grindstone in the drab, drab world of the law. (If you Make Law Review, though, you can take at least one off-the-wall course without fear.)

However, if you're truly interested in an offbeat subject for its own sake, proceed. Although the odds against your ever being able to practice in this area are overwhelming, the course/s can still be a nice treat.

Options

Even if you go into law school absolutely certain what it is you want to do as a lawyer, please keep an open mind. For example, future visiting professors' courses aren't listed in the catalogue, for obvious reasons. So even if you know what you want to take and have confirmed its availability, there will be opportunities you'd not anticipated. Some of them will even come from the regular faculty, when a professor decides to offer something new, for the very first time.

Also, sometimes law students fall in love...with a subject. (I'll never forget one fellow student who raved about how surprised he was to find administrative law was the most wonderful thing there is. He is very happy now, practicing only within certain areas of administrative law. To this day, I find it repulsive. But it takes all kinds.)

Even though, above, there was a warning about not wasting your slots, do consider exploring the Law. If you follow the recommendations of chapter 23 about working for a lawyer, you might've already gained exposure to one area of the law—which you might or might not have liked. Regardless, the possibilities within the Law are far, far greater than anything anybody could possibly be aware of before starting law school. Unlike the recommendation in chapter 23 regarding playing it safe and sticking to what you know with respect to your college courses, in law school that's impossible: it's *all* new to you, really.

Further, most attorneys concentrate their practice in areas they never expected to get into. For some, this means a broken heart. But often, it means he or she fell (or got pushed) into something and ended up staying in it by inertia, increasing returns on their investment—and maybe even by heartfelt choice. Come job-hunting time, unless you're set on practicing in just one narrow specialty, you might want to have had *some* diversity in your law studies.

—Just be sure that most of your courses are "respectable"—i.e., job-hunt-oriented.

Getting a Head Start—Again

The approach recommended at the start of chapter 5 is valid even beyond first-year. Chapter 5 and the addendum to chapter 7 discussed sources of self-help materials for independent study of first-year subjects. Vendors have materials for advanced courses, too. Blond's®, Fleming's Fundamentals of Law, Gilbert, and Sum & Substance also do tapes for post-first-year subjects. So, you can again get the edge by prepping before the semester even begins. Whether you use it to get the jump on the adversary—again—or to cut down on the time you have to spend on your courses, it works. Even though first-year grades are the ones that count the most, by far, you want to keep your average up in years two and three, also. (In fact, if you Make Law Review, getting high grades while working as a second-year slave will possibly enhance your chances of getting a top editorship in third-year. —But grades are less important than your social skills.)

Aspen Law & Business, for example, has its series of books whose subtitle is always "Examples and Explanations," and another one subtitled "Problems and Answers." They also have a good book by Mark Reutlinger called *Wills, Trusts, and Estates: Essential Terms and Concepts.* (He also did *Evidence: Essential Terms & Concepts,* discussed in the addendum to chapter 13.) Matthew Bender has its wonderful *Student's Guide to /Whatever/* series, with titles on the Uniform Commercial Code, the Internal Revenue Code, and evidence. Matthew Bender also has its *Understanding /Whatever/* series. West Publishing, of course, has titles on everything—the most useful of which (for you) are its *Nutshell*™ series. Law school bookstores carry the West books. The ones from Aspen and Matthew Bender are harder to find. You might need to call these last two and order direct.

If and when you call, ask for a copy of each publisher's *law school* catalogue. Look for titles that indicate their potential for independent study, as indicated above. However, the catalogues don't put these books in a separate section. That's because these catalogues are for law *professors*, not students. With Aspen, for example, you have to carefully search for books with the subtitles mentioned—as well as for other self-help books that don't have *either* of the subtitles listed above, such as the Reutlinger book. With Matthew Bender, the only sure way to find them is to look at the end of the description of each book. There you will find *small* type in italics, saying if the work is a casebook, textbook, or part of the Student's Guide series. You do *not* want either of the *first* two. As with Aspen, some of Matthew Bender's independent study books aren't labeled as part of a self-help series, even though the book's description clearly indicates that's what the book can be used for. (Fortunately, both publishers have begun to print lists of other available self-help titles on or inside the covers of their independent study books. But for a complete list, you have to check the catalogue.)

Commercial outlines are published for advanced subjects, too. And software disks are available for them, such as West's (with its published outlines) and Numina's (using the Emanuel or Smith's Review material), and Lexis.

By the end of each semester, you'll know what you'll be taking next semester. So, that's when to get the commercial outlines, the books, and the tapes. Then read (and listen) to them during the vacation before the next semester starts.

Even if you Make Law Review and then get access to the editors' outline collection, these materials can help you. Use them to quickly get up to speed in the subject matter, which in turn will help you to *quickly* grasp what's in the outlines from the Law Review collection. That way, you won't lose any time getting yourself oriented once the course begins.

Toll-free numbers for all vendors are in the appendix. Get their catalogues and see what they have.

> *If you're undecided as to what courses to take, you might even consider choosing some of them based on whether or not you can prepare for them before the semester begins. It'll certainly make it a lot easier to do well.*

To Your Credit

If your law school is affiliated with a university (as nearly all are), you can often get credit in your law school for courses you take in another graduate program. Sometimes these are listed in your law school catalogue. The usual examples are from graduate schools in business or public policy—whatever these schools are called at your university. However, whether or not something's already been approved, you can still seek out other courses. You can even create your own. For example: You have a strong undergraduate background in economics. Find a sympathetic law professor and arrange for independent study credit in "law and economics."

If you're taking a course elsewhere in your university that's not already been approved for law school credit, or if you're creating your own unique project, you must get the approval of whoever handles such things in the dean's office at your law school. Usually, it isn't a problem—as long as your proposal is within reason.

Also, you'll probably find it's not as hard to get an "A" in some other school—and especially in an independent study project—as it is in a regular law school course. No guarantees, though.

Warning: The major law firms don't like to see these on your transcript. So think carefully about it. Then have a good explanation as to why you took it. And have plenty of "approved" courses—and top grades—to go with it.

* * *

Through it all, your highest priority is having the freedom to *choose* the job after graduation that's right for *you.* Everything else is just a means to that end. As chapter 16 explains, *once you have a job,* what's (probably) most important to your future is the ability to research well and to write well—even if you become a trial lawyer. That's why most of the particular *courses* you take in law school are of secondary importance—unless, as mentioned, you want to have a particular type of career in the Law.

The commercial outlines, Matthew Bender's "Understanding" series, West's "Nutshells," etc., will still be of value to you in practice. When you have to do something in a new area of practice, you'll use one of these "study aids" in order to get your bearings. And don't forget the legal encyclopedias. Also, in every state there are CLE (Continuing Legal Education) courses. Many of these programs are put on by national organizations such as NITA or ATLA, by vendors of legal research materials, or by your State Bar. (Another entity, the Practicing Law Institute, sells books and regularly puts on programs in New York City.) Some of these are advanced courses, for those who've long been specialists in a particular area of the law. Others are for those who want to get into a new area, and so are intended for beginners.

So, don't get the idea that if you don't take a particular course in law school, you'll never again get the chance to study it. Quite the contrary. (For example, for aspiring trial attorneys, there are NITA and ATLA programs in trial advocacy. Although these are generic, and not state-specific, they're better than most law school courses in trial ad and most mock trial programs. That's one reason why, when you're in law school, it's better to do the court internship if you must make a choice.)

While you're in law school, *grades* count most—especially *first*-year grades. So you want high grades, regardless of subject, because:

With *very* few exceptions, once you're out—and have a *job*—*the subjects you took won't count:* no one will care.

Chapter 15 - Foreign Studies

Even if you're planning a career that has nothing to do with other countries or international law, a foreign study program can be worthwhile. Most law students have the equivalent of cabin fever by the time they're in third-year. At the very least, a foreign law study program is a nice—though expensive—change of pace and scenery from your home school. Also, except for the brief annual vacation or occasional foreign convention, conference, or business trip, once you begin practicing law you're probably going to spend nearly every day of the rest of your life in America. The USA's a great place, but it's also great to have a final fling before you settle down.

Besides, as chapter 14 noted, the courses you take after first-year are unimportant—with the exceptions as noted. So you certainly don't have to take all of them in the United States.

Whether or not you have already traveled abroad, you know such trips are usually just a glorified (and fun) tourist deal. But if you attended school in another country, you had opportunities denied the typical tourist. And if you go as a *law* student, you can have some amazing opportunities denied the typical student in a foreign studies program.

Foreign study is also a matter of your post-graduate intentions. If you want to be an "international lawyer," then it might help to put your money where your mouth is and go.* If you already speak a foreign language, then it can be *invaluable* for you to study law in a country that speaks that language, and to learn various legal terms in the local tongue, along with local procedures. But rarely do you even have to know the language.

Closing the Gap

I knew a guy who went on a summer law program in Japan after his first year of law school. He then took a leave of absence from his law school and spent the next academic year in Japan, studying the language full-time. Then he participated in another Japan summer law school program, and worked as a paid clerk for a Japanese law firm. He returned to his home school in the fall, and sought a clerkship for the following summer. Even though his first-year grades weren't great, he got some offers—including one that specifically stated he would be sent back to Japan, at the firm's expense, to do his clerkship there. He accepted that one. He is now in the

---

* Most "international" lawyers, though, stay put in the States. They advise foreign corporations regarding U.S. law, for the benefit of those corporations' American subsidiaries. To understand foreign law, American corporations usually hire foreign firms—or else the U.S. firms they normally use will farm the work out to a foreign "corresponding" firm. Very few American lawyers get posted to foreign offices of their firms.

Tokyo office of another, prestigious, firm...and his entry-level starting salary was $70,000 a year. The moral here is that, even if you aren't in the top 10% of your class, foreign studies might help make up for the difference come hiring time. They might even give you the edge.

For example, consider the typical job interview with a law firm. Recruiters see the same person over and over, in effect: same appearance, same courses, same grades, etc.. They get tired of talking about the same things again and again. When a job applicant comes in who has something unusual in his or her background, the interviewer will focus on that, just to have something new and different to discuss. If that "something unusual" is law-related, so much the better.

Granted, this doesn't justify spending the money to go on a foreign program. Nor will it get you the job unless everything else looks reasonably good—and perhaps not even then. But it might help make you stand out from the crowd, to stick in the interviewer's mind. Every little bit helps.

Warning: If you talk about how exciting, glamorous, stimulating, etc., it was where you went, the interviewer will be worried that you expect to find your job to be likewise. No way. Virtually no job in the law—and especially in the first year—is like that. You might have just aced yourself out of an offer. So what you do instead is to emphasize all the negatives—but without sounding like a grouch. Talk about how much you just loved grinding away on the law books, to escape the temptations and delights of, say, Paris. Don't lay it on too thick, though. Lawyers tend to be pinheads, and pinheads definitely do not like to be mocked—especially by those hoping to join their ranks in the law factories.

At the other extreme, if you talk about your studies at Serbia's Slobodan Milosevic Center for International Law, Justice, Psychiatry, and Humanity, the interviewer might figure you have your heart set on a career in the Balkans. So, no matter where you were, stress how different it was from America, and how this resulted in all sorts of inconveniences. But again, don't sound like a pampered lout. Rather, emphasize how pleased you were to find the law school grind is the same, no matter where you are. And you found happiness in the sheer predictability of the drudgery, amid all the confusing cultural differences of the country.

In short, you—subtly—emphasize you are a legal robot who can steadily produce billable output under all kinds of conditions, pleasant or unpleasant. If you can say these things with a straight face, your interviewer might well make you an offer on the spot. (The foregoing assumes, of course, that you have not actually set your sights on a career in a specific country—unlike the Japan program student mentioned above. But even he did not take the attitude of "Tokyo or Bust" during his interviews. He let *them* spot the possibilities—which, of course, were staring them in the face.)

If You Have the Yen for It

If you're interested in foreign study, be mindful it's expensive. Usually the programs are put on by American schools, in cooperation with a foreign institution. Each school gets a piece of the action. So, the tuition is a lot higher than the normal tuition at the U.S. school—plus air fare, room and board, etc..

You can use federally-guaranteed student loans, though. You don't have to get approval for your specific program. As long as you're going to get law school credit, you're eligible. Further, because these funds exist for "educational purposes," you can use the proceeds to pay for room and board, as always…and for the air fare. (But don't forget, you have to repay those loans someday, with interest.)

The final consideration regarding money is that foreign law study programs are not a "now or never" thing. Even though most of them don't advertise the fact, nearly all are open to licensed attorneys, too. Sometimes, however, students get first priority; licensed attorneys get in only if there are unfilled slots at the time of the application deadline. Check this out. Sometimes it requires a phone call.

Other than cost, the main negative is that you're usually limited to a total of just a few credits. That's fine if you want to spend a lot of time sightseeing and carousing with the locals. But if you're paying a lot of money, and coming back with only a handful of credits compared to the time you were gone, you need to weigh the cost v. the benefit. And, of course, you might need to do something to make up the difference when you return (or before you go): take a heavier credit load than normal in one semester, or attend a summer session. So, be sure to find out the maximum number of credits you can get out of it, and plan your home credit load accordingly.

Shop around to find the best deals. Even more important, check with your law school before you even apply to one of these programs. Make sure you can transfer the credits home. Get it in writing. You have to move fast on this, because most foreign study program slots fill quickly. (And you usually have to pay a hefty, *non-refundable* deposit with your "application.") By the time you get confirmation from your school, it might be too late to get in.

When to Go

If you think you can swing it financially and regarding the transfer of sufficient credits, the other major thing to consider is whether to go on a summer program, a semester program, or an academic-year program.

Nearly all the programs are summer-only: some for just two or three weeks, others eight to twelve. For the shorter programs, it's possible for you to work a summer job at home and still go.

If you Make Law Review, and you hope to become an editor in third-year, you should remain at your school throughout second-year. If you're chosen at the end of second-year to be a third-year *editor,* there goes year three. The problem is that the deadline for most foreign studies programs is anywhere from late January to late March—long before year-end finals. Keep that in mind if you're in first-year and are interested in foreign study but hope you have a shot at Law Review. (And if you follow the recommendations of *this* book, you definitely will.)

In that case, if you think you can stand to immediately extend your studies, the best time to go on a summer program is probably after your *first* year of law school. (The courses you'll take will be vastly different than the Big Six you will have just endured.) After either first- or second-year, you can do a summer clerkship *and* a foreign study program, if you wish: as mentioned in chapter 12, clerkships are usually for just half the summer, either the first or the second. (Then again, as also mentioned, you might prefer to do two clerkships in one summer, back-to-back; or, your sole clerkship one year might be summer-long.)

With the semester and academic-year programs, chances are good they will not be under the auspices of an American school. So you'll be transferring credits directly from the foreign institution. Again, be sure to check this out ahead of time with your own school. However, your own school might have semester and academic year programs with a foreign "sister school." Naturally, your school would prefer you to go on one of those, because then *they* get a piece of the financial pie. For that reason, they usually make it easier to get more credits than you would if you went elsewhere. Sometimes, they make their own funds available for this—as loans, with interest. (Less frequently, you can get an outright grant.)

The best time to go on a semester program is the *second* semester of either your second or third year—preferably the former. You will need the first semester to line up a job, whether it be just a summer job or a "permanent" one, to start after the academic year ends. However—as chapter 12 said— most law firms that hire summer clerks as part of a formal program make their decisions about whether or not to extend permanent offers at the end of that summer, rather than in the fall. So, you might be one of the lucky few who starts third-year with a job already waiting for you at graduation. Also, perhaps you will *not* be chosen for a Law Review editorship for your third-year. Then, you might not want to stay on as a cite-checking slave. And perhaps you do *not* intend to apply for a judicial clerkship in lieu of going to work for the law firm that offered you the job. If all these conditions exist, you are then free to go where you wish in your final semester—and perhaps for your entire third year.

* * *

While in law school, I participated in two programs, one in Europe, one in Asia. In Asia, classes were followed by an (unpaid) internship at a local law firm. Although each was very expensive, I would do it all over again. All of those in the Asian program were fellow law students, although one of them had been a practicing attorney who was then getting an LL.M.. (LL.M.: Master of Law.) In the European program, again one of the participants was an attorney, but not a student. He was in a two-person firm that had recently won—and collected its fee in—a very large personal injury case. The program was his treat to himself, a unique vacation.

The schools arranged for us to do the usual tourist things. However, many activities were unique to our status. We met with prominent attorneys, government officials, and judges. We got to sit in on a criminal trial. We visited with corporate counsel of local and American companies doing business in the country in question. In Asia, we toured a couple of factories. I found the professors in foreign studies programs to be superior to those back home. Nearly all the foreign professors who participated (usually as guest lecturers) were excellent. The assigned materials were wonderful—and voluminous. The assigned workload was heavy, but not oppressive. (Then again, it's well known that even lousy wine always seems to taste better in a foreign locale. Your happiness with the local scenery and the girls—or guys, as the case may be—clouds your judgment.)

* * *

To find out what and where these programs are, check the December and January issues of *Young Lawyer* (published by the ABA Law Student Division) or *National Jurist,* an independent magazine for law school students. (See chapter 20 for information on these.)

If you can afford it, I recommend it.

Chapter 16 - Critical Skills:

Case Investigation—and
Legal Research, Reasoning & Writing

Case Investigation

Cases turn on *facts*—especially in a *jury* trial. What the jurors relate to are facts, especially insofar as the facts help the jurors decide whom to blame. Even trivial facts can loom large in their deliberations.

Perhaps the name "Leona Helmsley" means something to you. There was a TV movie about her. She was sent to prison for income tax evasion, not so long ago. (She's out, now.) Income tax evasion is hard to prove when the evader is sophisticated. I don't know how sophisticated Leona Helmsley was or is. But I'll bet I know the key fact that got the jurors to vote "Guilty": Ms. Helmsley's maid testified that while she was serving food and drink to Ms. Helmsley and a visitor, Ms. Helmsley said to the visitor, "Only the 'little people' pay taxes." Helmsley may have been pure as the driven snow, but I'm sure the jurors' minds were irrevocably poisoned against her when they heard what she'd said. Someone had discovered a bit of evidence that, objectively speaking, was almost irrelevant to whether or not the defendant had committed the crime. But it was enough to put her away.

Most lawyers, sooner or later, have to rely on a private investigator—or, at least, they *should*. But forget the detective novels and movies. Rather, for once, *The Perry Mason Show* was (almost) accurate: Paul Drake was (nearly) a typical investigator. Yet, today, depending on what type of law you practice, you're also likely to be dealing with a large firm such as Kroll Associates, of New York City. Such firms, among their many services, perform "due diligence" before one corporation acquires another, for example.

However, most investigations involve a search of public records, especially courthouse records. America is an amazingly open society. Many public records are compiled by private information services, and are available on-line or on CD-ROM: marriage licenses, voter registration, drivers' licenses, mortgages, creditor filings for consumer goods, etc..

It behooves you to become familiar with how to do case investigating yourself. True, the CD-ROMs will be beyond your budget. But the old-fashioned gumshoe approach is not. You need to learn how to search through court-house records. —Granted, if you do well in law school, and go to work for a big-bucks law factory when you graduate, it will almost never be worth your time to do any of this yourself. But that's why you should learn how to do it while you're still in law school…or better yet, even before you go.

Four reasons why: One, if and when you do rely on an investigator, you'll be better at evaluating that person's competence—and in spotting padded bills. (There are a lot of nincompoops and charlatans in the business—just as there are in the law itself.) Two, in a given situation you might not want to make someone else privy to what's up. Then you better be able to do it yourself. (Unfortunately, some investigators are quite indiscreet, either habitually or occasionally; just like lawyers. You're always taking a chance, even if you've worked with someone enough to think he or she is close-mouthed.) Three, your client might not be able to afford it, or is too cheap to authorize it. If you *need* the information, you can get it yourself—even if you do it on your own time, at no charge. (You certainly won't want to make a habit of that, but sometimes that's the only way to go.) Four, it will make you a better attorney. You will be aware of sources of information others might not have thought about. And you'll do a better job of sensing when "something's wrong with this picture." You'll have the edge.

For example, during a lawsuit, each side conducts "discovery"—formal procedures whereby each side seeks information *from* the other side *about* the other side. I'm sure it will come as no shock to you that adversaries (both lawyers and laypeople) *lie*. Or, they just keep the truth all to themselves.

That's unethical. There are rules against it. There are penalties for it, sometimes severe. But it happens all the time.

However, if *you* have *already* conducted *informal* discovery, without the other side's involvement, you'll be better prepared for the *formal* process—and will get more out of it. It will help you catch the other side's deception. It will help you trap them at it. (This is especially delightful when you do it in front of a jury. Then it's called "impeaching the witness.") And once in a great while, you might even find a judge who cares about such things; who will do something about it besides going "Tsk, tsk. Shame, shame."

Example: I handled a breach-of-contract lawsuit that involved fee-splitting. One of the key issues was how much the "bad guy" had charged for a service he provided in years past. His current rate was available, but of limited use. I foolishly did not do any informal discovery before taking his deposition. At the deposition, he lied, and it was obvious. Only then did I come to my senses and start digging. Come to find out he had, over the years, filed suit several times to collect fees owed him for the service in question. The case files contained ample documentation. Reviewing his own evidence, it was easy for me to establish what his standard rate had been. That was crucial to establishing "damages" in the case—i.e., how much he'd ripped off. Although the suit settled before trial, I'd really been looking forward to nailing him on this point in front of the jury. (In hindsight, if I'd known the truth *before* the deposition, I would have kept it all to myself anyway. But I would have done a much better job of pinning him down in his lies. As it was, I'd done poorly, and had left him a lot of wiggle room.)

And here's how it can work for you in a different way: Sometimes, your *own* client is the deceitful one. Or sometimes your client is afraid to tell you the *whole* truth, thinking you'll refuse to pursue the case with zeal. Or sometimes your client just has a bad memory, or doesn't recognize the vital importance of something you need to know. You can only get so far by asking questions and looking over documents you get from the client. Sometimes, if the case is important enough, you need to run an independent check. (God knows the *other* side will.) And there are few pains worse than getting blindsided because of you own client's omissions...especially when it happens right in front of a jury.

Today, as standard operating procedure, I search out 1) other litigation the opposing client has been involved in, 2) other litigation the opposing client's *attorney* has handled—to see how he or she operates, and 3) other litigation my *own* client has been involved in—just in case my client says something now that *contradicts* what's in the public record.

Okay. Say you don't want to be a trial lawyer, and you won't be involved in lawsuits. Even so, case investigation can come in handy. Example: Your client wants to sign an important contract with a firm that he or she has never done business with before. The client has checked out the firm's credit rating, bank statement, etc.. The "due diligence" seems complete. However, you—being a conscientious attorney—decide to check the courthouse records. You already know the other guy moved into town five years ago, and started this company of his from scratch. But the guy's 50 years old. Curious, you check him out where he lived before. Lo and behold, he went through a bankruptcy eight years ago—and took his former company down with him, leaving a lot of *its* bills unpaid. You then discover that he'd lived in another city before that—where, gee, he'd started a new company. *That* company had signed a five-year lease for a warehouse...and was evicted and sued a year later for not paying rent. And so on. Yes, you wouldn't have done this case investigation without your client's agreement to pay the cost of it. And the client certainly didn't need *you* to do it. But *you're* the one who thought of it. *You're* the one who knew what to look for. And even if someone else did the work, it was *you* who saved the client a bundle.

One more non-litigation example: Normally, a real estate sale includes "tracing the chain of title." Specialized companies do that. But sometimes they screw up. Or, more often, they do it "by the book," and fail to go beyond the routine. If there's an odd deed or easement "outside the chain of title," it can cause big problems later. If you hope to have a real estate practice, intimate knowledge of the way the system actually works will enable you to check the specialized company's diligence. (I know of one real estate attorney who regularly embarrasses the title insurance firms by finding *important* things they've *missed*. He's very successful.) An ounce of prevention is worth a pound of cure.

As a lawyer, it probably isn't worth your time to do any of this investigating yourself. But if you know how to do it before you get your license, it will stand you in good stead. (See chapter 23, item 8, for more information.)

Legal Research

Chapter 1 noted that legal research has two purposes: to bring yourself up to speed on a new subject, and to Find Authority to back up your arguments. Both of these are especially important in your first few years of practice.

The law is supposed to be predictable. That means it's supposed to apply in the same way to everyone in similar circumstances. A lot of people have invested a lot of money in various things, based on the existing law. They've organized their lives and planned their futures based on the existing law.

Anytime the law changes, it upsets some applecarts. Maybe a particular applecart *should* be upset. But even so, it means a lot of other changes must be made as a result—a ripple (or perhaps *tsunami)* effect, to mix metaphors. Legal change is disruptive, period. That's why judges usually try to make their rulings as narrow as possible. They fear the Law of Unintended Consequences. (That's also why, when judges *do* change the law, they sometimes pretend they *haven't.)*

Finding Authority means you're putting the monkey on the judge's back. And you're forcing that judge to go out on a limb if he or she doesn't rule in your favor on the point in question. As with most of us, judges are (usually) "risk averse." They don't like to take unnecessary chances. It goes like this: If you're a judge, you're already somewhere in the judicial hierarchy. However, unless you're already one of the Supremes, you can aspire to a judgeship on a higher court. Maybe you'll get there by rocking the boat— but only if you rock the right boat in the right way at the right time. But this is something that's obvious only in hindsight...and by the time that occurs, your chances for promotion may already be sunk. The advocate, by Finding Authority, lets the judge play it safe. That's what judges like. And, in general, that's what society likes—for good reasons.

So, you better be able to find that existing law, including the exceptions, the exceptions to the exceptions, and all the nuances of every bit of it.

There are lawyers who lie to a court, even in writing. They cite cases having absolutely nothing to do with the point at issue. They completely misrepresent the holding of a case. They cite statutory law that has long since been repealed, or cases long since overruled, and claim such law is still in force. They know better. Sadly, there are judges who know they're being lied to, but do nothing about it. Maybe this is because the deceitful attorney has a special relationship with that judge. Maybe it's because the judge is determined to make a case come out a certain way, no matter what the law is. However, in general, if you Find Authority that's *decisive,* then that authority is "controlling." The judge *has* to follow it (supposedly). You win.

In law school, you look for the Highest Authority, usually U.S. Supreme Court cases. But in practice, you will seldom find a High Authority that seems to fit your situation. And if you do, you'll probably also find (or your opponent will find) other High Authority that also seems to fit your situation—and goes against you. However, the farther down the authority hierarchy you go, the more detailed the law becomes. There may have been only one U.S. Supreme Court case in history that seems to fit your situation—but chances are good there have been dozens of cases in your *state's* supreme court. With luck, you'll find one that's "on all fours"—and favorable.

You usually want to find the *lowest* authority that appears to control your situation: a state statute, a regulatory agency's rule, etc.. The "controlling" authority that's closest to your client is the *easiest* to deal with. If you have a municipal ordinance that explicitly governs your client's situation, chances are pretty good that's the end of the matter. It's a safe bet you don't have to worry about trying to apply a U.S. Supreme Court ruling that concerned facts quite different from yours. You still check the higher authority, of course, to make sure it hasn't trumped the lower. But most of the time—unless there's a Constitutional issue involved—the controlling municipal ordinance allows you to wrap things up quickly. Clients (and bosses) like that... as long as you weren't hasty about it and thus overlooked something vital, a land mine that will eventually cause them to lose an arm and a leg.

<u>It Ain't Over 'Til It's Over</u>

As you will discover, a case won at the trial court level is not necessarily a case won. A civil court trial judge can overturn a jury's verdict. (A criminal court judge can do this only if the verdict was "Guilty.") And an appellate court can overturn the result of the trial, even if the trial judge is with you. It isn't enough just to win at trial. You have to protect your victory in case there's an appeal. And, of course, if you lose at trial, you want to have a record showing that the *law* was on your side and you *should* have won. If you can't box the trial court in, you want to at least try to box the appellate court in.

However, only about two percent of all civil cases ever go through trial. (There are even cases where the parties settle while the jury is deliberating.) Your skill as a negotiator plays a big part in determining the nature of the settlement. So do the facts. And so do things like how believable your witnesses are versus how believable the other side's witnesses are. But if the law is clearly on your side—and you know it, and can prove it—your position is a lot stronger than it might otherwise be.

Say you don't want to be a trial lawyer? Even if you never do anything in connection with litigation, the documents you draft may someday be subject to litigation. And a lot of lawyer-negotiators handle business deals. They try to make sure their clients get the long end of the stick. If you've done your homework, and can prove that things "have to" be done *your* client's way because the law says so, you will do very well indeed. An ounce of prevention is worth a pound of cure. Part of what legal research involves is being aware of potential problems that have occurred in similar situations, and being aware of how those problems were resolved in court. You then draft your document or tailor the business deal in question in such a way that your client knows, up front, that if push comes to shove the law is on his or her side.

However, the best victory is the one that occurs without fighting. If a dispute arises, and goes through litigation, your client will probably have to spend a lot of money to prevail. Even if you're eventually proved right, your client will not appreciate the fact that it took a long and expensive court battle to achieve final success. To change the metaphor yet again: if you've done a good job on your legal research, you can at least make sure all your client's bases are covered.

Time is Money

Legal research takes time. Most lawyers bill by the hour. And most clients will get very annoyed when they get a big bill that includes a lot of legal research. After all, you're a lawyer—and most clients (wrongly) think lawyers are supposed to know the law, *all* of it, off the top of their heads. No way.

As a good lawyer—if you are a good lawyer—you have two major skills: 1) You know how to Think Like a Lawyer, which (by the time you've been in practice long enough) includes a good "feel" for any given situation; and 2) You "know what you *don't* know"—and *how to find out* what you *need* to know. Thinking Like a Lawyer, you will know *what* to look for and *where* to look for it, which involves Legal Research.

In contrast to the client, your supervising attorney knows that a lawyer can't provide all the answers off-the-cuff. He or she knows it takes research. However, you better be efficient at it. Otherwise, it might take you five hours to locate what a good researcher can find in fifteen minutes. Your boss may end up writing that time off as a loss...and you will be made aware of his or her displeasure.

It isn't just a matter of holding the client's legal bill down, either. Sometimes, you have to be able to find an answer *fast*—such as overnight, or even within a few hours. If you don't know where to look, or what to look for, your client's troubles (or your boss's) will get much, much worse very quickly...and *your* troubles will *begin*.

Learning How

As was pointed out in Chapter 12, if you Make Law Review you will learn how to do legal research *very* well. It will be part of your on-the-job training as second-year slave labor. So, if you do Make Law Review, you (probably) do not need to take any courses in legal research. (However, you still might want to consider a course in an arcane area such as administrative law, because few Law Review articles involve this subject. Administrative law is *hard* to research. And as more and more areas of the law are handed over to bureaucracies for conflict resolution, knowing how to Find Authority in administrative matters gets more important.)

If you do not Make Law Review, you should take all the legal research courses you can.

CALR

In most law schools, students get a quick introduction to "Computer Assisted Legal Research." Chapter 5 introduced the two companies with on-line CALR: Lexis and Westlaw. (I've heard there's now a third, but I haven't confirmed this.) If you know what to look for, and where to look, you can find some answers mighty fast by using an on-line service. However, it tends to be expensive. It can easily run hundreds of dollars an hour. So, as a law student, you can't count on being able to use Westlaw or Lexis when you're a practicing attorney.

However, for law school students, there's *no charge* for time spent on-line. (More accurately, as mentioned in chapter 5, the law school pays a flat fee for this, covering the entire student body.) —And these days, you better be good at both the Westlaw and Lexis systems. You don't know which one your future employer will have...and your future employer will definitely not be patient as you try to get the hang of it.

The Intermediate Step: Legal Reasoning

This is a short section, but the skill it concerns—legal reasoning—is as critical as the others.

To understand the relevant law once you're in practice, you'll be reading various reference materials that will bring you up to speed. But the law changes, constantly. True, major changes to an entire subject area are rare. However, new wrinkles constantly appear; old ones get smoothed out— especially in sub-areas of any given legal field. So you have to keep up with the case law.

Chapter 3 discussed "briefing a case." Once you're beyond your first semester of law school (and sometimes even before then), you almost never do it the way you did then. But once you're out of law school altogether—or even before, as in a summer clerkship—you'll very often be "briefing a point of law." This combines case investigation, legal research, legal reasoning, and legal writing.

If you're going into a trial or a hearing, and anticipate a dispute will arise over a point of law, you do a "bench memo" for the judge. If you're going into a negotiation, you might want to do a memo to enlighten the other side and get them to abandon some ridiculous position they're holding that's based on their incorrect understanding of the law. Most often, though, you'll be doing a memo for a supervising attorney or a client. Here you discuss what the law is, and whether and how it applies to the problem at hand.

Above, under "Legal Research," it was mentioned that judges are "risk averse," and like to stick to precedent. It was also mentioned that you need to be able to find all the existing law on a point, including the exceptions, the exceptions to the exceptions, and all the nuances of every bit of it. That way, no matter what you're trying to accomplish, you can argue that it's justified under *existing* law—or under a logical extension thereof. (An alternative is to argue that the specific "controlling authority" in question is actually an imprudent departure from the overall pattern of existing law. All you're trying to do, you say, is to get this court to make an *exception* to this controlling law…but this exception will actually be in line with the rule. Seriously.)

The only way you can truly be on top of things is to know how to "parse the cases" *in light of the facts of your client's situation.* It is vital that you be able to grasp the *crucial* aspects of a given case. It is equally vital that you be able to grasp the *distinctions* among cases. Something that at first appears to be "on point" turns out to be completely irrelevant. The section in chapter 5 on legal reasoning discussed all this. But it's worth the reminder here. (Hence, another mention of John Delaney's book, *Learning Legal Reasoning,* introduced in chapter 5; and Ruggero Aldisert's *Logic for Lawyers,* discussed in the addendum to chapter 7.)

If you can't do a sophisticated briefing of a point of law, your analysis might fall short…in which case you may take a fall.

Legal Writing

Most of the cases you'll read in your casebook are poorly written. They tend to use stilted, pompous language. Latin phrases are frequent. Even the English is convoluted. This is what the typical layperson associates with legal documents. Unfortunately, many law students get the idea that this is the way lawyers *should* write. They say it conveys the "majesty" and the "mystique" of the Law. Don't you believe it.

No lawyer should <u>ever</u> write legalese. Granted, there are times when a bit of legal jargon is the most <u>concise</u> and <u>precise</u> way to express something. But then, you're just using a term or a phrase as legal shorthand, to save time and avoid misunderstanding. (For example, you might refer to the "Equal Dignities Doctrine" in property law, or to "res ipsa loquitur" in torts. You *could* use plain English, and spell out what each of these is. But if you did, opposing counsel and the judge would think you're talking down to them. The effect would be counter-productive.)

However, I've met attorneys who say they *deliberately* use the most obscure legal bafflegab they can in their writings. They give two reasons why this is supposedly a good thing. First, they say it makes it very difficult for opposing counsel to follow the argument. This, in turn, makes it very difficult for opposing counsel to *respond* to the argument. Second, they say it makes it *impossible* for the *client* to understand it. This, in turn, supposedly confers two benefits to the lawyer: a) the client is impressed by the attorney's mastery of the Magic Words of the Law—and is therefore inclined not to protest a large bill from the lawyer for writing such drivel; and b) if the lawyer made a mistake, *the client won't catch it!*

To take these one at a time…

Never Forget Your Audience

If *opposing counsel* has trouble following the argument, so will the *judge*. You want to have the judge on *your* side. That means you want to start off on the right foot. If what you present is obscurantist garbage, you won't even get your foot in the door. This is especially so with trial courts. (Judges are very busy—and impatient.) Finding Authority is paramount. But that's just the start. It is necessary, but not sufficient. You next have to let the judge know what you found, and present it in a manner that's convincing. Hence the importance of *good* legal writing.

As chapter 1 said, advocacy takes two forms: oral and written. Of these, oral is—nearly always—the less important. (Heresy for a trial lawyer to say, but heresy is sometimes also the truth. And in this case, it is.)

Television and the movies make it appear that the most important part of a trial is what goes on in the courtroom—the testimony that's heard, the physical evidence and documents that are presented. Maybe; but even when that's true, it's often true only in a formal sense—especially in a civil trial. Long beforehand, opposing counsel will have tried to frame the issues in such a way as to favor the outcome they desire. They also try to get rulings in advance of trial as to what testimony and tangible evidence will be allowed during the proceedings. In a (civil) jury trial, by the time the jury hears the case the issues have often been cut down in size, and cut down in number. Sometimes the courtroom appearance is just a wrap-up for the client's benefit. (Again, heresy for a trial lawyer to say, but—again—true.) Even though *all* trials are dicey, each side tries to narrow the unpredictable possibilities to as small a range as it can. That way, even if the worst comes to pass (i.e., you lose) you will already have succeeded insofar as you've exercised "damage control" even before the damage occurs.

Example: You're defending two parties, one rich, the other not-so-rich. The other side seeks exemplary (a.k.a. "punitive") damages. If your clients are found liable, the jury will take the extent of your clients' wealth into account when deciding how much to award in punitives. You, naturally, want to minimize the potential loss. So you try to get the rich defendant dismissed from the case before the trial starts. That way, even if you lose, the jury will only consider the assets of the not-so-rich defendant. It's virtually certain the jury will award far less than it would if it could also consider the "deep pockets" of the rich (ex-) defendant. If you can Find Authority that's controlling, and that authority shows it's improper to have your rich client involved in this suit in the first place, you've already won a great victory, of a sort. Here's why: Under the circumstances, both the rich defendant and the not-so-rich one are covered by the same insurance policy. It's the *insurance company* that hired you, and pays your bill—and it's the insurance company that will pay the winner if you lose the case. (The jury doesn't know that, of course. They're not allowed to. If they did, they'd naturally overlook the fact that the not-so-rich client doesn't have deep pockets.) So, by getting the rich defendant taken out, you've just saved the *real* party-at-risk a bundle—no matter what the outcome at trial.

The written arguments an attorney submits, whether to a trial court or an appellate court, are (usually) read before the attorney gets a chance to utter a word in the courtroom. Occasionally, if what's written is bad enough, the judge won't even let the attorney come in to the courtroom to be heard. And even if he or she does, quite often all the lawyer gets to do is answer the judge's questions—and the questions are sometimes based on what the lawyer wrote. Granted, with two advocates evenly matched in legal research and legal writing skills, with equally strong cases, before open-minded judges, the better oral advocate will win. But that constellation of circumstances never happens in the real world. If you've won the battle on paper, the battle is probably already over—if not at the trial level, then on appeal.

Even though, as mentioned, nearly all civil suits are disposed of without trial (they're "settled out"), that doesn't mean a judge isn't involved. Quite the contrary. Sometimes a case gets *"poured* out"—by the judge. Your client doesn't even get his or her day in court. It's called "Summary Judgment."

If the judge rules against you on anything (including summary judgment), you can eventually take it up on appeal. However, appellate courts are reluctant to reverse or remand most rulings of trial judges. This is especially so if the record includes a well-researched and well-written argument from the attorney who prevailed on the point in question. (Besides, appeals are very expensive and take a long time. Most clients, for some reason, don't like that.)

All judges work amid mountains of paperwork. In truth, modern judges are really just glorified, bureaucratic paper-pushers. The other branches of government have not made sufficient resources available to the judiciary for most judges to be able to truly *deliberate* any more. They have to keep processing paper, as fast as they can, to dispose of cases and move these documents out the door...because more are coming in all the time. "Case management" is the name of the game, especially as to the parties' pre-trial maneuverings.

However, even though any one case will perhaps not get the attention it deserves, that does not necessarily mean it will be dealt with quickly. Judges review dozens of documents, hundreds—perhaps thousands—of pages, every week. Most judges can take a long time, if they wish, to make a decision on something—without giving it a moment's thought in the meantime. (I read where one state appellate court took *four years*, from 1992 to 1996, to decide a case. I do not know why.) They don't have to decide matters in the order received. Nor do they even have to read documents in the order received. Say you turn in a piece of legal writing that's opaque. It goes into the hopper, along with dozens of other pieces of legal writing from other attorneys on other matters. When the judge is considering what to read next, he or she looks through the piles of documents. If the judge picks up *your* masterpiece of obfuscatory fecal matter and quickly scans the first few paragraphs before deciding whether to continue, it will quickly go back into the stack. Quite possibly it will deliberately be placed at the *bottom* of the heap...and will stay there for months, and months, and months.

I know of one federal judge who not only refuses to read legaldygook, he has his clerk return the material to the lawyer who submitted it. There's always a form letter with it, bluntly telling the lawyer that the judge will not read crap. So the lawyer then re-writes it in plain English...if he or she wants that case to be heard. Even if the attorney then satisfactorily re-writes the document, that lawyer now has an uphill battle to win the judge to his or her side. I know of another judge who's even worse: the document written in legalese is neither returned nor read. Instead—assuming that opposing counsel's brief is intelligible—the judge automatically rules in favor of opposing counsel. Tough on the lawyer. Tougher on the client...who hasn't a clue as to the truth of the matter. (The client's lawyer might not either; but even if he or she does, the client will never be told.) —Then again, I know of at least one judge who never bothers to read *anything*— including the rules of evidence and civil procedure.

In the higher courts, more and more, the lawyers' briefs are read only by a judge's *law clerk*. Then the clerk prepares a very "brief" summary for his or her boss. Thus, as an attorney, you're writing only for the eyes of someone who's been out of law school even less time than *you*. And while judges' law clerks tend to be the cream of the academic crop, that doesn't mean they'll be any more patient than their bosses when it comes to trying to make sense of legal gibberish. (*They* have mountains of paperwork to process, too.) If you can't lay it all out, clearly and *concisely*, you're almost *asking* to lose.

Making Your Client Part of the Team

We've now arrived at the second reason short-sighted lawyers give for writing in legal bafflegab.

Clients are often a pain in the neck, because they don't think like lawyers. (If they did, they probably wouldn't have gotten into a situation that called for a lawyer in the first place.) Being laypeople, clients often get all excited about things that are totally irrelevant from a legal perspective. Sometimes it's hard to get a client to accept this. So, it can make life easier for the lawyer if the client doesn't even know the attorney has omitted from a document something the client thinks is so important. Hence the legaldygook. But this can come back to haunt you.

As chapter 6 explained, Thinking Like a Lawyer involves selecting the relevant law to apply to a given set of facts in the correct way. And as the discussion of hypotheticals in chapter 7 showed, sometimes changing the facts only slightly will cause a change in the legal outcome. (That's a big part of what "parsing the cases" is all about.) The layperson client will obviously never understand the law as well as the attorney does. But even if the attorney *understands* the facts better, from a legal perspective, the attorney will never *know* the facts as well as the client does. And the client will always know *more* facts about the case than the lawyer ever will.

Unless your client is somewhat dim-witted (which happens), by writing in plain English you ensure that the client can follow your argument. (You can always explain, orally, the meaning of the few terms and phrases of legal jargon that are unavoidable.) If you've made a mistake regarding the facts, the client can catch it and you can correct it. By this, I don't mean simply that you've stated an incorrect date or something:

Modern law is, for the most part, common-sensical. As you read this book now, you're (presumably) a layperson. Yet, if you were informed of the facts in a given dispute, there's a very good chance you would have the same "gut feel" for what the outcome should be as any lawyer would. This is so even if you thought certain facts were very important when they actually were irrelevant. The trend in the law has been toward *justice*, not the continuation of mere legal technicalities as the basis for resolving disputes. (The legal technicalities still exist, of course. But today, they tend to serve the interest of justice rather than being mere ends in themselves. A given example might seem arbitrary, picky, and unfair if you heard of it all by itself. However, it's almost a sure thing that if it were explained to you in context—including the reasoning behind it—you would agree that it's a desirable technicality after all.)

—So, when I refer to "making a mistake regarding the facts," what I mean is that the lawyer may have overlooked something important, or included something that was not important. A client, reading the document, will then probably say, "Why mention this?" or "But what about ————?" Whatever it is, it might be something the lawyer hadn't thought about at all, or hadn't thought about correctly. (Or, let's hope, it's something the lawyer did consider, and dealt with correctly.) In this sense, then, your client's reaction to what you (the lawyer) said serves as a reality-check. That can be a priceless gift to you as an attorney—because, other than your client, there's no one else who can perform this service as well, if at all.

—And that's why the lawyer's documents should minimize the use of legaldygook.

Now take it a step farther: If what you've written is a pleading in connection with a lawsuit, but it doesn't make sense to your client, then it won't make sense to a jury. Granted, the pleading is only for the judge's eyes, not the jurors'. But the argument you make to the court is the same argument you'll make to the jury—only when you argue to the jury, you'll hardly be using any legal terms at all. So, if it isn't clear to the layperson who's your client, chances are it won't be clear to the laypeople who are your jurors, even when you cut out the legalese.

And what if the document *isn't* in connection with a lawsuit? Say it's a letter. Well, for all you know, the sender and recipient of that letter might have a dispute someday. That very document might be relevant. If what you drafted for your client was clear (simple and direct), there will be no disagreement as to what it means. It may be that, according to what's in that letter, your client is wrong and the other party is right. If so, it's better for your client to give in now, at minimal cost, than to let the disagreement grow into a lawsuit. If your client goes to trial and loses, the total costs will be much, much higher. "Eating crow" is a lot cheaper.

It also might be that your client is clearly right, but the other party won't give in. In that case, the document is headed into court, eventually. It might end up in front of twelve jurors' eyes. Now, you tell me: If what you wrote is entirely in legalese, and the other side is complaining about that very legalese, who has the jurors' sympathy?

A client who is intelligent, and who also has common sense, is an extremely valuable asset. Unlike most writing (such as the drafts of the manuscript of this book), you can't show your work to other people and ask them to critique it. (True, if you work for a law firm, or a corporate law department, or a government agency, you can—and *must*—hand your work over to your supervising attorney before it leaves the office. But your supervisor will not have your client's or the jurors' frame of reference, and will be looking at it in an entirely different way.) You have to ensure that the work you do for a client will be held confidential—until and unless the final document (such as a will, or a pleading in a lawsuit) is made available to outsiders. So, use the client as a critic. The client will never be able to criticize your understanding of the *law,* anyway. You won't lose face because you misunderstood the implication of a fact or two. And the client will probably appreciate you all the more for having extended an opportunity to participate in a meaningful way. (That doesn't justify a large bill. But I'll bet it makes the client more willing to pay, because the client has a better understanding of what you did to deserve your fee. —And good client relations can nip many a potential problem in the bud.* They can also bring in referrals.)

More Pedagogical Malpractice

Other than the perfunctory introduction to Legal Research you get in first-year, there are no required legal *research* courses in law school. In fact, there are few legal research courses at all, even in the big schools with numerous faculty members and impressive library resources.

Other than the perfunctory introduction to Legal Writing you get in first-year, there are no required legal *writing* courses in law school. In fact, there are usually no other legal writing courses at all.

This is more pedagogical malpractice. Incompetent solo practitioners, especially, who are recent graduates often poorly brief a point of law or

---

*   For one thing, the client will be less inclined to sue you for malpractice if that client had a hand in what you did.
     Machiavellian of me to note this? You bet. "Saint Nick" was no fool—and the client who worships the ground you walk on when you first take the case can turn into the client who wants to see you burn in Hell for eternity if you fail to work the miracles he or she was expecting.

poorly draft a key document. Sometimes they later lose a malpractice suit, as a defendant, because of this. Someday, one of these lawyers will sue his or her legal alma mater for damages because that attorney had been so poorly trained in these areas. And if *I'm* presiding in the court that hears that case, I will grant summary judgment in his or her favor. (Yes, I know, it would be reversed on appeal. But it would be a shot heard 'round the American legal world.)

If legal research and legal writing are the two most important skills a lawyer should have, why do law schools—everywhere—habitually ignore them? If you'll recall chapter 4 and part of chapter 14, you know. But just in case:

It is simply impossible to correct students' papers in a casual way. Remember chapter 3's discussion of how easy it is for law professors to grade final exams? To properly grade a legal *writing* assignment, the instructor must *edit* it. This involves a lot more work than just making a "model answer" checklist and awarding points based on how well a student "spotted issues." Also, if *everyone* in the class were expected to learn to write at least reasonably well, then it would be extremely difficult to decide who gets the "A" and who gets the "A-." And it would be much more subjective than an issue-spotting checklist. (Legal writing courses are nearly always on a pass/fail basis—so students give it *bottom* priority.)

And remember chapter 3's discussion of how students don't get any meaningful feedback? The essence of learning how to do legal writing involves extensive—and often intense—1:1 feedback. (Correcting and instructing with regard to legal research is much easier, in comparison.)

Legal research and legal writing, properly taught, involve *many* homework assignments, not just a final exam. A proper legal writing course, for example, could easily take up an entire year. During that year, students would draft letters and memos, contracts, deeds, wills, agreed divorce settlements, releases, pleadings, motions, responses to motions, proposed court orders and injunctions, bench memos, trial briefs, and appellate briefs.

To teach legal research and legal writing *well* requires a substantial commitment of resources. The student-faculty ratio for the class has to be very low, or else each instructor has to put in far more hours than the average professor in order to do the job right.

—But you can't use just an ordinary writing teacher. You have to have teachers who are trained in the Law, who know how to Think Like a Lawyer. In general, such people are not available. There are few attorneys who are really good at legal research or legal writing. It isn't worth their while to teach, given that doing the job right requires such a huge commitment of time and effort...and a huge pay cut, probably.

However, it *would* be worth their time if the law school itself valued it. The typical legal writing instructor is very low on the academic totem pole, below assistant professors. Whether or not a licensed and experienced attorney, he or she is paid only chicken-feed. And if the school has a full-time "Director of Legal Writing," the chicken feed becomes chicken *shit* when you calculate it on an hourly basis. With few exceptions, the only attorneys who apply for such a job are those who probably can't write at all. (At my school, the attorney was the underling. The Director was a non-lawyer Ph.D. in English...who wrote some of the dullest and most obscure prose I have ever read.) Meanwhile, as mentioned in chapter 4, the regular professors are pulling down $50,000-$100,000 a year for 6-8 hours a week, max, of "teaching." (And at my school, a full prof's *base* salary was considerably higher than $100,000.)

If a law school valued legal writing, it would allocate at least $120,000 to hire a director of legal writing who would work 30-40 hours a week...and the school would hear from many *qualified* applicants for the post.

As chapter 13 noted, most law schools provide real-world clinics only grudgingly, to placate alumni demands. The quality of the clinics, as a learning experience, is typically low. But if the law schools were to allocate the resources necessary to make the clinics more valuable, it would cut in to the law schools' net profits. The bottom line is the most important thing. As chapter 14 stated, the profits a university makes off its law school are important to it. The same bottom-line consideration applies regarding legal research and legal writing. On a cost-benefit basis, it simply isn't worth it to the law school—no matter how disastrous its effect on future lawyers... and on those future lawyers' future clients.

Of Insecurity—and Snob Appeal

However, I believe there's a second (and perhaps more important) reason why the law school powers-that-be all but ignore these crucial skills: legal research and legal writing are too bound up with the *real* world.

Before the rise of the law school, future lawyers learned their skills by serving as apprentices to practicing attorneys. It was training-in-the-trenches, learning-by-doing (under the presumably watchful eye of the Master). As chapter 3's discussion of Christopher Langdell showed, law school went to the opposite extreme: the retreat from the real world into the ivory tower.

Law school professors fancy themselves intellectuals. Yet, they're just law school graduates who now teach the law; nothing more. (Once in awhile, a professor is not even a licensed attorney.) They aren't Ph.Ds. Granted, most Ph.Ds aren't intellectuals, either, but at least a graduate school in the liberal arts or natural sciences does require at least some intellectual ability...sometimes.

Do not get me wrong: It's pretty hard to survive law school if you're a dum-dum. The average lawyer is more intelligent than the average lay person. And the average law professor is more intelligent than the average lawyer. But high intelligence does not necessarily mean intellect. There is a difference. Richard Hofstadter, the historian, made a distinction between intellectuals and "intellectual journeymen."* (He borrowed the distinction from Max Weber, the German legal theorist, sociologist, and economist.) An intellectual, he said, "lives *for* ideas." The "intellectual journeyman," in contrast, "lives *off* ideas." Lawyers are in the latter category. —So are law professors, though they would never admit it. Let's get real: How "intellectual" is a subject such as "commercial paper"? —or "agency"? —or "real estate transactions"? —or "federal income tax"? Sure, they require intelligence. Reasoning, too. But so does auto mechanics, especially today.

Law school professors know that they aren't engaged in a genuinely intellectual endeavor. And they seem to think there's something wrong with that. I don't. But what *is* wrong is that law professors like to *pretend* they're intellectuals. Because few of them really are, though, most apparently haven't any idea of what the life of the mind is all about—in the sense discussed by, say, Hannah Arendt (or Richard Hofstadter and Max Weber). Yet, they want to be *thought of* as intellectuals, and they know that professors are *supposed* to be intellectuals. And so, they mistake form for substance. They believe that if they don't allow anything "practical" (such as a worthwhile legal clinic) then this somehow makes them more "intellectual."

For the same reason, they write in an "academic" style. (And it's the style of the Ph.D. Director of Legal Writing I just mentioned.) You know what I'm talking about. They apparently believe that verbal garbage is the mark of a real egghead. If you can use big words that ordinary people can't understand, and put them together in sentences that even well-educated people have trouble comprehending, you must be an intellectual...or, at least, a lawyer.

So, lawyers write legaldygook to impress their clients—and to maintain a superior position *vis-à-vis* mere laypeople. Law professors write in "academic" style, for similar reasons. Neither lawyers nor law professors have any interest in seeing law students learn how to write *well*.

The "only" people who do have an interest in seeing law students learn how to right well are *your* future clients, juries, and judges. —But in the *real* world of the law, those are the *only* people who *count*.

---

* The term "journeyman," by the way, is from the old crafts guilds. A new worker started as an Apprentice. Upon learning the basics, he become a Journeyman—and stayed a Journeyman for years, perhaps for the rest of his life. ("He" and "his" are correct. There were no women in the old crafts guilds.) Few achieved the title of Master, as in Master Carpenter. Today, in labor unions, the move from apprentice to "master" is routine, and automatic.

The Traditional Argument

There are those who say that it's a waste of time to compose a legal document that's intelligible. Unless you go solo, your supervising attorney will not allow you to create your own documents. Instead, you'll be pulling documents from the files. This "boilerplate" did the job for other lawyers in previous matters. And all you'll be doing, in effect, is cutting and pasting. You'll just be changing things here and there to adapt the "model" to your client's needs. Last, they point out that "form documents" (*generic* forms, where you just fill in the blanks) have, along with the model documents, been *tested* in court and have stood up to judicial scrutiny.

All true. However, in a larger sense, all false.

First, there are some documents for which there will be *nothing* in the files, and for which there is *no* generic form. The most complex example is a trial brief or an appellate brief; the simplest, a progress report to a client. If you can't write well, what you'll provide will not exactly make a favorable impression on the recipients.

Second, while it's (usually, but not always) true the model and form documents have been successfully tested in practice, that's not necessarily to their credit. Often, if the documents had been drafted better in the first place, no one would have challenged them. There should have been no need to put them to the test, at all. Further, even though *one* court interpreted a convoluted document *one* way, some day some *other* court might choose to emphasize a *different* part of the bafflegab—and interpret the document's meaning *another* way. Happens all the time. (Oil and gas leases are notorious for this.) If the document is simple and direct (relatively speaking, of course— considering that this is a legal document), it's hard for a court to contradict its "plain meaning." (However, that happens too—-but rarely.)

Third, once you've created a *well-written* document for a specific situation, you can use *that* as your model, or turn it into a generic form and store it on a disk. So, your initial investment of time and effort will save you a lot of both in the future, and will yield a good return. Besides, you don't have to create your first document from scratch. In fact, it would be risky to do so. But you're almost never completely on your own, anyway. In addition to the documents in the files, you can turn to "form books." These contain hundreds of samples—a form for nearly every purpose. In any given state, probably at least one or two publishers prepare these. So, start with the model document or generic form. If all else fails, search the courthouse files (they're open to the public) for cases similar to yours. Make copies of what you can use. Then cut the unnecessary words, taking out as much of the legalese as possible. Turn it into plain English. Add what your client needs.

Fourth—and related to the third—a document that's readily understandable lets you *think* about it more clearly when you want to use it as a model or form. Even though a lawyer understands legaldygook, no attorney in his or her right mind wants to go through such muck. There's a tendency to grab and use anything that seems relevant. Without the legalese, it's easier to spot what fits the new situation, what doesn't. You can more easily see what to add, delete, or alter. This saves time, without turning into a situation where haste makes waste.

If you also consider the advantages of making the client part of your team, the argument for legalese fails.

However, if you work someplace where you *must* use boilerplate legaldygook, so be it. But you still should avoid it any chance you get—such as in letters to clients.

Don't Leave It to the Paralegal

There has been an unfortunate trend in the law in recent years: the rise of the legal assistant. The legal assistant (a.k.a. paralegal) is supposed to be analogous to the dental assistant or medical technician. However, such dental and medical personnel have clearly-defined and clearly limited duties. What's more, most often, their work is done in the presence of both the patient and the supervising professional. None of this is so regarding paralegals.

Instead, attorneys have been using paralegals as cut-rate associates, letting the assistants do the work that only a *lawyer* should do. This way, the attorney can bill at the *lawyer's* rate for work the *paralegal* did. Because the client is not present, the client is none the wiser. (One partner in a law firm, who is trial lawyer, told me she hates to go to court, even though she's very good. "When I'm in court," she said, "I can only bill the *one* client for my time. But when I'm in the office, I can have five paralegals simultaneously doing work that goes out over *my* signature. So I can turn *one* hour of my time into *five*." She makes a lot of money. I don't see why she doesn't go the extra step and bill other clients even when she's with only the one client in court. Maybe this minimal honesty enables her to keep her conscience clear. And I know a solo practitioner whose one paralegal does all the work in a certain area of law. The attorney himself knows absolutely nothing of that area of law, and has no intention of learning. With clients, he refers to the paralegal as "my associate." The clients assume the paralegal is a lawyer. They never realize the significance of the fact that the "associate" never signs off on anything. Only the licensed attorney does that—although the assistant signs for him, above the attorney's typewritten name. This paralegal, naturally, makes more than the norm. So far, this duo has gotten away with their fraud, as has the trial lawyer just mentioned.)

I do believe this is a big reason why many law school grads are having such trouble finding jobs as attorneys. Why hire a lawyer to do legal work when you can hire a paralegal—many of whom are sharper than many lawyers—at a fraction of the cost? There have even been recent law school graduates, licensed attorneys, who have—in desperation—applied to law factories for jobs as legal assistants—and have been willing to be paid accordingly.

Granted, paralegals haven't started representing clients in court yet. But this is small comfort. (Besides, I know of some cases where *that's* happened, too, in routine hearings—with the knowledge of everyone but the absent client. Nor were the legal assistants licensed attorneys.)

Paralegals know the procedures for doing legal research. And they know how to crank out documents. But they don't have the understanding a lawyer has—or, rather, the understanding a lawyer *ought* to have. They miss things. Important things. The significance of a passage in a case reporter can escape them. And they don't know how to "parse" the cases. The significance of a passage in a document can escape them.

Don't *you* do business this way. (But if that's the way you are, we both know there's nothing to stop you.)

If you intend *not* to do business this way, learn how to do legal research and legal writing yourself…and how to do it right. Then you'll be less tempted to rely on a legal assistant when you shouldn't—and you'll know enough about *good* legal research and legal writing to realize that what most paralegals (and attorneys) do is sub-standard work. If you have any self-respect at all, you won't accept anything less than quality work…not from your subordinates, and not from yourself.*

—Which brings us back to the law schools' pedagogical malpractice: If you haven't the foggiest idea of what really *good* legal research is (i.e., beyond a superficial perusal of the standard sources), or what *good* legal writing is, how can you be expected to be able to tell good work from bad?

Contracts Craftsmanship

I am unable to sufficiently emphasize the importance of being able to draft contracts well. Very few lawyers can do it. (Before I went to law school, I'd hired an attorney to write one for me in a business deal. It was so poorly written—even containing misspelled words!—that even I, as a complete layman, knew it was worthless. I refused to accept it, and sought out a new attorney. The first one, wisely, did not present me with a bill.)

Here's an example of poor legal drafting that ended up costing a client a bunch of money. It involved an agreement between a builder and the intended householder. They made a deal whereby the householder would

---

* Lest you get the wrong idea: A paralegal can be excellent for doing routine legal work. (And computer programs contain checklists anyone can follow to make sure he or she does the work correctly.) Examples would be simple wills and simple divorces. There are many others. Today even the small-time practitioners have all but priced themselves out of the market for these. So, many people are doing without. Instead of requiring legal assistants to always work under the supervision of a licensed attorney—with the higher bill that automatically entails—I believe the paralegals who provide *these* services should be free to set up shop on their own.

pay on a cost-plus basis: The cost of materials and labor, plus a 20% fee as the builder's profit. They also put a "cap" on the amount the householder would have to pay. This is the relevant passage from their contract:

> It is specifically agreed by and between the parties that notwithstanding the agreement hereinabove the owners shall not be required, under the terms of this agreement, to pay the contractor any amount in excess of the sum of Three Hundred fifty Thousand Dollars ($350,000.00), which is the estimated cost of construction, plus the fee provided herein.

Do you see the problem? —Ambiguity: Was the $350,000 the cap? Or was that just the maximum total of *costs* (materials and labor)—on which the builder was then *also* entitled to a 20% *fee* ($70,000)? Because of that one comma after the phrase "which is the estimated cost of construction," the court ruled the agreement meant the latter. The householder had to pay $420,000, plus prejudgment interest, postjudgment interest, court costs— and his own attorneys' fees, which were substantial, because this case went up to that state's supreme court.

The contract was filled with crappy legalese. I'll bet whoever drafted it— probably working with boilerplate—lost sight of that vital comma amid the gibberish. (Sometimes, though, I wonder if this isn't part of some great make-work scheme on the part of the legal profession. Good drafting would probably cut the number of contracts lawsuits in half.)

Some Rewards
You Might Not Have Thought Of

If you've learned how to write fairly well before you start law school, and then you make sure you learn how to do *legal* writing—and legal research— quite well in first-year, you will have the edge regarding other possibilities...

First, it may be that when you return in the fall after year one, you'll find that you did not Make Law Review on grades. But you'll still have a good shot at Making Law Review in the *write-on* competition (discussed in chapter 12).

Second, as a general rule, only those who've Made Law Review have a chance of getting a student Note or Commentary published. Even then, the only Law Review that would consider it is the one the author works for. So it's a long shot. But it sure Looks Good on the Résumé if you succeed, especially if you want to become a professor. (And if your "write-on" essay is good enough, you might be able to turn that into a Note or Commentary.)

Third, every year there are dozens of legal essay contests for law students. Typically, the winner gets a few thousand dollars. If you win, that achievement Looks Good on the Résumé, too—and don't forget the money.

The next-to-last reason to learn to get good at legal research and legal writing, though certainly far from the least, is this: More and more, especially in the higher courts, judges ask their *clerks* to write the court's Opinion. (Judicial clerkships—as contrasted with judicial internships—are discussed in chapter 20.) Sometimes the judge asks the clerk to do just a first draft, and has told the clerk what he or she wants in it. But sometimes the judge asks the clerk to do even the final draft—which the judge then just touches up here and there. (Without mentioning any names, it is known that at least one Opinion of the U.S. Supreme Court was written entirely by a 25-year-old clerk.)

Part of the reason for this is that at least some judges can't write worth a damn. But the bigger reason, especially today, is that the judges themselves don't have time for it. Yet, they want their Opinions to make them look good. So, they want to hire clerks who can write well—both as to style and as to logic, etc..

If you can do that, and can provide writing samples to your prospective judicial employer, you'll have the edge in getting the job—all other things being equal (which they seldom are). And once you're on the job, if it turns out you can write better than the judge's other clerk/s, guess who becomes the judge's favorite? (If you're clerking for a federal appellate judge who serves as a "feeder" to the U.S. Supreme Court, this can make all the difference in the world. And even if you aren't, it can have a big impact because of the favorable remarks he or she will make about you to other judges and attorneys—and to faculty members at prestigious law schools where you just might be hoping to get an offer to teach.)

The favorable remarks, most likely, won't emphasize your writing or research ability. Instead, they'll concern you skill at conducting a "lawyer-like analysis" of the facts and the law. But your acumen will have manifested itself primarily in your formal legal research, case parsing, and especially in your legal writing—which combines them.

The final reason for you to get good at legal writing and legal research is that, quite often, Very Important Lawyers like to have articles published with their names on them, on topics within the law, as a form of public relations. Naturally, such lawyers are too important to do the work themselves. So—as often happens with professors in law school—they turn it over to an underling. That could be you. Sometimes you even get "co-" authorship credit when it's published. Regardless, the boss knows who did the work. And as long as the work was well-received upon publication, the boss will continue to Take Good Care of You.

One More Time:
Getting the Jump
on Your Adversary

As chapter 1 said, Legal Research and Legal Writing are courses that don't count "now"—i.e., in law school...but which can make or break your legal *career*. These skills are indeed crucial.

As mentioned in chapter 6, final exams test your skill at legal writing—sort of. But the legal writing you'll be doing once you get out into the real world will be different. For one thing, you'll have more time in which to do it. But the subjects you'll be writing about won't be as "simple" as first-year exams will be (if only in hindsight).

The first point at which these skills can make or break your career might be as early as your summer clerkships while you're still in law school. Chapter 12 said each firm will assume you already have what it takes to be a good lawyer, because you got good grades in first-year; and what they're mainly interested in is your character and personality—to see if you're a good "fit" with that firm. True. However, they'll be paying you a lot of money while you're a summer associate, and they might want to test your efficiency.

They'll do this by giving you tasks in briefing a point of law. Often these will be quasi-make-work, simple projects. But how quickly you complete your assignments, and how well, helps the firm gauge your potential productivity. No matter how good your social skills, if you don't make the grade with respect to the bottom line, your law school grades won't save you.

If you clerk at a firm two summers in a row, this test will intensify during your second time around. In any event, get good at these critical skills by the time you finish your first year of law school. And as with everything else, your law school will do very little to help you: your first-year courses in legal research and legal writing will be quickie introductions, not serious skills-building programs.

Legal Research - On-Site

Because legal research doesn't count in first-year, you might think there's no point in getting a head start on it. However, if you already know how to do it right before you even set foot inside the law school, it will save you time and perhaps even trouble. (Legal Research is usually just pass/fail. But that doesn't mean it's a snap.) —And don't forget how important it might be to the success of your summer clerkship/s.

If you follow the recommendations of chapter 5, and visit law school book-stores before you enroll, you can pick up the assigned textbook then, perhaps even a used copy. (It's a real textbook, not a casebook.) However, if you're still in college (or high school), here's a better buy— *Legal Research: How to Find and Understand the Law,* by Stephen Elias and Susan Levinkind. It's $20, paperback from Nolo Press. It contains a number of research exercises—and then, separately, tells you what you should have found and where you should have found it. The book also has information on how to do on-line legal research. You can find *Legal Research* in—or order it through—a regular bookstore. Another good book is the *Legal Research Guide: Patterns and Practice, 2d ed.*, by Bonita K. Roberts and Linda L. Schlueter. It's an $18 paperback, from the Michie Company.

If you already know how to do basic legal research, the American Bar Association's Law Student Division has a couple of booklets that will help you perfect a systematic approach. Both are called *A Streamlined Briefing Technique,* by Clyde Emery. The first, the "White" edition, has 45 pages. It's for those in the following 11 states: California, Florida, Illinois, Indiana, Maryland, New York, Ohio, Pennsylvania, Texas, Virginia, and West Virginia. The second, the "Blue" edition, has 38 pages, and is for those in all other jurisdictions. I went to law school in one of the "White" states, and now practice in another. In both, I found Emery's *Streamlined Briefing Technique* (White Edition) invaluable. (I've had no need to use the Blue edition, and haven't seen it. However, I assume it's comparable to the White.) It tells you everything you need to do, step by step, and how to do it right. It was published in 1973. It has not been updated. But that is no problem. Just keep in mind that, for example, the most recent *American Law Reports* series is now the 5th rather than the 4th. (ALR is a legal encyclopedia.)

Whereas the ABA itself overcharges for each of its publications, its Law Student Division charges too little, really. Each edition of the *Streamlined Briefing Technique* is just $2.75. (That's no misprint. It's two dollars, seventy-five cents.) Get the one for your jurisdiction. In terms of publications for law students and lawyers, either of these is the best retail buy you will *ever* find.

More on CALR

Legal research in a three-dimensional library is very time-consuming. But legal research in an on-line (or CD-ROM) library is comparatively fast— if you know how to do it right. (And, of course, you can use the materials mentioned above to guide your CALR, too.) You can save a lot of time and tedium. The book you need is *always* on the "shelf," with no pages cut out (which sometimes happens). And the ability to import material on-line will, alone, be a big help, because you don't have to photocopy hard-copy materials and then type their contents into your computer.

In law school, you get minimal training in on-line legal research. (At my school, we got one session of about 90 minutes. That was it.) Even if you're a whiz with computers, it takes a lot of practice to master CALR. So, you will need to put in *much* more time on it beyond the perfunctory training session. As mentioned earlier, you can do this at no charge to you.

Take advantage of such a wonderful opportunity. After you've had your initial training, find out when the Westlaw and Lexis reps will be at your school other than when they're conducting more training sessions. Then try to get them to help you, so you can improve your skills beyond the rudimentary ones you acquired during your own training session. You don't have to rely solely on the visiting rep, though. The services have toll-free numbers to call for assistance in conducting your search. You can learn a lot from the person at the other end of the line—especially if you call during the grave-yard shift. (That person is an attorney, by the way.)

Further, in some cities, they provide additional training for free, at their local office. (They're trying to get the paralegals to come in, so the paralegals will make greater use of the on-line services their law firms subscribe to.) But *these* training sessions allow you to work on *your* legal research tasks, not merely the made-up exercises you will have done as part of your train-ing in law school. You might have to be persistent to find out where and when the sessions are held. The best time to take advantage of this, for you, is while you're on vacation from law school. (But if your law school is in a city that has these sessions, the Westlaw or Lexis people might let you in even during a semester.)

Once you're in practice, you should carefully weigh the costs of any on-line research against the benefits. (CD-ROMs, in contrast, are clearly cost-effective...unless you have to buy them yourself.) The best time to use the *on-line* research is when you want to see if anything's happened in the law since the date of the last hard-copy materials you have. (There's always a lag between the time a regulation, statute, or court decision is issued and the time it's available in hard-copy. But the "computer research" services often have these texts available on-line within hours.)

If you're going to a hearing to discuss a crucial point of law you've been researching, it's worthwhile to do some quick on-line legal research a day or two before. You don't want your opponent to pull the legal rug out from under you, especially right in front of the judge. (Sometimes, by the way, your opponent will pull a case out of thin air, claiming that it was just decided within the past few days or the past couple of weeks. Surprise, surprise, the case is supposedly "on all fours"...and goes against you. It's truly gratifying to be able to call this liar's bluff—and you can do that only if you've done some final checking of your own.)

Westlaw does two programs that can make you look *real* good in your employer's eyes. Both are intended to help you do cost-effective CALR. The first is the "Summer Associate Program," the second, the "Judicial Clerkship Program." (I assume the latter is also available for those doing court *internships*.) Call Westlaw at (800) 850-9378 for more information.

Steven L. Emanuel, the commercial outline entrepreneur, has written *Lexis-Nexis for Law Students, 2d ed..* Published in 1995, it's a $17 paper-back, available through Lexis. The Lexis toll-free number was in chapter 5, and is repeated in the appendix. West has similar publications.*

---

  * My research assistant and I spent two months trying to get copies of product literature about these. We were referred to someone in the Media Relations department there. During two months' time, she repeatedly

Legal Writing

As for legal writing, any law school bookstore will have a selection in this area. But most of them will be textbooks for that school's course. That means they'll probably be somewhat expensive.

Here are three books that, while not specifically for legal writing, are 1) invaluable, and 2) cheap. The first is *The Elements of Style,* by William Strunk, Jr., with additional material from E.B. White. It's just six bucks, in paperback. The second is *Simple & Direct,* by Jacques Barzun, a $15 paperback. The third is *Essentials of English: A Practical Guide to the Mastery of English.* The author is L. Sue Baugh, and the book is a seven-dollar paperback. You can't go wrong by getting these, reading them, and applying their lessons. (I own, and use, all three.)

There are also several good books that get into the technical nitty-gritty of writing. In alphabetical order, the first is *The Associated Press Style Book,* which costs $14 in paperback. Second is the *Chicago Manual of Style*, now in its 14th edition. The price for this hardcover book is $34. Next is the *Gregg Reference Manual,* with William A. Sabin listed as author of the 7th edition now in print. Available in paperback for $26, it also comes in a spiral-bound format for $19. Fourth is the12th edition of the *Harbrace College Handbook*. Published in hardcover ("cloth"), its price is $23. Then there's the *The Little, Brown Handbook,* a hardcover title in its 6th edition, which sells for $27. Sixth is the *Merriam Webster Style Manual,* an $18 hardbound work. Seventh and last is *A Practical English Grammar,* 4th ed., by A.J. Thomson and A.V. Martinet, for $13 in paperback.

As chapter 6 mentioned, normally, in expository writing, the "KISS" rule applies: "Keep It Simply, Smarty." These books help you adhere to that rule. But in legal writing, the rule becomes "KISS-A-MIC." —"Keep It Simple, Smarty...and Make It Complete." That is, you must try to cover all the bases. The following books will help you do that...

There is at least one book written specifically for legal applications, which is not a textbook. This is Bryan A. Garner's *The Elements of Legal Style.* As you can see, it's modeled on the Strunk & White book for laypeople. It's $25, in hardcover. I have a copy, and recommend it. (Garner also compiled the *Dictionary of Modern Legal Usage,* mentioned in chapter 5.)

The "grand old man" of clear legal writing is David Mellinkoff. His book, *Legal Writing: Sense and Nonsense,* is published by West in paperback, for $19. I don't recommend it, though. It seemed boring to me.

either promised to send material, or else said that it had already been sent. We never got anything. I realize that—with sales close to a billion dollars a year—West's employees perhaps can thumb their noses at anyone they choose. But if this is a taste of things to come now that Thomson has acquired West, then a lot of customers are going to have a very bad taste in their mouths about West Publishing.

A third work is Richard C. Wydick's *Plain English for Lawyers, 3d ed..* This paperback from Carolina Academic Press costs just under $10.

My favorite is *Plain English Pleadings,* by Carol Ann Wilson. It's a Prentice-Hall paperback, just over $26. However, it's written for those who already know their way around a legal document, and who are familiar with legal terminology. So don't get it as your first book on legal writing. Wait until you're ready to go from apprentice to journey-person status; then Wilson's book will be the best one you can get.

I haven't found a book exclusively on contract-drafting that's both excellent and cheap. Scott J. Burnham, of the University of Montana Law School, has done a book called *Drafting Contracts, 2d ed.* (1993). The price is about $18, in paperback. It's published by the Michie Company. (*Drafting Contracts* is also available on disk, through Lexis, for the same price.) It provides lots of exercises—which is good. However, it's a textbook. Because it's a textbook, there are *no answers.* (The answers are all in the teacher's manual, which you can't get...unless you're sneaky.) Unless your school has a course that uses the Burnham textbook, you're out of luck. Even so, it is very good. As part of learning how to draft better contracts, you will find yourself understanding contract law much better, too.

Michie does a second Burnham book, *The Contract-Drafting Guidebook.* This one's for attorneys. It contains additional material not found in the student book. But this one is $60, and hardcover. If you can't spare the money in law school, let it go. But if you enter the private sector, especially as a solo, this book is a *must.* And even before you become a lawyer, it's good to have, because it's never too early to start practicing on the drafting of contracts. (Even if your school doesn't have a course in contract drafting, your legal writing instructor might be willing to critique your work. —Just try to make sure that your instructor knows his or her craft.)

As you will see in chapter 20, you should subscribe to publications for lawyers, and should join organizations for lawyers and law students. Chapter 20 recommends this in connection with your job search. However, there's another reason, and it's relevant here. By joining organizations and subscribing to publications, you get on mailing lists. For most people, "junk mail" is a nuisance. But you should *welcome* direct mail advertisements that relate to the Law.

Because the law school is not on your side, the law school will do little to help you become a good lawyer. (For example, the *Streamlined Briefing Technique* was never mentioned in my legal research class. My Moot Court partner discovered it, and shared the news with me. And remember the anecdote in chapter 7's addendum regarding *O'Connor's Federal Rules.*) But those who already *are* lawyers (sometimes) want to get good, or better, at what they do. And so, the lawyer publications have ads for workshops, books, CD-ROMs, etc.. And by getting on mailing lists, you will receive direct mail solicitations. *Take advantage of these.* With student I.D., you can often get a discount.

For example, when I was still in law school I signed up for a class just because the course description promised that it would devote time to learning how to draft contracts in that subject area. That was just a come-on. We had only *one* contract-drafting exercise, and it was a joke. (The professor was the guy I mentioned in chapter 4, who loved to lead students on and then leave them empty-handed. Much later, I learned he had never drafted a contract in his life.) It was beginning to look as though I'd graduate from law school with absolutely no training whatsoever in contract drafting—just like all my fellow students.

However, I had subscribed to a newspaper for lawyers, and that got me on a mailing list. One day I got a piece of "junk mail" announcing a two-day workshop in contract drafting. I called, arranged for a student rate, signed up, went—and loved it. Later, I took another two-day workshop, at a student discount, on how to draft litigation documents—and loved that, too. Because it was just a local thing, I'm not listing the vendor. However, if you subscribe to publications or join organizations, you will likely have similar opportunities, wherever you are.

I know of just two firms that operate nationwide. The first is Kinder Legal. (The "i" is short.) Its founder is Gary Kinder. His program is called "Getting the Judge to Say 'Yes.'" He charges $275 for a day-long session.

Kinder Legal can be reached as follows: 1326 Fifth Avenue - Suite 440, Seattle, Washington 98101; telephone (206) 622-3810; fax (206) 622-3866; and the e-mail is gk@kinderlegal.com..

The second firm is Law Prose, Inc.. Its founder is Bryan A. Garner, author of *The Elements of Legal Style (*discussed in this chapter) and *A Dictionary of Modern Legal Usage* (discussed in chapter 5). He does two separate writing programs, but does them back-to-back. The first is "Advanced Legal Writing & Editing." This covers general legal writing, including litigation documents. The second is "Advanced Legal Drafting." It's geared more toward legal instruments such as contracts. Doing just one program, or doing them separately, costs $295 for one day. But take them back-to-back, and it's $550, a saving of $40.

Law Prose, Inc., can be reached as follows: 5949 Sherry Lane - Suite 1280, Dallas, Texas 75225-8008; or by fax to either (214) 691-9294 or (214) 696-2611.

I have taken all these courses, and highly recommend them.

Yes, this seems like a lot of money. But as you've surely noticed by now, anything associated with the Law tends to be costly. True, there's no way to directly measure the benefit. However, I do believe this is "bread" upon the waters, that'll come back to you tenfold.

Perhaps, for law students, Gary Kinder or Bryan Garner would be willing to discount the fee. It's worth a try. (Nothing ventured, nothing gained.)

Part IV:

Lift-Off for the "Real" World of the Law

Chapter 17 - MBE, MPRE

In all but four states (Indiana, Iowa, Louisiana, and Washington) and in Washington, D.C., you must take the Multistate Bar Examination (MBE) as part of your bar exam. It lasts one day. It's given twice a year: the last Wednesday in February and July. It has two sets of 100 multiple-choice questions; one's in the morning, the other in the afternoon. Each session lasts three hours. That's an average of one question every minute and 45 seconds.

The MBE covers six subjects: Contracts, Torts, Property, Constitutional Law, Criminal Law, and Evidence. All except Evidence are *first-year* subjects. (Evidence replaces Civil Procedure, the other Big Six subject of year one.) Of the 200 questions, Contracts and Torts each has 40. All the others have 30 apiece.

The distribution of sub-topics is also known. For Con Law, six questions concern the separation of powers within the federal government; six concern federalism itself. In Torts, half the questions deal with negligence. In Crim Law, five cover what are called "inchoate" crimes; six, homicide. Seventeen of the Contracts questions ask about contract formation and consideration. Nine of Property's questions deal with Estates and Future Interests. Hearsay is the subject of one-third of the Evidence questions; five involve impeachment and rehabilitation of witnesses; two ask about writings as evidence. Et cetera.

There's no order in which they're presented. You might get a series of questions each of which is in a different subject from the one before. Or, you might get ten in a row on the same subject.

MBE questions range in difficulty from easy to hard. On a scale of 1-10, the easiest is probably about a two, the hardest, about an 11. The Multistate people analyze candidates' performances for consistency. Those who score, say, below 50% ought to have incorrectly answered a disproportionately large number of the hardest questions—and vice-versa. Sometimes, the Multistate people discover something's wrong: for example, what they thought was a question of medium difficulty turns out to have been very confusing; even the best candidates often got it wrong. Sometimes, they throw that question out. *Everyone* gets credit for it, regardless of his or her answer.

Each time the MBE is given, 30 questions are taken from each of the two preceding exams and repeated in the new one. These 60 questions vary in difficulty. For each of those sets of 30, there was a relationship between candidates' overall performance and their performance on those 30. (That's a big reason why they were selected for later use. No doubt, at least a few of the 60 questions taken from the preceding two exams were questions that appeared on *both* of them.)

Each exam mostly contains completely new questions, of course. The questions repeated from old exams function as a "control." The new questions are supposed to come out the same way as the control set: Those who do poorly on the overall exam should also do poorly on the new questions that are really hard, while doing better on the less difficult ones. Those who do quite well on the overall exam are expected to do quite well on the new questions, too. Sometimes it doesn't work out that way. Then, once again, some of these questions are tossed out and *everyone* gets credit for them.

The Multistate folks feed all of this into a computer and do some very fancy statistical work for what they call "equating." It's supposed to equalize the overall difficulty of the MBE, from one exam to another, in measuring the results. (The matter is further complicated by the fact that the typical performance on the February bar exam is considerably lower than that on the typical July bar exam.) You get two scores: raw and scaled. The raw score is pre-equating. The scaled score is post-equating. It's the one that counts. So, if you get a 70% scaled score on your Multistate, this means you would have gotten a 70% if you'd graduated from law school five years earlier and taken it then. That's what they say—for what it's worth.

The average raw score is around 128. That's just 64%. "Equating" typically adds 10-20 points. However, because each point is just 0.5% (remember, *200* questions), the average scaled score in recent years has been between 136 and 145. Even *that's* just 68% - 72.5%.

Picky, Picky, Picky—and Tricky, Tricky, Tricky

The Multistate has many, many trick questions. But even the straightforward questions usually aren't easy. They test *very* narrow applications of legal rules. Often, the correct answer is a very narrow *exception* to a legal rule. If you don't know "everything" backwards *and* forwards, you'll screw up. That's a big reason why the average score is so low. It's not that candidates are lazy about preparing for the bar exam, nor are they stupid. They're just overwhelmed by minutiae. (It's said that the Multistate examiners regard *10,000* points of law as fair game.)

The potential choices nearly always include at least one *incorrect* statement of the law. If you've mastered the material, the incorrect statement/s can be quickly eliminated from consideration. Quite often, however, at least one of the choices will be a *correct* statement of the law—but that correct statement is *irrelevant* to the question. Frequently, each potential answer states an element of a cause of action that's relevant to the question. Each of these elements is correctly stated. However, you have to spot the one element that's the *key* to the problem. Or, *all* the possible answers state the *same* proposition of law—just in different ways. You have to select the one that's *most* correct. This is the one statement of the law that most *exactly* fits the facts of the question, the statement that hits the nail right on the head. The "wrong" answers are the ones that are unnecessarily broad—or too narrow. Or, it's the other way around: All of the answers are *wrong*. You're told to pick the one that's *most* wrong. So, you have to *reverse* your normal way of thinking.

As if that isn't bad enough, the "fact patterns" are often *bizarre*. The MBE Examiners want to *disorient* you. So they sometimes present facts that *defy* common sense, that *contradict* anything that could be called reasonable. It's like Lewis Carroll's poem, "The Walrus and the Carpenter"—

> "The time has come," the Walrus said,
> "to talk of many things: Of shoes, and ships,
> and sealing wax; of cabbages, and kings...
> and why the sea *is* boiling hot,
> and *whether* pigs have wings."*

That way, the only thing you can rely on to answer the question is your own knowledge of the legal point at issue.

—And all of this concerns the *"straightforward"* questions.

One type of *trick* question relies on candidates' proclivity to jump to conclusions. For example, there's a lawsuit. Two answers say the plaintiff wins, two say plaintiff loses. You know, from reading the facts, that plaintiff wins. Yet, both of the answers that say, flat out, that "plaintiff wins" are *wrong*. One of the answers that starts off by saying "plaintiff *loses*" is the correct choice. Here's why: the "plaintiff loses" answers include the word "unless," or "if," followed by some basis for plaintiff to *win*. One—and only one—of these two is the *right* answer. The examiners really like to play with your mind this way. Any candidate who's feeling rattled probably won't even have the presence of mind to catch the phrase that turns one of the "wrong" answers into the only *right* one.

My favorite among the trick questions is when two choices are in legalese, two in plain English. *Both* of the legalese answers are made-up nonsense (usually in Latin). The first of the plain-English answers is nonsense, too— and sometimes it's the very first choice presented. You read that, immedi- ately see it's nonsense—and perhaps subconsciously assume the other plain- English answer is also nonsense. To further throw you off the track, the second answer written in plain English is too broad, or too narrow, or other- wise just a little bit odd. *So, all four answers are bad answers.* The "right" answer is the only one that isn't *total* nonsense—even though it just barely makes sense itself. Thus, you're supposed to make the best of a bad situa- tion, choose the least of evils. Obviously, unless you know the ins-and-outs of everything, *cold,* you'll blow that question. The right answer (in this example) is the second one in plain English. Most students concentrate on the legalese choices, trying to figure out which one is right. Not only do they lose a point whichever of the two they pick, they also waste valuable time.

Here's another one that's barrels of fun: You get a *long* fact pattern,

---

* I have taken liberties with the punctuation, condensed the spacing, and supplied emphasis.

taking up half or three-fourths of the page. Then you get a series of as many as eight questions based on that one fact pattern Not only do you have to know the relevant law extremely well, you have to be able to keep that one set of facts in mind as you work through all the questions. But wait—it isn't just *one* set of facts: Instead, for the next question in this set, you'll get something like this— "FOR THIS QUESTION ONLY, assume that everything is the *opposite* of what we just told you." (Actually, it isn't quite that bad, but it feels that way during the exam.) Then, right after you've *un*-memorized everything because they changed the facts for one question, the very next question will be something like, "FOR *THIS* QUESTION ONLY, assume everything's back to the way it was at first—except that the *following* facts are different from *either* of the previous questions…" And so on.

Clever, these examiners. Only a twisted mentality could concoct many of these questions. When I was a child, some of the neighbor kids were really sick, mentally: They'd take a cat to an abandoned building and place a heavy weight on its tail, right up to the point where the tail joined the body; or they'd rig a harness and hang the cat by its hind-quarters upside-down from a rafter. A week or so later they'd return. You know what they found. Sometimes I strongly suspect that as adults they're drafting questions for the Multistate Bar Exam. They're far more perverse even than law school professors.

You have to be able to *very* quickly spot the key factor and the right answer. I've already quoted Scott Turow's statement, in *One L,* that first-year essay exams are "an intellectual quick-draw contest." but *One L* was written long before its author took the bar exam. Seems to me that description applies even better to the Multistate: Above, it was mentioned that you have about a minute and 45 seconds for each question. However, with four possible choices per question, you're going through *400* possible answers in 10,800 seconds (three hours). That's one possible answer every *27 seconds—* including the time it takes to read the *fact pattern!* Worse, the MBE comes at you from every imaginable angle, to throw you off balance.

The Multistate people "release"—i.e., divulge—some of the MBE questions they use, every year. For each, they announce what the right answer was and explain it. However, the questions they release are nearly always just the easy ones. The non-official sample questions are just as good, often better—and always harder.

In recent years, there have been candidates who got only one question right of the 30 on Property, or three right of the 30 on Con Law or Evidence, or five of the 30 on Crim, or just six of the 40 on Contracts. There have also been candidates who correctly answered *all* the questions in a given subject area. (I assume those are people from the bar review organizations, who regularly take the MBE to memorize questions so they can include them as practice questions in their bar review materials.)

By now, you have the idea. If passing the bar exam is supposed to be a measure of competence, then the Multistate ought to be a measure of competence. It isn't. Instead, the mental games the examiners play have subverted the substantive aspects. From law school to "barzam," the more things change the more they stay the same regarding lawyers-to-be.

Yes, it tests what it's supposed to: the things lawyers need to know and understand. Even "coming at you from every imaginable angle, to throw you off balance" also serves a purpose. —After all, in the real world of the Law, you'll encounter some amazing situations and arguments. And there are those who argue that the time pressure separates the men from the boys (or whatever the non-sexist phrase is that has replaced that one). But the gamesmanship of the examiners has long since overwhelmed the substantive aspect.

Each state chooses how much the MBE will count in computing the final score. The lowest weight appears to be 30%, the highest, one-half. (I'm sure it's possible to determine this for certain. However, based on the materials I obtained regarding various states' procedures and policies concerning their bar exams, it seems many states do not make these things clear—intentionally.) Irrespective of how the MBE and other portions of the bar exam are weighted, most states require a combined *scaled* score of 65% - 70%. (The lowest passing grade appears to be 55%; the highest appears to be 76%.)

It Doesn't End with the Multistate

Most states have other tests as part of their bar exam. These are given on the day/s before or after the MBE. At least one full day is devoted to essay exams. You're given a set of facts. You have to prove you can Think Like a Lawyer, state the relevant Black Letter Law, and apply it correctly. So far, sounds like a law school essay exam. But on a bar exam essay question, you're told who all the parties are and the nature of the problem/s. Your job is to figure out the solution/s and to explain why you're right. (If there is no solution, you also have to explain why.) Also unlike a law school essay exam, you have to show you know the *fine points* of your *state's* statutory and case law on the subject. You have between ten minutes and one hour per question.

Virtually every state administers its own essay questions. In addition, roughly a dozen give the Multistate Essay Exam (MEE—but the term "Multistate" always refers only to the MBE). As with the MBE, the MEE tests six subjects, but different from the MBE's: Business Organizations (the principal-agent relationship, corporations, and partnerships), Conflict of Laws, Commercial Transactions (commercial paper, sales of goods, and consumer goods credit), Family Law, Federal Civil Procedure, and Wills-Estates-Trusts. The states' essay exams cover a lot of the same ground, but—as mentioned—they test state-specific law in those areas. Typically, there are at least 12 subjects. New York's bar exam is said to be the hardest in the country. In part, it's because—so I am told—its essay portion tests *34* subjects. Nebraska is the only state that administers just the MEE for the essay portion of its bar exam, without additional state-specific questions.

Many states' bar exams continue into a third (or even a fourth) day (or half-a-day). This usually concerns that state's civil and criminal procedure, federal civil procedure, or various other matters. So, you've not bid adieu to your first-year civ pro course after all, even though it isn't on the Multistate. Instead, it's back—with a vengeance: because now you have to know that *and* your *state's* civ and crim pro rules...and often the subtle differences among them.

(California and Colorado also have a "performance skills test." You get a packet that includes a description of a fact situation, copies of cases and statutes, etc.. You then analyze everything, using the supplied cases and statutes as legal research. Then draft a legal document. It could be a letter advising a client, a memo to a supervising attorney, a motion for a trial court, or an entire brief for an appellate court. Rote memorization is not the key factor in a performance skills test—or in the real world. So, this part of these states' bar exam is more real-world-oriented than either the MBE or an essay exam. Interesting that only two states have it. —However, in Colorado, at least, it's supposedly so easy that it's almost a joke.)

* * *

In several states, if you get a high enough score on the MBE, you automatically pass the entire bar exam—regardless of your performance on the essay portion, etc.. In others, if you get a certain minimum score on the MBE, every point above that can be used to offset a low score on the state-specific portion of the barzam. (In these states, it does not work the other way around.) In still others, if you *don't* get a certain minimum score on the MBE, you fail the entire bar exam, no matter how well you do on the state-specific portion.

A high score on the bar exam doesn't bring you rewards the way high scores on first-year finals do. And no one ever asks how well you did. Their—and your—only concern is whether or not you *passed*.

* * *

By the time you've finished your first-year finals, you'll think you've seen the limits of stress. Just wait 'til you get to the bar exam. (One candidate, during the February '93 barzam in California, had a heart attack.*) Law school finals are often spread out over two weeks: two to four hours per final, usually with a day off in between. The "barzam" is six to eight hours a

---

* Other candidates came to his assistance. Those who helped the victim were not allowed extra time to finish, to make up for the time they spent trying to save his life. —It had a happy ending, though, at least in the short run: After getting a lot of bad publicity, higher officials decided to "review" the scores of those who'd helped the victim...And the victim himself had *shown up the next day* to take the MBE portion of the exam. (See what law school does to you?)

day, two to four days straight. It's grueling, a gauntlet. By the end of just the first day, the fatigue factor has already set in.

Even during a formal bar review course, the mood is often one of sheer desperation—and the mood can be contagious. Many employers provide time off for new graduates to study full-time for the exam. However, there never seems to be enough time to prepare. Sure, the passing grade is (usually) less than 70%, and that's the *scaled* score. And yes, roughly four out of five people do pass it on their first try (except in New York and California). But there is simply no way to master everything the bar exam can test. Everyone sweats it.

If the bar exam were a serious measure of one's knowledge of the law, the minimum passing score would be set much higher. And the pace would not be hectic. Reflection is one of the hallmarks of a good attorney. In the real world, there is usually ample time for reflection. The "barzam," in contrast, forces "instant analysis"—as does the typical law school final. Based on what I've seen in practice, this instant analysis becomes habitual. Thus, the artificial time constraints might actually be *counter-productive* in the long run. Out in the real world, a client might suffer because his or her lawyer was content with an instant analysis that was erroneous.

The bar exam is a hazing ritual, and nothing more. Instead of being forced to drink too much alcohol or to perform ridiculous physical acts of self-degradation, future lawyers are forced to "drink in" an endless stream of legal lore—and to endure a nerve-wracking gauntlet spread over several days.

The "Ethics" Exam

Once upon a time, there was a President of the United States named Richard Nixon. His nickname was "Tricky Dicky." In 1972, living up to his sobriquet, he assembled a group of (supposedly) former CIA agents who played "dirty tricks" on the Democratic Party. These dirty tricks were discovered and traced to the Oval Office. The Watergate Scandal resulted. (It was named for the building in which the Democratic Party's national headquarters were located: the target of the agents' repeated burglaries.) As the scandal unfolded, the American public was astonished to see that nearly all of the President's men who supervised the (ex-?) CIA agents were *lawyers*. This further besmirched the reputation of an exalted calling that had long been badly misunderstood by an ungrateful laity. The noble profession's response was to create a test of future lawyers' knowledge of "legal ethics"—an oxymoron. Hence the Multistate Professional Responsibility Examination (MPRE), first administered in 1984. (The MBE was first administered in 1972.) Today, to get a law license in any one of 45 states (and, of course, the city in which the Watergate complex is located) you must take it. Thus, it is one of Richard Nixon's unintended gifts to all his future fellow attorneys (along with several Supreme Court cases limiting the use of executive privilege).

As with law school itself, the MPRE is largely a make-work exercise, intended to *exalt* the legal profession rather than genuinely trying to *qualify* students for the (ethical) practice of law. It tests a "Model Code" and a model set of "Rules" of lawyer ethics. It also tests the Model Code of Judicial Conduct. You'll probably take this exam while still in law school. Many schools now require students to take a so-called "Professional Responsibility" course, the subject matter of which is the same as the MPRE's. ("Professional Responsibility" is abbreviated "P.R.." "P.R." normally stands for "Public Relations"—as in blowing smoke. The P.R. course is definitely part of the legal profession's P.R.. —MDs take the Hippocratic Oath; JDs take a "hypocritic" oath.) The MPRE is given thrice annually (March, August, November). Most students take it around the time they're in the law school course. (As with the bar exam, you can take a preparatory course for it— whether in a formal setting or via home-study materials.)

You get two hours to answer the MPRE's 50 questions. Compared to the Multistate, the pace is leisurely. Instead of being asked whether something is right or wrong, you are usually required to state the correct degree of the relevant rule's application. As with the MBE, you have four choices. Here is a typical set of possible answers:

> A. The rule requires this.
> B. The rule encourages this.
> C. The rule discourages this.
> D. The rule forbids this.

As with the MBE, there's a raw score and a scaled score. The scaled score range is 50-150. The lowest passing mark, scaled, is 70; the highest is 85. Most states set their passing score from 75-80. Future lawyers sweat out the MBE; for most, the MPRE is a breeze—and there's no stigma even if you fail it a time or two. But try to get it out of the way before you take the barzam.

Chapter 18 - Lookin' Toward the "Barzam"

As chapter 17 said, the bar exam is in two parts, MBE and non-MBE, and each part is further sub-divided. You will have studied as many as five of the six MBE subjects as part of first-year. You should get a firm grip on these subjects *long before* you graduate. Because most states combine the MBE score with what you get on the rest of that state's bar exam, a high Multistate grade can (sometimes) make up for a lot of shortfall in other areas. (And remember, you pass in most states if your combined average, however weighted, totals just under 70%, scaled.)

Yet, most students pay no further attention to first-year subjects after year one, except insofar as first-year concepts come up again in advanced courses. Then, nearly two years after saying "Good riddance!" to Torts, Criminal Law, Contracts, Property, and Civil Procedure—*especially* Civil Procedure—and (maybe) Con Law, they find themselves having to learn it all over again. But *this* time around, they're expected to "review" things they never *heard* of (but should have been taught) in first-year.

Bar Review Courses

Most law school graduates take a bar review course, to prepare for the exam. I know of two people from my law school—and one from another—who sat for my state's "barzam" without first taking a prep course of any kind. All were brilliant. (One was editor-in-chief of the Law Review.) All flunked. From reading chapter 17, you can understand why.

The typical bar review course presents law school professors, either live or on video, who lecture—straight lecture, no Case/Socratic Method crap. There are also practice exams to work, both multiple-choice and essay. Usually there's a feedback mechanism, to find out where you're weak and need more review. The practice-exam sessions are usually all day Saturday.

There are two approaches. Both involve cramming. The first is part-time. A bar-prep course that covers both the Multistate and the essay portion (and anything else) lasts five to six weeks. Lectures are held on weekday evenings during a three-hour time slot. Typically, it ends about ten days before the bar exam. Then candidates cram even *more* frantically than they did during the bar review course.

The second approach is *full*-time cramming. Students attend 6-8 hours a day, at least three days straight. Because this involves a smaller timeframe, they're offered more often than the part-time course.

Some prep courses offer both MBE and state essay review; you have to take both. Others offer both, but you can sign up for either. Still others offer only one or the other. Several have a "home study" option, and some are exclusively so.

BarBri, a subsidiary of Harcourt Brace, is to bar review what West is to legal publishing: Goliath. BarBri's market share is huge, perhaps 90%. Its sales tactics are *quite* aggressive.)* As of this writing, its full bar-cram course costs about $1100. Others charge anywhere from $800 to $1800.

The cram-courses devote more than half their time to the first-year material the MBE covers. (Granted, Evidence is not a first-year subject, but the argument still holds.) Seems to me that—at least regarding the MBE subjects—these aren't review courses at all: they're *remedial*. Astoundingly, the law school professors habitually *justify* their spotty coverage of the first-year subjects by saying "Oh, well, your bar review will go over all the omitted topics anyway." Imagine the outcry if for-profit remedial programs sprang up to teach *elementary* schoolkids how to read, write, and do basic arithmetic in the summer between sixth and seventh grades—because the nation's primary schools had not attempted to teach these things themselves. Picture the reaction if elementary schoolteachers habitually excused their negligence by saying, "Oh, well, the for-profit course will cover all this anyway." Yet, for legal education, there's hardly a murmur in protest. Once you have your ticket, who cares? —Just the clients ill-served by attorneys who have a license to practice, yet who are almost as functionally illiterate in the law as many of America's high school graduates are with respect to the 3Rs. (However, unlike those who deal with people who are illiterate and innumerate, clients seldom can tell the difference.)

Professors say the essence of legal education is learning how to Think Like a Lawyer. So, they say, they don't need to cover the entire spectrum of substantive law in any given course. In fact, they continue, any one topic—almost any one case—can function as a prism, creating a rainbow of legal enlightenment.

They're right, insofar as legal reasoning is concerned. But if that's the only important thing students are to acquire in law school, it raises some obvious questions: Why does law school last three years, if the essence of learning how to Think Like a Lawyer can be acquired during first-year? — And if it takes some students all three years to acquire this skill, why don't the law schools make *sure* that *everyone* has it before they graduate? (I doubt it would take three years.) If the substantive aspects of the law aren't important, why have the Big Six of first-year? Why not let *students* pick their subjects? Why have even more than one subject in the first place?

The professoriate plays both ends against the middle...and guess who's in the middle? The typical new attorney's analytical skills are poor—and his or her substantive knowledge is almost zero. Yet, while it's seemingly only the new attorneys who suffer as a result, the real victims—the worst victims—are the clients.

---

* Even the mighty West was no match for BarBri. In the mid-'90s, West started its own bar-cram course. Despite investing a lot of money, it found itself completely outclassed (as it were). West soon decided to cut its losses, and withdrew from the bar review market.

The bar review's cram-course does indeed help you to get a law license. But its purpose is to provide jam-packed short-term memory. After the exam, students "pull the plug" on what they've studied…and nearly all of it quickly drains away.

Getting a Head Start, Yet Again

Do not wait until your bar review course to start preparing for the bar exam. You won't have time to learn all the law you should have learned long ago. This is especially true regarding such arcane topics as the Rule Against Perpetuities in property law. By the time you get into a bar-cram course, it just isn't worth your while to spend time and effort on topics that you didn't understand *at all* before. You're looking for the *maximum* return on your investment, not a *diminishing* returns situation. You need to make sure you *totally* understand things you *thought* you understood before. However, by starting on the MBE practice questions before your third—or even second—year of law school, you can do both: fill in the big gaps in your knowledge *and* nail down the stuff you'd only "sort of" understood before.

An on-site bar-prep course is a business. They're in it for the money. Nothing wrong with that, in and of itself. But they want to maximize their efficiency—which is another way of saying they want to minimize their costs, for the highest possible profits. So, they schedule their courses accordingly. In any given state, there are several law schools. The cram companies don't start their courses until all the schools have recessed. This means, for a summer course (which is what the vast majority of students take), it won't begin until the first week in June. Everything is scheduled for the *company's* convenience (i.e., profits), not yours. They hire a lot of temporary help to put these things on, and they want to have those people on the payroll for the shortest time possible. (For example, the materials aren't mailed out to bar exam candidates until shortly before the course begins, even if students finished their final exams in law school *several* weeks before.) So, they end up making your bar review even more frenzied than it would otherwise be, unnecessarily.*

If you can head into your bar review having already *mastered* the five

---

* Another way they maximize their profits is by getting students to pay a "course reservation" fee during first-year. In return for this deposit, students get a "locked-in price" for the course two years hence, even if the company has raised the price in the meantime. This "reservation fee" is, in effect, a two-year, interest-free loan to the corporation. Without mentioning any names, let's say there's a bar-cram company that has 35,000 students a year taking its course—and all those students paid a "deposit" of $100 in the spring of first-year. That's $3,500,000. If the firm invests that at, say, 10%, its income during the two years, compounded, is nearly a million bucks. While not exactly astronomical, it's pure profit—and goes straight to "the bottom line."

first-year topics the MBE covers (as opposed to merely having passed your first-year courses in them), you won't have to spend much time on them. Bar review in those subjects will truly be a *review*. Here's how to do it:

- First, follow the recommendations in chapter 5—preferably before you even start law school.

- Second, re-read your Master Outline for the five first-year subjects on the MBE from time to time in your remaining two years of law school. (Your Master Outline is just supposed to *trigger* your memory regarding all the *details*. You need to keep this stuff fresh in your mind. *This review might help you in many of your advanced classes, too.*)

- Third, if you haven't already done so, get the student edition of the *Restatements* on contracts and torts, discussed in chapter 5. (Those two subjects total 40% of the MBE.) Read them at your leisure between the end of year one and the start of your bar review course. And if during first-year you did not get the property materials discussed in chapter 7's addendum (shame on you), get them later and study them before graduation.

- Fourth, whether or not you take a course in evidence, get the independent study materials on it, discussed in the addendum to chapter 13. As with the other materials, study them while you're still in law school.

- Fifth, from time to time, review your flash cards: those that you made yourself, and those you bought ready-made, as mentioned in chapter 7's addendum.

Store-Bought Multistate Q&A Materials

However, there's only so much effort you can put in to reviewing your old Master Outlines, etc.. Besides, as is clear from chapter 17's discussion of the tricky-picky nature of the MBE, "merely" knowing *everything* about the law *isn't* enough. You need to get comfortable with examsmanship, MBE-style. That means you have to work Multistate practice-questions, which are multiple-choice. This is the best way to *test* your knowledge—and to cope with the devious nature of the MBE. At some point, you'll find it far more worthwhile to work through the questions and then see why your wrong answers were wrong, than it will be for you to simply keep studying the same old outlines, etc.. You'll pick up a lot of nitty-gritty—and it's the nitty-gritty that the MBE tests. Because you'll be proceeding at your own pace, you don't have to worry about brain-overload.

One of the really nice things about the Multistate subjects is that (as the name implies) they're nationwide in scope. Unlike the state-specific part of a bar exam, no state legislature can overhaul the law, or even make minor changes. (The only exception to this is Con Law, where the U.S. Supreme Court sometimes changes a rule or two, one year to the next. But the Con Law questions are only 15% of the Multistate, which itself is—at most—50% of your combined final score on your state's bar exam. Thus, each Con Law question counts, at most, a mere one-quarter of one percent of your overall barzam score—and there are only two or three Con Law questions whose answers will change because of a new Supreme Court decision. Besides, the "lead time" for the examiners to prepare the MBE is a *year.*) So, you can safely work through "old" questions.

Today, you don't have to wait until your bar-cram vendor provides you with materials shortly before its course begins. You can get such material on your own, from other sources:

Chapter 5 mentioned Blond's®, the Sulzburger & Graham subsidiary that does commercial outlines. It has a book titled *Blond's Multistate Questions,* with 1,000 practice multiple-choice questions and answers in it. It costs about $30 in paperback, and is available on disk for $50.

Chapter 5 also mentioned Emanuel, another commercial outline publisher. Emanuel does a book called *The Finz Multistate Method.* (Steven Finz, its author, does the Sum & Substance cassettes on torts mentioned in chapter 5.) The price is around $34. It contains nearly 1,200 practice multiple-choice questions (with answers and explanations) for the MBE.

Steven Finz also does a 1-tape, 1½ hour lecture on audio cassette as part of the "Outstanding Professor" series of Sum & Substance (which, as mentioned, is a subsidiary of West Publishing). It's called *Mastering Multiple Choice (MBE),* and costs $25.

Chapter 5 spoke of products from Gilbert, the Harcourt Brace subsidiary. Gilbert does a 210-page book titled *Gilbert Law Summaries: Multistate Bar Exam,* for $18. Richard Conviser, who does Gilbert's "Legal Legend" torts tapes, is the author. It has 200 sample questions are in it—so it appears to be more of a "how to" book than a practice-questions book.

Law-in-a-Flash® (whose parent, as mentioned in chapter 5, is Emanuel) has a volume called *Strategies and Tactics for the MBE,* by Kimm Alayne Walton. This includes 550 Multistate questions and answers. It costs $35. Walton gives *excellent* advice on "How to Attack the MBE," including a great discussion of all the traps the MBE examiners set for the unwary. Even though her book only has 550 questions in it, it would be worth the price even without *any* questions. As you've seen, there are thousands of questions available in other materials, but her examsmanship discussion is unique. *Her* questions, for example, tell what sub-area each of the possible answers is in. That's *enormously* helpful as you try to pinpoint your weaknesses and work on them. Further, she gives points for each possible answer—and tells you whether you scored a hit, a near-miss, were wide of the mark, or failed to aim in the right direction in the first place. This too is of enormous help. If you're trying to decide which of these books to get first, this is the one.

Siegel's was mentioned in chapter 5 as yet another publisher of commercial outlines (and as an imprint of Emanuel). The Siegel's outline for each subject costs about $16 or so. Each includes multiple-choice questions with answers, as well as sample essay questions with model answers.

You should get *several* MBE Q&A books, and work through them one after the other during your remaining two years of law school. If you can't find them in a law school bookstore, check the appendix of this book to get the toll-free numbers of these vendors.

You can save money by making a deal with one or more fellow students—such as those who were in your first-year study group. Split the cost evenly. Then each of you takes one book. Part of the deal has to be that you won't put *any* marks in these books: You will not underline or otherwise mark any portion of the fact patterns, nor will you X out what you think is a wrong answer, or circle or put a checkmark next to what you think is the right answer. That would destroy the clean slate the next person should have. (Make your own answer sheet.) The same thing goes for marking anything in the section that discusses the answers. Set a deadline. When the deadline arrives, you swap books. Repeat the process until everyone's worked every book. Then *start over.*

Bar-Prep Vendor Materials

You can get books of practice questions from the bar-cram vendors too, of course. Harcourt Brace is the parent company of both BarBri and Gilbert. Candidates get two Multistate Q&A books, one from each subsidiary. The BarBri book has over 1100 practice questions; the Gilbert, slightly more than 1300. During a BarBri course, students make use of both of them. You can too—on your own.

But you can also get *substantive* materials. These contain text-only. They cover the law itself: torts, property, etc.. The self-help materials discussed in chapter 5, etc., *don't* cover *everything*. The *bar-prep* materials *do*—but *their* goal for you is memorizing, not *understanding*.

You should have gotten the self-help materials long ago. Then, right after first-year, you should get the bar-cram Q&A *and* substantive materials. *You get them from someone who took the most recent bar exam.*

The bar review outfits don't want their materials floating around, because too many people would be tempted just to get the materials (and maybe some of the self-help tapes mentioned above) instead of paying $1100+ for a bar review course. So, when someone takes a prep course, he or she has to pay a "materials deposit" of $75-$100. The deposit is refunded when the materials are returned to the bar-cram company. (It doesn't make any difference what condition the items are in when they're returned: The bar-prep people destroy them. They just want to keep these things off the market.) If you try to buy these items separately, without signing up for the bar review course, they cost $100-$150 *per book*—and there are several volumes. Students, quite rationally, decide it makes more sense to pay the extra money and get the lectures as well as the materials.

Here's how to get them cheap: Make a deal with a third-year student who's about to graduate. If the materials deposit is $75, you offer—say—$125 for them. The student forfeits his or her own deposit, and makes a 67% profit off you ($50). If you don't know any graduating third-year students, post notices on the bulletin boards at your school, offering to buy the materials. (You aren't limited to seeking only BarBri's stuff. There are several bar prep firms.)

Generally, these people don't get their hands on these materials until they've already graduated. That means they probably won't be around the law school anymore. So, you have to connect with them before they leave. Further, bar exam results aren't announced until months later. (For those who take it in February, the results are announced in late April, usually. But because most people sit for the July bar, it usually takes a month longer to grade all the tests; scores don't come out until late October.) Most students will probably want to keep their bar review materials until they find out if they passed. Therefore, you have to plan on a lag between making your deal with someone and getting that person's stuff.

Do not pay in advance, not even a deposit. Also, have more than one prospective supplier lined up: Law students (and lawyers, for that matter) are notoriously unreliable about keeping their promises. (However, you should be up-front about the fact that you have more than one potential supplier.) First-come, first-served.

Make sure it's understood you will be getting *clean* materials, with *no* marks in them. (That's one reason why you offer a nice premium over the materials deposit.) Different people like to mark different passages, and usually mark things in different ways, too. As with preparing your own personal outline, you want to be able to do what works best for *you*. The person who had these books can mark them in pencil. There's no need for him or her to use ink, including highlighters. Then you erase the pencil markings before using these books—and marking them up—yourself.*

If possible, you should get the substantive texts and the Q&A materials from at least *one* bar-cram vendor *far* ahead of time. It's worth paying $125 or more to get these from a graduating student, even though you'll be taking a bar-prep course later and getting (updated) materials then.

If you're splitting the cost with one or more other students, the same rules

---

* True, if someone circled or crossed out answers in pencil, you can still see the mark after you erase it. However, the way to deal with that is to put the *same* mark by *every* answer. Then erase these, too. You (usually) won't be able to tell which was the original. As for the pencil-markings of passages in the text or the answer-explanations section, don't worry about it: you'll be doing your own markings, in ink, and you won't notice the traces of the pencil marks you've erased.

apply to the substantive materials as to the Q&A materials: no marks. That means no highlightings, no underlinings. Instead, make your own notes, *extensive* ones. By getting the materials far ahead of the bar review course, you'll have plenty of time to do this. (During a bar-cram course, you won't.) Your note-taking will help you learn the law much better than you would otherwise. So, it's worthwhile to get the substantive materials as well as the Q&A materials—*early*.

Consolidate Your Strengths, Eradicate Your Weaknesses

By dealing with the Multistate's narrow questions, you will be amazed at how you'll see connections you would otherwise have missed. You will often find yourself simultaneously understanding *both* the big picture *and* the nitty-gritty, in a comprehensive way you would not have dreamed of. Eventually, everything will come together for you. Several times, I had a "Eureka!" experience: "So *that's* what that point of law was all about!" Despite commercial outlines, *Restatements,* independent study books, and even the lectures during my bar review course, it was only the discussion of the answers to the MBE practice questions that cleared up many of the *finer* points of the law for me. *That's why you should start on this as soon as possible.*

It's just like doing your personal outlines: it takes time for the material to sink in. The earlier you start, the longer you'll work with it; the greater the likelihood it'll become second nature to you. Then, during the real thing, you'll *immediately* spot the possible answers that contain incorrect statements of the law. That saves you some time. You use that time to go *again* over the facts, *carefully.* (Very often, the answer is based on some seemingly-minor detail. If you miss that detail, you miss the question.)

Another important consideration is "the *call* of the question"—what the question is really asking. Sometimes, what at first seems to be a property question turns out to be a torts question, for example. And quite often, many of the facts given are completely irrelevant to the correct answer. By understanding the call of the question, you can immediately separate the useful from the useless.

When you test yourself, don't *guess* at any of the answers. Save that for the real thing, where a question not answered at all counts the same as a question answered incorrectly, i.e., zero. (So, the MBE rewards good guessing, and doesn't penalize bad guessing any more than it does a thoughtful answer that's wrong.) When practicing, it's better to leave the answer blank—and fill in your knowledge later—than it is to guess correctly and then fail to review the answer at all because you got it right. You may have guessed wildly and correctly on the practice question—but you almost certainly won't get so lucky on the real thing.

On practice questions, separate those you missed because *you didn't read the facts carefully enough* from those you missed because you honestly thought the wrong answer was the right one. The day of the MBE, your concentration will be much better—although you should try to improve it beforehand. However, missing questions because you didn't understand the *problem*, or didn't know the *law,* is more serious. (Yes, a wrong answer is a wrong answer, regardless of the reason why. But the ability to keep your mind focused is something you'll either have or you won't. And if you've truly mastered the law—and the quirks of the MBE—you'll find your concentration has improved. One hand washes the other.)

> Because there are only 200 questions on the Multistate, there are only so many points of law *your* MBE *will* test. If you've been working multiple-choice questions *far* in advance of the barzam, you'll have tested yourself on virtually every conceivable point of law that might be on the real thing. You will have answered many, many questions in each area of the law. If you don't know a given point of law, the pattern will become painfully obvious. So, put some time in on it, to improve your understanding.
> *Take careful notes on what you missed.*
> *Save your corrected answer sheets.*
> Then, assuming you started practicing far enough ahead, you'll be able to take each practice exam a *second* time. Check to see if you're still missing questions in the same sub-area, especially if you're giving the *same* wrong answer each time. If so, you'll know what to do.

Although the right answer to any given question will be the same regardless of which company prepared the materials you're using, the different vendors sometimes explain the answers in somewhat different ways. Sometimes, one book's way of explaining a point of the law just won't "get through" to you. But some other's might. At least, that's the way it was for me. (And, surprisingly and culpably, you'll sometimes see the explanation one company gives *contradicts* that of another. If you start preparing for the MBE far enough in advance, you can find out which one is right.)

Unfortunately, and hard to believe, you will unintentionally start to memorize answers if you work through the same set of questions too soon after your previous round with it. That's bad. But if you get Q&A materials from several vendors, not just one, it will be much harder for you to accidentally slip into rote. It's also a reason to do your first round shortly after you finish first-year...and to then set the materials aside for *months.* In your spare time between vacations after year one, you should keep re-reading your first-year Master Outlines and the *Restatements* on torts and contracts. You should also review the do-it-yourself study materials on evidence and property—especially the really difficult areas (hearsay in evidence, Estates and Future Interests in property).

If you can stand it, begin working Multistate practice questions during the summer vacation after your *first year* of law school, while the first-year curriculum is still fresh in your mind. Start with sets of questions that are all in the same category (contracts, torts, etc.). Definitely get the do-it-yourself evidence materials and study them during that same vacation. Before returning to law school in the fall, you should have worked practice MBE exams with 200 questions drawn from all six Multistate categories, just like the real thing. During your winter vacation in second-year, answer the same questions all over again (another reason not to mark your question books up).

Believe it or not, you will find this process *enjoyable*. To return to the analogy used at the start of chapter 5: it's like the pleasure you'll feel when you find you're actually *thinking* in the *foreign* language instead of mentally *translating* all the time. You'll feel a truly deep sense of satisfaction from this sense of *mastery*. ("Good God, I'm *getting* there. I might have 'what it takes' after all!")

The areas where you *repeatedly* made the *same* mistakes are the areas which you want to *especially* review before the bar exam.

During the real thing, you'll want to write down the numbers of the questions where you're not sure what the right answer was. If you have time left over after going through all 100 questions in a session, review the difficult ones. (I set up two columns on the cover of the exam booklet. In the first, I wrote down the numbers of those questions where I didn't have the foggiest idea what the right answer was, the first time through. I had guessed at the answer.) *Completely* skipping questions is dangerous—because when you go back you can easily lose track. Then you fill in the blanks for the wrong questions. And you might not even have time to go back. So, better to fill in anything the first time around, then go back and erase if and when you have time and decide that some other answer is superior to the one you'd originally guessed.)

In the second column, I wrote down the numbers of the—many more—questions where I thought I knew the answer, but wasn't sure. I'd also filled in an answer to each of these, of course.

At the end of the first pass-through, I still had about 20 minutes left. So I went over all the questions in the first column. Time ran out before I'd finished reviewing my answers to the questions in the second column. (One attorney who read this book in manuscript said he'd done it the other way around: He put his extra time in on those questions where he thought he'd picked the right answer earlier, and now just wanted to make sure. On those questions where he'd just made a random guess, he left his answers as they were, without a second look. As he explained it to me, "Why waste time on complete unknowns?")

Develop a system *you* feel comfortable with. Then use it during your timed *practice* exams.

If you already know the points of law, and can concentrate on the facts and the call of the question, it will make a *big* difference to your state of mind during the exam. While you can't exactly lollygag, you're just naturally much calmer, and more clear-headed. It's hard for me to explain this, but perhaps you've already had the feeling yourself—in which case you already know what I'm talking about. It's the difference between approaching something in fear and trembling, and approaching something with a quiet confidence. Then, even if you have a bad day, you'll still do all right. It's the difference between anxiety as to whether or not you'll even pass it, on the one hand, and being curious as to whether you'll *ace* it, on the other. (Notice the similarity concerning first-year finals ?)

State-Specific
Essay Exam Preparation

If you concentrate on Multistate materials and working MBE questions between the end of first-year and the end of the first semester of third-year, you'll be 'way ahead of the game. In your final semester, you should continue working MBE questions. However, in that final semester you should begin *studying* (not just reading) state-specific materials. Then, in the time between your graduation from law school and the barzam, you want to concentrate on the state-specific materials. These are the "advanced" subjects.

The biggest decision most students must make regarding the bar exam is whether to take law school courses that cover subjects the barzam tests. If you hope to have a career in estate planning, you should take wills, estates, and trusts anyway. If you plan to be a trial lawyer in the state where your law school is located, you should take courses in that state's civil procedure anyway, not just for the bar exam. And so on. The question is whether to take something just because it's on the barzam, even though you're not at all interested in that subject.

No matter what courses you take in law school, however, you will still be hit with a lot of strange and completely new material as part of your bar review course. (Having read chapters 3 and 4, you know why.) In that sense, it will almost be like first-year, all over again—at a *much* faster pace. The more that's completely new to you, the worse it will be for you in trying to memorize all of it in time. Therefore, better something (a course in law school) than nothing.

After first-year, I took only one course in a subject on my state's bar exam. It made a big difference concerning bar review, and I wished I'd taken more such courses. However, when I was in law school, I was unaware of the do-it-yourself materials mentioned in the addendum to chapter 13 (regarding evidence) or in chapter 14 (various subjects). My law school's bookstore did not stock them. Indeed, many of them did not even exist then.

So, you do not have to make the difficult choice I did. (But for those of you who go where Con Law is just an elective, you should take the Con Law course, period. Who knows? —Someday you might be under consideration for a federal judgeship. Imagine how embarrassing it would be at your confirmation hearing if it were disclosed that you were not interested enough in Constitutional Law to even take one course in it in law school.)

Whether or not you take a course after first-year that will be included on your state's bar exam, you should *still* get the (generic) books and tapes mentioned in chapter 14. If you *do* take a law school course in a bar exam subject, study these materials during the vacation before the semester in which you'll be taking that course. (The same thing is true if you get materials for a course that will *not* be a bar exam subject.)

If you do *not* take a particular law school course that covers a bar exam subject, but have the materials mentioned above, then you should begin studying them during the summer vacation before your third year. —And if you have summer (law-related) employment, these materials just might help you on the job, too.

At the latest, you should begin studying them during the winter vacation in year three.

The generic materials are good advance preparation. However, they won't be enough, because they aren't state-specific. To the best of my knowledge, though, the only people who do *state-specific* materials are the bar review organizations. You should get these materials at the same time you get their MBE materials mentioned above. (The materials deposit covers *everything*. So, when you pay a premium over that deposit, *you* should get everything too. —To make sure you don't get cheated by the law school graduate who's your supplier, call the prep firm and ask them to list all the materials candidates get in return for the materials deposit.)

And in your last semester of law school, you should *begin working essay questions from past bar exams*.

Bar exam candidates are not allowed to walk out with the *MBE* exam question booklets when they leave each session. (This is because some questions will be repeated in later exams.) But in most states, those who take the *essay* exam *are* allowed to keep the questions. The bar-cram courses have been collecting these for years. Their materials for the *essay* exam subjects include actual essay questions from dozens of previous bar exams, and a model answer for every one of them. There are only so many major points of law the essay questions can test. So, if you work old essay exams, and compare your answers to the model answers, you *will* be prepared for *anything* on your state's essay portion of the barzam. (Exception: when the state legislature overhauls the law. However, even there, the lead time for preparing the essay exam is at least six months. Those who prepare the exam questions know what areas of the law are in flux. They'll *avoid* asking questions in those areas.)

<u>Misc. Materials</u>

National Jurist, Inc., has a package deal for $79: a 250-page book, *Scoring High on Bar Exam Essays,* with a three-hour set of audio tapes, *How to Pass the Bar Exam.* Both are by Mary Campbell Gallagher. If you want just the book, you can get it from the publisher, Sulzburger & Graham, for $25. (Looks like the tapes aren't sold alone.)

Chapter 7's addendum listed the *First Year Law School Survival Kit,* by Jeff Adachi. His company, Survival Series Publishing, also does a paperback volume for the bar exam. Not surprisingly, it's called *Bar Exam Survival Kit.* The price is $40, and it's available from Legal Books Distributing, (800) 200-7110. As with his First Year Kit, Adachi provides strategies and memory aids. He also does a book called *Barbreaker,* which sells for $100, and a *California Bar Exam Survival Kit* for $40. But I have not seen either of these, so I can't comment on them.*

Tape, not Live

If you've done well in law school (i.e., Made Law Review), you'll already have a good job lined up before you graduate. If so, your future employer will almost certainly pay for your bar-cram course. In that case, take a bar review course—the most thorough one you can get, even though you've already done the things recommended above. But get it on *tape*.

On-site courses are often *presented* on tape—videotape. But nearly *all* of them do *audio* cassettes. (For those whose lectures are also on video, the audio cassettes have identical content, other than the absence of the picture, of course. The audio is taken from the video. —And, by the way, there are no visual aids on the videotapes.)

Listening to bar review tapes confers two big advantages over attending on-site lectures:

1. *You save a lot of commuting time.* You can spend this time studying, instead. Why spend 1-2 hours five or six days a week going to and from lectures that last 3-4 hours? (Actually, they're even shorter than that, because of breaktimes.) For a five-week evening-weekend course, that could total *30-60 wasted hours.* (There are the full-time bar review courses, too. For these, the ratio of class to commute time is much more favorable.) If you're working full-time, you normally would not be able to leave early enough to make a 6:00 bar review lecture every night. So, if you're doing an evenings-weekends bar review course, you'll be cutting back on your job.

---

* Note: Chapter 17 said that California and Colorado have a "performance skills test" as part of their barzams. One of the Gilbert commercial outlines is called *California Bar Performance Test Skills.* It's $18. Even though it's for California, seems to me the advice it contains might work just as well for Colorado.

With tapes, you minimize the amount of time you're spending away from your tasks at work.

2. *You can progress at your own rate.* You can stop a tape to look something up in your written materials. And you can *replay* any portion of any tape. Can't do *that* with on-site live lectures or videos. Best of all, perhaps, you can listen to the cassettes when you're in a receptive mood, at your convenience. (By now, you know how hard it is to absorb lecture materials when you're in no condition for it.*) So, you can start reviewing far ahead of time—such as during your final semester of law school.

'True, the on-site courses offer "real world" test conditions for taking mock exams. But you can always time yourself, and limit yourself to three hours for a 100-question MBE set. And you'll already have been through several high-stress time-pressured exams: your first-year finals, for example. You'll have already been through a less stressful multiple-choice exam, the MPRE.

However, as always, it's your call. (Also, be advised: you need to be highly self-motivated to get your bar review just from the tapes, without attending lectures. It's very easy to procrastinate when you're on your own. The best way to protect yourself against this is to have a study group. Each of you takes the cassettes for one or two subjects. Just as with the MBE Q&A books, set a deadline. Each of you listens to his or her cassettes before that deadline. Then you get together and exchange them. Repeat until everyone in your group has heard all the tapes. This externally-imposed discipline might make up for your own possible lack of self-discipline.)

Mnemonics

Mnemonic. Here's one: "MADAM—Mnemonic: Any Device Aiding Memory." See? ("KISS-A-MIC," in chapter 16, is another.)

Mnemonics aren't much help on the Multistate. But they're vital for the essay exam. Like a Master Outline for first-year courses, you should be preparing them long before it's time to take the exam. But like the Summary Outlines for year one, you should be able to regurgitate all of them, very fast, on scratch paper before you start to work the essay questions during the bar exam. (As mentioned above, you should have largely finished your study of the first-year Multistate subjects *before* your *final year* of law school, and you should spend most of your final *semester* of law

---

* If you're working full-time (or even part-time) while preparing for the bar exam, you can listen to the cassettes while commuting. However, I found it difficult to absorb the material while in traffic. For me, listening while behind the wheel was something reserved only for subjects I already knew pretty well…of which there were very few. However, if you commute by bus, train, subway, or carpool where someone else is driving, you can listen (through headphones) without distractions.

school studying for your state's essay exam. This final semester is when you should be developing mnemonics.)

Before I sat for the bar, I *bought* a set of mnemonics from someone who'd developed hundreds of them...only to find out the hard way that what worked so well for him didn't work at all for me. So I then made up my own. Often, I just reworked the mnemonics of others—including the ones I'd just bought, plus a smaller set I got from the bar review course. Here are two of my own:

Q: What are the general intent crimes?
   (Mnemonic: "The General Intended to BARF.")
A: Battery, Arson, Rape, and False (Imprisonment)

Q: Who can be excused from jury duty (petit or grand)?
   (Mnemonic: "APES can be excused from Juries.")
A: The Aged (over 65), a single Parent with sole responsibility for a child under 10, any other Excuse the court thinks okay, and full-time Students

One way to practice these is to do two sets of flash cards. The first set consists of 3x5 index cards cut up into 1x3. On one side, put an abbreviated form of the question. On the other, put just the acronym of the mnemonic, all by itself. Example: Front— "General Intent Crimes" Back— "BARF."

The second set consists of 3x5 cards, too, but full-size. On the front, write out the entire question. On the back, write the full mnemonic horizontally across the top. Then write the acronym vertically on the left side. Example: Front— "Who can be excused from jury duty, whether petit or grand?" Back—

   "APES can be excused from Juries."
A - Aged: over 65
P - single Parent with sole responsibility for a child under 10
E - any other Excuse the court thinks valid
S - full-time Student: high school, college, grad school, etc..

From time to time, take a few minutes and check the 1x3 cards, to see if you can still remember the MADAM. Then, less frequently, use the 3x5 cards to test your detailed knowledge.

(I have my doubts as to how well mnemonics work for first-year courses, because the memorization required there consists of the elements of causes of action. Besides, you should know them so well that you don't need mnemonics, any more than you need them to recite the ABCs. —However, recall chapter 7's brief mention of the woman who devised new law-related lyrics for various rock-and-roll songs in first-year. That approach might also work on the essay portion of the bar exam, if you have the talent for it. — And don't forget maybe rewording a poem you already know by heart.)

More on Timing — and Priorities

After first-year, try to arrange your credit load so that by the time you reach your *last* semester you'll only need to take the *minimum* number of credits required to maintain full-time student status. And try to make sure these are "gut" courses you can easily ace—although, *with the exceptions mentioned in chapter 14*, you should do this with *all* your courses. If you had a part-time job in previous semesters, lighten your schedule in your final semester—and, if possible, stop working altogether. (If you need the money, better to take out a student loan than to spend your time working on something other than the barzam.) If you're on Law Review, you can't do much to lighten your load there. If you're in Mock Trial or Moot Court competition, consider giving it up unless 1) you expect to do *very* well, based on your performance in second-year, or 2) you plan to become a litigator, and just can't get enough of it.

During that final semester, you listen to all your first-year and evidence tapes again. You review all your first-year Master Outlines again, and anything else you need—the primers, for example. Then you re-work all the MBE practice questions you did before. You should also review all the tapes and written materials for the essay subjects that will be on your state's bar exam. If you'll be tested on federal and state civil and criminal procedure, you should be memorizing all those rules. And you should be working on your mnemonics. Then get *new* materials and start going over those. This includes answering the new MBE practice questions and past real-life essay exam questions.

If you do this, then by the time you start a formal bar review course after graduation, you will already be in excellent shape for your state's bar exam.

* * *

Based on your educational experiences so far, by now you're thinking this entire book sounds crazy. And it *does*: "Classes are the least important part of law school," "Extra-curricular activities are the most important," "Making Law Review is the most important thing of all," and now, *"Start preparing for the bar exam as soon as you've finished first-year."* It's all topsy-turvy, and seems to stand common sense on its head.

Once you get into law school, you will see and hear with your own eyes and ears, and you will know that's the way it has to be—if you want to *thrive,* not just *survive.*

I did not design this crazy law-school set-up...and if I were King of the Forest, I would certainly do some clear-cutting and removal of deadwood.

As it is, all I can do is show you the "easiest" way through this thickest of all the groves of academe.

The fact of the matter is that, other than your first-year finals, the single most important exam you'll take as a future lawyer is the bar exam. But by preparing for the MBE part of it as soon as you've completed first-year, it will stand you in good stead in years two and three of law school. Even though many advanced courses are highly specialized, and have nothing to do with first-year topics, there will still be some that specifically build on year one topics. (This is especially true with Wills-Estates-Trusts. But you never know when first-year topics will pop up in other courses.)

Further, assuming you Make Law Review, complete mastery of your first-year topics will enhance your performance as second-year slave labor, because you'll know more than your fellow slaves. That, in turn, will impress your superiors—and give you a better shot at being selected as an (important) editor in third-year.

Perhaps you're thinking, "Hey, 'Atticus,' this is too much work." Fact is, you're going to have to work hard in law school, no matter what...if you hope to do well. But—to again quote the Opening Statement—the question is whether you'll be working *smart*, too. Even though working smart is also hard, it's actually *less* hard than *just* working hard. The choice is yours.

* * *

Come bar review time, your employer might give you a mini-sabbatical to study for the barzam. However, you won't get *much* time off. (Try to at least cut back to half-time during the six weeks before the barzam.) —And if you do *not* get time off, or not *enough*, you will probably be a nervous wreck by the time of the bar exam. In the meantime, you will probably have neglected your duties at work. Regardless of whether or not you get a break, you don't want to get into a frenzy.

Although most students pass the bar exam on the first try, a substantial minority fail. (Interestingly, most who fail it the first time fail it the second time, too.) The stigma of having failed the bar exam is severe. John F. Kennedy, Jr., could afford it (literally—and *twice*) but for the average person, flunking often leads to a pink slip at the office. (You'll have to wait roughly six months for the next exam; and don't forget the months afterward, before the results are announced. In the meantime, without a license, you can't perform some of the work you were hired to do. This includes signing off on documents as attorney of record, and making occasional court appearances.) It's very embarrassing for your employer to have a flunker around—and lawyers *hate* to feel embarrassed.

Even if you don't get fired, failure hinders your career prospects. Your dossier will always remind your supervisors that you flunked the bar the first time around. However, failure—even repeated failures—don't necessarily doom your career prospects: several prominent lawyer-politicians flunked it more than once. (Perhaps, though, that's why they went into politics; maybe they were forced out of the firms they worked for.)

You ought to start on the bar exam early—much earlier than you would normally think prudent—because 1) you want to make sure you pass it the first time, and 2) when you're pouring it on in the home stretch of your bar review, you want to still be able to take it in stride.

There are even more good reasons to start early. They're discussed at the end of this chapter.

If You Have to Go It Alone

It's at least theoretically possible that, despite following the recommendations of *Planet Law School,* you will *not* be an exceptional law school student. (Maybe, for some reason, you will have put most of your energy into your love life. Or maybe you're one of those people who always "freezes up" during an exam. —But if so, how did you get good enough grades to get *into* law school?) Or maybe, for whatever reason, you've decided not to practice law, but want to get the law license anyway, just in case whatever it is you *do* want to do doesn't work out; so you're sloughing off on grades. In any of these circumstances, you must either then pay for a bar-prep course yourself, or else forgo it. I recommend the former. A bar-cram course is a well-structured program. And it makes you work harder than you otherwise would.

As above, I recommend you get it on tape—even though a program on tape costs more than the same program presented on-site. In addition to the advantages already stated, you can split the cost with fellow bar exam candidates. As mentioned, use the same rotation system as was recommended for sharing first-year tapes and Multistate Q&A books.

However, if you're *really* pinched for funds, consider getting only the *state* bar review tapes. (For the MBE, don't forget all those first-year cassettes, recommended in chapters 5 and the addendum to chapter 7; plus the evidence tapes mentioned in the addendum to chapter 13. They cover almost exactly the same material as the bar review, at a much lower cost.)

Let's say you can get state-only materials for $540 (a realistic figure). If you can get just two other people to go in with you, that's $180 apiece. Each of you has saved over $350 right there. (Each of you will also have to chip in for a refundable security deposit on the tapes.) Then share the tapes, as discussed above.

How to Get a Free Bar Review Course

If you don't find a patron to pick up the tab, here's how to get a free bar review course anyway.

Most of the bar-prep firms have on-site student representatives at each law school. In large schools, they have a rep in each section of the first-year class. The sales push begins in the very first semester of law school. If the student rep signs up *x* number of his or her fellow students, the rep gets a free bar-cram course.

So, as soon as you know you're going to a particular law school, call the bar review companies. Tell them you want to be a student rep at your school. (If you're going to a large school, maybe you should find out what section you're assigned to before you call. —And when you call, don't refer to them as cram courses: they take offense at that.) See if you can get the name and phone number of a current rep at your (future) school, and then talk with that person.

Try to get an exclusive agreement in *writing*—i.e., a contract saying you will be the only rep for your section, or the only rep for your entire first-year class, as the case may be. Make sure there's a clause concerning the grounds for getting fired, and what compensation you receive based on your performance to date. If you exceed the number of sign-ups you need to get a free course, you ought to get a cash commission for the extra ones. If so, be sure to find out *when* you get the money. You should also try to get a *free* set of Multistate Q&A (and substantive) materials at the end of *year one*. Get your state essay review materials early, too. —And get the course on tape, during your final semester of law school.

Because BarBri is the biggest, start there. Then go down the list. But even if BarBri is receptive, don't stop there. You might be able to get a better deal from another firm. —Some of them might not presently be using campus reps. If so, the first test of your ability to make a sale is to sell the firm on the idea of making an exception for *your* school, using *you* as its rep. (This can work even with home-study courses, if you do it right.)

Another thing: find out if any of the lecturers for a given bar-prep course are professors at *your* school. *That's* the firm you want to represent. (Chapter 10 said professors can be just as petty and vindictive as you or I. One way to find this out for yourself is to be in a course with a professor who's a lecturer for a bar review company that you don't represent. —Because of my law school's prominence, several of its most important faculty members do bar prep lectures. All work for the same bar-cram company. Their clout with the administration is such that for years the dean's office tacitly banned all other bar-prep firms from soliciting business within the walls of the law school.* Then these professors used *class* time to urge students to sign up with the bar-cram company *they* lectured for. No rival company's student rep dared speak up in protest. —This is a big-bucks business, and hardball tactics are the norm. The image of the law school as an ivory tower is deceiving...And no, I was not a student rep for one of the shut-out firms. I was just privy to what was going on.)

Another advantage of a being a bar-prep rep is that you have far more occasion to talk with students than you otherwise would. This isn't a matter of mere socializing. As chapter 8 mentioned, you'll be dealing with these people, lawyer-to-lawyer, someday. The better you know them, the better.

---

* Things are not as they were in Dean Langdell's time at Harvard Law School. Today, in all university-affiliated law schools in America, the faculty—not the deans—are in charge. Deans are hired to do three things: 1) raise money, 2) deal with the university administration, and 3) run such mechanical operations as alumni affairs, student admissions, placement, and the hiring of non-faculty staff. The typical dean doesn't stay on the job very long—and even many of the top schools are having trouble getting the best people to accept an offer.

Bar Review Courses - Vendors

I am aware of seven bar-prep firms that operate on a national scale: America's Bar Review (a.k.a. the Reed Law Group), BarBri, Micromash-Nord, PMBR (which—as chapter 5 mentioned—stands for "Preliminary Multistate Bar Review," though they never spell it out), The Princeton Review, and The Study Group. There are others that operate only within one or several states. You will need to find these on your own, when the time comes. I will mention one now, though: Fleming's Fundamentals of Law (FFL), originally listed in connection with tapes on first-year subjects and an examsmanship course. FFL's bar review course is only for California— and is perhaps the best. (It's certainly the most expensive.)

Some of these vendors are "full-service," offering both MBE and state-specific materials; you must take both. Others offer both, but you can pick and choose what to take. Still others are only one or the other. Some are just on-site, others just on tape or via home study, and still others offer both. Some will give you practice essay exams and will then grade each answer individually and tell you where you're strong, where you're weak. Some give a money-back guarantee or a reduced rate for a re-run if you fail the bar exam. Be sure to ask. And if the answer is "Yes," get it in writing.   (It should be part of the standard contract, though.) All are listed in the appendix.

> Assuming that you do take a full-scale bar-prep course, remember: any bar-cram course stresses only the key points. These are the items that have repeatedly been tested on your state's bar exam (and the MBE). That's the nature of the beast, given the time constraints of the course. The odds are that those points of law *will* be tested again on *your* exam. But if you've been studying *well ahead of time,* you'll already know *all* the key points and a lot *more*. That way, if what your bar-prep course emphasizes gets slighted on *your* bar exam, you'll *still* be prepared—because you studied the "possible" *as well as* the "probable" exam material. That's called *insurance.*

Killing Two Birds with One Stone

Even if you take a *full* bar exam preparatory course (MBE plus essay), whether free or not, try to follow the recommendations of this chapter. By doing so, you kill two birds with one stone.

The first is what's already been said: by starting early, you minimize the strain of studying for the bar exam—and maximize your chance to pass it the first time around.

The second involves a longer-run view. Chapter 3 asked, "Have you ever suspected that a given lawyer was actually quite ignorant of the law...? Well, many of them *are.*" Chapter 3 (among others) discussed how law school ill-serves the future lawyers of this country—and thereby ill-serves the future clients of those attorneys. Low as the image of lawyers is, laypeople still *trust* lawyers to *know the law.* —They have *no choice,* at least in this regard...because that's why a layperson goes to an attorney in the first place.

There are many, many basic principles of the law that any lawyer *should* know. Even if you leave out specialized areas such as Estates and Future Interests, and Evidence, there are hundreds of basic principles of the law that *every* lawyer should know. But in fact, few do. (No attorney can know it *all,* however. In fact, no attorney can know more than a tiny percentage of the law. Even so, my statement still holds, regarding basic principles.)

Students were supposed to have learned these basic principles in law school. But, as chapters 3 and 4 showed, the reality is otherwise. Later, the (future) attorneys were supposed to have learned these things for the bar exam. And maybe they did. But that "learning" involved cramming thousands of points of law into their heads. They held them there just long enough to get a passing score. After that, they forget nearly all of them. And once they have their ticket (i.e., law license), there's little incentive to go over any of them again. They—maybe—look up what they need to know to do what they have to do; the rest is out of sight, out of mind.

So what's wrong with that?

—For one, people always hit on attorneys for free legal advice. It's a real ego trip to have someone sucking up to you because of your (supposed) expertise—especially if it's someone who's a big-shot, or someone you find sexually attractive. It's just human nature to puff oneself up a bit when the opportunity arises. No reason why lawyers should be any different.

However, most attorneys practice in only one narrow area of the law. When they get hit on for free advice, they're rarely asked questions about their own narrow area. Instead, they're asked questions all over the place...but usually in the thorny subjects of family law, probate, or employment law.

Few lawyers have the humility to say "I don't know" when asked a question—especially if the person asking the question is someone you want to impress. Regardless, few people want to appear ignorant—especially if they know the other person thinks it's something he or she *ought* to know, cold. Most laypeople will resent it if a lawyer says "That's not my area of the law" and then explains that it would take some legal research to find the answer. They'll think the lawyer's a "typical greedy bastard attorney," who doesn't want to give anything away he or she can charge for. They honestly believe there are some things *any* lawyer should know, just by virtue (ah, the irony) of being a lawyer. And they're *right.*

So, the attorney gives an answer off the top of his or her head. Usually it's the *wrong* answer. It might not be *dead* wrong, but it's seldom *as* right an answer as it *should* be.

Okay, say you don't care about giving bad advice to freeloaders. Say you don't care one of them later finds out how wrong you were, and bad-mouths you to anyone who'll listen. Say you don't care you might lose some potential business as a result.

Okay. So here's the second thing wrong with not knowing basic legal principles. Here's something you *definitely* should care about:

If you work the Multistate questions regularly, and set aside ample time to truly master the state-specific material for the essay portion of your state's bar exam, *you'll gradually build up a general awareness, a sense of additional relevant points of law in any given situation.* And so, when you're working on a problem on behalf of a *paying* client, there will be things that will come to mind you might not otherwise have thought of. "Seems to me, I remember—somewhere in the back of my mind, something about…" *Your gut feel will alert you* to the possibility of something "out there" that you might be able to use. (For example, you might be in an unusual situation in some specialized area of the law: you have a problem that has no standard analysis or potential solution. But if you'd made sure you had a thorough grounding in *all* the subject areas of the barzam, you might be able to *borrow* a concept from some other area of the law and apply it—by analogy— to the situation at hand. That's called "creative lawyering"…and will enchance your reputation.) If you check it out, you might get a pleasant surprise.

If you truly *know* the basic principles of the law, you will be constantly amazed at how ignorant so many of your fellow attorneys are regarding those same basic principles. The general level of ignorance of this "learned profession" is truly astonishing. *You* be the *exception* to the *rule.* This is where you can out-maneuver your opponent. This is where you can build a reputation as a *good lawyer.* (Having a reputation as a good lawyer will often get you the benefit of the doubt in a close-call situation.)

It may be hard for you to imagine it now, but being well-respected by other *attorneys* as a craftsman (craftsperson) of the law might someday be important to you. After all, other lawyers (particularly in your specialty, if you have one) will know the law better than your clients will, by definition. The respect of your clients will be crucial, of course. But they're like the audience at a jazz nightclub: the musicians are there because the audience is willing to pay for the performance. And the musicians respond with tunes that are "crowd-pleasers." That's as it should be. However, the really *good* musicians are actually playing for *each other.* It's great for them to be making money, and to be popular. But what they *most* value is the *respect of their fellow-musicians.*

You will find that what truly warms your heart as an attorney (other than a fat check that doesn't bounce) is the awareness that other *good* attorneys respect *you.*

And if you don't care about *that,* then please do the world a favor: don't go to law school. There are far too many lawyers in this country as it is… just far too few *good* ones.

Chapter 19 - Life After Law School

This is a book about law school, not the practice of law. However, because you're thinking about becoming a lawyer, you should think about what you want to do as a lawyer. This in turn will affect the choices you make while in law school, as to activities, courses, etc..

What follows is a *very* brief survey of various career paths in the Law.

The Groves of Academe

There's a saying, "The smartest law students become law professors; the second-smartest, judges. The rest become lawyers." I do believe that if you pull the grades in law school, and then get a prestigious judicial clerkship, you would be certifiably insane not to try to become a law professor. As chapter 4's example of Larry Tribe of HLS showed, you can have your cake and eat it too: a faculty post and a private practice, simultaneously. Unlike a lawyer who's a solo in private practice, you don't even have to pay your legal assistants, whether secretarial or what would otherwise be called paralegal (i.e., your student aides). (Be sure to wait until you get tenure before you take on a lot of outside work, though.)

However, given that affirmative action is still going strong, if you're a white male you might as well forget a faculty position at a prominent school— unless you clerked for a Justice of the U.S. Supreme Court, or at least for a top judge on a prestigious Circuit Court. (See chapter 20 for more information on getting a federal clerkship.)

In fact, most who become clerks for a U.S. Supreme Court Justice started out by clerking for a "justice" (judge) on one of the top circuits. Certain justices on these (and a few others) function as conduits to the High Nine. Only graduates of Harvard, Yale, etc., can go directly to Washington from law school…and it's rare even then.

Private Practice

It used to be there were only two respectable careers in the Law. The first was private practice, preferably with a prestigious firm. A new associate went from junior to senior associate, then either Made Partner—junior partner, at first—or was expected to leave the firm. (Paul D. Cravath, of Cravath, Swain & Moore—the ultra-prestigious firm in New York City—pioneered this "up or out" rule. He copied it from the officer corps of the U.S. armed forces, where—if you get passed over for promotion more than twice—you're expected to resign your commission.)

The other respectable career was the judiciary, preferably the federal judiciary. This was in part because most state judiciaries were and are tainted with corruption or incompetence. (Federal judges, in contrast, are tainted—

when they're tainted, and most *aren't*—only with incompetence.*)
However, at least some judges—whether state or federal—do have integrity
and ability.

It used to be that if you weren't a partner at a prestigious firm—or on
your way to being so—or weren't a judge, you were nothing. And because
most judges came directly from a partnership at a prestigious firm, there
was really only one path in the Law. The few exceptions, such as famous
trial lawyers like Clarence Darrow, were rare indeed. That's changed.

For example, some people—called "staff attorneys"—are hired with the
understanding that they will *never* Make Partner. I have no idea what they
do. And whatever it is, they don't get much respect for it.

Another designation is "Of Counsel." Back when, this described an unoffi-
cially retired Partner. It was sort of like being a "Professor Emeritus" at a
university. Or it might refer to a bigwig retired politician or judge, who'd
joined the firm as a rainmaker.

Today, that type of "Of Counsel" still exists, but rarely so. Now it's usually
someone who's regarded as more important than a staff attorney—and is
paid much more, relative his or her *work* at the firm. (Often, the Of Counsel
just moonlights at the firm, while maintaining a completely separate
practice of his or her own. What the Of Counsel has in common with the
staff attorney is that neither has a shot at Making Partner.)

Another change is in the nature of the law firm. Today, there aren't many
law partnerships left like the old ones were. They were general partnerships: Each partner could be held *personally* responsible for all the firm's
liabilities—and any partner could incur *unlimited* liabilities. So, each partner
could wipe out the net worth of all the others with the stroke of a pen or a
moment's thoughtlessness. Therefore, it was vital to be able to trust your
partners completely. Today, no one trusts anyone else at all in the Law—let
alone completely. The intense pressure to make money (also known as greed)

---

* You probably think I'm being a smart-aleck again...Well, in his first year as
President, Richard Nixon nominated a federal appellate judge, Clement F.
Haynsworth, Jr., to be an Associate Justice on the Supreme Court.
Haynsworth was described as "mediocre," and the U.S. Senate rejected the
nomination (in November, 1969). Two months later, not having learned the
lesson, Nixon named a federal district court judge, G. Harrold Carswell, to
the Court. He, too, was called "mediocre," and his nomination was also
rejected. What makes this episode amusing was the way in which Senator
Roman Hruska of Nebraska came to the defense of his President's nominees.
Exasperated by the repeated charge of "mediocrity," he finally exclaimed,
"There are a *lot* of mediocre judges and people and lawyers. Aren't they
entitled to a little representation?" —Lord knows they have representation
in the *Senate*. (Both judges remained on the federal bench after the defeat
of their nominations to the Supreme Court.)
    And don't forget the state judge mentioned in the footnote on page 36.

virtually guarantees there will be mistakes and "irregularities." Big ones. So, firms have transformed themselves into limited liability partnerships, professional corporations, professional limited liability partnerships, professional limited liability corporations, etc.. This way, the partners still get all the rewards for undiscovered incompetence and unethical behavior— and pay none of the costs (other than the deductible on their malpractice insurance) if and when these are exposed.

However, even though you might not be called a "partner" when you make the grade, there's still some distinctive transition. It appears the terms "junior" and "senior" partner are not used today. Instead, there are "non-equity" v. "equity" partners; or "non-participating" v. "participating" partners; or "employee" v. "shareholder" attorneys. The former, in each respective pairing, get only salary and bonus, just like the junior and senior associates. The latter get a piece of the action.

But there's an even bigger change. In the old days partners were like tenured professors. They couldn't be fired. Today they can, and are—when they don't make enough money for the firm.

As mentioned in the addendum to chapter 13, the general division in private practice is between litigation and a "transactions practice." Litigation includes trial and appellate law. (For the difference, see again chapter 13, regarding Mock Trial and Moot Court.) In a transactions practice, you rarely set foot in a courtroom. (But neither do many so-called "litigators," these days.) Your work involves preparing legal documents such as contracts, deeds, and wills. A transactions practice and a litigation practice have two things in common. The first is that both involve a lot of paperwork. The second is that both involve a lot of negotiating (with the exception of certain transactions practices, such as wills).

I won't discuss specific areas of practice (such as labor law or products liability litigation). There are too many of them. Chapter 20 presents tips on finding a job. One of those tips concerns information-gathering. That's where you'll learn of specific areas of practice, far better than I could describe them to you now.

<u>Corporate Counsel</u>
In the old days, becoming a corporation's *employee* as an attorney was embarrassing. The only lawyers who did that were those who hadn't Made Partner at a firm—but who didn't have the nerve to go out on their own. Those in private practice sneered at corporate counsel. Corporations allowed their legal departments to handle only *routine* matters. Anytime a corporation had a *serious* legal situation, it called in the "real" lawyers—the ones in private practice, nearly always those at a prestigious law factory.

Times have changed. For one thing, many corporate executives finally wised up and realized they'd foolishly bought into the mystique of the prestigious law firm. Today, corporate attorneys get a *lot* more respect than before…and more money. Many corporations still turn to outside attorneys, especially for major litigation. (This is often because the major firms have the connections to subtly influence the outcome.) Corporate counsel don't have to put in the hours—or put up with the stress—that attorneys in the law factories do, either. If your family is a high priority, corporate work is even better than being a staff attorney at a law firm; staff attorneys don't get the respect "line attorneys" do. And on a pay-per-hour basis beneath the partner level, the average lawyer in private practice quite often makes *less* than corporate counsel. Further, the general counsel at several corporations now make *millions* of dollars a year—as much as partners at even the biggest, most prestigious firms. And don't forget stock options.

If you like business, and have a flair for it, going to work for a business firm can be much more satisfying than working for a law firm. However, as a general rule, you should get some experience with a law firm first—the bigger, the better. (This is how you meet your future corporate employer, for one thing.) Corporate legal departments, in general, are not so interested in training their new people. —But this, too, may change.

Public Interest Law

This usually involves working for a non-profit corporation, at relatively low pay. In general, it doesn't get much respect…because of the low pay. Usually, those who graduated at the top of the class don't bother to apply for such jobs. —Nor do they bother to apply for jobs as prosecutors, for that matter. But there are always exceptions to the rule…especially for those who are already living off a trust fund. The two easiest examples of public interest law are the American Civil Liberties Union (ACLU), for liberals; and the American Center for Law and Justice (ACLJ) for the "religious new right." Anything that Ralph Nader is associated with also qualifies.

Contract Work

In recent years, a new area of private practice has opened up: contract work. This does not necessarily involve *drafting* contracts. Rather, it's "temp work"—being placed by an employment agency to do temporary work for an attorney or law firm on an "as needed" basis. It appears to be used heavily in connection with litigation. For example, contract attorneys pore over documents, looking for important facts. It's dull stuff. —But then again, so is most work in the Law. All the temp firms supposedly require you to have made good grades in law school.

The big advantages of being a contract attorney are: 1) you have much more control over your time, from month to month; and 2) you don't have to get caught up in the office intrigue that affects any law firm over a given size. As with being "Of Counsel" or a staff attorney, contract work is especially popular with those who want to spend at least as much time with their families as they do with other lawyers.

The big disadvantage is that you don't get much respect—if any—from other attorneys. This is because most contract attorneys took up that role because they couldn't find work anywhere else.

Government

Government employs a lot of attorneys; the total is much higher than the private sector. Big surprise. This includes everything from municipal regulatory agencies to the Attorney General or Solicitor General of the United States. Usually, it involves administrative law. Government work is usually transactional. However, prosecutors and full-time public defenders are an obvious exception (along with others). There's also the Judge Adjutant General (JAG) Corps of each branch of the armed forces. (Civilian attorneys can work for the armed forces even if they aren't members of the JAG Corps.)*

As you already know, the staffs of state legislators and members of Congress have *lots* of lawyers on them. In Congress, various committees and sub-committees often have their own separate staff, accountable to the committees themselves. Usually the staff members are lawyers.

Politics

I hardly need comment on this. Lawmakers make laws. Lawyers are trained—albeit badly—in the law. But if you're thinking of politics, don't forget judicial politics. (See below.)

The Judiciary

This does not necessarily mean *being* a judge. For one thing, courts have staff attorneys. Unlike a judicial clerk, who works for one specific judge for only a year or two immediately out of law school, the staff attorney works for the entire court. (Because there's only one judge to each trial court, there are no staff attorneys at the trial court level, only the appellate.) You can have an entire career as a staff attorney with one court.

And there's another option short of the typical judgeship: "Magistrates" and "Court Masters" are, often, lawyers who act as "associate judges," of a sort. For example, under the Constitution, the Supremes have original jurisdiction over certain kinds of cases. That means those cases *start*—and, obviously, end—in the U.S. Supreme Court. As you can imagine, the High Nine have better things to do than presiding over a trial. So, when a case of that type comes up, they turn it over to a Court Master.** The court master presides over the trial just as a regular judge would. Then, when it's over,

---

* The armed forces also have *summer associates,* even if you haven't enlisted. However, the Pentagon folks usually refer to these as summer "internships." Check your local yellow pages, your law school's Placement Office, or the publications mentioned in chapter 20, for listings of the JAG Corps for each service. You can then call to get more information, even about non-JAG internships.

** Sounds like a video game, doesn't it? I can see it now...

everything goes to the Supreme Court Justices. They read all the testimony, look at the evidence, etc.. And then—as always—they meet as a committee and decide the outcome. At lower levels of the judiciary, both federal and state, magistrates or court masters occasionally preside over entire trials.

Federal judges entitled to lifetime tenure are called "Article III" judges (because that's the part of the Constitution that authorizes them). Other federal judges, who lack lifetime tenure, are "Article I" judges (because Article *I* authorizes them). They also lack the power to declare that any litigants and their attorneys are in contempt of court—and to punish them for that contempt. Bankruptcy Court, Tax Court judges, and others are Article I judges: they're appointed for a limited term, and can be re-appointed. If you like working with financial statements and taxes, these are a good business-related alternative to being corporate counsel. But as with almost any other judicial appointment, you need good political connections to get one and keep it. (And note: Article I judges don't get near as much respect as Article III judges.)

As administrative law has increased, there's been a need for more "Hearing Officers" to resolve disputes. At the higher levels of the administrative appeals process, these Hearing Officers are always lawyers, and they're called Administrative Law Judges (ALJs). Most proceedings are governed by the rules of evidence as though they were regular trials.

In many states, judges are appointed and have life tenure. In others—those that use the "Missouri Plan"—they're initially appointed, but then must stand for election and re-election to keep their jobs. And in still others, prospective judges must stand for election, period.

Judicial politics aren't as bruising as normal politics. They're more like an election for County Clerk. However, you have to be "in good" with your political party's hierarchy—*and* with the local bar organization—to win.

In most states, you have to have been a lawyer for *x* years before you can become a judge. But the lower the judgeship, the lower the required time. For some posts, all you need is a law license.—In fact, I know of at least one state where you can be a county judge or a justice of the peace without even a law degree.*

As portrayed in the media, judges are learned, wise, etc.. I can think of only a handful of judges I've dealt with who fit that description. Most are political hacks, who got their jobs by doing enough favors for the right people in the right party. The wonder, then, is that the judiciary is as relatively good as it is. However, the stereotypical exalted image of a judge lingers. And "Judge" is, along with "Admiral," "Colonel," "Ambassador," and a few other terms, a title of address that survives even after you're no longer active in that role. It's a nice ego-trip.

And who knows? —You might even get to dispense *justice*...once in awhile.

---

* And by the way, federal judges—including *U.S. Supreme Court Justices*—don't have to be lawyers, either, or even law school graduates.

Mediation, Arbitration

In recent years, as the courts have clogged, the time it takes to bring a case to trial has stretched into the Great Beyond. Costs of litigation have skyrocketed (because there's so much pre-trial "discovery"). So, many disputants have turned to mediation and arbitration as a way to deal with their problem quickly and (relatively) inexpensively.

The mediator or arbitrator presides over a meeting between the parties. Sometimes, the parties' lawyers are also involved. Unlike a judge, a mediator or arbitrator is much more actively involved in the proceedings. If it's *binding* arbitration, the arbitrator has more in common with a judge than with a mediator. Otherwise, the arbitrator's recommendations are just advisory. So are the mediator's.

The big problem is if you're mediating or arbitrating between special interest groups. If you have a pattern of making honest recommendations that completely favors one side over the other, word gets around. Then your future as a mediator or arbitrator may suffer. This is because the mediator or arbitrator must be acceptable to both sides. No matter how reasonable your recommendations were, you will become known as "pro-" or "anti-" whatever. Therefore, mediators and arbitrators nearly always try to split the difference. Thus, if one party was absolutely in the wrong, that party comes away with more than it deserved.

In the past, to become a mediator or arbitrator, you had to have some background in the field. That's not so true, today. In some communities, there are now Neighborhood Dispute Resolution Centers. No expertise is required to serve there. (I don't think you get paid, either...but it's a good way to pick up referrals.)

If you want to help people resolve their differences, and to do it in a non-confrontational way, consider eventually working as a mediator or arbitrator.

Legal Journalism

America's love-hate relationship with lawyers shows no sign of waning. Journalists cover the law and lawyers more than ever before. And the most knowledgeable people to provide the coverage are...lawyers. There's a host of specialized legal media now, such as *The American Lawyer*, *The National Law Journal,* and Court TV. But even general interest publications, such as newspapers, are devoting more space—and sometimes a regular section— to lawyers. All these need reporters and editors. Even though you wouldn't be directly practicing law, you would still be working *with* "the law."

The Legal Information Industry

Technically, legal journalism is part of this. However, legal journalism is distinct enough that I listed it separately, above. The legal information industry includes materials provided to law students and lawyers. This is everything from textbooks and casebooks to loose-leaf services and on-line services. The "headnotes" in West's case reporters, for example, are prepared by West, not the court that issued the opinion that's printed in the reporter. All those headnotes are done by West's legal analysts, who are attorneys.

A separate sub-division is research-for-hire. It's similar to the contract attorneys mentioned above. The difference is the client hires a firm, rather than hiring specific lawyers. Usually, the *client* is a lawyer who's looking for some *fast* research.

Then there's the legal seminar biz. Usually, this involves lawyers making a presentation to other lawyers, such as in Continuing Legal Education seminars. However, it can also involve attorneys making presentations to laypeople. It can even involve presentations to those who are "in between"— i.e., law school graduates studying for the bar exam.

Others
You might eventually give up on the law altogether. Peter Ilych Tchaikovsky did, as did Gustave Flaubert. Studs Terkel, the columnist and author, was trained in the law: University of Chicago, Class of '34. So was televangelist Pat Robertson (founder of the ACLJ): Yale, '55. —And don't forget Geraldo Rivera (*née* Gerald Friedman): Brooklyn College of Law, '69.

In the alternative, there are also those who used their law degrees as a springboard to a career *related* to the law. Steven Brill, the entrepreneur who founded American Lawyer Media, Inc. (parent of *The American Lawyer,* Court TV, *et al.,*) is a licensed attorney. So is Ralph Warner, founder of Nolo Press, which distributes and publishes lawbooks-for-laypeople. Jack Crittenden, founder of *National Jurist,* is another law school alumnus.

U.S. Senator Robert Byrd of West Virginia, currently the Senate Minority Leader, is a law school graduate…who never took the bar exam. (And speaking of leaders who were trained in the law: there's Nikolai Lenin, Fidel Castro, Mihail Gorbachev…and Mohandas Gandhi.)

No need to mention the hundreds of lawyers who started as *outside* counsel to corporations—and then were brought inside to run the whole show.

* * *

To get an even better idea of what it's like in the real world of the law, there are several books about lawyers in any well-stocked bookstore. Here are two:

The first is a smorgasbord—*At the Bar: The Passions and Peccadilloes of American Lawyers,* by David Margolick. It's a 1995 paperback, and sells for $13. It's not systematic, and in fact is a selection of Margolick's work when he had an "At the Bar" column for the *New York Times.* But as a way to do to some literary browsing in the law, it's a fun read—and informative. (I believe Margolick is a licensed attorney.) Not as good, but still interesting, is *My First Year as a Lawyer: Real-World Stories from America's Lawyers,* edited by Mark Simenhoff. This 1994 ten-dollar paperback is a collection of 18 essays. (I had the impression many of these were written as a chapter from a novel-in-progress.)

* * *

I shall end this chapter with an apology. Virtually everything in this book talks in terms of your becoming a licensed attorney. More significantly, it talks in terms of your going to work for a law factory—rather than, say, becoming a solo practitioner or joining a public interest law firm. Yet, nearly *half* of all attorneys in private practice are *solo* practitioners. And as mentioned, many lawyers put their law degrees to work outside the legal profession.

As you saw in chapter 9, there's a tendency to get caught up in the "group think" mentality, early in law school. And this book certainly contributes to that. But it doesn't have to be that way, for you. Please do not get the idea that I think it should. Just keep in mind that, as the Opening Statement said, what this book is ultimately about is increasing you freedom of choice. (See the section on "Creating Your Own Job," in the next chapter, for an example.)

Chapter 20 - Tips on Finding a Job

As chapter 19 said, this is a book on law school. Anything else is noted just in passing. That goes for a mere chapter on finding a job, when there are entire books on this one subject. The purpose of this chapter is twofold: first, to pass along to you information about resources to aid your job search; second, to share some thoughts you perhaps won't encounter elsewhere.

Your law school will have a Placement Office. It's primarily for graduating students who seek "permanent" employment after graduation. Perhaps it also assists those who want to be summer associates. The Placement Office arranges for on-campus interviews with prospective employers. Make use of whatever help you can get from there.

The Winning Approach I

Make Law Review.

Then Get a Judicial Clerkship. No matter what you want to do with your law degree in the long run, in the short run you should get a judicial clerkship.

A judicial clerkship is similar to a court internship, discussed in chapter 12. However, a judicial clerkship is a full-time job after graduation. If you did very well in law school, you have a shot at a clerking with one of your state's higher courts, or with a federal court. And you should go for it. In fact, if you hope to become a law professor, you *must* go for it—with the highest court you can get.

But you don't just work for "the court." You apply for a post with a specific judge. (As mentioned earlier, for a district court, there's only one judge per court. At higher levels, there are many. Either way, you have to choose whom to contact.)

Usually, a graduating law school student who's good enough to get a federal appellate clerkship has already lined up a job with a prestigious law firm. He or she joins the law firm after finishing the clerkship. (Sometimes, as chapter 19 mentioned, there's more than one clerkship. Usually, though, only future law school profs do more than one—especially if the second one is with the U.S. Supreme Court.)

However, even if you don't have a private-sector job lined up, you should still try for the clerkship. This is because your judicial boss can pull strings to get you an offer you'd otherwise completely miss. Not only does a clerkship Look Good on the Résumé; it can also provide a safety net if all else fails.

Two Tips re. (Federal) Judicial Clerkships

First, if you didn't use *O'Connor's Federal Rules - Civil Trials* (see the addendum to chapter 7) to help you study first-year Civ Pro then you should get it and read it before you apply for any clerkship.

Second, be sure you know where your judge is…literally. A federal *district* court judge lives and works in the city where the district courthouse is. Such is not necessarily so with a federal *appellate* (circuit court) judge. (The district court is the trial court at the federal level. The circuit court is the first level of federal appeal.) All but one of the federal circuit courts cover several states. The judges on the court often continue to reside in the city where they were living before they were appointed to the court. They conduct most of their business by phone, including conference calls, and get together in person—in the city where the circuit courthouse is located—only when they're hearing oral argument in a case. So, if you're particular about where you want to live, find out where the circuit court judge you're interested in is *really* located.

The *Federal Judiciary Almanac* lists *every* federal judge in America: Article I judges as well as Article III. It's published twice a year by Prentice-Hall's Law & Business Division. It should be in your law school's library.

Chapter 15 mentioned *The National Jurist,* an independent magazine for law students. It does a newsletter, called the *Judicial Clerkship Insider.* It's a monthly, for $97 a year. Your law school library might subscribe to *Judicial Clerkship Insider.* If so, no charge to you.

Magazines and newspapers for lawyers also run occasional feature articles on specific courts and judges.

Obviously, you need to be prepared to discuss individual opinions the judge in question wrote. You read them in the case reporters. To find out what those cases are, you can use Westlaw or Lexis and do a search.

Your research should be nearly *complete* by the time you *start* third-year.

The Winning Approach II

Regardless of what you do your first year or so out of law school, you'll probably be working for a law firm after that.

The places where you apply for work know that you want a job. But they—quite rightly—suspect you really don't much care *where* you get work, as long as the money's good. You have to show them that you're after the *right* job, not just a "good" job—and that you've carefully selected this firm as your potential employer, whether summer or "permanent." The more you know about the legal industry, the particular law firm, and perhaps even individual senior attorneys there, the better.

Most of the major firms have promotional material. You should read this, of course. But anyone in his or her right mind will have read that material before the interview. So, it won't get you very far in distinguishing yourself if all you know about that firm is what you read in its own literature.

During the typical job interview, the student talks about himself or herself, usually in response to questions from the interviewer. The interviewer talks about the student's answers, and about the firm. You want to turn that around, to gently *take charge. You* talk about the *firm,* and in such a way that you prove you know what you're talking about, instead of the usual nebulous nonsense. In passing, you show why *you're* right for *them.*

By carrying on a well-informed conversation during your job interview, you'll prove you selected this firm carefully. (And you certainly want to find a way to show off the extent of your knowledge. Just be sure to leave out any bad stuff you've discovered in your research.) This shows two things: 1) you're sincere, and 2) you did some real homework. (If you've read John Grisham's *The Firm,* you'll perhaps recall how detailed the hero's knowledge was. He casually strutted his stuff in a pre-hiring encounter with the partners. They were impressed.)

Look Before You Leap

As chapter 12 noted, even if you Make Law Review, that doesn't necessarily put you on the road to happiness. Most law students get caught up in the snobbery of the Law. They go for the status. In terms of a job after graduation, they go for the most prestigious firms. If they get an offer, they have bragging rights. But bragging rights are small consolation if and when they realize, too late, that they joined a firm that's wrong for them.

Most job candidates come into an interview prepared only to talk about themselves. Other than grades and the résumé, there's not much for the firm to go on. Down the road, both parties are often disappointed. It's *your* responsibility to make an *informed* choice. In part this is because you will suffer more—*much* more—than your employer if the two of you were wrong about each other.

You need to know what's happening in the legal world. However, in the context of a job hunt, the "legal world" means what's happening in the "legal industry," the "law *market."*

Say you're looking at a particular law firm that's prestigious, high-paying, etc.. However, unbeknownst to you, the firm is on the verge of dissolving; big egos are clashing. Naturally, as always happens in these matters, the firm's official spokesperson denies this, and no one at the firm will speak on the record. But it's common knowledge the firm's days are numbered. Meanwhile, to keep up the front, the firm continues to interview prospective associates. Do you really want to have one of your summer clerkships *there?*

Second example: Say you clerked at a firm, and have received a permanent job offer. You learned, while a summer associate, that the senior partners are big boosters of certain political causes and the candidates of a particular party. No problem for you, as it turns out, because you more or less believe in the same causes and candidates. But there were a couple of things you *weren't* told: 1) all employees are "encouraged" to contribute generously in money and effort to designated causes and campaigns, and 2) those who don't will receive assignments that are more and more thankless, tedious, etc., than otherwise. In short, you're expected to be more than an avid fan. You're expected to buy season's tickets, in expensive seats. If your prospects with that firm depend on this, do you want to make such a commitment?

On a much larger scale, here's a third and final example: It used to be the law factories hired new associates in the belief that all of them were "partnership material." Sure, they knew some of the new people would eventually leave or be asked to leave, but each new associate was expected to have a future with the firm. That's no longer true. For one thing, there's more lateral hiring—at *all* levels—than ever before. Firms actively try to recruit one another's star performers, even entire departments. "Honor among thieves" has given way to back-stabbing and throat-slitting.

More and more, though, law firms engage in "bait and switch" regarding their new employees—the entry-level associates. I'm sure you've heard that many corporations replace mid-level (and middle-aged) managers with younger (*cheaper*) people; age discrimination laws to the contrary notwithstanding. The same thing now happens in law firms. An associate works at a "wholesale" salary, but his or her time is billed out at "retail." A $70,000 expense yields maybe $200,000-$300,000 a year in revenues to the firm. Once the associate makes Junior Partner (whatever it's called at that firm), or perhaps even just when he or she becomes a senior associate, the firm's profit margin shrinks. That person's salary has increased more, in percentage terms, than his or her billing rate has. So, at several firms, mass firings and replacements of nearly *all* associates who've been there awhile is nearly *routine* procedure. As you do your job search, find out if a firm you're looking at does this.

I've never gone through a job change in the Law, but I've been told that the process of trying to go from one firm to another, even on your own initiative, can be pure Hell. Keep that in mind before you choose your initial employer…and before you (voluntarily) decide to seek a job with a new firm.

Scanning the Horizon…Constantly
There is at most barely a year between the start of law school and the start of your first interview season. As chapter 11 noted, you can take four summer clerkships, max—and the offer of a permanent job probably comes (if it's made at all) at the end of the summer after your second year. So, you need to choose those summer posts wisely. And that means you need to start looking at law firms and areas of practice long *before* you start interviewing—which could be as early as the second semester of *first*-year. (Besides, if things don't "click" for you in your summer clerkship/s after year two, you sure don't want to be starting your job search from scratch in the fall of year *three*.) Most students wait until it's almost too late. Then they grab the first thing they can get that looks decent. "What we do in haste we regret at leisure" (or something like that).

Once you're in law school, join the special-interest clubs in areas that interest you. You might be able to pick up some good leads as to particular firms. However, keep in mind that everyone in that club is your competitor *vis-à-vis* the job market; so don't expect much.

Even before you start law school, you should consider getting a subscription to *The National Law Journal,* a weekly newspaper for lawyers. It normally costs $124 a year, but the student rate is half-price. *NLJ* will be a great source of information as to what the "hot" (and "cold") areas of the law are. It also runs articles on specific firms. This will help you pick up information as to a given firm's "culture." And *NLJ* runs a column on recent articles of interest that have appeared in academic law journals; these can help you in school, and out. (*NLJ* has also run reports on which federal judges get the most respect...and which ones serve as "feeders" of clerks to Justices of the U.S. Supreme Court.)

Another excellent publication is *The American Lawyer* Magazine. It's published ten times a year. The subscription rate for students is $99. Every year, in one of its fall issues, *The American Lawyer* runs the results of a survey it conducted among summer associates at the most prestigious firms. Although the responses for any given firm are not consistent from year to year, this information can be a big help to you in deciding where to interview—and which summer clerkship offers to accept. (Of course, your best source of information is always friends from law school who "think like you do," and who've clerked at the firms in question.)

Depending on where you're located, there are state-specific publications. (Examples: *California Lawyer, New York Lawyer, Texas Lawyer, Chicago Lawyer,* and the *Lawyer's Weekly* for Massachusetts, Michigan, Virginia, and other states.) These are even more likely to have articles on law firms in the area. If you know where you intend to practice, you should perhaps subscribe to a legal newspaper for that jurisdiction, if one exists. Call or visit a law library in that jurisdiction to find out what's available. (Many times, practicing attorneys don't know.) Be sure to speak with a real librarian, instead of a student assistant. Many of these publications also have a student rate.

Even while you're still in college, it would be a good move to subscribe to *The National Jurist*. It costs $18 a year, for six issues. (Once you get into law school, you should be able to get it for free, set out in stacks in the lobbies.) You should definitely join the American Bar Association's Law Student Division, first mentioned in the addendum to chapter 13. As noted there, dues are $15 a year. This gets you an automatic subscription to *Young Lawyer,* the ABA/LSD's magazine, *and* to the *ABA Journal.* (As mentioned, joining the ABA/LSD provides other benefits, too.)

Official bar association publications usually are little help. They always play it safe. (*Young Lawyer* is, in general, an exception—but it doesn't profile specific firms, anyway.) Even so, once in awhile you can learn something from them that will aid you in your job search. If you know where you intend to practice, join that state's bar association if you can while you're in law school. (Many state bar associations have something similar to the ABA/ LSD.) This should get you a subscription to that state's bar journal. Most major cities have their own bar association, too, with a "house organ." Join, and you get an automatic subscription.

If you can't afford all these dues and subscriptions, don't worry. You can read the various publications for free in a law library. Don't limit yourself to your law school's library, though. Depending on where you're in law school, there will be other law libraries, and these are open to the public (though the public doesn't know that). If you're in a major city, the city or county or its bar association might have its own law library. If you're in a state capital, the state supreme court will have its own law library. (By the way, if you can't find what you need regarding *books* in your law school's library, you might check in these other places.)

Many of the law newspapers have columns on significant cases won by a given firm, or on big new clients a specific firm has obtained. Use this information to impress your interviewers. The same thing is true if a firm has opened a new department. Even if you have no desire to work in that department, it will please your interviewers that you're *aware* of it— especially if it's still a relatively new development not yet reflected in their own literature. (You can also avoid disaster. For example, you'd look pretty bad if you told them how much you wanted to join their securities law department...and the entire securities law department just defected to a rival law firm.)

> Make a clipping file. (Save it even after you get a job following graduation. —It might come in handy some day, if things don't work out as you'd planned.) If you're reading these publications in the library, photocopy the relevant item, for your clipping file.

Phone Numbers (repeated in the appendix):

The American Lawyer	(212) 973-2800
The National Law Journal	(800) 888-8300
The National Jurist	(800) 296-9656
Young Lawyer (ABA/LSD)	(800) 285-2221

Detailed Profiles

Clearly, you want to read up on a firm in *Martindale-Hubbell,* the law directory.

You can also do law firm research on-line. West's Legal Directory™, accessed through Westlaw, gives a profile of the firm you select. You can also access the National Association for Law Placement / *Directory of Legal Employers* database. Through this, you can get information on a specific office of a firm—for example, a large national firm with many locations. With Westlaw's access to the "Dow Jones - All Database," you can search out recent news media mentions of the firm or specific attorneys in it. Last, you can use Westlaw to obtain a list of litigation in which a particular firm or attorney was listed as counsel of record. Lexis has similar capabilities.

The National Jurist, Inc., does a newsletter for law school students who seek jobs with private firms. Its *Employment Insider* is published biweekly. The company regularly polls every law firm in the country that has between ten and 75 attorneys. (These are the firms that are less likely to interview at law schools.) If and when you sign up, you immediately get the most recent edition of another National Jurist publication, the *Hiring Directory*. This is published three times a year. For first- and second-year students, the *Directory* they get lists firms looking for summer associates. That for third-years lists the firms looking for permanent employees. Each subsequent issue of the newsletter then supplements the latest *Directory*. The *Directory* typically lists between 400 and 600 firms. Each issue of the newsletter then covers another 20-35 firms that say they're looking to hire at least one new attorney. That way, you get leads you wouldn't otherwise have known of. *Employment Insider* is available in four editions: Northeast, South, Midwest, and West Coast. Your choice. A year's subscription is 24 issues, and costs $97. If you don't get a full-time job within the period of your subscription, you get a full refund. (Note: This money-back guarantee does *not* apply to the judiciary newsletter.) I've not seen an issue. You might want to call and ask for an old back-issue as a sample. (Your school's Placement Office might have a subscription. If so, no charge to you.)

There's one book on the market that gives profiles of 200 firms in 11 cities. It's *The Insider's Guide to Law Firms,* from Mobius Press. The editors are Sheila Malkani and Michael Walsh. The information in their book is almost as candid, and perhaps more useful, than the summer associate surveys in *The American Lawyer.* The 11 cities covered are: Atlanta, Baltimore, Boston, Chicago, Dallas, Houston, Los Angeles, New York City, Philadelphia, Pittsburgh, San Francisco / Palo Alto, and Washington, D.C.. As of this writing, the second edition, published in 1993, is the most recent. It's $29, in paperback.

A Tip for Summer Associates

If you work as a summer associate in a "law factory," and you like the firm, and you think you have a shot at getting a permanent offer, be sure to do the following during your clerkship: 1) become very familiar with the library—especially the materials not available through CALR, 2) get on good terms with the librarian/s therein, 3) get on good terms with any and all secretaries and staff you deal with.

Your survival as an entry-level associate is officially in the hands of your supervising attorneys. (It goes without saying that you must also get on good terms with any and all attorneys you deal with...so I won't say it.)

However, your skills re. #2-#3 can have a big impact on your job performance. This is true even when things are going smoothly. But it's especially true when you're in a crunch situation. This will happen—and usually when you least expected it. (The first one is important for its own sake. But it's also important because your firm's librarians will be more likely to help you if they know you've already familiarized yourself with the library—and thus don't have to be led around by the hand.) Members and veterans of the armed forces know that non-commissioned officers—the corporals, sergeants, petty officers—are sometimes in a position to make or break a commissioned officer's next promotion...or entire career. Be mindful of the Golden Rule.

Using Your Connections

Chapters 12 and 13 spoke of judicial internships, research assistantships, etc.. Sometimes the judge or professor or faculty litigator you worked for is asked to recommend someone. He or she just might recommend you. And sometimes, the judge or professor you worked for takes a more active role, and will pull strings to get you an offer—or at least a job interview—that might you never have been able to get on your own.

Of course, if you've been active in the ABA/LSD, ATLA, etc., you will have made contacts there. (See also the "Inns of Court," mentioned in chapter 21.)

Résumés

Do not rely on one all-purpose résumé. In these days of software and laser printers, there's no excuse for that. If you've done your research, prepare a *customized* résumé for almost every potential employer. Granted, most law firms look for the same things. But if you have a good feel for the distinguishing characteristics of a particular firm, you can put something special in the résumé for that firm. (The same thing goes for your cover letter.)

For example, if you're trying to get a job at a law factory known for its political connections with a major party, your résumé for that firm should list your own involvement with that party (assuming you have indeed been involved). If you notice that all the (male) senior partners at the firm belong to the Masonic Order, and you belonged to De Molay or Job's Daughters in high school, list it on the résumé you submit to *that* firm. (A good way to find out such things is to check publications such as *Who's Who* or the biographical index of the local paper.)

Do not list your membership in law-related organizations that might raise your prospective employer's eyebrows—unless you're *sure* your target firm will like it. Sometimes these are liberal organizations (The National Lawyers' Guild), sometimes conservative (The Federalist Society). In fact, don't list anything that *might* trip you up. Always do your homework first.

Even if you can't customize your résumé for particular firms, you can do so for particular types of work. The résumé you prepare to try to get a job that involves work as a trial lawyer should be quite different from the résumé you prepare to try to get a job that involves work in the patenting and copyrighting of computer software. (Future barristers, for example, can list their membership in the student division of the Association of Trial Lawyers of America, or similar state and local organizations—even if you intend to apply to a firm that only does defense work. What you learn from ATLA is just as useful for aspiring defense counsel as it is for future plaintiffs' attorneys. —Just make sure you mention that in your interview, so they know which side you're on.)

Most of your competitors as applicants will present the same credentials as you: outstanding grades, Law Review, etc.. You need to have something on your résumé that causes the firm to want to interview *you*.* If there's a way to make you stand out from the crowd, do so—as long as it isn't something weird. (Warning: It's very easy to be "weird," by lawyer standards.)

—Of course, if you've Made Law Review, they'll probably interview you without further ado. Then your task is to make sure *you're* among those they want to *hire.*

A Tip for Minorities re. Your Résumé

Most firms—and *all* judges—choose whom to interview after screening applicants' résumés. Sometimes, they engage in affirmative action (or reverse discrimination, depending on your point of view). If you're Hispanic, and have an Hispanic surname, no problem. But if you're of Asian ancestry, with an "American" name such as Lee, your prospective employer won't have a clue. Same thing if you're black. So, the way you tip them off as to your minority status is to join your minority group's student association and then list it on your résumé. (You're probably welcome to join one of these clubs even if you're not a member of the minority group in question. But if that's the case, don't list it on your résumé: It will be assumed that you're trying to pull a fast one, and retribution will be swift.) If your school doesn't have an Asian-American Students Association, or a Black (or Afro-American) Students Association, start one—even if you're its only member. Then you get to list yourself as its president, too. (This is the sole exception to the rule that becoming an officer in a student organization is a waste of time for the purpose of Looking Good on the Résumé.)

—Also, if you're Jewish, with a "Gentile" name, and want to apply to a heavily Jewish firm, join—or start—a "Jewish Law Students Association."

---

* I heard of a guy who won $67,000 on the TV show *Jeopardy* shortly before he started law school. He put that on his résumé. I doubt that's what *got* him interviews. However, *during* his interviews, *every one* of the firms asked him about it. In one or two cases, that's almost the *only* thing they wanted to talk about. (And don't forget the discussion of foreign legal studies, in chapter 15.)

List that on your résumé for the target firm. (Or skip this, and just list your involvement with other Jewish activities, such as synagogue, UJA, and JCCA.)*

<u>A Tip for Women re. Your Résumé</u>

If you have a first name that could be that of either a man or a woman, clear up any possible confusion on the résumé itself, and in your cover letter. Example: Your first name is Sidney. Your name is at the top of your résumé. The assumption will be that you're male. If you're female, put "(Ms.)" in front of your name. Do the same thing where you type in your name below your signature on the cover letter. (But when you sign, leave off the "Ms.," of course.)

If you're a feminist, you might object to my statement about the presumption that you're a man. Maybe you think a man whose first name is Sidney should put "(Mr.)." Forget it. —Although, if you're a man, and your first name is *Lynn,* it might be wise to put "(Mr.)" in front of your name after all. Besides, women have an advantage, although these days they seldom have an opportunity to use it… Example: You're married, and you want to get a job with an outfit you know is *very* conservative (traditional family values and all that). You signal your own conservativeness in part by putting "(Mrs.)" before your (married, not maiden) name—even if your given name is clearly that of a woman. (You should also belong to something like the Daughters of the American Revolution—and list that on your résumé for that firm.)

—An alternative to this, regarding announcing your gender, is to just use your full name if it includes an obviously female name in it. "Sidney Jennifer Jones," for example. However, at some point, you'll have to let them know you go by "Sidney"; it would sound pretentious to always seek to be informally addressed as "Sidney Jennifer."

Odds & Ends

<u>Looking—and Sounding—the Part</u>

The words that follow I find distasteful. You will too, probably. However, the first part of the subtitle of this book is *What You Need to Know*. In the interest of telling you the truth, the whole truth, and nothing but the truth, I have to include this sub-section.

Discrimination on the basis of looks—appearance—is a fact of life. The movies and TV people understand this quite well. Villains nearly always have displeasing physical features. Heroes and heroines are nearly always good-looking. Studies have shown that mothers of newborns are less affectionate with their infant if the baby is ugly. And to get elected to public office these days, you'd better be photogenic.

---

* The same thing works for a student who's Christian and wants to work for a firm heavy with those active in "Christian causes." Et cetera.

The same sort of discrimination exists in the Law. Chapter 13 discussed how jurors favor the side whose attorney they like. More often than not, the one they like is the better-looking. Potential employers hire those they like. More often than not, the better-looking applicants are the ones they like, all other things being equal.

This is not to say that you must have the physique of a model to be a success in the Law. But if your physical qualities are not within the parameters of a particular firm, chances are you won't get a summer clerkship, no matter how good your grades.

In one sense, this isn't the problem for men the way it is for women. The range of what's acceptable is greater for men than for women. But there are limits. It's okay to be a large man. In fact, it's a plus: tall men, especially, are more admired, automatically—even by other men—than short men are. But large women have a problem. Fat people, of either gender, are discriminated against, but fat women moreso than fat men. Those with disfiguring birthmarks or scars are shunned, typically. Those with disabilities, especially something as salient as cerebral palsy, but even as relatively subtle as a gnarled left hand, are also subject to avoidance.

The more prominent the law firm, the more likely its employees are winners in the genetic lottery. Keep that in mind. "Lookism" is especially important for rainmaking (bringing in new business).

This is particularly important for two groups of lawyers. The first is trial lawyers, for reasons already stated.*

The second group where appearance is particularly important consists of those who deal with highly successful people—corporate executives in the area of business law, and wealthy individuals in the area of estate planning. In either, "All-American good looks" count heavily. (In the latter, as an alternative, it helps to resemble the stereotypical, elegant aristocrat.)

However, while a truly handsome man has an advantage, a truly handsome woman has a number of disadvantages. I don't need to spell them out.

---

* However, as elsewhere, there are exceptions to the rule. Too many male trial lawyers look too slick: the $1,000 suit, the Rolex watch, the silver hair and the $50 styling thereof. It obviously hasn't hurt them in court. But jurors resent the privileged status of attorneys. And so, often, they find the unpretentious lawyer more likable. One guy I know of wears decent but obviously inexpensive suits...and he has a very crooked set of teeth. He obviously came from a family that couldn't afford braces. Many jurors have a similar background, so they identify with him. (What they don't know is that this guy makes almost a million bucks a year, year in and year out.) Gerry Spence, one of the most successful trial attorneys in America, constantly wears a silly fringe jacket in court—and keeps his hair long even today. (He's cultivating an image of rugged frontiersman, of course. If he could get it past the metal detectors, I'm sure he'd keep a Bowie knife in a buckskin sheath tied to his belt. And if he thought it would help, he'd probably wear a coonskin cap. By extension, this contrivance extends to his client's image. And it usually works with juries.)

But speaking of women: this sub-section includes "sounding" the part. Many young women (and even some older ones) talk with high-pitched "little girl" voices. Such voices carry little credibility as authority figures—and a lawyer is supposed to be an authority on the law. (A high-pitched voice in a man is also a problem, obviously. But it's much less frequent, obviously.) If you have a voice like that, work on changing it.

Next: Male or female, if you come from a lower-middle-class (or downright poor) background, you will need to learn how to act and sound like an upper-middle-class professional. Although I have repeatedly condemned the portrayal of lawyers on TV and in the movies, I must admit that the "crispness" these actors exude in their attorney roles (when they're portraying the *good* guys—and gals) is exactly the sort of air you want to have. So, whatever your background, if you don't already come across this way, watch and learn from show business: *not* how the attorneys act in *trial,* but how they talk and carry themselves *outside* the courtroom.

Related to this is learning how to handle yourself in an interview. If you have little or no experience dealing with upper-middle-class bosses when seeking a job, you'd better get some practice at it. Perhaps your school's placement office conducts "mock interview" sessions. If they don't, try to arrange it through a student association or a young lawyers' group. Obviously, if you blow the interview, you blow the job. Don't let poor interviewing skills cost you an opportunity for which you're genuinely qualified.

Back to women: Far too many female attorneys seem to believe that the way to gain respect from men is by acting like jerks. Somehow they think that an outward show of macho toughness, perhaps including off-color jokes, makes them one of the boys. It doesn't. There's a difference between the no-nonsense approach and that of a pit bull. The women attorneys who are most respected are those who can be tough as nails when the occasion demands it, but who are always polite and even genteel. I think that's the way men should be, too. But unfortunately, it's still acceptable for men to be otherwise. It isn't for women. Instead of trying to descend to the level of a male jerk, women should be setting a better example. (So should those males who aren't jerks.) You don't have to be an asshole to gain respect as an attorney.

Two other groups merit special attention. The first is racial minorities. Racial discrimination still exists, as you know. And, unfortunately, affirmative action all too often puts members of minority groups under a cloud of suspicion as to their competence. It used to be said that a *woman* had to be twice as good as a man to be regarded as an equal. I doubt that's true anymore. But I'm willing to bet it's true for racial minorities.

Because of blind grading in law school, you can objectively prove your academic worth. But once you're out in practice, it's a whole new ballgame. And it starts when you're looking for a job. You *have to* look and act and sound like a professional...and being professional is not a matter of race.

I've dealt with two blacks—one a man, one a woman—who are among the best examples of "crispness" I'll ever meet in my life. (One is a federal judge.) My hunch is that they're both involved in programs whereby they can serve as role models and mentors to aspiring black attorneys. If you're a member of a racial minority group, ask around: wherever you are, there should be at least one such person, and he or she might be willing to help *you*.

For the average man or woman, it's rough being a non-white person in American society, even now—and even if you come from a family that's upper middle class. (But this is hardly news to you.) Just be advised that the world of the Law is still overwhelmingly white, and part of the lingering racism of our society is that a non-white attorney will not get the benefit of the doubt the way the average white attorney will. (Recall the discussion—on page 136 in chapter 10—of the incident involving an overtly racist professor at my law school and a black student in one of his classes.)

The other group that merits special attention is homosexuals. For homosexual women, there's not much of a problem. For homosexual men, there is. I will not urge you to stay in the closet. Just don't *flaunt* it. Your private life—including your sex life—is none of your employer's business, anyway. Please avoid an in-your-face attitude...unless you've found a law firm composed entirely of gays who cater to a gay clientele.

This really isn't a matter of sexual preference, though: "straight" males who are playboys will also find that it counts against them if they flaunt their sex lives at the office. The difference, as you know, is that many straights get up-tight just at the knowledge that a colleague is "gay."

Life is unfair. Life is cruel. And life is rough. So is a life in the Law. I can't do much to change it, and neither can you, although in our own small way, each of us can try. If you fit any of the descriptions here, perhaps my random comments will help you to evaluate your situation, and your prospects...and to plan accordingly.

I'm no expert in any of these matters. No doubt I'll get at least a few angry letters accusing me of being insensitive, at the very least, or bigoted, at worst. I'm not trying to pick a fight or to be condescending. I share these thoughts with you in the spirit of letting you know what you're up against. If, as a male WASP who's straight, *I'm* part of what you're up against, so be it. I apologize for whatever offense I've given.

Of Dual Degrees

The job market for lawyers is tight, and likely to remain so. Many prospective attorneys wonder if they should get a second degree. Sometimes this takes the form of a combination degree. For example, you go four years straight, taking courses in business school and law school. You end up with an MBA and a JD—in one year less than it would take you if you got the one and then the other. Another option is to pick up a second law degree, such as an LL.M. in Taxation. That takes a year.

I advise against either. For one thing, if you follow the recommendations of *Planet Law School,* you almost certainly will not have to worry about finding a good job. Regardless, the MBA has lost its luster, unless it's from a top school. Unless you plan to eventually work as corporate counsel, I do believe it's a waste of time and money. As for the LL.M., you should have a practice concentration *before* getting the Master's—in which case, why bother getting the Master's? Having the LL.M. might get you a job you wouldn't otherwise get, but I doubt it. Both options are great money-makers for the law schools, though—*which is why they promote them.*

It seems to me that most people who get the Master's are junior faculty at lower-rated law schools. Often, their J.D. is from a school that isn't ranked high, either. Even though their grades were good enough to become law professors at "regional" schools, they know they face a "glass ceiling," to use a buzzword. So, they go to a place like Harvard, Yale, or Stanford to pick up the LL.M.. The Master's itself isn't what's important to them; nor is the subject area. What's important is where it's from. They hope the prestigious credential will give them a better chance of being hired at a more prominent school. (I also knew a guy who picked up a Master's because it enhanced his résumé for a judgeship he wanted.)

Finally, it appears that a lot of LL.M. candidates are those who went straight into the Master's program after getting their J.D....because they couldn't find a job when they got out of law school. *The law firms know this.*

Pro Bono

"Pro bono" is short for "Pro bono publico"—"for the public good." It's where an attorney provides legal services free of charge, usually on a one-shot basis, for organizations or individuals who can't afford any attorney at all. This became quite fashionable during the '60s. There are still lawyers who do it. (Technically, public interest law—discussed in chapter 19—is sort of a full time pro bono publico. However, because those who do it are getting paid for it, "pro bono" does not include public interest law. —After all, those who successfully represent an employer who busts the workers' union will tell you, with a straight face, that *they're* acting for the public good, too —at $250 an hour.)

Over the past few decades, it's become standard procedure for big firms to talk about opportunities for new associates to do pro bono work. I urge you to forget it. You're not qualified to be practicing law on your own—which is usually what a pro bono case involves, in effect. Get good at what you're supposed to be doing for money, first. It's better to wait until you and your firm know if you're worth what they're paying you, before you start asking them to let you work for other people for free while you're on the firm's time.

Don't put the cart before the horse. There will always be plenty of pro bono opportunities. Show your sophistication by making this very argument if the subject comes up. (Your prospective employer doesn't like pro bono anyway—unless it's a high profile cause that adds to the firm's image.

They talk about it because they think it's expected of them. But it's a trap for the unwary. If you stress pro bono, you probably won't get a job offer. And even if you do get the offer, you'll never be allowed to do pro bono anyway—with the exception just noted.)*

Do not get me wrong: I think any attorney who graduated from a *public* law school (i.e., taxpayer-subsidized) ought to be *required* to do a minimum amount of pro bono every year. "Much is expected from those to whom much has been given." Everyone should do at least some pro bono. I urge you to, also…but only when you're experienced enough to be able to do it *right*. ("We are not the first who with best meaning have incurred the worst." — Cordelia, in Shakespeare's *King Lear*.)

Creating Your Own Job

By "Creating Your *Own* Job," I do not mean hanging out your own shingle; or rather, not *just* that. And I've put this section in *this* chapter rather than the one about "Life After Law School" (chapter 19) because *this* chapter has talked of "Looking before You Leap" and "Scanning the Horizon." I now share with you how one law school student did exactly that, to his immense satisfaction…

During his second year, his state's legislature rewrote its Family Code. The overhaul was an upheaval for attorneys who'd specialized in family law. It was no longer business as usual for them; they had to re-learn everything. The revisions were complete by the end of this student's second semester in year two. He then spent the entire summer analyzing the new code and comparing and contrasting it with the old. He met with legislators (and with their assistants, who'd actually written the code). He made the rounds of the law school professors who'd served as consultants to the legislature, and openly informed them of what he was doing. He solicited their expertise—and got it, free. They indulged him because he was a mere student. Cleverly, he also consulted some of the leading members of that state's family law bar, with the same result.

That fall, before the new code went into effect, his analysis was published in the state's bar journal. It was a godsend to the family law practitioners. He then expanded his work into a manual, which was published in his third year of law school. In short, he scooped all the family law *experts* in the state: he himself became the *authority* on the new code. Even though he had not Made Law Review, he got several wonderful job offers from family law specialists. They wanted to be able to brag that *they* had him on *their* payroll. (And he'd already met all the top practitioners, who thus already

---

* Then again, there are some firms that take pro bono quite seriously. In fact, a handful have hired a full-time pro bono coördinator to try to match lawyers' desires to available opportunities. So, if you really are serious about doing pro bono, look for these.

knew him from a *formal* but non-job-interview encounter; all by itself, that gave him an edge. —And I'm sure his interlocutors had already been evaluating him as a potential future employee when they first spoke with him.) A bidding war ensued. (Too, he was already collecting royalties on the sale of the manual.) *One year* after he got out of law school, he was chosen to head the Family Law Section of the State Bar—at the ripe old age of *26.*

—Nice work, if you can get it...and maybe you *can* get it, if you're alert (and work your butt off).

Hanging Out
Your Own Shingle

I strongly advise you not to set up shop on your own, fresh out of law school. You should at least get some practice under the guidance of a more experienced attorney. However, for whatever reasons, there are people who hang out their own shingle before the ink is dry on their law license. If and when you go solo, here are two books that are the best. The first is *How to Start and Build Your Own Law Practice,* by Jay G. Foonberg. The American Bar Association publishes it—which naturally means its price is high: $40, in paperback. It is now in its 3d edition. Foonberg covers almost everything, but covers it rather quickly. Another book, less costly, is *The Young Lawyer's Handbook.* This one's also in paperback, and costs $16. The author is Polly McGlew. It's hard to find it in a regular bookstore or to order it through one. The publisher is Future Horizons, Inc.. You can reach them by phone at (817) 277-0727. The McGlew book covers fewer topics than Foonberg's, but covers each of them more thoroughly, especially the nuts-and-bolts of setting up and running your own office. If you can afford to, get them both.

Many state bar associations also have their own books on going it alone. And nearly 20 states now have mandatory courses for new attorneys on "the basics of practicing law." So, although I still advise against going solo while you're still wet behind the ears, at least there are some good do-it-yourself guides out there.

Miscellaneous
Helpful Materials

Carolyn Nutter did a great book years ago that's still in print, *The Résumé Workbook: A Personal Career File for Job Applications.* It's not specifically for graduating law students or lawyers. However, I think it's the very *best* book of its kind. Nutter tells you how to create a résumé that gets you an interview. (If you don't get your foot in the door, you can't make the sale.) I've used it myself, and *always* got called in. I was astounded to learn that this book is still just ten dollars, in paperback. It's easily worth five times as much. Get it—*even if you decide not to go to law school.* It's that good. But it's hard to find in bookstores, and many won't even special order it. The publisher is Sulzburger & Graham. Their toll-free number (repeated in the appendix) is (800) 366-7086.

I've heard that two other books are excellent, but I've not read them yet. The first is *Guerrilla Tactics for Getting the Legal Job of Your Dreams,* by Kimm Alayne Walton. It costs $25. (Walton also wrote the Sum & Substance book, *Strategies and Tactics for the MBE,* mentioned in chapter 18.) The second is *The Legal Job Interview,* by Clifford Ennico, which sells for $18. You will have no trouble getting either one through a bookstore.

West's Sum & Substance division does an audio cassette called *Interviewing With Law Firms.* It lasts an hour-and-a-half, and costs $20. But I've not heard it, so I can't vouch for it.

It's already been mentioned how important it is for you to come across as a crisp (future) professional, and how this includes looking the part, as much as you possibly can. It's even more important, of course, to do so when you're around prospective employers—especially when you show up for your job interviews. John Malloy wrote two classics that are still in print. Both are now in paperback. His original book was *Dress for Success,* now in a revised edition. There's a companion volume, *The Woman's Dress for Success Book.* The men's book is $14; the women's, $11. As with *The Résumé Workbook,* each is easily worth five times its price. Even if you decide not to go to law school, you'll probably be applying for a job someday where you have to look like a professional. You'll also need to look like a professional during your Mock Trial, Moot Court, or other competitions—and at any official school functions where you mingle with faculty and deans in a formal setting. So, get the Malloy book for your gender, and do what it says, period.

If you're planning to be a trial lawyer (and maybe even if you're not), be sure to get Kenney F. Hegland's *Trial and Practice Skills in a Nutshell, 2d ed.,* first mentioned in the addendum to chapter 13. Its chapters on interviewing clients, legal problem-solving, counseling clients, negotiating, legal argument, and legal writing are all magnificent. It's the best one-volume reference you can find on these topics. It's especially good for solos.

There's something else you should read. It's *The Young Lawyer's Jungle Book: A Survival Guide,* by Thane Josef Messinger. It is truly wonderful. It was written mostly for entry-level associates at law factories. (Do not confuse it with *The Young Lawyer's Handbook,* by Polly McGlew, mentioned above. That's for those hanging out their own shingle, whether as a solo or starting up a small firm.) No matter where you are, the ladder to the top gets narrower as you move up, and the rungs get farther apart. Messinger's book will be *invaluable* to you in avoiding a misstep. But the lessons it contains apply to *anyone* who practices law, no matter whether you go to work for a law firm (big or small), a corporation, the government, the armed forces, a judge, or what have you—even solo. Don't wait until you've been hired for a permanent job before you get *The Young Lawyer's Jungle Book,* though. On the contrary: it's important for you to know how to function smoothly even in a judicial internship, a judicial clerkship—and *especially* in a *summer* clerkship. As with *Planet Law School, The Young Lawyer's Jungle Book* gives you the benefit of everything the author learned the *hard* way. Foresight is always better than hindsight. Messinger shows you how to be "professional" in fact as well as in job title. His book costs about $19 —one of the best bargains you'll *ever* find in a book for lawyers.*

---

* Yes, it's published by the same company (The Fine Print Press, Ltd.) that published *this* book. But that's not why I'm recommending it. In fact, I got the idea for doing *Planet Law School* while reading Messinger's book, and then contacted his publisher. (And by the way, the "g" in Messinger is hard.)

Part V:

Countdown to Law School

Chapter 21 - Should You Really Do This?

Tort law makes much of the concept of "notice"—in the sense of someone having been put *on* notice of a situation that could cause harm to others. The purpose of this chapter is to put you on notice of a situation that could cause harm to *you*. Going to law school, and becoming an attorney, is that situation. Before you make the commitment, ask yourself: "Should I really do this?"

Here's a short quiz:

1. Do you like to get emotionally involved with your work?
2. Do you dislike or attempt to avoid conflict?
3. In resolving conflict, do you prefer deciding what's fair based on the circumstances of each situation?
4. Do you like to create or start projects and let others finish and / or maintain them?
5. Do you dislike paying attention to details?
6. Do you prefer short-term projects?
7. Do you value efficiency?
8. Do you like to do things your own way, on your own schedule, and in order of your own priorities?
9. Do you get more satisfaction being part of a team than being a solo act?
10. Do you want to change the world?

The is taken—with her permission—from Deborah L. Arron's book, *Running from the Law: Why Good Lawyers are Getting Out of the Profession.* (Arron practiced law herself for a decade before her own departure. She now has a consulting and counseling business, helping attorneys who also want to bid the bar adieu.*)

After posing her questionnaire, she says this:

> *"A 'yes' answer to <u>any</u> of the above questions*
> *ought to raise <u>serious reservations</u>*
> *about the wisdom of entering law school,*
> *and especially about planning to use your degree*
> *to <u>practice</u> law."* (Emphasis added.)

---

* You might want to save the following information, either for yourself or for an attorney friend: Deborah Arron's office phone is (206) 285-0288. The fax is (206) 213-0750. Her e-mail address is dlajd@aol.com. She's written other books for lawyers. One's for those who are wondering what they'd do if they left the profession. It's called *What Can You Do with a Law Degree?* A 1994 paperback, it costs $32.

I did not discover her book until after I'd been practicing awhile. I took the quiz—and answered a *strong* "yes" to *five* questions, a "yes, but it depends" to *four*...and a "no" to only *one*. So, there's a high probability I too shall eventually join the exodus from the profession. (And maybe this chapter is my first step.)

The Gauntlet

Perhaps you're interested in going to work for a prestigious firm. (That's where the big bucks are.) When Richard Kahlenberg was still in law school, he asked a friend—an attorney with a prestigious firm in Boston—about what big-firm lawyers do. After thinking it over, his friend left this message on Kahlenberg's answering machine:

> Labor law is basically oppressing laborers. Estates and probate work is largely planning the estates of very wealthy individuals in the Boston area. Corporate and business law tends to be helping large corporations take over small corporations, and therefore leads to the oligopoly of the wealthy and basically screwing the workers over to make enough money to pay for the loans they have to take on, which lawyers negotiate, incidentally. Corporate work also involves giving middle managers and the above what they call "golden parachutes," which tend to be extremely large payments to management so they will not object and try to bar a takeover attempt.
>
> Real estate law involves helping large corporate developers buy up property at low prices, usually by using the mechanism of the state to rake in huge tax write-offs. Municipal bond work involves floating bond issues which are bought by wealthy individuals in the United States and produce tax-free benefits for wealthy individuals at high marginal tax rates...

Doesn't all that sound fulfilling? This statement has far more truth than jest...as you will discover if and when you join a major law firm.

In *Broken Contract,* Kahlenberg reported a survey of his entering class at Harvard Law School (1986). Seventy percent wanted to go into public interest law. Yet, three years later, Kahlenberg himself was perhaps the only person in his entire class (of roughly 550) to do so.

This is not to say that most students *should* go into public interest law. But obviously there'd been a sea change between first- and third-year. Students entering law school often want to serve the most progressive and compassionate ends. However, they nearly always end up serving the regressive and callous.

The change occurs because *law school itself <u>deliberately</u> causes it*—everywhere, not just at Harvard. First-year is the crucial part of this.

It starts with the Case/Socratic Method's intentional confusion and mystification, as discussed in chapters 3 and 4. But there's more than that to it. Far more. Chapter 4 quoted the first edition of a book by NYU Law alumnus George J. Roth, *Slaying the Law School Dragon*. Here's another passage from it:

> *Intimidation* is the law school dragon. It is nurtured on a mother's milk so soured by the catalytic action of incompetent and sadistic professors that its chemical composition is changed from what could be enlightenment and pleasurable acceptance of knowledge into anxiety, inordinate competition, and deep frustration.
>
> The anxiety comes from not knowing what you're doing, not knowing where you stand academically in the class for weeks at a time, and not knowing where you're going to find time to do all the things which are expected of you.
>
> The inordinate competition is engendered by a system of daily recitation which is *designed to make you look stupid, cause traumatic embarrassment, and make you feel like you were never cut out to be a lawyer in the first place.* The big pitch is to get high grades so you can get a job in a good law firm when you graduate. Every classmate is a potential enemy. (Emphasis added.)

Granted, the second edition of Roth's book (11 years later) deleted this. However, Roth obviously felt it had been true of *his* experience in law school or he wouldn't've put it in the original edition.

Now here's a passage from a book by Mark H. McCormack, a Yale Law alumnus. It's called *The Terrible Truth about Lawyers*.

> /T/he Socratic Method...can also be thought of as **The Professor Always Wins, and the Student Lives in Terror.**
>
> Make no mistake, *terror is an integral part of the law school experience...*
>
> (The emphasis—both the bold print and the italics—is in the original.)

The Terrible Truth about Lawyers was not written for prospective law students. McCormack, like Arron, left the Law and became an entrepreneur. His book is for business people who regularly deal with outside attorneys. (The title he originally wanted for it was *What They Don't Teach You at Yale Law School.* —McCormack's first book, *What They Don't Teach You at*

Harvard Business School, had been a best-seller.)

Roth got his NYU law degree in 1942; McCormack, his Yale law degree in 1957. Yet, the tone of the two passages is almost identical, even though their authors' graduating classes were 15 years apart, at different schools.

Recall another quotation in chapter 3, from Goodrich's *Anarchy and Elegance*: "/L/aw school was intended to confuse, to intimidate..." He also spoke of the "horrors of law school." Goodrich finished his Yale law degree in 1987—30 years after McCormack. Yet, his description of law school was similar to McCormack's (and Roth's).*

Now for another quotation from Scott Turow's *One L:*

> In order to reach the second and third years, students must pass through the first year, and by then have already had the stuffing kicked out of them. They have been treated as incompetents, terrorized daily, excluded from privilege, had their valued beliefs ridiculed, and in general felt their sense of self-worth thoroughly demeaned.

Chapter 5 quoted Richard Kahlenberg's *hatred* of Harvard Law School, because it put first-year students through hell. Turow's Harvard law degree came in 1979; Kahlenberg's, ten years later.

By now the pattern should be apparent. Law school has not changed in decades. "The Gripes of Roth" (whose first-year was in *1939-40*) are still universally valid. (The overt terrorism may have lessened, but the intimidation continues unabated.) Further, it's the same virtually anywhere you go. (As chapter 3 discussed, Harvard was the cookie-cutter.)

The following incident happened less than a decade ago: On the first day of law school, my section's very first class was in torts. The professor was afflicted with the Kingsfield Syndrome (discussed in chapter 9). He skipped any greeting. He did not even introduce himself. Instead he immediately chose a student, and interrogated him at length and without mercy. Later that day, the student dropped out of law school.

I well recall the response of his classmates, myself included, when we heard the news that he'd left. I wonder if *anyone* felt sorry for the guy. Instead, all that I saw (and shared in) was a sense of elation that *we* were

---

* By the way, Goodrich did not go to Yale Law intending to become an attorney. As the editor of a newspaper for lawyers, he just wanted to understand the law better. So he entered a one-year program leading to a Master of Studies in the Law (M.S.L.) degree. His one year of law school, though, was the same first-year curriculum that the J.D. students had to endure. I find Goodrich's book all the more amazing because he reached such profound insights about law school and the Law even though he was only at YLS for the two semesters.

the *tough* ones, the "survivors" who could take the heat—while the drop-out had fled in terror from the kitchen. Of course, *we* hadn't been subjected to the psychological torture *he'd* been forced to undergo. *We* hadn't "survived" anything.

I've often wondered what he did with his life after that. And I've often wondered how he dealt with his embarrassment, perhaps even his shame. I still remember his name, and hope our paths cross someday. I want to apologize to him, even though I never had the chance to speak with him the one day he and I were in law school together. And I want to compliment him on his wisdom...and his courage. It took a lot of guts to walk away from that, not to continue in the role of willing victim.

> Do not mistake me: Believe it or not, I am not trying to talk you out of going to law school. Quite the contrary.
>
> But I am definitely trying to talk you out of going to law school if you don't understand what it is you're letting yourself in for—the *risk* that you'll be running. And as chapter 4 explained, my purpose is to tell you the bad stuff, so it won't come as a shock when it happens to you. There are plenty of other people to tell you about the good stuff—such as it is—as though no bad stuff exists.

The movies, the TV shows, the novels—and even most of the books for prospective law students—simply don't tell you the truth about law school, and what it's really like to be an attorney.

The *law schools* won't tell you, either. *It's not in their interest to do so—* for reasons you have seen. And God knows the law *firms* won't tell you— especially if and when they're trying to recruit you. They'll let you find out for yourself, the hard way. Sadly, even most solo lawyers won't tell you, either. Instead, they too try to keep up the pretense, the facade—in part because if they admitted the truth, they would think they're showing signs of weakness, that they couldn't hack it.

But perhaps you're *already* some kind of macho (or "macha") fool who really gets turned on by the idea of running such an academic gauntlet. Perhaps you think *you'll* be the one who thrives on this, while the "weaklings" go to the wall or go down the tubes. Well, pal, good luck. It's always the *other* guy (or gal) who gets cancer, who gets killed in the car crash, right? You're immune, because you came into this world with a Privileged Status known only to yourself. (On the other hand, it's true that you in fact are *not* as likely to get lost and intimidated, let alone terrorized—because you have the benefit of *Planet Law School.)*

None So Blind

Given the fact that class discussion plays no role in your grade for the course, why do law professors use "terrorism" and intimidation in the first place? What purpose do these serve?

Goodrich hit on the answer. Speaking of a particular professor's use of the Socratic Method, he said:

> His <u>inducement of mental vertigo</u> was so complete, so far beyond the necessary, that I had no difficulty believing that a <u>deeper agenda</u> lurked beneath the surface orientation. Many critics of legal education use the word *brainwashing* to describe the process, and I began to understand what they meant. By <u>eliminating all non-legal points of reference</u>, /the professor/ forced us to accept his word about the law; by implying that every assumption students had made prior to law school was presumptively wrong, <u>he made us doubt our self-worth.</u> And when he hinted at the existence of a legal framework that could encompass *all* thoughts and ideas, <u>accessible only to those who adopted the legal point of view</u>—courageously and altruistically, by implication— <u>he had us eating out of his hand.</u> In those early weeks, we were so relieved to be told that certainty existed somewhere in the legal world that <u>we didn't care whether it was valid.</u>
>
> (Italics in the original; underlining supplied.)

I disagree only with Goodrich's statement that it's just in the "early weeks" of law school that this attitude exists among the students. On the contrary: one of the *major purposes* of law school is to ensure that this attitude is *permanent*—especially the part about not caring if the "legal point of view" *is* valid. That's the "deeper agenda."

There's a famous saying, attributed to Edmund Burke, that "The Law sharpens the mind—by narrowing it." Perversely, lawyers often cite this with pride. There's certainly nothing wrong with narrowing the mind concerning one's calling, if that enables a person to become more adept at his or her craft. But the Law—and especially law *school*—also strives to harden the heart...and to obliterate the soul.

In 1970, Charles A. Reich's book, *The Greening of America*, was published. In it, he said this about law students:

/In law school, students/ discover that they are expected to become "argumentative" personalities who listen to what someone else is saying only for the purpose of disagreeing; "analytic" rather than receptive people, who dominate information rather than respond to it; and intensely competitive and self-assertive as well. Since many of them are not this sort of personality before they start law school, they react initially with anger and despair, and later with resignation. In a very real sense, they "become stupider" during law school, as the range of their imagination is limited, their ability to respond with sensitivity and to receive impressions is reduced, and the scope of their reading and thinking is progressively narrowed.

As a professor at Yale's law school, Reich was in a position to know. His book (a product of the "counter-culture" of the era) presented itself as part of the solution. Yet, Reich himself—as a law professor—was part of the problem.

Benjamin Sells is a former "law factory" attorney who is now a psychotherapist in Chicago. He counsels attorneys. Chapter 3 quoted his book, *The Soul of the Law: Understanding Lawyers and the Law*. In it, he also made this statement:

Here we come to another reading of Justice's blindfold. It isn't only passion or prejudice that the blindfold obscures, but perception itself. Justice can no longer look out upon the world, can no longer appreciate its subtle variations and delicate distinctions. Instead, the blindfold turns vision inward so that Justice's struggle to comprehend reality becomes necessarily solipsistic. Of course Justice *must* "see" things in its *own* terms— *that's all that is left it*. Memories of how things looked before the blindfold begin to fade as the out of sight becomes out of mind. Abstractions, idealized systems, and coldly objectified facts replace sensory awareness, and *gone from view are all chances for shared vision*. With blinders in place, *"I don't see your point"* comes to mean *"I cannot look through your eyes."* (Emphasis added.)

Elsewhere in his book, he said "Because non-legal experiences cannot help but remind the lawyer of his or her broader connections to the world beyond the Law, such experiences, like bad recruits, must be drummed out."

The Law is a haughty discipline. It assumes that anything and everything *worth* discussing can somehow be understood and discussed within the framework of the Law, using legal concepts and legal analysis.

Elsewhere in *Anarchy and Elegance,* Goodrich expands on that insight. "/I/n law…what one said was largely dictated by what the limited forms of the law allowed one to say, anything left out automatically being considered second-rate or useless." Like the Bed of Procrustes in the ancient Greek myth, whatever doesn't fit within it is cut off—or, at the very least, held in contempt as being unworthy of serious consideration.

Why is this important? As Goodrich put it, "/L/egal education has a way of replacing everyday human values with what I can only call 'legal' values— values that sustain the system of law *rather than the people that system was created to serve."* (Emphasis added.) "Lawyers resolved conflicts by placing them in a hermetically sealed, self-referential loop that *ignores* precisely what it should *encompass—the views of the millions of nonlawyers whose lives their decisions affect."* (Emphasis added.)

True, the objectivity and rationality of the Law is necessary to properly deal with controversy. However, Law is not supposed to be an end *in itself,* but a *means to an end*—actually *ends,* plural: truth, justice, humanity, for starters. While it's understandable how the Law has become an end in itself for attorneys and judges and law professors, this does not mean that our society has to go along with that, or let it continue. Here's why…

The Existentialism of the Law

From 1914 to 1945, Europe did its best to destroy itself and make a mockery of the word "civilization." One of the intellectual by-products was the rise of a philosophy called "existentialism." It became quite influential after the war—even fashionable, among those who fancied themselves the cultural *avant garde.* Existentialism says there is no meaning to life, to the universe, to humanity. Everything is just a cosmic happenstance— including the cosmos itself.

Law has become an existentialist discipline. But unlike the philosophers, the fundamental nihilism of the law professors has an ulterior motive. The *main* goal of law school, especially what occurs in first-year, is *to destroy students' belief in morality,* and to replace it with cynicism and amorality. At that, it succeeds very well. *The "terrorism" and intimidation are a crucial part of this process.*

Future lawyers are indoctrinated that there isn't *really* any such thing as "right" or "wrong." There are only legal maneuvers. Those who persist in a sincere belief in ethics are treated with the same disdain—or alarm—as a 16-year-old who still believes in Santa Clause or the Tooth Fairy. Students are left in no doubt that concepts such as "truth," "justice," "humanity," and "morality" are just emotionally charged words to use when trying to *manipulate others.* Anyone who takes them seriously is obviously a mental defective, unfit for a life in the Law.

The acid of the Case/Socratic Method dissolves students' old way of relating to the world. Then the students are manipulated into adopting what Goodrich called "the legal point of view." This is more than just Thinking Like a Lawyer in the sense discussed in chapter 6. It's a way of looking at oneself and at life. The methods for accomplishing this radical transformation *have* to be *drastic* if they're to succeed. The passages quoted from Roth, Reich, McCormack, Turow, Goodrich, and Kahlenberg do—as Goodrich said—describe techniques of brainwashing.

If professors were to have a normal dialogue with students, trying to convince them that there really *isn't* any such thing as right or wrong, the students would put up a spirited resistance. There would be few converts. But by using the classic indoctrination techniques—"treated as incompetents, terrorized daily, excluded from privilege, had their valued beliefs ridiculed, and in general felt their sense of self-worth thoroughly demeaned" (the Turow quotation, above), the professors make the students receptive to "the existence of a legal framework that could encompass *all* thoughts and ideas, *accessible only to those who adopted the legal point of view*" (the Goodrich quotation, above). As Goodrich put it (above), the professor *"had us eating out of his hand..../W/e were so relieved to be told that certainty existed somewhere in the legal world that we didn't care whether it was valid."* (Emphasis added.)

The law school professors inculcate the attitude that rules have no *intrinsic* value, and that *no higher values exist*. Students leave school believing that the Law is just a game. The only thing that counts is winning. Winning, in turn, means prize money—and, of course, prestige. You help the client to "get his" (or hers), and thereby "get yours." Then take the money and run.

Goodrich put it in personal terms: "Law school hadn't turned me into a jerk, but it told me that if I felt the need to be a jerk, I should be a first-rate jerk, and not feel guilty about it."

Of course, if you're really *good* at being a jerk, and it gets you where you wanna go, then it's awful easy to feel the "need" to be a jerk. (That includes what in effect involves cheating one's own clients.)

Goodrich then provides the transition from the personal to the societal: "Legal training doesn't create selfish, aggressive people—but it does provide the intellectual equipment with which recipients can justify and give force to beliefs and actions most people would wholeheartedly condemn."

> This ensures that those whose goals involve *wrong-doing* will have no difficulty in hiring the "best" and brightest law school graduates to work on their behalf.

You've heard of Gresham's Law? (Not "Grisham's," as in the lawyer-novelist.) Gresham's Law concerned money. (Then again, Grisham isn't exactly writing for free.) Gresham's Law says, "The bad drives out the good." And that's certainly what's been happening in the legal profession. (Recall that the subtitle of Arron's book is "Why Good Lawyers are Getting Out of the Profession.") Even the "transactions practice" attorneys, more and more, tell the client only what the client wants to hear, even if what the client wants to do is flat-out illegal. And more and more, the trial lawyers, especially, fight dirty to win. Often they began fighting dirty in law school.

Here are three incidents from *my* legal alma mater...

1) In one of my first-year courses, the prof was a new member of my school's faculty, and had previously taught at a law school some distance away. There were no old exams of his on file; no model answers. Shortly before the final exam, one of my section mates started telling people that she'd acquired the professor's old exams and model answers from a friend of hers at the other law school. However, there were no such old exams and model answers, because— as the prof announced after the final—he had never taught this particular first-year course before, ever. The creep who invented the story was just trying to give herself a big psychological edge over everyone else during the final. To her, vice in the pursuit of victory was a virtue.

2) I was serving as a witness for a couple friends of mine who were taking a course in trial advocacy. They were a team, and were good enough to be selected to give a demonstration. They had a real "mock jury," composed of college students. They also had a real judge. The course had its own unique rules for trials, in addition to those of civil evidence, etc.. All the students in the course knew the "local" rules. However, the professor who taught the course hadn't told the judge about these rules. The prof was at the demonstration trial. The opposing team repeatedly violated the course rules. My friends could not make objections to the judge about this, because the judge didn't know anything about these rules. The professor knew full well what was going on. Yet he did nothing about it, even though it would have been quite easy for him to do so without creating a scene. His unspoken message to his students was clear: Vice in the pursuit of victory is a virtue.

3) There was a special Moot Court intramural competition for second-year students only. I chose not to compete. The student who won the grand championship lied to the presiding judges about a key fact of the case during the final round. Everyone knew it except the judges (who were visiting attorneys, and had not studied the information packet). Because the liar was the final speaker in the competition, there was no chance for his opponent to set the record straight. The liar knew that. Hence the lie. Again, the faculty advisor was aware of the truth. The faculty advisor did nothing. The winner's name is now on a plaque near the main entrance to the law school. The message was again clear: Vice in the pursuit of victory is a virtue.

This attitude then carries over into the real world, on the part of *all* students—who learned the lesson from the triumph of those who sacrificed integrity to victory.

One of the excellent points Sells makes concerns what he calls "developmental ideology."

Developmental ideology has thoroughly infected the legal profession...Before the law student has ever opened a book or read a case, the placement office, career consultants, job manuals, and the profession in general have already defined the proper path: good grades / law review / interviews / summer job / offer / associate / partner / corner office.

...

Nobody says to the hapless law student: "Learn contract law because it represents the age-old struggle to shield ourselves from uncertainty. Listen carefully to the deep, binding concerns that contracts are really about: of making offers and looking for acceptance, of how lasting agreements depend on mutual consideration, of how difficult it is to reach accord and find satisfaction, and how painful are broken promises..."

No, development ignores the poetry and art of legal education and cuts to the chase: "Get the grades or forget the corner office."

—And, of course, the corner office (which comes from having a senior partnership at a prestigious firm) is the be-all and end-all of an attorney's existence. The passage from Roth spoke of this, too: "The big pitch is to get high grades so you can get a job in a 'good' law firm when you graduate." (Quotation marks around "good," supplied.)

Sure, there are always one or two law school profs who play the role of token idealist, exhorting students to do good works when they graduate. Such professors are frauds. They're smart enough to discern the origin of the problem, yet they keep quiet about it. If they wanted law students to retain something of their pre-law-school humanity, they'd—for example— teach contracts in the manner Sells just discussed, above. (Or, in Roth's words, they'd emphasize "enlightenment and pleasurable acceptance of knowledge," rather than drudgery and anxiety.) Instead, they, too, often serve the very clients they urge their students to go out and fight *against*. In fact, they serve as *role models for hypocrisy* to future lawyers. The more sophisticated students understand the *real* message conveyed.

Chris Goodrich, in passing, again hit upon the truth when he said "Law had made me less human, asked that I *dismiss my moral center* as a dangerous, incomprehensible Pandora's box." (Emphasis added.) And in *Broken Contract,* Richard Kahlenberg had this to say: "That phenomenon is unnatural. The human condition does not require that smart people, when they reach a certain age, must jettison their convictions (even as they mouth those abandoned beliefs with greater vigor)."

Kahlenberg ends his epilogue to *Broken Contract* with a passage that explains the title of his book:

You can blame the individuals for breaking their personal contracts—the agreements they had with themselves that they were pursuing law not for the money but to do good. You can blame the institution, Harvard Law School, for breaking its implicit contract, proclaimed on the walls of its buildings, that law is about justice, and then fostering an atmosphere where it is hard not to be a hypocrite. But no matter who is ultimately responsible, the sad truth is that every time an idealistic law student turns into a hardened attorney for the wealthy and powerful, she brings closer to the breaking point another agreement —the social contract*—and that is simply unacceptable.

No disrespect to Kahlenberg, but it *is* acceptable, very much so—to those who benefit from it.

Obviously, not all law students end up serving the wealthy and powerful. In fact, only a handful do. But by the time they graduate, virtually all of them *want* to. And those who *do* end up serving the wealthy and powerful have huge advantages over those who want to resist the continuing depredations of the vested interests.

The Payoff

Students do not learn in law school what they need to know to adequately serve their future clients. Take trial lawyers, for example. Chapters 3 and 14 cited then-Chief Justice Warren Burger's famous speech at Fordham University's Law School in 1973. Here's part of what he said:

> Many judges in general jurisdiction trial courts have stated to me that fewer than 25 percent of the lawyers appearing before them are genuinely qualified; other judges go as high as 75 percent. I draw this from conversations extending over the past 12 to 15 years at judicial meetings and seminars, with literally hundreds of judges and experienced lawyers.

Then, in a footnote to the published version of his speech, he added this: "One former colleague of mine on the Court of Appeals...puts the figure at *two* percent." (Emphasis added.)

Granted, Burger made that speech roughly a quarter-century ago. Since then, many schools have added trial ad classes, and the National Institute

---

* The addendum to this chapter discusses, in part, the "social contract."

"ATTICUS FALCON," ESQ.

for Trial Advocacy has held thousands of workshops for licensed attorneys. However, the level of competence is still amazingly low. (And unlike Burger, I would include judges.) Even for those who want to get good at it, it's still largely a matter of trial and error: the client's trial, the lawyer's error.*

There are far too many cases where the attorneys on *both* sides are incompetent. It becomes a battle of the mediocre. One side wins, and one side loses, only because (in a trial) there *has* to be a winner and a loser. But often the client who lost would have won if he or she'd had a decent attorney; or the client who won gained far less than he or she was legitimately entitled to. As a wag once said, "Ignorance of the law is no reason for an attorney not to collect his or her fee."

The wealthy and the powerful are usually represented by attorneys from the law factories, which hire only those who graduated at the top of the class. However, these new attorneys aren't any better at practicing law than the rest. The law factories know this. With respect to aspiring litigators, they don't let them handle cases (except trivial ones, if any) until they're sure the neophytes are up to it. They make their new lawyers serve a *long* apprenticeship, to make up for the lack of worthwhile trial ad training in law school.**

More important, the major firms know that the lawyers who *don't* go to work in the law factories do *not* have the resources to methodically develop *their* skills. The law schools, too, are well aware of all this. They like it that way, because the major law firms like it that way. "He who pays the piper calls the tune." So, the law schools willfully continue to neglect the needs of *all* aspiring trial lawyers, knowing that 98% of them will not be getting the post-graduate training the major law firms provide.

Those who are the victims of the wealthy and the powerful, or who want to challenge the wealthy and the powerful, can seldom afford any attorney at all. Often they can only afford one who's hopelessly outclassed by the litigators from the major firms. Granted, if the stakes are high enough, a truly good trial lawyer who's an independent will take the case on a contingency fee basis. However, cases worth taking on contingency are rare,

---

* The law school programs are nearly always superficial. NITA's programs are better than most of the academic ones. However, even the NITA programs only last 10-11 days, at most. Further, they're very expensive. Few newly-licensed attorneys can afford them. True, NITA provides "scholarships" for beginners who can't pay in full. However, most new lawyers work as solo practitioners or in small firms. No one can fill in for them if they take off a week—and their schedules are so unpredictable that they would have a hard time setting aside, far enough in advance, time for a NITA program.

** And the big firms can easily afford NITA's tuition rates. They regularly send their new would-be barristers to a *lot* of workshops, or else hire experts to conduct programs in-house. The *cumulative* effect of so much training makes a big difference.

and the best plaintiff's attorneys carefully pick and choose among them. So, usually, it's David v. Goliath. But in a modern courtroom, unlike ancient Israel, there is no divine intervention. Goliath wins. (In part, this is because the big law firms are very good at currying the judges' favor behind the scenes, between trials.)

It isn't just a matter of inadequate training, though. The cynicism and amorality also play a significant role. With their idealism eradicated by law school, few lawyers have any interest in "fighting the good fight" for the sake of a worthwhile cause. If there's no money in it—or at least some free publicity—they just don't give a damn.

Further, as Turow noted—in *One L*—regarding those who'd already gone through first-year:

> If you get knocked down often enough, you learn not
> to stand up, and after being a Harvard 1L, a silent crawl
> to the finish line looks to many students to be the better
> part of valor. Looking around the hallways, I often saw
> the 2Ls and 3Ls as a sad, bitter, and defeated lot. I met
> repeated instances of those attitudes all year.

Remember, he's talking about *Harvard* Law School—the *top* of the academic legal heap. (I assume he was speaking of those who did not Make Law Review—but that isn't necessarily so.) Granted, if you follow the recommendations of *Planet Law School,* you won't end up the way Turow describes—at least, not in law school. But it could easily happen to you in your career, especially (and ironically) if you go to work in a law factory.

Chapters 3 and 4 presented the case that law school does not teach the Law. Chapter 14 stated that learning How to Think Like a Lawyer could easily be taught in much less than three years. If you don't share those conclusions now, you will by the time you get out of law school, if you go.

However, the opportunity to get a law license is restricted almost exclusively to those who've graduated from law school. By the time they graduate, virtually *no* future lawyers have the "fire in the belly" that it takes to go up against those from the prestigious firms. Law school deliberately extinguished whatever flames once burned within them. If the terrorism and cynicism of first-year haven't "done the job," then the *tedium* and cynicism of years two and three will.

As chapter 16 mentioned, the best victories are those won without a fight. The bad guys win without a fight, time and time again, because the prestigious firms that represent them make sure their attorneys are at least reasonably good—in the sense of knowing their craft. Few potential challengers are willing or able to take them on, unless the stakes are quite high, or they figure to get a quick and easy settlement.

> So, *the <u>ultimate</u> purpose of the
> pedagogical malpractice of law schools
> is to subtly <u>rig the system</u> in favor of
> the major firms—all of which represent
> the powers-that-be in society.*

I am not saying there's a "conspiracy" between the law school faculties and the senior partners at the major firms. True, the law schools do get their money from the major law firms. But it's just a case of "You scratch my back, and I'll scratch yours." The law schools and the firms know that *a*moral students become the best attorneys to have when furthering the interests of *im*moral clients.

Unfortunately, many of those who *are* willing to take on the powers-that-be are fanatics. Their own lack of humanity easily matches that of the vested interests. Self-righteous, they feel that they have a monopoly on the truth, and that justice exists only when they win. For them, too, the end justifies the means. It's like John Brown—that crazed, bloodthirsty thug of American history—trying to launch a holy war of extermination against the slaveowners of the South, and provoking them to intransigence in return. A couple of lines from Yeats's poem, "The Second Coming," fit such a situation: "The worst are filled with passionate intensity, / While the best lack all conviction."

No doubt, I will be accused of being one of the worst, a self-righteous fanatic. Well, I *am* filled with passionate intensity—at least once in awhile, such as right now, maybe. But as the footnote on page 136 mentioned, "All 'A' are 'B'" does not necessarily mean "All 'B' are 'A'."

The Sacrifice

In their book, *No Contest: Corporate Lawyers and the Perversion of Justice in America* (published in 1996), Ralph Nader and Wesley J. Smith made this observation:

> Young lawyers at big firms also face substantial pressure to specialize—and specialize early—in a very narrow area of the law. They become experts on a single provision in federal pension law or the tax code. They become part of an *insular, myopic* community.
> (Emphasis added.)

Sound familiar? They continue:

They never gain the kind of breadth of legal experience, not to mention other types of human experience,
that produces better public citizens. They also become
more anxious in their drive for partnership, fearing that
their narrow sets of skills may limit their options if they
are thrown back into the job market.

Back to Sells:

So often I hear lawyers say they would like to step off
the track, slow down a bit, maybe do something different for awhile but they fear the *loss of face* and worry
that family and friends might *think less of them* if they
made less money, had a smaller office, or worked for a
less "prestigious" firm. (Emphasis added.)

There is a caste system within the legal profession. It starts in law school.
There, the snobbery and one-upmanship concern whether or not you Make
Law Review, whether or not you get a Prestigious Summer Clerkship, etc..
(And if you encounter students or graduates of other schools, the
one-upmanship concerns what everyone's law school is or was.) After graduation, it still concerns these things. But now it will also concern whether or
not you got a Prestigious Judicial Clerkship, and which firm you work for,
and whether or not you Make Partner. This quest for status, as an outward
source of self-esteem rather than relying on self-esteem that comes from
within, is hardly unique to law students and lawyers. But it's especially
prevalent among them.

Law students' desperate search for status is the direct result of the
terrorism and intimidation of law school itself. As with a child's traumatic
experience that echoes throughout the rest of his or her life, future lawyers
perhaps never really get over first-year. The fear and trembling of law school
is internalized. Above all, lawyers live in fear of being *embarrassed,* of
losing face. Hence the bluffing and the refusal to admit mistakes and apologize for them.

Sells was quoted earlier regarding "developmental ideology." Almost
from Day One, law students have it drilled into their heads that they will be
"nothing" unless they get that corner office someday (and then manage to
hang onto it). By emphasizing such status symbols so heavily (including Making
Law Review), law school distracts attention from its soul-destroying nature.

(It reminds me of how, for centuries, girls were told there were "nothing"
unless they got married, *stayed* married, and "raised a family" as a full-time
housewife when they grew up—even if the grown-up girl did not want to get
married, or the marriage proved horrid. Even today, parts of that attitude
are still common.)

Goodrich, when speaking of a particular professor, commented as follows:

"ATTICUS FALCON," ESQ.

> He knew that the law's version of logic was no better than any other—and perhaps worse, because it pretended to be better. Surely he knew that many lawyers clung to law out of *fear,* not belief; that they grew to love law because it was the one thing they were allowed, indeed encouraged, to love *without question.* They found new faith—perhaps ironically, perhaps inevitably—in the very system that *destroyed* their native faith.   (Emphasis added.)

"Existentialism" was discussed (briefly) above. It sought to "wipe the slate clean" regarding beliefs in values, meaning, etc.. Søren Kierkegaard was one of the earliest and most influential of the existentialists. He said that it's impossible for human beings to live without believing in *something.* So, he suggested we make a "leap of faith"—to more or less arbitrarily *choose* to believe in something, and then build everything else around that.

That's what law professors do, too. But whereas the existentialist philosophers were *honestly* arguing that there really is no meaning to life, period, the law professors *dishonestly manipulate* students into rejecting any meaning outside the Law. (Sells calls this the "Life-begins-at-Law-School Syndrome.") Then students are manipulated into making a "leap of faith" to the Law—and never looking back.

Once they're in law school, and certainly once in the Law, the participants believe that they have "no place else to go." They often eventually convince themselves that to leave the Law—or to have a law practice in any way unconventional—is not "respectable." So they try to make the best of what for most of them is a very bad situation. They cling to the security blanket of a job with a prestigious firm, no matter how much they secretly detest it.

Early in this chapter, Kahlenberg's discussion of the survey among the members of the 1986 entering class at Harvard Law School was cited—along with what happened three years later. Although Kahlenberg didn't say so, Alexander Pope, the English poet, came up with the words to describe this transformation (in his *Essay on Man, Epistle II*):

> Vice is a monster of so frightful mien,
> As to be hated needs but to be seen;
> Yet seen too oft, familiar with her face;
> We first endure, then pity, then embrace.

Change "Vice" to "The Law," and the fit is *perfect.*

Now here's another passage from Sells:

Many lawyers overly invest their personal individuality in their professional identities. In the parlance of professionalism, they have "become lawyers." Once this identification is made, the person will do anything to maintain the professional persona because it has *become* them, expressive of their very being. Indicators of this condition include not being able to turn it off at the end of the day, feeling lost and uncomfortable in non-work settings, and imposing professional attitudes on all aspects of life...This substitution of professional persona for individual personality can go on for years; <u>some lawyers never get past it</u>.
    (Italics in the original, underlining supplied.)

I think Sells is being charitable. *Most* lawyers never get past it. That's why the average lawyer strikes the layperson as being such a pinhead. With regard to what goes on in law school, Sells added:

This kind of training creates a cult of individualism that leaves lawyers no way out. Expected to be forever self-sufficient, strong, knowing, aggressive, and confident, the lawyer is expected to be more than human. Even in situations where one would expect to find communal effort and collegiality—say in a law firm or among a group of lawyers representing the same client—we see the cult of individualism at work, transforming collegiality into competition and community into a mere collection of "I's."

The dog-eat-dog attitude that starts in law school thus continues well beyond graduation.

But the basic problem is that the style of individuality taught in law school is <u>false</u> individuality. At base it has little if anything to do with individuality as a psychological reality. *From the perspective of soul, individuality has to do with uniqueness and eccentricity, not self-confident isolation.* That lawyers *as a group* display this kind of <u>in-your-face individualism</u> is proof that this kind of individuality is conformism <u>masquerading</u> as individuality.
    (Italics in the original. Underlining supplied.)

Now here's the killer:

/C/ombine the objective coldness with the constant circumspection and caution with which lawyers are taught to face the world, and you have an overwhelming combination that *closes the lawyer in on himself or herself.* Add the unspoken but clearly conveyed *sense of aristocracy that law school encourages* and you have a prescription for *an alienated profession made up of lonely men and women.* (Emphasis added.)

> *You won't hear (until after you've become a lawyer) that the rate of clinical depression among lawyers is four times that of the general population, that the rate of alcohol and drug addiction is higher for attorneys—especially trial attorneys—than for any other profession. (Various surveys show that it's perhaps as high as 60%.) And the suicide rate among attorneys—again, especially trial attorneys— is second only to that of psychiatrists.*

Lawyers are in a double bind. Because of the hyper- and pseudo-individuality of the Law, attorneys tend to live each in his or her own little world— just as law school and the Law itself is its own little world: on another planet, as it were. And because they've so thoroughly internalized the values of the profession, they often engage in self-destructive behavior rather than finding a way to heal their soul. But this *self*-destructive behavior is just an acceleration and an intensification of the destruction the *law professors* began. And for those who complete the process of destroying themselves: the victims get the blame—"they couldn't hack it."

The <u>Cult</u> of the Law

By now, perhaps you've noticed that the pieces begin to fit together in a way that makes sense—with a twisted logic:

1) Make students believe they're stupid, worthless, etc.—and make them feel, by implication, that their old values are childish, ignorant, foolish.
2) Make them believe that "for those in the know," there is no such thing as truth, justice, humanity, etc., and that really savvy, sophisticated, superior people reject such nonsense in the same way they reject the idea that babies are brought by storks.
3) Make them believe in a realm that is all-knowing, all-encompassing, a realm above all others—isolated from ordinary reality, rejecting the common perceptions of ordinary reality.
4) Make them believe that as lawyers, they will enter that realm and will henceforth be members of a learned and noble self-made aristocracy.

5) Make them believe that the only values that exist in this realm—the values they must serve—are those of power, prestige, and profit. Winning is everything. Even vice, when in the pursuit of victory, is a virtue.

6) Make them believe image is more important than reality. Loss of "respectability," loss of "face," are anathema.

7) Make them believe their very identity will disintegrate if they ever question the Cult of the Law. And if they *leave* the cult, then it's obvious they're inferior beings—because they "couldn't hack it."

As Benjamin Sells put it:

> Although legal training performs the first phase of initiation, that of separation, it then veers from the initiatory pattern by beginning *to limit rather than expand the lawyer's sense of broad-based community.* The results are familiar to anyone who has been in or observed other groups of inductees. Although in-fighting might occur, a fierce loyalty nonetheless develops within the group *vis à vis* those not in the group. (I have heard more than one lawyer refer to non-lawyers as "civilians.") The group is likely to develop ideas and practices designed to accentuate and glamorize its separateness while ensuring its continued existence as a closed order. Rigidity and bureaucracy become problematic as the order establishes its own ways for doing everything. (Within the group, these highly stylized practices are accepted as necessary for maintaining the group's internal security, and even become carriers of great nostalgia.) *Revealing internal secrets to outsiders becomes a cardinal sin, and criticizing the group in front of outsiders borders on outright treason.* (Emphasis in the original, except for that last sentence.)

The Downward Spiral

But now we must return to the terrorism and intimidation of the Socratic Method.

Mark McCormack's book, *The Terrible Truth about Lawyers,* as quoted earlier (page 285), said that "terror is an *integral* part of the law school experience..." (Emphasis added.) But the quotation presented was only partial. Here's the rest of that sentence, plus the two sentences that followed:

> *and the long-term consequence of that terror is to make*
> *it very difficult for lawyers to admit when they've made*
> *an error or when they simply don't know something. The*
> *ultimate sin is being at a loss for words.*
>   Law school has taught them to hide uncertainty at
> any cost.   (Emphasis in the original.)

Sells, the lawyer-turned-psychotherapist, also talked about this in *The Soul of the Law:*

> For a lawyer to admit ignorance is to admit weakness,
> and to admit weakness is to open oneself up to attack.
> People who are close to lawyers can attest to the depth
> of this training and often comment how rare it is to hear
> a lawyer admit to not knowing something. Lawyers are
> taught to bluff, expected to bluff. Lawyers must always
> give the impression of knowledge and confidence, must
> always know.

This leads to what Sells calls the "impostor syndrome."

> The roots of the impostor syndrome begin in law school,
> where lawyers are taught it is better to bluff than to
> admit ignorance...*At first,* the lawyer feels merely
> inadequate and dishonest. But the next step is *cynicism.*
> *The lawyer decides everyone else is faking it too,* and
> begins to relate with people on the assumption that
> everyone is lying and posturing. (Emphasis added.)

And in fact, with respect to other *attorneys,* that assumption is usually correct. The lawyer who is somewhat ignorant and incompetent rationalizes his or her own inadequacy by saying that others are no better. Then he or she uses that as excuse for *not trying* to get any better.

Some trial attorneys even take *delight* in *not knowing the substantive law.* They pride themselves on having "forgotten everything I learned for the bar exam." It's as though they're belatedly rebelling against what law school put them through. They rely on little more than hot air—and their ability to ingratiate themselves with juries. When involved in litigation, they "throw everything against the wall—to see if something sticks." Unfortunately, since many judges don't know the law very well, either, sometimes something *does* stick—something that should have brought *sanctions* against that attorney. (Usually, such nonsense won't hold up on appeal. But most cases, even cases that have gone to a verdict at the trial level, are settled out rather than going up on appeal.)

However, the failure of the law schools to properly educate students in the substantive law and skills has another effect: the rise of "Rambo tactics"—the vicious and petty practices of many trial attorneys.

Example: I know of one trial lawyer who, when asked to provide documents to the other side, sends them by fax. But first he shrinks each 8½" x 11" page of the originals, so that *four* of them will fit on *one* 8½" x 11" piece of paper. He then faxes this. The other side complains, of course—but he forces them to go to the judge to get a court order telling him to cut out the crap. That takes time—and runs up the opposing client's bill. So far, no judge has ever punished him for this. (In general, judges don't want to be bothered with such "trivial" complaints. In fact, they habitually refer to complaints as "whining"...and insinuate that the complainants "can't hack it." These same judges then turn around and denounce Rambo tactics.)

Yet, it isn't just the law schools' failure to educate students in the substantive law that gives rise to Rambo tactics. The law school professors themselves provide the *role model*—in the form of the terrorism and intimidation of first-year.

Rambo tactics are what Anna Freud called "identification with the aggressor." Psychiatrist George Vaillant explained it in his book, *Adaptation to Life*: "Through such an identification, an individual who hitherto has felt safe only by prostrating himself before a potential aggressor, now achieves mastery by *incorporating or identifying with the very traits in the aggressor that he used to fear.*" (Emphasis added.)

For several years now, commentators have deplored the rise of Rambo tactics. Many of these commentators are law school professors. They pretend to be "holier than thou." However, to understand the origin of the phenomenon, they need look no farther than the nearest mirror.

All of these things, combined, cause lawyers their well-deserved reputation for being arrogant, obnoxious, self-important, and brusque, given to ego-driven one-upmanship, regardless of the situation (including non-legal situations); in short, for macho bullshit.

As a journalist, Goodrich elsewhere makes another interesting point that's relevant here:

> /B/oth law and journalism thrive on the pretense that they are transparent, neutral interpreters of reality. And that, surely, is a major reason the general public mistrusts law and journalism more than other professions—because lawyers and journalists assume airs of authority they have not earned, because the images they provide are often too neat, too convenient, too arrogant.

A License to Steal

Ironically, this is especially true for solo practitioners, or for attorneys in small firms. Unlike the junior associates who live in dread of their superiors in the law factories—who in turn often live in dread of their big corporate clients—the small-time attorney has little to fear. The "pedigreed" law firms treat their clients with respect. Most solo practitioners, in contrast, treat their clients the way adults treat small children, the way hospital personnel treat patients, or the way nearly everyone treats the aged in an old folks' home: with condescension bordering on contempt.

Further, if a *major* firm "blows" something for a major client, the firm—and the lawyers who mishandled the matter—suffer a major blow. But if a small-time lawyer blows something for a small-time client, the repercussions are minimal. Unlike the law factories, the nature of his or her practice seldom involves "repeat business." There are always plenty more small-time clients where that one came from. These attorneys are virtually *unaccountable* to *anyone.* (Sure, a disgruntled client can file suit for legal malpractice. But the legal deck is *really* stacked against anyone who tries to take a lawyer to task in court.) And yes, a lousy lawyer doesn't get word-of-mouth referrals. However, most of the "little people" choose a lawyer almost at random anyway.

Sells noted that it's rare to hear a lawyer admit ignorance. It's even rarer to hear a lawyer *apologize,* for *anything*...unless he or she is in court, and is trying to curry favor with the judge or jury.

Nearly all lawyers—big firm or solo—spread themselves too thin. As a result, they seldom provide the quality of service their clients have a right to expect. These attorneys' attitude is, "Better a steady dime than a seldom dollar." Oddly, this is true even of many trial attorneys who take cases on contingency. Usually, they try to perform just enough work to get a settlement out of the other side. For them, it isn't cost-effective to put in the effort that would enable them to win big at trial. They still get 40% (yes, it's that high now, in many jurisdictions) even if the case settles after just a phone call or two. On an hourly rate, the return on their investment of time and effort is staggering. Trials, in contrast, are much dicier...and (from a cynical point of view) usually not worth the trouble.

Perhaps you've seen the 1972 movie, *The Godfather.* (It was re-released in 1997.) It's based on a novel of the same title by Mario Puzo. In the novel, there's a line that—unfortunately—did not make it onto the screen. The old Godfather, when talking to his adopted son (who became the new Godfather's consigliere), says, "A lawyer with his briefcase can steal more money than men with guns." Amen. Sometimes the lawyer is helping his or her clients steal from others. But lawyers also steal for themselves, from their clients.

When your car isn't working, you take it to an auto mechanic. Many auto mechanics are rip-off artists. But at least you either get your car back in good working order, or you know the mechanic hasn't done the job right.

When you're ill or have a broken arm or a bad gash, you go to a doctor. Some doctors are also rip-off artists. But at least you either get your condition corrected, or you know the doctor hasn't done the job right—or you then get an *independent* and *objectively verifiable certification* that what ails you *cannot* be corrected.

With lawyers, it's different. After all, at least for litigation, the Law is the only profession where there's someone on the other side trying to prevent everything the attorney on the one side is trying to accomplish. Plus, there's the judge. So, if things go wrong, the attorney can always tell the client that the client didn't have a good case to start with, or the judge was ignorant or prejudiced. The client is none the wiser.

Until 1947, India was ruled by Britain. But for a long time before India officially became a British colony, it was a corporate domain—run by the British East India Company. All the Company's managers regularly skimmed off huge sums. In the late 18th century, Robert Clive was in charge. He took so much for himself that his political enemies in London convened Parliamentary hearings in 1773 on his alleged breach of fiduciary duty. His defense? Addressing the committee of investigation, he sincerely announced "By God, Mr. Chairman, at this moment, I stand astonished at my own *moderation.*" Robert Clive would feel at home as a modern American attorney.

Do not get me wrong: I am *proud* of the knowledge and skills I possess as a lawyer, and of what I've been able to do for people. But I am *ashamed* of the legal profession in general, and of what I see so many of my fellow attorneys doing. In a way, I am even *more* ashamed of those lawyers who have *integrity*—but who do nothing to come to terms with the problem of how corrupt the legal profession is, generally. Despite the profession's P.R., it isn't just a few bad apples. The barrel itself is bad, as it's presently constituted. And it's the *law schools* that are most to blame for this.

The judiciary could clean up the legal profession if it wanted to. True, in jurisdictions where judges are elected, they're beholden to the lawyers who appear in their courts. However, even in jurisdictions were judges are appointed, they do little or nothing to reform the profession. The reason is that their way of thinking, like that of the practicing attorneys, was indelibly shaped by law school.

The Labyrinth—
and the Minotaur

Once upon a time in the ancient world of the eastern Mediterranean, the Minoans were the dominant sea power. They lived on the island of Crete. Their navy gave them a veto over the movements of the merchant ships of the cities along the shoreline of the mainlands. The Athenians of that era were a relatively unsophisticated and powerless people.

A Greek myth says that every year, Athens sent tribute to Crete: seven young men and seven young women, whom the Minoans would then use as sacrifices. The King of the Minoans was named Minos. He owned a monster, half-human (male), and half-bull. Its name was "the Minotaur" (from "Minos" plus "tauros"—bull). Its favorite diet was human flesh. The Minotaur dwelt in a huge maze. The captives were put inside it. They'd wander around, terrified, with no way out. The Minotaur would hunt them down, one by one.

In the ancient Greek myth, only 14 young men and women were sacrificed each year. In America today, over 40,000 young men and women enter the labyrinth of the Law each year. Recall Chris Goodrich's statement quoted from *Anarchy and Elegance:* "/O/ur professors *wanted* us to get *lost* in the legal wasteland, apparently..." (Emphasis added.)

But there's a big difference: Once they've started law school, most students begin to *mutate into* Minotaurs: each half-human, half "bull" (as in B.S.). Then they *devour their own former selves.* This self-cannibalization continues throughout their careers, eating away at their heart and soul.

...Which reminds me of more poetry, this a complete poem—"In the Desert"—by Steven Crane:

> In the desert
> I saw a creature, naked, bestial,
> Who, squatting upon the ground,
> Held his heart in his hands,
> And ate of it.
> I said, "Is it good, friend?"
> "It is bitter—bitter," he answered;
> "But I like it
> "Because it is bitter
> "And because it is my heart."

After the passage on individuality quoted earlier, Sells made a startling remark: *"The true individual, one who has a sense of his or her own uniqueness, is perceived as a potential danger to the established order."* (Emphasis added.)

The significance of this comment apparently escaped Sells. But in the context of this chapter, it is fraught with enormity. The law schools are law factories in their own right, turning out lawyers-as-pinheads, legal robots. That is because the major law firms, along with the law schools—for which they provide the major funding—are very much a *part* of the established order, and seek to support it. Law school graduates who are truly individuals are indeed potentially dangerous to that "order."

By breaking a student's spirit in law school, professors needn't be much concerned that he or she will become a threat to the established order. And by perpetuating the Cult of the Law, the law schools and the legal Establishment constantly reinforce the loss of genuine individuality.

But, of course, some students might somehow manage to survive law school with their humanity and morality intact. They will then refuse to march lock-step through a career that's a living death, where they're embalmed long before they're *officially* pronounced dead. So the law schools try to ensure that *no* graduating students will be *effective* as attorneys—at least, not without expensive and time-consuming training. Thus, even those who would challenge the status quo...cannot. Instead, they often end up with the attitude, "If you can't beat 'em, join 'em." ("I've got *mine*.")

If you think you can join a major firm, in order to accumulate power within the system, and then try to reform the system from above, forget it. The firms themselves hold this out as a lure—knowing full well you will be co-opted long before you're in a position to even think about making a move. The following words from an Antebellum spiritual applied to the slave system, but they're applicable to any thoughts of reforming the legal establishment by going the big-firm route:

> So high, can't get over it.
> So low, can't get under it.
> So wide, can't get 'round it.
> Oh, rock my soul.

(There's not much I can do about it, either. I am not a member of the legal Establishment, and never will be. My successes come on a case-by-case basis, and are merely a drop in the bucket. I am no threat to the established order. But writing this book is better than nothing.*)

In the Greek myth, one year the son of the King of Athens volunteered to be one of the young men who's sent to Crete as a sacrifice. His name was Theseus. As sometimes happens in myths, the daughter of King Minos fell in love with him...and found a way to help him avoid succumbing to the Minotaur. Her name was Ariadne. She told him about the labyrinth, and gave him a ball of string so that he (and the other intended victims) could find their way out of the maze after they'd been put in it. Somehow (as also happens in myths), Theseus found a way to kill the Minotaur. He and the others escaped, and the Athenians never again provided human sacrifices for the Minoans.

The Opening Statement of this book began with a quotation from Scott Turow's *One L*: "...I knew I needed help—somebody, something to show me the way through." All of Part II of *Planet Law School* is your ball of string. It contains information and advice to help you avoid becoming a victim of what happens in the law school labyrinth. Make use of what's in chapters 5 and 6 even *before* you start law school. During first-year, take advantage of

---

* Then again, maybe it's just a way of washing my hands of the matter. ("I've done *my* bit.")

what's in chapters 7-11. If you follow the recommendations, you will not be lost. *That's half the battle.* "To be forewarned is to be fore-armed."

Sun Tzu was a 5th-century B.C. Chinese sage. He wrote a book called *The Art of War.* Apparently it's the greatest such book ever written (better even than Clausewitz's *On War,* which is the Western classic). In *The Art of War,* these lines appear: "Know yourself, know your enemy—and in a thousand battles you will never have to fear a major defeat." Notice: no guarantee of victory, just a guarantee that you will avoid disaster.

Most of this book has presented material to help you to know your enemy—and to prepare for battle. Unlike Theseus, you will not be able to slay the Minotaur. But you will stand a good chance of not becoming a sacrifice, turning into a self-made Minotaur.

Due Diligence

If you are serious about maybe going to law school, five books are "must reading." The first is by Stefan Underhill. It's part of the *"Majoring in..."* series from Noonday Press, which is an imprint of Farrar, Strauss & Giroux. This one's called *Majoring in Law: It's Not Right for Everyone. Is it Right for You?* A 1995 paperback, it costs $11. If you're only going to read one of the books recommended here, that's the one. (However, if you do read *only* one of the books recommended here, even if it's Underhill's, you're making a mistake.) He has some key chapters concerning the myths about what it's like to be an attorney and what attorneys do. And as his book's subtitle says, he has some good information about seeing if you're really cut out to be a lawyer.

This chapter has heavily quoted the second work you should read: Chris Goodrich's *Anarchy and Elegance.* (It might be hard to find a copy, though, because—as mentioned earlier—it's out of print.)

The third work has also been quoted a lot in this chapter: *The Soul of the Law: Understanding Lawyers and the Law,* by Benjamin Sells. It was published in 1994. It's in paperback, $15.

And the fourth was also quoted above: Deborah L. Arron's *Running from the Law: Why Good Lawyers are Getting Out of the Profession.* Published in 1989, it's $14 in paperback.

The last one I'll strongly recommend is Richard Kahlenberg's *Broken Contract: A Memoir of Harvard Law School,* which this chapter has also quoted from, a lot. It's a 1992 paperback, $12.

I've said it before, and I'll say it again—such as right now: If you go to law school, you'll be giving up tens of thousands of dollars, and three years of your life. You owe it to yourself to know about what you're thinking of getting yourself into. Do not be penny "wise" and pound foolish. Spend the money—or, if you can, get these books for free from libraries. Perform "due diligence" by reading them and thinking seriously about what they say.

The "must read" works just listed aren't the only ones that are good. They're just the best. Another worthwhile book is *The Lure of the Law: Why People Become Lawyers and What the Profession Does to Them*. Its author is Richard W. Moll. A 1990 hardcover, it costs $19 (or, at least, my copy is hardcover, and cost $19).

There's *Law v. Life: What Lawyers are Afraid to Say about the Legal Profession*. Walt Bachman is its author. The subtitle gives the impression the book contains comments from many attorneys. It would be more accurate were it "What *Other* Lawyers are Afraid to Say about the Legal Profession," because it consists entirely of Bachman's own thoughts. The book, published in 1995, is an $18 hardcover.

Another one is *Proceed with Caution: A Diary of the First Year at One of America's Largest, Most Prestigious Law Firms*. It was published in 1997, and costs $18. The author wrote under a pen name, "William R. Keates."

And I shall again mention Mark McCormack's *The Terrible Truth about Lawyers,* which this chapter also quoted. Its subtitle is *How Lawyers Really Work and How to Deal with Them Successfully*. Whether or not you go to law school—in fact, especially if you *do* go to law school—*The Terrible Truth about Lawyers* is a good book to read, despite the exaggerated title. It's available in paperback for just under $5.

If you're intellectually inclined, there's *The Lost Lawyer,* by Anthony T. Kronman. He's the Dean of the Yale Law School. As far as being an intellectual goes, he's the genuine article. (And I mean that in praise—even though his book is tough going in some places, and I take issue with him on several points.) Its subtitle is *Failing Ideals of the Legal Profession*. Published in 1993, it's a $17 paperback.

A final item you might want to consider is a monthly publication called *The Rodent Newsletter*—"The Official Underground Publication for /Law Firm/ Associates." Its editor, who uses the pen name "The Rodent" (as in "rat race") is a former associate at Baker & McKenzie, a *mega*-firm headquartered in Chicago. He prints news and facts sent in by attorneys in law factories around the country. The picture it presents ain't pretty. ("The Rodent" also did a book, *Explaining the Inexplicable: The Rodent's Guide to Lawyers*. Published in 1995, it's in paperback for $10. It's a humor book, but includes a lot of real-life stuff. I didn't much care for it, in part because the author gets too many of his facts wrong. But I do recommend the newsletter.) A year's subscription is $16. Perhaps you could get just a sample issue for three or four bucks. The address—repeated in the appendix—is Rodent Publications, 2531 Sawtelle Blvd. - No. 30, Los Angeles, Cal. 90064.

Most of the books about what a drag it is to be a lawyer are written for those who *are* lawyers, not for *prospective* lawyers. And most of them are written by people who have left the Law—and thus are safe from reprisals.

Most people thinking about becoming attorneys have stars in their eyes. Their attitude is "don't confuse me with the facts; my mind's made up." They've bought into the myths Underhill discusses. (Either that, or they can't think of anything else to do after college.) Only *attorneys* read Arron's book and most of the other ones. That's because those attorneys feel bad about themselves. They think there must be something wrong with themselves because they're so unhappy in their chosen career. So they read *Running from the Law,* and the other books, to help them realize that they aren't alone. This helps them build up their determination to either change things in the way they practice law, or else—more likely—to leave the profession.* The bad drive out the good.

The Opening Statement of this book quoted Omar Khayyam's *Rubaiyat* (F. Scott Fitzgerald's translation). Here it is again:

> *The Moving Finger writes, and having writ, moves on.*
> *Nor all your wit nor piety shall lure it back to cancel half a line,*
> *Nor all your tears wash out a word of it.*

You should seriously consider reading those books now, instead of waiting until you're an attorney. By reading them, you will get to know yourself better—and to know whether or not you should go to law school in the first place. If and when you do go to law school, what you've learned from these books will help you as you try to maintain a *healthy* perspective, throughout your career.

Fool's Gold

The Opening Statement of this book also spoke of Knowing Yourself—which is the other half of what Sun Tzu recommended, above.

In his book, *Explaining the Inexplicable,* "The Rodent" quotes an attorney from a mega-firm: "I'm at Skadden, Arps," the woman had said, "and we pride ourselves on being assholes." Well, I didn't write this book to help you succeed at being an asshole. (But we both know if that's what you want to be—or already are—then so be it.) Regardless of what sort of person you are now, or want to be, though, there's a very high probability law school and a life in the Law will turn you *into* an asshole (especially if you become a trial attorney). At the very least, it's likely to turn you into a pinhead. The major purpose of this book is to help you avoid that, if you so desire.

A couple of those who read this book in manuscript pointedly asked if I knew of some way to light one candle rather than constantly cursing the darkness. Well, forgive me for sounding like *Sesame Street*'s "Oscar the

---

* Note that three people writing about the Law felt compelled to use assumed names: "William R. Keates," "The Rodent," and yours truly, "Atticus Falcon." The reason for this is clear from the Sells quotation, above: "Revealing internal secrets to outsiders becomes a cardinal sin, and criticizing the group in front of outsiders borders on outright treason." We're not interested in being martyrs. But don't you find it at least somewhat disconcerting that all three of us felt compelled to hide behind anonymity in order to tell the truth?

Grouch," but the only thing to be done is to overhaul the American system of legal education. Because jousting with windmills is not my idea of a good time, I'll pass on that. Instead, *Planet Law School* is intended to help *you* make the *best* of a very, very bad situation.

However, I will comment on two things that, in my opinion, offer false hopes…

Inns of Court

As with the origin of the term "hornbook" and the meaning of "lex," here's another bit of legal trivia: The first Inn of Court was started in 1292 by King Edward I as a place where out-of-town barristers could stay while they were trying cases in London. Over the next several hundred years, there came to be several Inns of Court, and they evolved into training schools for apprentice trial attorneys. The United Kingdom still has them.

The modern American version started in 1980. Warren Burger, then Chief Justice of the Supreme Court of the United States, had been inspired by the civility and gentility of the English barristers he'd encountered. He thought establishing Inns of Court throughout America might counter the trend toward what would later be called "Rambo tactics."

There are now a few hundred Inns of Court in this country. In keeping with their original purpose, most are for trial lawyers. However, attorneys with "transactions practices" now have their own, too. For all, the guiding words are "Legal Excellence, Civility, Professionalism, Ethics."

As Patrick E. Higgenbotham, of the 5th Circuit Court of Appeals, explained: "The American Inns movement is not an elaborate public relations campaign aimed at salvaging the declining image of lawyers. Rather, it is an effort to define and embrace the underlying values of the legal profession—a positive claim that the law is a learned profession." He also said, *"This movement is carried by a felt need to save our professional souls."** (Emphasis added.)

However, it appears that many Inns have already degenerated into just another social organization for lawyers, for the purpose of "networking" and career advancement. You have to apply for membership as though it were a country club—and enrollment is limited. (Dues vary from Inn to Inn. But the lowest I've heard is more than a hundred dollars.) An Inn has become an "in" thing for one-upmanship and *social climbing,* too, just as with country clubs (or charity groups for society matrons). It isn't just enough any more to belong to the "Inn-crowd." Now you have to be in the "right" Inn.

Several Inns are affiliated with law schools. Law school students can even join Inns *not* affiliated with law schools. (Law students and those attorneys who've been licensed for less than five years are called "pupils." —As I said, there is a caste system in the Law.) If you're interested, call the American Inns of Court Foundation (in Alexandria, Virginia), at (703) 684-3590. They'll send you an packet that includes a list of all the Inns in the land.

---

*   Lawyer's Citation: 25 Colo. Lawyer 41, 42 (1996). Layperson's: *The Colorado Lawyer,* November, 1996, page 42.

IAHL

The International Alliance of Holistic Lawyers was founded by an attorney in Vermont named Bill van Zyverden. As with the Inns of Court and most other associations of attorneys, it has a very noble-sounding "mission statement." Unlike other attorney associations, its members (supposedly) try to live up to it. Gee. Wonder how long that will last. (I can already foresee that many lawyers who favor Rambo tactics will join IAHL if it starts to become a prestigious organization the way the Inns of Court are. Then they'll proclaim their membership in it in the same way that the wolf paraded about in sheep's clothing.) So far, it appears that this organization doesn't *do* much of anything. Its newsletter and annual convention are given over largely to New Age psychobabble.

In fact, it seems to be the very sort of wimpy, "touchy-feely" group that macho lawyers point at when justifying their own insensitivity, lack of compassion, etc.. To re-work a line from comedienne Lily Tomlin, if IAHL is the answer, then we badly need to rephrase the question.

If you'd like to check it out, IAHL can be reached at P.O. Box 753, Middlebury, VT 05753, or by phone and fax at (802) 388-7478. The e-mail address is HJCI@AOL.COM. (This information is repeated in the appendix.) Ask for a sample of their quarterly newsletter. Student dues are $15 a year.

However, "The only thing necessary for the triumph of evil is for good men to do nothing."* Law school intentionally and continually ensures that "good" lawyers—whether in the sense of good at their craft *or* good in the moral sense—are few and far between. Yet, as the quotation from Patrick Higgenbotham—and statements from IAHL's founder Van Zyverden—show, there are at least a *few* good men (and presumably, women) in the Law.

Perhaps some of *you* will have the determination to be *good* attorneys—both in the sense of skills, and in the moral sense. If so, you must—above all else—avoid wearing your "goodness," in the moral sense, on your sleeve. (Yet another reason why I've written this book under an assumed name.) As H.G. Wells said, "In the 'Kingdom of the Blind,' the one-eyed man is…blinded."

To Thine Own (Better) Self, Be True

Chapter 9 quoted from Tennyson's "Charge of the Light Brigade." Here again are those lines: "Theirs not to reason why, / Theirs but to do and die."

Notice, it isn't "do or die," but "do *and* die." And if you're familiar with the real-life charge of the light brigade (in the Crimean War), you know that all they did do was charge—and die—in vain.

---

* This has been attributed to Edmund Burke. However, he never made this statement. But he (perhaps) once wrote a highly convoluted sentence that has been rephrased into this one.

Forgive me for raising the subject, but someday—no matter how young you are now—you are going to die. (Yes, it's true. Trust me: I'm a lawyer.) If and when you know your time is almost up, you will no doubt look back on your life. When you do, what will you think of it? Will you feel smug because you made it to the top in some prestigious law firm? Will you take satisfaction that the net worth of your estate will perhaps be in the millions of dollars? Will you be proud that your actions—and inactions—helped to make the world a *worse* place?

Here's the last piece of poetry I'll quote. It's from Robert Frost's "The Lawyers Know Too Much"—"Tell me why a hearse horse snickers, hauling a lawyer's bones?"

—Or, as some guy from Nazareth said, nearly 2,000 years ago: "What is a man profited, if he shall gain the whole world, and lose his soul?" (This goes for women, too.)

Before you decide what path to pursue in the Law, if any, you might want to read Leo Tolstoy's *The Death of Ivan Ilych*. Ilych was a lawyer.

There's a difference between idealism and utopianism; between skepticism and cynicism; between objective detachment and amorality.

However, the law schools pretend that these differences do not exist...and the legal profession itself gives them only "lip service."

If you want to make the effort to retain your humanity as you become an attorney, please keep these distinctions in mind.

ADDENDUM to CHAPTER 21:
LAW SCHOOL and "The LIFE of the MIND"

As with most future law students, I was a member of my schools' debate teams. I can still remember how, when I first started, I held the varsity advocates in awe. They were highly intelligent and articulate, clever and quick on their feet. They were also very well-read and well-informed about current events. Somehow I got the idea that *lawyers* were like that. And because I wanted to be around such people, I decided that someday I would go to law school.

Lawyers are indeed articulate, occasionally clever, and often quick on their feet. But they are not well-read, and often not even well-informed about current events. Intelligent though they may be, they are not necessarily highly so, let alone intellectual. The Life of the Law is not The Life of the Mind. Because Chapter 16 has discussed this already, this addendum will only take up what passes for the Life of the Mind in law school.

"Intellectual activity" in law school is a sort of Monday-morning quarterbacking with regard to U.S. Supreme Court cases. ("Scalia always votes to expand police powers. And Thomas always votes the way Scalia does—no matter *what* the issue is.") It's political analysis, really, like the commentary on election night.

However, there are three schools of thought that are struggling amongst themselves within the Ivory Tower of the Law...

Law & Economics

This is a book about law school, not economics. So this is not the place to discuss economic theory. However, in America, economics is secular theology. And, as often happens in theology, the orthodox dogma is intolerant. Those who see things differently are branded "heretics." Although they're not burned at the stake, they are driven from the universities (and politics).

Individualism, in an extremist form, is at the heart of American capitalism (at least, in theory), just as it's at the heart of the American Dream. To this, Law & Economics adds another principal article of faith: each individual seeks "utility maximization"—i.e., maximum consumption. And consumption is maximized when efficiency is maximized. The Law & Economics school of thought seeks to use this dogma as the basis for public policy, and for determining the outcome of cases in the courts.

Thus, if one party to a contract can make more money by breaking his or her word and contracting anew elsewhere, the Law & Economics people say "Go for it." Traditional morality, as in keeping one's promise, has nothing to do with it. Neither does the hardship that a breach inflicts on the other party, even including driving it into bankruptcy, perhaps. The guiding principle is "Get yours—and the Devil take the hindmost." Granted, this has been the driving force for almost the entire human race, throughout history. Capitalism merely accepted this reality, and found a way to put it to productive use, literally. The famous "Invisible Hand" said public benefit would arise from private selfishness: a greater good (and more goods) for a greater number.

However, even Adam Smith, the father of classical economics, argued for a *visible* hand, too. This would enforce policies on behalf of the common good when the Invisible Hand was inadequate. (Prior to *The Wealth of Nations,* he'd written *A Theory of Moral Sentiments.*) But the Law & Economics theorists will have none of that. I do wish they'd spend some time in a country where business people, employees, and government officials all feel no obligations toward those who pay their salaries, or with whom they have a contract. Nothing works, nothing runs on time, nothing gets repaired. Paradoxically, the ultimate result of the Law & Economics school's support for the "efficient breach of contract," as they call it, would be a society of maximum *in*efficiency: a downward economic spiral into anarchy. This in turn paves the way for "*Mafia* capitalism."

It's quite interesting, too, that the Law & Economics theorists conveniently overlook the cost of litigating breach-of-contract cases. Perhaps they have an ulterior motive. —Encouraging parties to break contracts certainly puts more money into the pockets of law professors who write about contracts and do consulting work for trial attorneys who handle breach-of-contract cases. "Utility maximization," indeed.

Critical Legal Studies

All of Critical Legal Studies is based on their great "discovery" that law and the legal system serve as tools of the Establishment. Gee, who'da thunk? It brings to mind the sardonic definition of a management consultant: someone who uses your own watch to tell you what time it is...and then keeps the watch as his or her fee. The fact that the "Crits," as they're called, still trumpet this great "insight" shows just how isolated their ivory tower is from reality.

Unlike the Law & Economics advocates, CLS maintains that a "commonality" approach is just as valid as individualism. However, they don't promote it. Instead, they simply turn up their noses at the individual *and* communal approaches, and take a "holier than thou" attitude. ("He too serves a purpose who only stands and *jeers.*") Critical Legal Studies attempts to provide a new foundation for legal theory. We might call it "Zero-Based Jurisprudence," i.e., starting from scratch.

Ironically, the Crits, too, start with the individual as the basis of their thinking—despite their declarations to the contrary. In this, they are far more the children of the American culture than they would have us believe. They differ from the L&E school in refusing to accept, as "received tradition," the secular theology of Western capitalism. Yet, their own approach is quite theological.

Indeed, although it might not seem possible, they carry the dogma of individualism to an extreme that exceeds even that of Law & Economics. They hail what might be called "person-as-process." By this, they mean that each of us can constantly re-make himself or herself, breaking free from the past, whether cultural or personal. However, this is a *very* old (and romantic) notion in Western culture, and especially in American culture. —As so often happens when radicals proclaim the "New Man" (or "Womyn"), the self-proclaimed revolutionaries are merely putting aged wine into new skins.

For the Crits, the purpose of the Law, paradoxically, is to destabilize society. They want to use the Law to smash up the established arrange-ments and procedures—and especially the established hierarchies. In this way, individual freedom will somehow be maximized, they say. Although they don't admit it, *anarchy* would be "the best of all possible worlds." — They would do well to ponder the nihilistic line in the song "Bobby McGee," about how "Freedom's just another word for nuthin' left to lose." This down-ward spiral into chaos is something else they have in common with the folks in L&E, their alleged arch-rivals.

—Of course, the Crits do not want to smash up the cozy nest they've made for themselves in the ivory tower (heavily subsidized by education's tax-exempt status and alumni contributions). One thing at a time, perhaps. Save the law schools for last. However, even before that final step, there would no longer be any law…nor would there be any society, or even civili-zation—other than the "families" of organized crime.

* * *

These are the two schools of thought that dominate legal theory today. Like German Nazis and Soviet communists denouncing each other, they're really just two sides of the same coin.* Whichever wins, humanity loses.

There's one more, new and perhaps growing. If you think of L&E as the "right wing" of the Law, and the "Crits" as the "left-wing," then the "New Republicans" ought to be called the "moderates."

Neo-Republicanism

The "New Republicans" have no connection to the Republican Party. Hence, the name for this school of thought is misleading, and unfortunate. They're called Neo-Republicans because they claim to be the heirs of the classical republicans such as Aristotle. (Our word "republic" comes from the Latin words—"res" and "publica." —Literally, it means "the public thing." For the ancient Athenians, it meant the common good. The Romans borrowed this

---

* It's seldom noted that "Nazism" is just the verbal contraction of the German words for "national" and "socialism." It's also seldom noted that the original term for communism was "scientific *socialism*"—as chapter 3 observed. Although in some ways Nazism and communism were worlds apart, in practice they were almost identical, because they were both inescapably totalitarian.

concept.) Although the New Republicans give lip-service to Aristotle, their theoretical underpinnings are from Kant's moral philosophy, not Aristotle's political philosophy.

On the surface, the New Republicans seem quite reasonable and responsible, even noble. For example, they maintain that the phrase "for the public good" still has an objective meaning, and is not a mere hypocritical slogan used by special interest groups to mask their agenda. They agree with Aristotle that the essence of freedom is self- rule.

You've heard the expression, "Everyone's entitled to his or her own opinion"? The Neo-Republicans adopt that. But then they go a step farther. They say that one person's opinion is *worth* just as much as another's. This is another obvious variation on the theme of "one person, one vote," which is indeed a valid belief. But while one person's vote is worth just as much as another's, one person's *opinion* ain't necessarily so.

This is where the New Republicans blow it. To them, all that counts, really, is "public opinion"—as in public opinion polls. Leadership is really nothing more than "spokespersonship." The idea that there might be some people more qualified than others to make decisions regarding public policy is heresy to them. It is, they say, "elitist." In this, of course, they—like the other schools of thought discussed above—merely reflect orthodox American political mythology...and then carry one aspect of it to an extreme.

Thus, a legislator or political executive is merely a vector, of sorts, expressing the consensus of his or her constituents. Red-blooded Americans shouldn't defer to the wisdom or experience of others in regard to a particular matter. Government officials are not elected or hired to exercise their own judgment. They should merely reflect "the will of the people."

But as anyone who has been involved in public issues knows, it is possible to *shape* public opinion, whether through a paid public relations campaign or through the cooperation of sympathetic members of the news media. So, those who control the content of the communications can manipulate public opinion—and habitually do. However, leadership, properly understood, often consists of creating and energizing a constituency to *oppose* the conventional wisdom—especially when the conventional wisdom is the result of manipulation by powerful interests.

The New Republicans, snug in their ivory tower, will have none of this. Theirs is a hypothetical construct. Their hopelessly naïve model plays into the hands of those who hope to manipulate the body politic even more than they already have. (And every dictator in history has claimed to merely represent "the will of the people.")

* * *

These three schools of thought are the closest thing you'll see to "the life of the mind" in law school...and yet, as a student, you probably won't even see these. No matter *what* school of thought, if any, your professors belong to, *you* will only be exposed to the Case/Socratic Method (unless one of your professors wants to mount a soapbox, as discussed in chapter 4). True, you can sign up for a seminar or two, as electives, before you graduate—and you might even find some intellectual content there. But in general, all you'll find in law school is mental gamesmanship.

(For more information on these schools of thought, see Anthony Kronman's *The Lost Lawyer: Failing Ideals of the Legal Profession,* mentioned in the main body of this chapter.)

* * *

Earlier, a quotation from Kahlenberg's *Broken Contract* referred to the "social contract." In the May, 1989 issue of *The Washington Monthly,* an article by Garrett Epps was published. Epps was then a first-year at Duke University's law school. He said this:

> The function of law, as many have rightly argued, is to fashion a public morality—a way of resolving contentious issues like integration, executive power, abortion, womens' /sic/ rights, and church-state relations without resorting to the naked ability of the powerful to impose their will.

Learned Hand, the great American jurist,* once said:

> I often wonder whether we do not rest our hopes too much upon constitutions, upon laws and courts. These are false hopes; believe me, these are false hopes. Liberty lies in the hearts of men; when it dies there, no constitution, no law, no court can save it; no constitution, no law, no court can even do much to help it. While it lies there it needs no constitution, no law, no court to save it.

"Liberty," as Hand knew well, doesn't just mean "rights." It means *respect for the rights and opinions of others.* It means a system for resolving conflict in a way that preserves the *social fabric.* This is what the social contract is ultimately all about. Law is supposed to be the servant of society, and humanity, and justice. And those things are part of the social contract. Otherwise, the system itself has no legitimacy.

---

* "Learned" is pronounced as two syllables: "Lern-Ed."

Ironically, with their contempt for basic concepts such as truth, justice, humanity, and morality, America's law schools and its legal Establishment are gradually reducing us to the primitive state of nature described in Hobbes's *Leviathan:* "No arts, no letters, no society, and, which is worst of all, continual fear and danger of violent death, and the life of man solitary, poor, nasty, brutish, and short." To counteract this, Hobbes called for "a common power" to keep people "in awe." Without it, he said, "they are in that condition which is called war: and such a war is of every man against every man."

Every law school encourages a state of war among its students. This state of war continues as the former students become practicing attorneys. Paradoxically, the law schools—and the legal Establishment—then try to set up the Law itself as the "common power" to keep people in "awe." ...And, of course, the legal profession, as the priesthood in the Temple of the Law, gets to bask in the reflected glory of the Awesome Power of the Law.

As mentioned in chapter 1, students get no course in "The Western Legal Tradition," or "The Basic Principles of Anglo-American Law." Nor are they required to have such knowledge as part of their pre-law education. They have almost no understanding whatsoever of the foundations of the Law, no acquaintance with the alternative value systems that have existed through history—and which now exist in various other countries. They have little appreciation for why the Rule of Law, *properly* understood, is so *wonderful*— a *magnificent* achievement of the human race.

What *scares* me about today's lawyers, law professors, and law students is that they regard *our* system of Law, and even the Constitution itself, as just more-or-less-arbitrary Rules of the Game. They seem not to care what the rules are really for, in a deeper sense, or how the rules came to be are as they are. They only want to know the contents of those rules so they can then play games with them (looking for loopholes, for example). They're almost completely ignorant of the entire Western political tradition, both historical and philosophical. For them, there is no real *meaning* in the Law, no higher purpose. It all might just as well be a product of pure happenstance.

"You don't know what you've got 'til it's gone." And if America's lawyers, law professors, and law students don't even *care* about what we have (as long as they can continue to "get theirs"), then they will easily switch their allegiance to a system of values that will mean the beginning of the end of the millennia-long struggle for individual freedom and dignity. Ironically, now that communism has almost vanished, the threat—from *within*—to the Rule of Law is even *greater*. ("In Hell there will be nothing but law, and due process will be meticulously observed." —Grant Gilmore, *The Ages of American Law*, 1974.)

Chapter 22 - Laypeople's Legal Myths

Just in case you decide not to go to law school, here are some common "myths" laypeople have regarding the law. (I had believed several of these myself, pre-law, and was surprised to learn the truth.)

Contracts

1. "An oral contract is worthless."

An oral contract *might* be worthless, under certain circumstances. The three most common are: 1) a contract for the sale of goods, where the price is $500 or more;* 2) a contract involving the sale or long-term lease of real estate;* and 3) a contract that *by its very terms* is *incapable* of being performed *within* a *year* of the date of the contract's formation.

Examples of that last one are an oral agreement to work for someone for two years; or to work for someone for a just a year—but starting *the day after* the contract is made. However, if (under an oral contract) one party promises to work for the other "for the rest of my life," that is *valid*. This is because there is absolutely no guarantee that anyone's life will extend at least a year from any given date. So the contract is not, by its very terms, incapable of being performed *within* a year.

With few remaining exceptions, not worth mentioning here, all other oral agreements *are* valid. (You've probably noticed that I keep writing "oral" instead of "verbal." "Verbal" just means "with words"—as opposed to a contract that's *implied,* based on the *conduct* of the parties; see below. A written contract is just one form of a verbal contract, although even many lawyers—incorrectly—use the two terms interchangeably. "Oral" always and only means "spoken.")

2. "To make a written contract binding, it should at least state that one party has given the other 'one dollar and other valuable consideration' in return for whatever he or she is getting from that other party."

---

* There are exceptions to this, however.

Nonsense. If the agreement is valid to start with, these "magic words" are superfluous. (Nowadays, you also see "for value received.") In fact, if *all* you have are the magic words, you might thereby make the contract *un*enforceable. If you're going to the trouble to put a contract in writing in the first place, you ought to just go ahead and spell out what the deal is. (The only time to use just the "magic words" is when you know that a third party will see the contract, and you don't want that third party to know exactly what that value consisted of. As an individual, such cases will be extremely rare—because, for one thing, most of your contracts won't be shown to third parties, and won't require any secrecy as to their terms even if third parties do see them.)

There doesn't have to be an exchange of money or tangible property. If each party just promises to do something in *exchange* for a *promise,* that's enough, usually. (And see next myth…)

3. *"Unless* both *parties provide something to each other—even if it's just a promise—there is* never *a contract."*

True, usually. (This is why the "dollar and other valuable consideration" shows up sometimes.) However, under certain circumstances, a one-way deal is enforceable.

Example: There's been a severe ice storm in your area. Large branches, under the weight of the ice, have fallen from trees, tearing down power lines, crushing the roofs of automobiles, etc.. Many more limbs have cracked under the strain, and clearly are in danger of falling. So, householders are scrambling to hire tree-trimming services to remove the limbs that might otherwise fall and cause damage.

You're a crew chief for one of those services. Things are so hectic that you're working 18-hour days, and rushing from job to job. You and your crew arrive at one house. You knock on the door. The householder comes to the door. You introduce yourself, name the firm you're with, and say you're there to trim the trees. You point out the limbs in danger of falling, and promise to get right on it. The householder doesn't say a word, but assumes a facial expression that you believe indicates his assent.

After you complete the work, you present the bill, along with a business reply mail envelope. The householder speaks up for the first time: "I never ordered your services. I never said anything to indicate my agreement to a deal. I don't owe you a dime." When you try to protest, he slams the door in your face. You check in at the office—and discover you trimmed the trees at the wrong address: you were supposed to have gone next door.

Well, your firm and that householder have an implied contract. It's enforceable. You told him what you were going to do. You believed he had contracted with your firm to do it. He knew (or should reasonably have anticipated) that neither you nor your firm normally do such things for free. And he accepted your services, without protest. While this does not mean that someone can go around doing things, unsolicited, for other people and then demanding to be paid for those services, the fact is that under these circumstances, your firm has enough of a "contract" to make the bill stick.

"Never say 'never,'" in the Law...well, *almost* never say "never" in the Law.

Evidence

"You can say whatever you want in a business situation, but as long as you aren't under oath, it can't be used against you."

Ha. I would like to be in court to see what happens when anyone who believes this tries to tell the judge and jury that yes, he or she made the statement in question, but no, he or she can't be held to it—because although it was a lie, it wasn't made under oath. Care to guess the outcome?

Torts

1. "It isn't slander or libel if you start out by saying, 'In my opinion,——————————————————.'"

Wrong. If you make a statement that otherwise fits the test of defamation, it's no protection to say it wasn't defamation merely because you were just expressing your "opinion" rather than stating something was a fact.

(Slander is defamation that's spoken, including live remarks on radio or television. Libel is defamation communicated in a recorded medium. Historically, libel just referred to written material, including personal letters as well as newspapers, magazines, and posters. Today it includes audio and video programming recorded prior to their broadcast or other means of electronic transmission. As for on-line computer stuff, including e-mail, I don't know. —But the distinction is important because recovering "damages" is usually less difficult for slander than for libel.)

2. "It isn't slander or libel if you start out by saying, 'What's-his-name says that ——————————.'"

Wrong again. It's no defense that you're merely passing along something someone else said. (More than one publication or broadcaster, which had assumed itself immune, has found this out to its sorrow.)

Civil Procedure

1. "In America, you can sue anyone even for some ridiculous reason—but even if the defendant wins, he or she still has had to pay all the costs of defending against the suit."

This is insurance industry propaganda. In nearly every jurisdiction, the winner usually recovers his or her costs. "Costs" includes expert witness fees, deposition expenses, copies of transcripts of the depositions and the trial itself, filing fees, subpoenas, etc. "Costs" excludes attorneys' fees. But even without attorneys' fees, they can run into the hundreds of thousands of dollars. And sometimes the winner *is* entitled to attorneys' fees.

Further, in most jurisdictions, a party who brings a frivolous lawsuit can be fined by the presiding judge. Such sanctions can include paying the defendant's legal bill. The judge can also sanction the *attorney* who takes a case that's groundless. True, very few judges ever use this power. But more of them should, more often. Plaintiff's lawyers are getting a bad rap that more properly should be directed to the judiciary. (And yes, the plaintiff's attorney should not have taken the case in the first place.)

Second, even in the absence of judicial punishment, the defendant who wins an utterly worthless suit brought against him or her can—in many jurisdictions—turn around and sue the former plaintiff for "malicious prosecution." (Historically, this was possible only in cases where a government official had brought baseless criminal charges against someone as an act of harassment. Hence the name. But this option is available in some jurisdictions in connection with *civil* suits brought as an act of harassment.) Turnabout is fair play—and the former defendant might possibly force the former plaintiff to pay the bills for both the former *and* the present suit.

Perhaps you've heard of the "British rule"—"loser pays." There, if the defendant is a big corporation, it can run up hundreds of thousands of dollars' worth of legal bills and expenses. The typical plaintiff is not a big corporation, and cannot afford to lose and then be forced to pay. So, not surprisingly, very seldom does David take on Goliath in Britain. In part because of the British rule, the fat cats there got fatter, and lazier. I'm sure you've heard about the decline of the British economy. One reason why that's happened, I believe, is precisely because of its "loser pays" rule. Now *America's* fat cats are licking their chops at the prospect of such tort reform here. But what's good for General Motors is not necessarily good for America. "Reform" can be *regre*ssive as well as *pro*gressive.

2. "Juries go crazy. Just look at that old woman who got millions of dollars because she spilled a cup of hot coffee on her crotch at the McDonald's drive-in window."

The media loves a good story, and will pick and choose among the facts in order to make a story good. (This goes for the news media as well as—obviously—for Hollywood.) They never told you that, in the McDonald's case, one of the key McDonald's witnesses testified that his corporation *knew* it made its coffee 'way too hot. It also knew that it was *statistically certain* that a given number of people would a) spill it, and b) get burned by it—

perhaps badly. In fact, there had already been more than *700* complaints about burns—just none as bad as the old woman's. McDonald's had been put on notice. It had then weighed the cost of fixing the problem against the benefit of doing so. It decided it wasn't worth it to fix it...even though this decision *guaranteed* that a (small) number of people would be *badly* burned.

The woman had only asked that McDonald's pay her medical bills. Nothing more. McDonald's had refused—even though it had known, in advance, that something like this was sure to happen.

I have read interviews with the jurors in the case. They said the key McDonald's witness was amazingly arrogant. So, they decided the *corporation* should get "burned," too. Had you been there, and heard and seen what they did, I'll bet you would have agreed with them.

The jury found the woman had suffered actual damages of $200,000. However, it also found that the woman was 20% negligent herself—something the media never reported. So, she got 80% of $200,000, i.e., $160,000. Then the jury added $2.7 million in punitive damages because of McDonald's arrogance. As it is, the other thing the media didn't tell you is that the judge was definitely pro-corporate and anti-plaintiff. He *overruled* the jury, and knocked the damages down to just $640,000. (Actually, the parties later settled for an undisclosed sum.) Of course, her lawyer probably took about half the proceeds, for his services and expenses. Most of whatever she got probably went for the numerous skin grafts she'd had to pay for out of her own pocket.

McDonald's no longer serves its coffee at a temperature of 190 degrees. Only that lawsuit—and the jury verdict—got them to do something they should have done on their own, long ago. That's the purpose of the tort law: Sometimes, to get the attention of a jackass, you have to hit it up-side the head with a 2x4. *Is that so bad?*

True, juries do go crazy. *But it cuts <u>both</u> ways.* There are "runaway" juries—and there are also what might be called "fall-away" juries. You never hear or see anything about the outrageous cases where an individual plaintiff loses even though it's obvious that the defendant has done serious harm to that person—often deliberately and irreparably. This is far, far more common. Sometimes, the defendant and his or her witnesses are very sympathetic—and the plaintiff, or his or her witnesses, are not. It becomes a popularity contest, and the plaintiff loses.

Further, as chapter 21 discussed, unless the case is a fairly big one, and not too messy, it's hard for any individual to find a *good* lawyer to take a case. And the "bad guys" usually can afford to hire the *best*.

Quite often, the bad guys *planned* everything, from the *beginning*. Every step of the way, they covered their tracks, because they knew there was a chance they'd get sued someday for what they knew they were *deliberately* doing. *They were preparing for trial before they'd even begun to harm the future plaintiff.*

The vast majority of civil wrongdoing in this country never ends up in litigation, because—most of the time—the bad guys are very good at being bad. (You rarely *become* a fat cat by being a nice little kitten.) Sadly and all too frequently, they get away with it. (And as a back-up if the victims *do* file suit, the bad guys often intimidate those victims, via "Rambo tactics," into dropping the matter...and settling for peanuts.)*

3. "America is lawsuit-happy. In the 'Good Old Days,' people just didn't sue one another at the drop of a hat."

Oh yeah? Read this: "The law makers and the law expounders have finally and recently perceived that the people of this country are the most litigious in the world." This comes from the opinion by one Justice Hallet in a Colorado federal appellate court case, *Hughes v. Green.* Sounds like #3 is correct. But check the date of this case: 1896: more than a *century* ago. And note that Hallet says "have *finally*...perceived," which suggests the pattern existed long before 1896—even in frontier Colorado. —For skeptics, the citation is 75 F. 691, 692 (C.C.D. Colo., 1896).

Criminal Law

1. "Criminals have too many rights. Cases are always being thrown out on technicalities."

At least 90% of all criminal prosecutions end up with the State *convicting* the accused, for something. Most accused persons have to settle for a hack lawyer who puts five minutes in on the case and then manipulates the defendant into "copping a plea," even if the State's case is as poor in evidence as the defendant is in money. (Old jailhouse saying: "Time is money—if you don't have money, you do time.") The real function of the criminal justice system is to process the losers. Guilty or innocent, the system doesn't care. Just keep processing the paperwork. Keep those people moving along the conveyer belt of "justice."

Granted, the cases that go to *trial* don't have such a high percentage of success for the State. But what's wrong with that? Think about it: What's the purpose of the criminal justice system? —To take the bad guys out of circulation, or at least to brand them as bad guys. Cops are overworked and underpaid. There are too few good detectives, and almost no decent crime labs—not even the FBI's, apparently. Put all that together, and you get a lot of mistakes and "irregularities." Cops are too quick to jump the gun—as it were. So are prosecutors (who are *also* overworked and underpaid). They

---

*   In case you've forgotten: I'm a plaintiff's attorney. And as you can see, I tend to root for the underdog.

"Atticus Falcon," Esq.

have to, because otherwise they get buried in the caseload. Same thing's true regarding criminal court judges (or almost any judges, for that matter).

The "technicalities" are there to make sure the cops and the DAs do their jobs right. If the bad guy really is guilty beyond a *reasonable* doubt, it'll be obvious in a courtroom. If the cops and prosecutors have to cut corners and violate rights to "prove" the accused is guilty, then maybe, just maybe, the accused is innocent. —And if the wrong guy gets nailed, that means the *real* bad guy is still out there, free as bird...a bird of prey.

I do wish the "law and order" types would give some thought to that—and stop their demagoguery.

Most of the time, when a conviction is reversed on a so-called technicality, it means the police, or the prosecutors, or the presiding judge *screwed up*. That is, they failed to do their job the right way. In criminal law, there are very few situations where the law is not clear. What happened is that one or more law enforcement agents either chose to ignore it, or were ignorant of it in the first place. Naturally, these folks won't admit that. So, they blame "technicalities" and appellate courts that are supposedly "soft on crime."

You've heard of indictments, right? As a general rule, the district attorney is not allowed to file an indictment on his or her own. Instead, the D.A. has to get a grand jury to vote to indict the accused—unless the accused waives it. What you probably *haven't* heard is that, in the grand jury proceedings, *none of the usual safeguards apply.** If the cops illegally arrested the suspect, *no problem*. If they interrogated the suspect without "Mirandizing" him or her, *no problem*. If they coerced a confession, *no problem*. If they seized evidence without a search warrant, *no problem*. None of the rules of evidence apply,* and *the suspect who's brought before a grand jury is not allowed to have his or her attorney in the room.*

Now, given the fact that the deck is so heavily stacked in favor of the State *prior* to trial, does it really seem so unfair to insist on a fair *trial?* —Besides, as anyone knows, the idea of "innocent until proven guilty" is a myth. We give lip-service to it as an ideal, but any criminal lawyer (defense *or* prosecutor) knows the jurors always assume that if the police *charged* someone with a crime, that someone is probably *guilty*—else why would the cops have filed charges? And if the accused chooses not to take the stand in his or her own defense, that's usually all she wrote. (O.J. Simpson beat the rap

---

* In most jurisdictions, matters of privilege are the only exception. The most common are the rules concerning attorney-client, parishioner-clergy, and intramarital confidential communications. (Of course, the 5th Amendment's right to remain silent also exists...but *not* if the State has offered immunity. Yet, there's "immunity" and there's *immunity*. Sometimes the former, known as "use and derivative use" immunity, proves to be no real immunity at all—but the witness has to testify anyway. *Real* immunity is "transactional" immunity.)

after asserting his 5th Amendment right—but it cost him well into six figures to get off—with a lot of help from the bungling of the police, prosecutors, and presiding judge.)

The problem isn't the "rights of the accused." It isn't "technicalities." It's our failure, as a society, to fight crime *effectively*. Instead of the sledgehammer approach of "more cops on the beat," "more prisons," and "three strikes and you're out" legislation, we need bigger budgets for the more subtle tools: more and better *detectives,* more and better *crime labs,* more and better evidence *technicians,* and more and better computers and "anticrime software." —Also, more and better prosecutors, and more and better criminal court judges. (More and better public defenders, too.)

For those who get upset about accused persons' having Constitutional rights, here's one for you: The Fourth Amendment's protection against unreasonable search and seizure *does not apply* where the suspect's property is in someone *else's* possession. So, if the cops believe a suspect put "the fruits or instrumentalities of a crime" in someone else's house for safekeeping, it makes no difference if they found it after they busted into the house without a warrant and trashed the place while searching for that evidence.

"Fine," you say?

—But what if it's *your* house? Think your insurance will cover the damage? (I doubt it. But even if it did, don't forget the deductible... and how many hours of pleasure you'll have trying to put the place in order again.)

Now let's change the facts: The cops are hitting the *wrong* place—*yours*—and they come busting in at 2 *a.m.*. Remember, they have no warrant. They also do not have to announce their presence—if they don't feel like it. In this case, they don't. They really can just come busting in—and that includes smashing down the door without warning. (The excuse the Supreme Court allows them to give is "The totality of the circumstances.")

Now change the facts some more: It's still 2 a.m., but you're a husband at home in bed next to your wife. You hear someone come crashing in. You have a pistol by the bed. You pick it up just as the bedroom door bursts open and a figure—obviously male, wearing a dark jacket—starts to rush inside, carrying a firearm of his own. Sure, he shouts "Police!" as he comes charging in. —But consider how many women have been stopped, abducted, and then raped by "police officers" in fake uniforms, carrying fake badges...but real guns. And in case you haven't watched any of the "Real Cops in Action" TV Shows, these guys who come busting in are often plain-clothes officers. They're wearing dark jackets. The word "POLICE" is written across the *back*. Now, if a bad guy can get a fake *uniform,* it's child's-play to get a jacket and write "POLICE" on it...as though anyone who's attacked is going to have a chance to read it.

Three guesses as to what you do...or rather, *try* to do. (Three more guesses as to what happens to you.)

—There's easily another book on more examples like that. They'd all be from real life, and real U.S. Supreme Court cases that give *bad* cops a license to make a mockery of "law and order."*

Time to get off the soapbox, and get to finishing this book.

---

* I was involved in a case where the cops came busting in at 11:30 p.m...because a guy had supposedly *run a red light five hours earlier*—even though they hadn't pulled him over at the time. Then they beat him up, in front of his wife and five-year-old son. The cops, the victim, and the victim's family were all white folk, of WASP ancestry. The guy was not involved in politics or political causes. So, no racial, religious, ethnic, or political bigotry. The victim had never met his assailants. Sometimes (some) cops just wanna have fun, I guess.

Chapter 23 - Pre-Law:
Laying the Groundwork

1. Background Reading

If I thought there was a book I could enthusiastically recommend to help you prepare for law school, I would not have written this one. Still, it doesn't hurt to read anything and everything that's available. Your local library or bookstore will have several titles.

As for books to help you understand the first-year curriculum, they were discussed in chapters 5 and 7.

And as for *general* background reading, there are many books available regarding the Law. However, none of them will help prepare you for law school. Nor will they help you get in to the school of your choice—at least not in the sense of improving your LSAT score, etc..

Even so, here are two books that can help you understand the "Big Picture." Both are paperbacks. The first is William Burnham's *Introduction to the Law and Legal System of the United States*. Get it from a library, 'cause it costs $50. The second is more easily affordable ($22): Lawrence M. Friedman's *A History of American Law, 2d ed..*

If you're thinking of going into trial law, you already know there are many, many books on criminal cases. So I won't list any of them. (They're usually the memoirs of victorious defense attorneys.) There's a shelf-full of books on the O.J. Simpson case alone, at least half of which are pro-prosecution.

Ironically, even though probably 98% of all trial attorneys practice *civil* law, writers have almost completely ignored civil litigation. Two noteworthy exceptions, though. The first is *Oil & Honor: The Texaco-Pennzoil War,* by Thomas Petzinger. Published in 1987, it's now out of print. The second is *A Civil Action,* by Jonathan Harr. It concerns a toxic tort class action against two big corporations—and the nightmarish experience of the plaintiffs' attorney. The $15 paperback was published in 1996. *A Civil Action* is a gripping tale. It reads like a good novel. (In fact, it was recently made into a movie, starring John Travolta.)

Last, F. Lee Bailey, the famous (notorious?) criminal defense attorney, has a book available in paperback, *To Be a Trial Lawyer.* It's useful for future civil barristers as well as criminal.

2. College—and High School—Courses

Some courses you should probably take just for their content—courses that will help you do well in law school, or in your law career. Some of them can be taken in college *or* high school.

Accounting: Much of legal work deals with business matters. Big surprise. This includes dealing with financial statements—balance sheets, income statements, sources & uses of funds statements, etc.. You would be amazed at how many lawyers don't even know the difference between a debit and a credit. If you understand accounting, at least through the master bookkeeper level, it will stand you in *very* good stead, both with your future law employer and with your future clients. (Even if you have no clients who are business people, most individuals' legal problems involve financial statements somewhere along the way.)

Economics: More and more, the law turns to economics as the basis for deciding cases. I think this is most unfortunate (see the discussion of Law & Economics in the addendum to chapter 21), but there it is. Enough said.

English Composition: "English Composition" means only non-fiction, expository writing—not poetry, short stories, plays, film scripts, or novels. As chapter 16 showed, it's crucial that you be able to write well. It's hard to get the hang of good writing—and the typical English Comp course is a real drag. However, if you have a good teacher at your school, and small classes, it might be worthwhile. Keep in mind, though, that *legal* writing is different from even *normal* expository writing. (Review chapter 16, if necessary. The last part of chapter 16 listed reference materials, for both regular writing and legal writing. These are repeated in the appendix.)

Philosophy: Yes, philosophy. It's the only undergraduate subject I know of that uses hypotheticals just as law school does. (Some high schools offer a philosophy course or two.) Even if you only take the basic "Introduction to Philosophy" course, you will have a good taste of what the Socratic Method is like—although your law school prof will not be anywhere near as gentle with you. If you can't do that, but your school has a religion department, try a basic theology course. (Theology is actually a branch of *philosophy*.) However, courses in the *history* of religion, or an introduction to various religions, will be of no use at all in this regard.

Another good philosophy course is *ethics*. True, law has little to do with ethics these days, in practice. But *juries* still believe in morals, so lawyers are forever insisting on the alleged morality of their clients' cases, or the need to do justice. An ethics course will cause you to think about this from several angles—and thinking about something from several angles is a big part of legal analysis.

Courses in philosophy, theology, and ethics, when properly taught, cause you to *question* nearly *everything*—and to look for hidden assumptions. These are the traits of a good attorney. (But be careful. As comedian George Carlin said, "If you study just enough philosophy in college, it'll leave you screwed up for the rest of your life.")

Also, you should take a course in *logic*, even though it doesn't use the

Socratic Method. If you're now in high school, and can take it there, you should. Legal reasoning is often based on syllogisms. Yet, most lawyers are not skilled enough in the art of reasoning to detect logical flaws in a sophisticated series of syllogisms. And so, the other side scores. However, although no lawyer—and not even a law student—ever uses the formal terminology of logic, you *will* be using logical reasoning. The better you are at it, the better you'll do. (For an example, see the footnote on page 136 in chapter 10, about how a white person's opposition to affirmative action does not automatically mean racism; it uses the verbal equivalent of a Euler Diagram.)

Note: Logic is especially important now that the LSAT includes questions that rely on (informal) syllogistic reasoning.

Chapter 7 mentioned Ruggero Aldisert's *Logic for Lawyers.* Whether or not you take a logic course, you should get his book *if* you're going to law school.

Statistics: As the saying goes, "There are lies, damned lies...and statistics." Like economics, statistics is being used more and more in the law, and often decides the outcome of cases. It's important for you to know the difference between a median and a mean; to comprehend what a standard deviation is; and to understand regression analysis, correlations, and confidence intervals. If you don't, some hustler will pull the wool over your eyes. —Or, even if you know something's wrong, if you can't explain it to a judge and jury, some hustler of an expert will pull the wool over *their* eyes.

Other: It's good to know something about American History, at a level more sophisticated than your high school course.

And if your high school or college has anything such as "Introduction to the Law," or "History of the Western Legal Tradition," take it. As mentioned in chapter 1 and the addendum to chapter 21, such courses either aren't offered at all in law school (oddly enough), or they're electives you might not be able to take because of schedule conflicts. Get them now. They can prove invaluable to you—maybe not in law *school*, but perhaps out in the *real* world of the Law.

* * *

Some of the courses mentioned above are not easy—especially statistics, accounting, and economics. For that reason, try to take them in a way that you don't get a grade—or at least it isn't included in your gpa.

Many universities have "continuing education" or "adult education" programs, where you can take academic-type courses that aren't for credit, and which won't show up on your transcript. (Often there isn't even a final grade.) Some of the people who teach these courses are wonderful. Check your own school and other schools in town for this. In many cities, there are private-enterprise adult education programs too. These are actually the best buy for the money. The best thing about taking a non-academic course is that you aren't "under the gun" to produce. But don't slough off the work just because you don't have your back to the wall. (In fact, if that's the way you operate, you'll probably be a lousy lawyer—though many lawyers do operate in exactly that manner...and it shows.) You can, of course, take classes during your summer vacation, instead. Otherwise (if you're in college), maybe you should get your own personal tutor. It'll cost you some bucks, of course. But starving grad students don't charge much. ("Will teach for food.")

If you do take such courses, you'll be taking them to *master* the subject matter. So, if you're not going to take them *seriously,* don't bother taking them at all—even if you *can* take them pass / fail or credit / no credit.

—Your parent/s will probably balk at paying for any of this. He, she, or they will probably insist you take such courses as part of your college work, and get grades. Have such person/s read this chapter.

The following were deliberately omitted from the list above:

Natural Sciences, Mathematics, Engineering: I know there are big differences among these three, and that there are several natural sciences. However, I lump them all together because they're all like the Law, in that they take facts and apply principles to them to arrive at a conclusion. Thinking Like a Lawyer has a lot in common with Thinking Like an Engineer, or a Mathematician, or a Scientist. (However, my personal experience with such types has been the that they only see things in terms of black and white, whereas the Law mostly deals in shades of gray. True, a trial lawyer *pretends* the situation is black-and-white, but he or she knows that in truth it—usually—ain't so.)

I suppose that knowledge of any of these can come in handy for a lawyer at some point. But they aren't essential, the way the other courses listed above sometimes are. Besides, they're *hard*—unless your school offers something like "Physics for Poets."

3. College Majors

Once upon a time, you had to major in something that sounded law-related: government, history, economics, etc.. Schools even set up specific "pre-law" programs, imitating "pre-med." Those days are gone. What counts now is your gradepoint average. Where you went to college also counts, sometimes heavily, but the main thing is the gpa (and the LSAT score). Perhaps, if you majored in "basket-weaving," you would not be well received. However, most schools now use an "index" system. The Law School Data Assembly Service (LSDAS), which administers the LSAT, gets your transcript and calculates your gpa. The law school then combines that with your LSAT score to yield an "index number." The higher this number, the better your chance of getting into where you want to go. However, some schools require a minimum gpa or LSAT score, so you can't use a high gpa to offset an LSAT score that fell below the cut-off, or vice-versa. The law school might never even notice what your major was. However, at the top schools, they're likely to look for it and take it into consideration.

Maybe there are still some people who go to college to get an education, but not many. People go to college to get a job. And if you're seriously considering getting a job as a lawyer someday, your key focus is on grades, regardless of major. That, in turn, implies that you should *take courses you can ace.* Sad but true, instead of exploring new realms of knowledge, you should play it safe and stick with what you already know.

For example, say you're fluent in Spanish. It would be too obvious if you majored in Spanish just to get easy "A's"—unless you're not obviously (by your name) Hispanic. But French and Latin are mighty close. Classical Greek is too, but to a lesser extent. So maybe you should major in one of those. (But you can't major in just Latin, or just Greek. You have to major in both, as Classics.) Or, let's say you've been a computer whiz since you were six years old, but you want to be a lawyer instead of a computer scientist. Major in computer science anyway. For one thing, it will help you get hired by a law firm looking for someone who can handle software patents. More important in the short run, it will help you get fantastic grades that'll get you into a top law school—even if you have no intention of ever getting involved with software patents. The same thing is true if your school offers a lot of accounting courses, and you've been doing post-closing trial balances for your family's business since you were nine.

You do *not* want to test out of the basic courses in a subject that you already know backwards and forwards. That means they'll start you out in a higher-level course, where you'll have to work hard—and maybe you won't ace it. So, *deliberately* do not do so well on the placement exam. (And if you were in Advanced Placement courses in high school, do not ask to be "placed out" of freshman classes in those subjects when you get to college.) *Then kick the bejeesus out of the basic courses.* (Granted, it might look odd that you didn't do so well on the placement exam, but then did real well in your basic courses. However, it is extremely unlikely that anyone will ever ask you about it. And if someone does, just say that you were ill when you took the placement exam.)

Yes, if you follow this advice you will miss out on a number of wonderful subjects (unless there's some way you can take such courses on a pass/fail basis). But if you're serious about law, at least consider this approach.

4. The (High School)
"We the People" Program

I'd mentioned that if you can take a course in the history of the Western legal tradition, you should. The "We the People" program is one such course. Its subtitle is "The Citizen and the Constitution." It's available at both the junior high and high school level. As its name implies, it focuses on the U.S. Constitution. However, it provides a good background as to what went into the making of the Constitution. It especially emphasizes political theory and history. At the high school level, students study this as part of a formal course, during regular school hours. (The course might or might not have the name "We the People" or "The Citizen and the Constitution.") I wish it had existed when I was in junior high and high school. It really is very good—especially for those thinking about going to law school.

But here's what makes it particularly neat: At the high school level, as many as 18 students from the class can participate in an interscholastic competition based on the material. The competition takes the form of a mock Congressional hearing. A panel of judges asks questions of members of the student panel. The students know some of the questions in advance, and have a "canned" answer ready. But then the judges ask follow-up questions. The students don't know these in advance, so they have to think on their feet. There's a district-wide competition in each Congressional district where schools are participating in the program. The district winners go on to compete for the state championship. The state champions then compete in the national championship, in Washington, D.C..

I've been involved in this, as a guest lecturer in high school classes participating in the program. And I've seen videotapes of a national championship team in action. This "We the People" program is better than high school debate, mock trial, moot court, Youth Court (discussed below), you name it. True, you won't get as much public speaking experience as you would in those other activities. However, the background knowledge you acquire more than makes up for that. (Ideally, though, you should be in a "We the People" course and competition, *and* in at least one of those other activities.)

If you're now in high school and your school does not participate, perhaps you can be the moving force to get it started there.

The "We the People" program is run by the Center for Civic Education. It's funded by the federal government. For more information, call the Center at (800) 350-4223.

5. Speed-Reading

No, no, no! Do *not* take a speed-reading course. If anything, you need to learn how to *slow down* your reading. Entire cases turn on the use of one word or phrase, or the location of one phrase or a comma within a paragraph. (Take another look at that excerpt from a contract, presented on page 212 in chapter 16.) Fine shades of meaning can make all the difference in the world. There's no such thing as reading something to get the gist of it. You have to read it so you know it all, backwards and forwards, inside out. Granted, this isn't quite so in law school—but it usually is in the *practice* of law. However, there is still absolutely *nothing* in law school for which speed-reading would be *appropriate.**

The most important reading skill of all is one that can't be taught anywhere: the ability to "read" *people*...especially jurors.

6. LSAT Preparation Course

If you bomb on the LSAT, your chances of getting into a good school are greatly reduced. —But then again, that doesn't necessarily mean you should forgo law school; you'll just need to give it some serious thought, relative to your career hopes.

Seriously consider an LSAT prep course. However, they're expensive (close to a thousand dollars—comparable to a bar review course). The Big Three vendors, in reverse alphabetical order, are The Princeton Review, Stanley H. Kaplan, and BarBri. They're listed in the appendix, with their toll-free numbers. There are other vendors, who operate just on a regional basis.

However, you have to weigh the (known) cost against the unknown benefit. A lot depends on where you hope to go to law school, too: If you know what your prospective law schools' required index scores are, and you have high grades, a high LSAT score isn't crucial. You can probably save your money. (That's the way I did it, and still hit a percentile that was high enough, when combined with my grades, to get me into where I wanted to go.) If in doubt, take the course. (One lawyer who read this book in manuscript wrote a comment in the margin: "No—take the course, period...and take it seriously.")

You can take the LSAT more than once, if you don't like the score you get the first time around. But note: LSDAS reports your *previous* score, too. So, if there's a big improvement, your prospective law school just might decide that the *later* score, not the earlier, is the fluke. It might be worth waiting a few years and then re-taking it. The LSAT people don't report scores more

---

* Yet, none other than F. Lee Bailey *strongly recommends* that you learn speed-reading. I don't buy his argument, but as between believing him or believing me, if I weren't me I'd believe him.

than three years old—but check to confirm this. (I went to college with a guy who got great grades, and wanted to go to law school. For him, it was "Harvard or Bust." He took the LSAT *before* he applied anywhere, and didn't have LSDAS report his scores to any schools. Wise move, 'cause he bombed. So he went to work after college, retook the LSAT a few years later, aced it...and went to Harvard Law.)

Better to hit the high mark your one and only time. An LSAT prep course will probably make a difference in your score—perhaps a *big* difference.

Chapter 18 discussed how to get a free bar review course. Can't say for sure, but the same thing might be possible with one or more of the LSAT prep courses. Instead of selling to fellow law students, you'd be selling to fellow undergrads. It's certainly worth looking into.

7. Gaining Exposure to the Law

Go to work for a lawyer, even just part-time. But "work" doesn't necessarily mean getting paid for it. Your goal is learning something about the Law. So, even if you end up working for free, it can still be worth it. (There's a potential problem with this, though: Your boss might well be worried about the possibility you'll violate client confidentiality. Then your supervising lawyer gets in trouble for what *you* did. If you're working at no charge, your employer has no way to put you in fear to make you toe the line. So don't expect to be permitted to learn much about actual cases—until you prove yourself trustworthy.)

When I was 16, and had just gotten my driver's license, I did volunteer work for the local Legal Aid Society. Most of what I did involved retrieving and shelving books. However, it was in my boss's interest to teach me the system of legal notation, and how to Shepardize a case. In my youthful innocence, I was thrilled—but even in hindsight, after all these years, *I* am grateful to *him*.

Of course, if you can get a *paying* job with a lawyer, so much the better. But then you'll be expected to perform tasks that don't necessarily teach you anything about the Law. Instead, you'll be typing, filing, answering phones, acting as a messenger, etc.. Whatever you're going to learn about the Law, you'll have to learn in your spare time. If the firm has a paralegal, perhaps he or she would be willing to teach you some things. In return, you'd help the paralegal do grunt-work, for example—although you'd be doing that anyway.

If you want to go to law school in the same city or state where you're attending college, get involved early with the local legal community. Help check in registrants at legal conferences, for example. The secretaries and clerks who work for the bar association, and so forth, don't like to do this stuff. And their bosses don't like to pay those people's normal rate for such low-level work. You find out about the activity ahead of time, and offer to help out for minimum wage, or even for free. You'll get to hang around and listen in. (You find out about the activity ahead of time by finding and reading publications exclusively for lawyers in your area. See chapter 20.)

Get involved in politics, even if you don't like politics. This includes political action groups and non-profit public interest law groups, whether liberal or conservative, including the ACLU or ACLJ. Lawyers are to politics and political causes what flies are to manure: they're all over it. Do a good job as a political worker, and someone might hire you as a law office worker—or generously let you work for free. If your state is one in which judges are elected rather than appointed, and you plan to be a trial attorney, then go for judicial electoral politics rather than the usual stuff. If you plan to return to this community to practice law someday, the connections you make now can prove *enormously* valuable. ("A *good* lawyer is one who knows the law. A *great* lawyer is one who *also* knows the *judge.*")

Another good place to find lawyers is non-profit arts groups. Get involved, and arrange it so you end up working on or for the same committee as a lawyer or two.

In any of these contexts, don't hit lawyers up "cold" about your desire to work for them. They'll immediately back off. Get to know them a little bit first. Give them a chance to get to know you. Impress them with your ability to handle whatever tasks the subject matter involves, be it politics, social issues, arts, etc.. (Besides, you want these people to help you learn something about the Law. So you need to check each of them out first, to try to find the ones you believe might be willing to give as well as take.)

Even after you get to talking with them, don't say that you've *decided* to go to law school. Instead, at some point casually mention that you're *thinking* about going to law school someday, but you aren't sure. And you *maybe* want to get your feet wet before taking the plunge. The lawyer you're talking with will get the hint, and will appreciate your subtlety. If he or she likes you, and thinks you can be a help at the office, you might just get yourself an offer.

Once you're doing anything for lawyers, get a law dictionary.* Keep it handy. Any time you see a new term, look up its meaning. Then, if you still don't understand it, ask the lawyer about it. But look it up first. Don't constantly bother your attorney about such relatively trivial things. (There's a good chance he or she won't know the answer, will be embarrassed

---

* Chapter 5 mentioned some law dictionaries that attorneys use. However, you might do better to get a law dictionary intended for use by non-attorneys. (But if you're working in a law office, you don't need to buy any law dictionary at all.) The *Real Life Dictionary of the Law,* prepared by Gerald N. Hill and Kathleen Thompson Hill, is good. It's a $20 paperback. Then there's *The Legal Dictionary for Bad Spellers,* by Joseph Krevisky and Jordan L. Linfield, a $13 paperback. (However, most of the time you encounter a legal term that's new to you, it'll be in print; you won't be *hearing* it on TV or some such…though, come to think of it, you might hear it around the law office. Regardless, be sure to consider the Hills' dictionary even if you are a poor speller.)

because of it…and will resent your presence as a witness to his or her ignorance.) To increase your knowledge of the law, get some of the books recommended in chapter 5. The more you learn on your own, the more inclined the lawyer will be to talk with you about the law, knowing you are able to carry on a fairly well-informed conversation.

Warning: Remember that there are all kinds of law practices, and all kinds of lawyers. Don't make the mistake of assuming that wherever you got involved is the way it is everywhere. Elsewhere it might be much better—or much worse. That's one reason why it's important to try to "hit if off well" with the lawyer you want to use as your mentor, before you approach him or her about a job. (Just watch out for sexual advances, though.)

8. Killing Two Birds With One Stone, Again

F. Lee Bailey says he worked as a private investigator while he was in law school. And I know an attorney who paid his way through law school by tracing chains of title in the deed records. Each of these two future lawyers picked up excellent informal research skills.

There's no reason why you can't try to do things like this, if you wish. It will pay off both in the short-term and the long. However, presumably, you're going to Make Law Review—*if* you follow the recommendations of *Planet Law School*. So, you won't have time for these other tasks during second- and third-year. And you certainly won't have any time for these during first-year. Presumably, also, you'll get Prestigious Clerkships. You won't have time for these other things then, either. So, the ideal time to do this is *before you even start law school*—if it isn't already too late for you. Then, if for some reason you don't ace first-year, you'll have some excellent (and rare) law-related skills. If you don't Make Law Review, you can then do part-time work for several lawyers in years two and three. Not only will you learn a lot about lawyering; you might even have a job waiting for you as an attorney with one of these firms.

There's no need to become a licensed private investigator. But maybe you can *work* for a private investigator who will train you in some of these research skills. (Just watch out for the sleazebags.) Or, you can work for a title insurance company, for example, that will teach you how to search the property records.

Many schools of continuing education, junior colleges, and for-profit adult education organizations offer courses in what I've called "case investigation." Call around and get their catalogues for upcoming semesters.

There are even a few—a *very* few—*law* schools that offer such courses, for credit.

Also, there are so many books on "investigations" that there's no point in listing them. Any well-stocked bookstore will have several of these titles in its reference section. However, be warned: most of them are of the "How to Find Anyone" variety. Often, they're quite superficial. So choose carefully.

But one title does deserve special attention: an organization called Investigative Reporters and Editors (IRE) does an *excellent* reference book. It's for professional journalists, but anyone can understand it. (IRE is housed at the School of Journalism at the University of Missouri - Columbia.) The work is *The Reporter's Handbook: An Investigator's Guide to Documents and Techniques.* The book's author is Steve Weinberg. It's a paperback, and costs $26 (IRE members get a discount). My first copy was of the original edition, and I found it extremely valuable. The new edition includes a larger section about on-line research. If you don't want to—or can't—get it through a local bookstore, you can order it by mail: IRE, Box 838, Columbia, MO 65211. (Add $4 for 1st class shipping, $2 for book rate.) Or, call IRE at (314) 882-2042. (The book's title and IRE's number are repeated in the appendix.)

9. School Visit

I don't see much point in this. One law school is like another, in terms of what happens there. If you want to find out what a law school class is like, visit a school close to home. A *college* visit while you're in high school makes sense, because you will have a life other than your school work, probably. Not so in law school. For nearly nine months a year for the next three years, regardless of where your law school is, you'll be living in books. It really doesn't make any difference what the outside world looks like. However, if you want to visit the place, no harm done. And if you've lived all your life in one type of environment (e.g., rural), you should check out any law school in a radically different environment (e.g., the Big City). (Also, as chapter 10 mentioned, if you're a disabled person, you really ought to visit the school.)

10. "Mini-Law School" - NILE

NILE is the National Institute for Legal Education. Lexis/Nexis and The Princeton Review are also involved in it. The two top officials at NILE did a book, *The Princeton Review Law School Companion,* with a third co-author. It ain't bad. (Do not confuse it with another book called *The Complete Law School Companion.*)

The National Institute for Legal Education is a "mini-law school." It's open twice a year: once in the summer, and once in the winter. You can take a six-, nine-, 11-, or 14-day program in the summer. All are offered on the East Coast, West Coast, and at a location somewhere in between. (So far, the summer East Coast program has been held at American University, in Washington, D.C.. The summer West Coast program has been held at Stanford University, near San Francisco. The summer program in the heartland might vary from year to year. The winter program is held in Boca Raton, Florida, which is near Palm Beach and Ft. Lauderdale. That's where NILE's offices are located. The winter program lasts five days.)

The six-day program gives a quickie introduction to half of the Big Six courses of year one. In the 11-day program, you get all of them. NILE also conducts workshops in CALR, P.R. (as in "Professional Responsibility"), Negotiations, and Communications. In the six-day program, you get half of them; in the 11-day, all. You can also take The Princeton Review's LSAT-prep course (for an additional fee). The nine- and 14-day programs include three days of (non-CALR) Legal Research and Legal Writing.

Naturally, in such a short time, you would not get a thorough introduction to the Law. However, I've spoken with several students who've attended NILE. Most were in law school when I spoke with them. Everyone said the Institute had served as an invaluable introduction, despite its brevity, to what law school is really like.

They have a very good point there. As this book has repeatedly said, law school is unlike any academic experience you've ever had before. You should get all the materials recommended in various chapters of *Planet Law School,* and take an examsmanship course. But only law school itself, actually being a student there (instead of merely visiting and sitting in on some classes), can acquaint you with what it's really like. —Until the National Institute for Legal Education came along, that is.

As this book has also said, the first few weeks of law school—especially the first few days—are a culture shock. NILE helps you deal with it. You're given real cases to brief—and then you're (gently) grilled on them in class, via the Socratic Method. There is no substitute for sitting in the "hot seat" yourself, if you want to get a feel for what the Socratic Method is like.

The program is intense: Classes run from 8 a.m. to 4 p.m., approximately, with only one full day off during the longer programs. The workshops are usually held in the evening, and run as late as 8:30. (In law school, the daily class load is lighter.) So, if you're thinking of signing up for Boca Raton in the winter in order to laze about on the beach, forget it. The NILE alumni all told me that they often studied from the time class ended 'til after midnight every night, breaking only for dinner. At the end of each course, they took a mini-exam in each subject, involving a simple fact pattern, just to get a feel for what a real law exam would be like.

You know how vaccines work, right? —You're inoculated with a mild form of the very disease the vaccine is intended to prevent you from getting. Your system then builds up antibodies against the germs in the vaccine. These antibodies remain in your system, and protect you against the full-strength germs of the disease if and when you encounter them someday. By attending NILE you can, in effect, inoculate yourself against the psychological virus of law school. Everyone I spoke with had already finished at least one year of law school. They all said that because they'd attended the Institute, they had a self-assurance that their fellow law school students lacked. And even though the program only covered a handful of cases for each course, many of them were later used in the law schools these students went to. The feeling of "been there, done that" came as a great relief amid the stress of the first few weeks of law school.

Other than the obvious, the biggest difference I heard between the Institute and law school was that all the professors at NILE were amiable. None are afflicted with the Kingsfield Syndrome. And all seemed sincerely to *want* the students to *learn* something. They even *helped* them. I'm astounded (and I'll bet those profs aren't like that when they're teaching at law school itself). You spend an entire day learning how to create your own personal outline. As you saw in chapter 7, that—along with getting the jump on your adversary and working hypotheticals with your study group—is the *key* to law school success.

Most of NILE's students are recent college graduates who will be enrolling in law school in a couple of months. That is when you should go too (assuming they're right about the quickie exposure to the culture shock of law school). As for The Princeton Review's LSAT-prep course at the Institute, you obviously should have taken such a course long before.

However, on the other hand, if you're not sure whether you want to go to law school at all, the Institute is a good way to get a small taste of the real thing before deciding whether or not to commit yourself to a more serious pre-law effort such as *this* book recommends. In that case, go before you even take the LSAT. (Then, taking The Princeton Review's LSAT prep-course at the Institute might be a good idea after all.) As was mentioned above, you don't learn much law at the Institute, because of the time constraints. So, if you go there while you're still in college, don't worry about forgetting what you learned. With the help of the materials mentioned in chapter 5, you'll have all the bases covered anyway, later. What counts is the Institute's "mini-law school" *experience.* —But even if you attend NILE (if you do) while you're in college, you should follow the recommendations of chapter 5 beforehand.

I was *very* skeptical when I first heard of the Institute. I called, and they sent a video showing actual classes from the previous summer's program. Fine, but I was still wary. However, the brochure they enclosed named dozens of their alumni who'd given permission to list them as references—and they even provided phone numbers. That's the first time I'd ever seen such a thing in connection with the Law: something approaching full disclosure.

—Being a cynical attorney, though, I then assumed they'd gotten a kickback for agreeing to this. However, I fancy that I've acquired a good B.S.-detector over the years...and I detected no B.S. from these alumni when I called them. And what amazed me was that these weren't people fresh out of NILE, who had yet to experience the real thing, who thus had no basis for assessing the value of the programs they'd been in. On the contrary, they'd already gone through a year or two of law school. And they appreciated NILE even *more* because of it. That kind of a recommendation is hard to come by—and is priceless.

Those I spoke with had all attended one of the long programs. But they went in the summer before attending law school. (If you do likewise, the longer you can stay at NILE, the better you'll be vaccinated against the madness of law school.)

If you're thinking of going while you're still in college, and you (or, more likely, your parents) are worried about the cost, do just the five or six-day program, if any. The three-day program on Legal Research and Legal Writing is the least valuable of the Institute's offerings. Chapter 16 recommended do-it-yourself books on these subjects...and you can't learn to do a good job of legal research and legal writing in just three days anyway. The workshops in Professional Responsibility, CALR, Negotiations, and Communications are not important, either. True, they don't comprise a separate offering. But you'll miss half of them if you only sign up for a short program instead of the long one. No big loss; you'll get P.R. and CALR in law school anyway. And you can't learn effective negotiations or communications techniques from just one workshop—even if NILE's workshops are good ones, which I'm told they are.

However, if you can't afford it at all, don't despair. Far better for you to spend anywhere from $50-$1,000 on the items recommended in chapters 5 and 6 (and the addenda to chapters 7 and 13) than to commit anywhere from $1,000 to $2,100 (or more) to NILE in one all-or-nothing chunk (and don't forget the air fare). The students I spoke with had not been aware of the do-it-yourself materials discussed in chapter 5, etc.. Also, prior to attending NILE, they had not they been aware of the examsmanship courses discussed in chapter 6.

Now, having said all that in praise, here are my reservations:

First, when I called for information, the person I spoke with thought *I* was a potential NILE student, and proceeded to give me the hard sell. That bothers me.

Second, they list at least one of their teachers as being a "Professor of Law" whom I know for a fact is not even an *assistant* professor of law.

Third, several months after my initial conversations with people at NILE, they sent me a new brochure. On one page there appears a quotation from a "Professor M. Kaufman, Loyola Chicago School of Law." It reads as follows: "I had several NILE students in my first year classes and they clearly had a competitive edge from the very first day." Three pages later, the brochure says one of *its* teachers is "Professor Michael J. Kaufman...a Professor of Law at Loyola University of Chicago School of Law." Nothing like an unbiased source, is there?

Fourth, NILE's materials gave me the strong impression that it is a non-profit operation. It isn't. The people who run NILE are indeed affiliated with a true foundation, the National Law and Leadership Foundation. It's incorporated in Illinois, where one of the officials is from, and is registered with Florida's Secretary of State. It runs "summer leadership programs for outstanding high school students." However, NILE itself is not under the auspices of that foundation. The National Institute for Legal Education is a separate, for-profit firm incorporated under the laws of Florida. Yet, each entity's promotional literature they sent me says it "gratefully acknow-ledges the following sponsors," and then lists Lexis/Nexis and The Princeton Review. When I called Lexis/Nexis and The Princeton Review, I could never find anyone who could tell me what the nature of their relationship with NILE was.

I have nothing against business people (or authors, obviously) making money off of prospective law students. And it seems to me that NILE's program is very good. It just bothers me a bit that their literature gave one impression when the reality is otherwise, with regard to their tax-exempt status.

Fifth, and even more serious, the official I spoke with refused to send a schedule of classes from the previous summer's session. "That's proprietary information," he said—which makes no sense to me. It can't be a trade secret—because every student who attended surely had a copy of the schedule, or could easily reconstruct it.

Sixth, NILE is expensive. The six-day program is roughly $1,000; the nine-day, $1,400; the 11-day costs $1,700; and the 14-day program is almost $2,100. Plus air fare. (If you live close enough to one of the locations, you can commute, of course, and thus avoid the room and board charge.)

Seventh, although it's good to get a (mild) taste of the Socratic/Case Method and the culture shock of law school, what happens in class (as chapter 8 pointed out) is almost completely irrelevant to your final grade.

Eighth, and last—and perhaps most significant—*not one of the students I spoke with had Made Law Review,* despite having attended the Institute. (Could it be that they became *over*-confident because they'd attended NILE—and then didn't work as hard in first-year as they should have?)

Despite my criticisms, if you can swing it financially without much strain, go—even if only for a short stay.

If you want to take a dip in the NILE before diving into law school, you can call for a brochure and a free video: (800) 394-6453.

11. "Project Out-Reach" (High School)

There have been many studies showing the relationship between frustration and aggression. Others have shown that where people do not learn how to cope constructively with anger, the result is often a destructive outburst. So it has been in our public schools, where—more and more—the authorities have adopted rigid policies instead of trying to deal intelligently with student rambunctiousness. The result has been, in general, a more obedient student body...but an increasing number of violent outbursts rather than mere disobedience. Though still rare, the violence of these outbursts has been increasing.

Part of chapter 19 of this book discussed mediation and arbitration. These are non-confrontational ways of resolving disputes—unlike litigation, or even typical negotiations. In mediation and arbitration, there is normally an objective third party who tries to find common ground between the disputants, to get them to reason together and to compromise.

The American Bar Association has come up with "Project Out-Reach" to try to deal with in-school violence. The idea is to help students set up and run their own "school-based peer mediation programs." As of this writing, at least one school in each of the following cities is participating: Atlanta, Chicago, Columbia (S.C.), Denver, Hartford (Conn.), Milwaukee, Minneapolis, Philadelphia, Phoenix, Portland (Ore.), St. Louis, San Antonio (Tex.), and Tampa (Fla.).

I don't know enough to say more about it, but it sure sounds good to me. If you like the thought of helping people to resolve their disputes, but don't like the thought of becoming a trial attorney, this is something you might want to get involved in—or to start—at your high school. The addendum to chapter 13 listed two books you might want to read: *The Art of Mediation,* by Mark Bennett and Michele Hermann; and *How to Mediate Your Dispute,* by Peter Lovenheim. If you like either one of those, then mediation just might be the thing for you as a lawyer.

"Project Out-Reach" is co-sponsored by the ABA's Section on Tort and Insurance Practice, its Section on Dispute Resolution, and its Young Lawyer Division. For more information, call the ABA at (800) 988-6386.

12. Miscellany

Typing and rudimentary computer skills are a *must.*

Sometimes, at hearings and trials, I wish I'd learned shorthand.

A memory course, in which you learn how to remember people's names and so forth, can come in handy.

Building your vocabulary is important. Attorneys—especially judges— use a lot of fancy words. You need to have a fairly sophisticated lexicon. (Throughout this book, I've used big words here and there—such as "lexicon." That's to get you to consider stretching your vocabulary, if you're not already familiar with these words. But what I've done is nothing compared to what you'll find in legal texts.)

As an example of how a poor vocabulary can hurt you: I once saw an attorney, at a hearing, read a legal passage that—he said—concerned providing material support to "indignant" people. The guy apparently didn't know the word "indigent," so when he saw it in the text he repeatedly read it as "indignant"—and thereby proved to the judge that he didn't know what he was talking about. Don't misunderstand me: despite my deliberate use of fancy words from time to time in this book, you generally *don't* want to *show off* your vocabulary. Leave such pretentiousness to Bill Buckley. But you do want to be able to take in stride *other* people's use of formidable words.

—And speaking of formidable words: you don't need Latin. Latin is fast disappearing from the law. It will be easy for you to look up in a dictionary what little remains of it, and to then memorize it. The only thing Latin could be useful for would be to correctly pronounce these words. But virtually all attorneys *mis*pronounce them—and you don't want to sound like a prissy schoolmarm by pronouncing them correctly. Go with the flow. (However, if you're already a Latin student, you might enjoy the *Latin for Lawyers* law dictionary, mentioned in chapter 5. It *only* contains legal phrases that are in Latin.)

As mentioned in chapter 21, attorneys tend to have some rather unpleasant habits regarding "interpersonal skills." Lawyers often take the attitude that the best defense is a good offense—and lawyers can be quite offensive. This is unfortunate.

The Gentle Art of Verbal Self-Defense, by Suzette Haden Elgin, is well worth your while. I have my own copy, which I re-read from time to time to try to restrain my knee-jerk negative reaction to criticism. And I've seen it in paperback and hardcover, for $5-$10, at various stores. There's a workbook available that goes with it, and Elgin has from time to time done workshops around the country. She's also done several sequels, but I've not read any of them, yet.

Whether or not you ever go to law school, *The Gentle Art of Verbal Self-Defense* is a good skill to have mastered. It may help you to resist forming a very bad habit...or to correct it if you already have it.

* * *

(Mostly) for Future Barristers...

> Even if you don't want to go into trial law, you will eventually be called on to make a presentation to a group, be it large or small, in a formal setting. Learning to stand up and speak well to an audience without peeing in your drawers is a very important skill to have, no matter what you end up doing with your life.

13. Teaching—and Storytelling

I know this sounds weird. However, for those who want to be barristers, it makes a lot of sense. After all, as mentioned, a trial is a storytelling contest. It's also a teaching exercise.

All of us tell stories, even when we're just relating an event to someone else: the play-by-play recap of a football game, or a report about how two friends got into an argument. A good story is a memorable story. Storytelling and teaching are obviously related to one another.

There's a saying, "If you want to find out how well you understand something, try teaching it to someone else." What I'm talking about is not hands-on teaching, of the sort that involves handicrafts or auto mechanics. But it still involves trying to impart and explain information to an audience in a way the audience will understand and *remember*. Without the hands-on experience, that's much harder to do. "Show-and-Tell" is the best example.

14. College—and High School—Forensics

If you're thinking about law, it behooves you to get some experience in forensics. Forensics, in the real world, usually has something to do with crime investigation (chemical analysis of crime scene evidence, for example). However, within academe, it refers to public speaking. This includes debate, interpretive reading, extemporaneous speaking, and original oratory.

Interpretive reading involves reading something aloud to an audience. Extemporaneous speaking consists of giving a speech from notes, without having memorized it word-for-word. In original oratory, you do memorize the speech word-for-word, and recite it. Debate—well, you know what that is. If your school has any of these activities, you should get involved; at least try one out. Some high schools even have Mock Trial programs.

However, just because you don't want to get involved in forensics, or don't do well if you do get involved, does *not* mean you are *not* cut out to be a lawyer. Trial lawyers—what we typically think of when we think of lawyers—are just a small minority within the legal profession, though obviously its most publicized. (Chapter 19, "Life After Law School," discusses alternatives.) And if you're interested in trial law, and have cable, watch Court TV. I guarantee you'll sometimes find yourself thinking, *"I* can do better than *that* jerk."

Other than Mock Trial itself, debate is closest to what a trial is. Although you don't have witnesses, you do present evidence, in the form of research material. And you argue your case, much as lawyers do at the end of a trial. A big difference is that each speaker gets to cross-examine "opposing counsel," directly—something lawyers never do. Debate is a wonderful way to learn how to research a problem, analyze your case, organize it, present it, and then think on your feet to defend it. (Actually, though, come to think of it, it's even better preparation for Moot Court than it is for Mock Trial.)

Caution: One time, I served as a judge for a high school interscholastic debate tournament. Much to my surprise, the students were deliberately attempting to speak as rapidly as they could. And they were trying to refer to as many sources of research material as they could, reading quotations aloud. They were going so fast that I could not understand what they were saying, even though I'd once lived in New York City. After that first round had ended, and I'd made my decision, I asked one of the participants why the fast-talking. She explained that I was supposed to have awarded points based on how many quotations were read, and how many sources they came from. (I had not made my decision based on that.) Reason, and persuasion, were—supposedly—to have nothing to do with it. Later, I confirmed her explanation with a high school debate coach…and never again served as a judge. If this is the way your school approaches debate, steer clear of it. It's a sure-fire way to lose a trial, whether to a judge or jury, and to lose an oral argument before an appellate court. *Don't* start a bad habit that *will* "kill" you someday. (However, other ways to get involved in public speaking were listed above.)

15. Youth Court

Youth Court is different from juvenile court. But as with juvenile court, it's only for those in their teens (under 18)—junior and senior high school students. (In that, it's similar to Project Out-Reach, discussed in #11 above.) In some places, it's called Teen Court, or Peer Jury. Even though it's a form of forensics, I'm discussing it separately. For one thing, unlike even Mock Trial, this is for *real*. It's similar to the Criminal Defense Clinic some law schools provide, as discussed in chapter 12. But in some ways, it's even better. As with the CDC, it deals only with misdemeanors. (However, in some places, it even includes the lesser *felonies*.) Unlike CDC, students get to be prosecutors as well as defense counsel, and can switch back and forth from case to case. Students also comprise the juries, and serve as bailiff, court clerk—and judge, sometimes.

It works like this: Students charged with minor criminal offenses can plead guilty and then elect to have their peers determine the sentence. Neither jail time nor a fine can be imposed. Instead, the typical punishment is *x* hours of community service, making a formal and public apology, or writing a penitent essay. (Contrary to my expectations, the student jurors did not go easy on these misdemeanants—even though nearly all the jurors are *themselves* misdemeanants: jury duty is part of their sentence.) However, Youth Court is a one-time-only option for the accused offender.

Because there's already a guilty plea, each session of Youth Court is concerned only with the punishment phase. Even so, the student attorneys make opening statements and closing arguments. They also present witnesses, and conduct direct and cross examinations.

Apparently, a given Youth Court might well be only for students who attend a given school. Those who serve as attorneys or judge (often changing roles from one session to the next) go through a—very—short training program at their school.

If you're thinking of becoming a trial attorney, this is a good experience to have. A few of the *Youth Court* students I've observed are better than trial attorneys I've seen who've been practicing for *decades*.

However, it has some very serious flaws. For one thing, what typically happens is that the student advocates imitate the "lawyers" they see in the movies and television shows. That is the *worst* possible way you can prepare yourself to become a trial attorney. As I've said already, what happens in a real trial has almost nothing in common with what happens in a movie or TV trial. I shall put it even more strongly, now: The movie and TV trials are total bullshit. (If you're interested in trial law because you fancy yourself as the center of attention in a dramatic role such as you see in the movies and TV shows about lawyers, become an *actor,* instead. Go to drama school, not law school. You'll be less disappointed.)

Another problem concerns the absence of *real* lawyers. Once the adult courts have sent students to Youth Court, there's no proper supervision as to what goes on. The adults involved in the Youth Courts are not attorneys.

The students do not follow the rules of evidence—they don't *learn* the rules of evidence. They learn almost nothing of court procedures. Yet, by law in most jurisdictions, these are still required in juvenile proceedings. The impression I got, from observing several of these from around the country, was that the attitude of the adult authorities was "Ah, they're just kids, so who cares about protecting their rights? —And who cares if a bunch of prima donnas want to pretend they're lawyers?" The message I got, loud and clear, was that it ain't broke, so there's no need to fix it by teaching even watered-down rules of evidence and court procedure to student advocates.

But what particularly bothers me about Youth Court is the message it sends to the *teens.* The adults involved say it "teaches kids to accept responsibility for their actions." I don't see how Youth Court is any different from regular criminal court in this regard—but admittedly, the repeat-offender rate seems to be lower among those who elect to be sentenced by a Youth Court. (However, I have seen no *reliable* study of this, nor any long-term survey.) I saw several instances where the adults involved—not one of whom was a lawyer—arbitrarily decided that the sentence imposed by the Youth Court jury was inappropriate. So, the adults nullified the sentence, and ordered the jury to come up with an acceptable one. I wonder: what sort of message does *that* send?

The students who get to pretend that they're lawyers love it, of course. The judges whose dockets are lightened love it, of course. But the criminal justice system is supposed to serve the interests of society, not the interests of overworked judges and lawyer "wanna-bes." And the word *justice* in "criminal justice" means the rights of the accused should be protected. I don't see that happening in Youth Court. Granted, the defendants aren't (necessarily) facing jail terms or fines (but see below). However, I fear trouble at some point because the Youth Courts are quite likely denying due process and the equal protection of the laws to those defendants who elect to be sentenced there.

Here's why: Youth Court sentences are based on what's called "deferred adjudication." As its name implies, judgment is deferred—i.e., there is no entry of judgment of a conviction—if the confessed offender serves out his or her Youth Court sentence. However, many people have the erroneous idea that "deferred adjudication" means there will be no criminal record once they've served the sentence imposed without the conviction. —Either that, or they think that, under deferred adjudication, they can eventually have the criminal record expunged, wiped clean.

Not so. In most jurisdictions, even under deferred adjudication *there will always be a criminal record—including the guilty plea.* Granted, juvenile records are often sealed, and not available to the public. But they're still available to the police, and to prosecutors. This prior guilty plea can influence them, if someone gets in trouble with the Law again. It will also influence the court or jury in passing sentence following a subsequent guilty plea or a guilty verdict after trial. (During the "guilt-determination phase" of a criminal trial, prior convictions are usually not admissible—and juvenile convictions aren't admissible, period. However, in many jurisdictions, during the "punishment determination phase," *nothing's* "off limits." This might include juvenile convictions.) More important, *the criminal record is sometimes available to potential future employers.*

And if—for whatever reason—the defendant sentenced by a Youth Court does not serve out that sentence as instructed, then he or she automatically goes back to the regular court: a *conviction* is *automatically* entered on that person's record, and the convicted misdemeanant is now sentenced anew— to a more serious punishment—with *no* right to *appeal.*

The juvenile courts are so backlogged that they bring a lot of pressure to bear to get the students to plead guilty (just as adult courts do). However, unlike the adults, the accused teens seeking deferred adjudication are not represented by a real lawyer at the hearing where they opt for Youth Court. So, they had no way to realistically evaluate the case against them before pleading guilty. In the sessions I observed, the discussion of the Youth Court option was conducted entirely in secret, in the judge's chambers. The students—and their parents—were scared stiff, and readily agreed to "copping a plea" in order to avoid having to hire an attorney and to avoid having a criminal conviction on the kid's record (they think). If they'd known the truth of the situation, they might not have been so meek—as the judge well knew. I even saw students plead guilty to offenses where, as a matter of law, they had committed no crime whatsoever. Their parents, laypeople, hadn't a clue...and the judge didn't care.

Even though Youth Court has serious flaws, you should consider getting involved. If your state allows local jurisdictions to set up a Youth Court program, but your area doesn't have one, and you're still in high school, you might consider trying to get one started. You could even do this if you're in college, either by getting involved with high schools where you're in college, during the academic year, or at your old high school during the summer. (You can't set one up for college students, of course, because they've— usually—reached the age of majority.) You might even be able to get college credit for it.

But if you do get involved, please be the exception to the rule, and try to see that it gets done <u>right</u>. Get some trial lawyers involved, preferably those who handle at least some criminal cases; they can count it as pro bono.

If you do become a Youth Court advocate, you might decide *trial* law is not for you after all. However, that doesn't mean you shouldn't go to law school. And the Youth Court can be a *very* impressive part of your eventual law school application. (You might have to explain what it is, though; it's still not well known.)

As of this writing, there are efforts underway to form a national organization of Youth Courts. However, it's mighty slow getting off the ground. Meanwhile, Ms. Paula Nessel at the American Bar Association's "Youth Education for Citizenship" Committee is acting as a one-person national clearinghouse for information. (The name of the committee is corny; Ms. Nessel isn't.) You can reach her by phone at (312) 988-6386.

Chapter 24 - Where to Go to Law School —and the Finer Points of Applying

Before you decide where you want to go to law school, you should have some idea of what you want to do with your law license. Chapter 19 provided a quick survey of the major career paths in the Law. But as chapter 14 said, there are many, many options in the Law. That's why chapter 20 stressed the importance of gathering information from magazines and newspapers for lawyers—especially the general commercial publications, as opposed to the official ones or publications for a specific area of the Law. You should choose your law school based, in part, on your career goals.

However, you should also choose your law school based, in part, on a realistic assessment of your situation. Your grades, for one thing. Your LSAT score, for another; so take the test far enough in advance of the law schools' deadlines for applications. (Law schools charge an application fee. These add up, fast. So, you only want to apply after you have a realistic idea of where to pin your hopes.)

Then there's the matter of money. How much do you have? How much can you get (loans and scholarships)? There are entire books on this subject alone. You can find them in a bookstore, a library, or a college financial aid or career counseling office. For most prospective lawyers, you'll need to weigh the costs against the benefits of going to a particular school. No matter where you go, you'll be giving up three years of your life. The only thing you can control is how much money you have to give up, as well.

I know someone who went to a private law school. Private schools are very expensive. She graduated with $100,000 in student loan debts...and no job offer. I also know someone who went to a highly rated state school that charged very low in-state tuition rates. (In fact, it's the guy I spoke of regarding Japan, in chapter 15.) He graduated with nearly $50,000 in the bank. (Partly, though, this was because he'd been clerking in Japan, as chapter 15 mentioned. When the dollar fell in value relative to the yen, the dollar value of his yen bank account increased by roughly 30%—with no effort on his part.)

If your finances are tight, you might consider joining ROTC in college, with an agreement that you'll be going to law school and then working for the JAG Corps. And it's something to consider even if your finances *aren't* tight: F. Lee Bailey spent several years in the Navy's JAG Corps as a Marine, trying cases involving anchorheads and leathernecks. (Back then, an officer could try cases without being a lawyer. Bailey, at that point, had not attended one day of law school. Things are different, now.) Edward J. Imwinkelreid, the U.Cal. – Davis law prof and author of the excellent book on evidence mentioned in the addendum to chapter 13, was in the Army's

JAG Corps. James W. McElhaney, the Case Western prof who wrote two trial ad books also mentioned in the addendum to chapter 13, was in the Air Force JAG. All of these advocates got twice as much experience in half the time, compared to the typical trial lawyer. (A public defender or prosecutor gets similar experience. The differences are that the armed forces' future lawyers get big subsidies while they're still in school—but their contract tends to be a bit more binding. —And by the way, you don't have to join ROTC to be eligible for the JAG Corps. You just don't get the stipend and extensive perquisites while you're in law school.)

If money is no problem, and you have the grades and the LSAT score, head for the top. If you want to go into private practice, and want to work for a prestigious firm, you'd *better* go to a prestigious school. Do some home-work regarding law *firms* even *before* applying to law *schools*. This is why you should read publications for lawyers while you're still in college. If you have your heart set on working for a prominent firm, or for a legal "boutique" that specializes in something, find out what those firms are. Then check the *Martindale-Hubbell* Law Directory, and see where their most recent associates went to law school. You'll need to go to one of those schools, because that's where the firms do their hiring. (However, be advised that the prestigious firms often insist that new associates have gone to a prestigious *undergraduate* school as well as a prominent law school. This is especially so in places such as Boston, or for careers such as Estate Planning—where you'll be dealing with clients who are quite wealthy. Many rich people seem to like to have servants who reek of "class." A few firms even prefer those who attended *prep* school. —And not just *any* prep school, mind you; only a *prestigious* one...of which there are very few.)

Attend a "national" school, if you can. —And if you can't, seriously consider whether or not you should attend law school at all. There are only a couple dozen "national" law schools, of the more than 200 law schools in America. The rest are "regional" or "local."

Depending on what sort of career path you have in mind, you should attend the *best* school *in the region where you want to practice*. Harvard, Stanford, Yale, and a few other national schools have recruiters showing up from all over the country. But as you'd expect, more top California firms recruit at Stanford than at Harvard or Yale; more top New York firms recruit at Harvard and Yale than at Stanford. (But note: these days, many firms are nationwide, with branch offices. Don't look only at where the head-quarters is, if you have your heart set on a particular firm or two, or a particular location.) Even if you want to stay in your part of the country during law school, chances are there's at least one "national" school relatively near to where you're living now.

If you want to be a law school professor, you really have no choice but to head for the top. I'm told (but haven't confirmed) that roughly 80% of all tenure-track law school profs came from just five of the top law schools. Most of the remaining 20% are graduates of just a dozen or so of the other top law schools.

No matter where you go, or how much money you have, be sure to include the following in your law school budget: study aids (which can run $500 or more), an examsmanship course ($65-$130), and a set of professional clothing. And don't forget a thousand dollars or so for bar review, in case you have to pay for it yourself.

If you plan on being a trial lawyer, here's something to keep in mind: Most plaintiff's attorneys are solo practitioners, or in litigation "boutiques." They're the lone heroes in the classic Western tradition. Many come from less-than-prominent law schools. (Examples: F. Lee Bailey, Boston U.; Joe Jamail, Univ. of Texas—back in the days before the Oil Crisis of the '70s yielded sufficient revenues to boost U.T. into the Big Time; and Gerry Spence, Univ. of Wyoming.) The big, prestige firms tend toward defense work—usually on behalf of insurance companies. They're the evildoing ranchers who want to steal the farmers' land—or the marauding gang that wants to take over the town. Almost the only time they take the plaintiff's side is when one of their megabucks corporate clients is involved in a contract dispute, or something like that. (Even then, they often bring in a top-notch litigator to serve as lead counsel for trial.) True, sometimes it's the ranchers or the gang who's right, and the farmers or townspeople *deserve* to lose. But right or wrong, the Bad Guys fight hard—and sometimes fight dirty. (And yes, even the good guys have also been known to fight dirty; the immortal Clarence Darrow, for example, tampered with a jury in a California case.) If you see yourself as the Lone Ranger, you don't need to go to a prestigious law school. Nothing wrong with it, of course. But given your career plans, it's not a *necessity*. (On the other hand: you might choose a lesser-ranked school and then decide, during law school, that you want the security of a big-firm paycheck. Well, pardner, it's too late for you, even if you Make Law Review.)

If money *is* a problem, that doesn't mean you *can't* go to a prominent school. It just means you can't go to a prominent school that's *private*. Several state schools (especially Michigan, Texas, Virginia, U. Cal.–Berkeley and UCLA) are in the top 20.* If you can establish state residency, you can qualify for the in-state tuition rate. At some state schools, there's even a set limit on non-residents as a percentage of the entering class. In effect, standards are lower for admitting in-state applicants than out-of-state. It might be worth looking into this, depending on where you want to go. Perhaps you should move there. Live and work in that state for a year or

---

* New York University (NYU), by the way, is a *private* school, and quite prominent. The State University of New York (SUNY) and the City University of New York (CUNY) are public schools. They aren't so highly rated—if that makes any difference to you. To make matters even more confusing, there's a school called the New York Law School. It's private, and not prominent. If you care at all about this, and want to try to keep them straight, the easiest way to remember it is to keep in mind that JFK Jr. went to NYU.

so before applying to law school. (If you do, be sure to register to vote in that state—and, if possible, do vote, even if it's just a local election for dogcatcher. Get a driver's license there. Put your new in-state address on your LSAT application, too. Admissions committees and bursar's offices sometimes look at all these things to determine whether you're a bona fide state resident— especially if you list an out-of-state home address on your application…which you shouldn't.)

If you want to practice in a given city, no matter what, you should go to a law school in or near that city. This is because the firms in that area will interview at the school. They'll come to you, in effect. Otherwise, you'll have a hard time getting your foot in the door. If you attend law school in North Carolina, but want to work in Oregon, it will be difficult to get an interview. In part this is because the law firm will be reluctant to pay your air fare. You can offer to pay your own way, of course. But then you have two problems. First, you want to schedule as many interviews as you can within one trip. That's hard—and, to your dismay, you'll find that sometimes an interview gets canceled at the last minute. Second, your offer will make you look desperate for a job. Human nature being as it is, the firm will naturally think there's something wrong with you that you haven't told them about, and they'll back away from you. —Unless, of course, you went to Harvard or some such, and maybe not even then.

There are readily-available books that discuss only the top law schools, and books that discuss every law school in the country. Among other things, they provide statistics on what sort of gpa and LSAT score each school demands. Do your homework.

Eggheads v. Tradespeople

Supposedly, there are two types of law schools: Those that emphasize Black Letter Law and practical matters, and those emphasizing Legal Theory. The higher the school's ranking, the more likely it supposedly emphasizes "theory." The implication is that schools of Black Letter Law are mere trade schools, while bastions of Theory are Noble Institutions of Higher Learning. The further implication is that students—and professors—in the latter are people of superior intelligence.

Yes, students at the "national" schools (i.e., the prominent ones, which always emphasize theory) *are* more intelligent, on *average,* than those at lesser schools. But they aren't so *because* the schools teach theory. Rather, it's because those schools get the pick of the litter.

Chapter 16 discussed, in part, the insecurity and pretensions of law school professors, and the difference between genuine intellectuals and "intellectual journeymen." The addendum to Chapter 21 discussed what passes for the life of the mind in law school, including Law & Economics, and Critical Legal Studies. But, as mentioned, these various camps are relevant only to the professors. *Students* always get the same old Case/Socratic Method.

There may be a Black Letter Law school that concentrates on teaching students how to fill out forms, but I doubt it. However, I do know there are law schools that "teach to the bar exam." Nothing wrong with that—as long as it includes *understanding* the law, not rote memorization of the legal status quo.

Watch the LSDAS

Chapter 23 mentioned the Law School Data Assembly Service, and how that organization combines your college gpa with your LSAT score to arrive at an index number that law school admissions people use. Usually this is a routine procedure. Your college sends in a certified transcript, and the LSDAS people do the rest. No problem.

But I want to share with you my own experience, which was unusual and unpleasant. My undergraduate school had some courses students could elect to take on a pass/fail basis. It also had some courses students could elect to take on a credit / no credit basis. The difference was that if you bombed in the former, it counted as an "F," just as the name implies. But if you bombed in the latter, it was almost as though you hadn't taken it. It was listed on your transcript as "No Credit," but it wasn't included in any calculations of gpa, etc.. There was no penalty attached. The only difference between getting credit and not getting credit was that the former counted toward total credits required for graduation. Most of the P.E. courses had the credit / no credit option. I signed up for one, a canoeing course, and chose to take it credit / no credit. Halfway through the course, I decided to drop it. As far as my undergraduate school was concerned, fine. It was simply entered as a "No Credit" on my record—and I had wasted some of my (parents') money.

However, when the LSDAS people got my transcript, they listed the "No Credit" as an "F." That hurt my gpa, and pulled down my index number. It also stood out like a sore thumb on the LSDAS report for law school. I called LSDAS and explained, and was told "tough." I wrote and explained, and got a written answer: "Tough." I got the registrar's office at my undergraduate school to send a letter, explaining the difference there between a pass/fail course and a credit / no credit course. LSDAS wrote back: "Tough."

Then I hired a lawyer. She sent those sweet and gentle people another letter. She informed them that 1) if the law school of my choice turned me down because my index number was not high enough, and 2) my index number was not high enough because LSDAS had used my "No Credit" as a zero when calculating my gpa, then 3) she would file suit against LSDAS on my behalf, for intentional infliction of emotional distress. She got a letter back: "Tough." (I just love a monopoly that knows how to act like it.)

I'd figured they wouldn't back down. But the admissions committee at the law school of my choice got a copy, from my lawyer, of her letter to LSDAS. I can't say that I wouldn't have been accepted but for that letter. However, I'm sure it caused my application to get special attention. The supposed "F" was explained. And I had demonstrated that I had the fighting spirit of a good lawyer.

I share this tale with you because those lovely folks at LSDAS may decide, arbitrarily, to screw *you*. Be alert. Enough said.

What <u>Not</u> to Say
in Your Essay

I didn't sit as a student member on my law school's admissions committee. But I have helped prospective law school students prepare their applications. (And every one of them has been accepted at his or her first-choice school.) Nearly every one of them wanted to say the same thing on his or her essay. "I want to serve society." "I believe in justice." "I want to do 'good' as well as doing 'well.'" Etc..

ZZZzzzzzzzz… I'll bet the admissions committee people have a separate file, just for these. It's called the "Goody-Goody File." And I'll bet more than half of all the essays they get take this approach.

If *you* do that, it will hurt you, for two reasons. First, you're obviously just another face in the crowd, at least as far as the contents of your essay are concerned. Second, sooner or later (probably sooner—like within three days of starting law school) you're going to be badly disillusioned—and the admissions committee knows it. All other things being equal, they probably think they're doing the goody-goody applicants a favor to turn them down. —And, maybe, they *are*.

Nothing wrong with idealism, compassion, humanity, etc.. But that isn't what the admissions committee is looking for, because it has almost no place in the Law—and *absolutely* no place in law school. Keep yours a secret. (But your *biggest* problem will be how to keep it, period.)

This is not to suggest you should come across as a potential legal pit bull, a future attack dog of the law. It just means you should let them know *you* know what you're trying to let yourself in for. (You might even tell them you've read *The Lure of the Law, Running from the Law, Law v. Life, The Soul of the Law, Majoring in Law,* and *Proceed With Caution*—all mentioned in chapter 21. That will prove you *really* know what you're doing—although you should tell them, briefly, what those books are about, because it's unlikely that they will have even heard of any of these. However, I suggest you *not* mention you've read *Anarchy & Elegance, Broken Contract,* or *The Lost Lawyer.*) And do NOT say that you've read *Planet Law School.*

Also, even if you plan to be a trial lawyer, do not say so in your essay. The admissions committee will assume your desire is based on watching TV shows and movies about trials. Even though probably no one on that committee has ever set foot inside a courtroom, everyone knows that the way the entertainment industry portrays life as a litigator is not the way it is. They'll assume you're buying into an illusion. Exceptions: if you were active in debate, mock trial, or Youth Court (all discussed in chapter 23).

What to Say,
How to Say It

Goals

You should admit to a desire to make money. Preferably, lots of it. But mention this only down the line, not at the outset.

Don't forget: most—maybe all—of the people who sit on the admissions committee are administrators and faculty. One of their major desires is to raise money for that law school. They get the money from the alumni. Then *they* can get pay raises, fancier offices, etc.. You don't want to be so crass as to say that you intend to donate megabucks to your legal alma mater as a show of gratitude for the *wonderful* legal education you just *know* you will have received there. But I guarantee you, they won't be too happy about it if you intend to have a legal career in a U.S. Trust Territory somewhere in the western Pacific, drafting livestock exchange agreements for members of a leper colony.

Traits to Emphasize

Above all, talk about your strong work ethic—though not necessarily with those exact words. And *don't* tell them how hard you're willing to work on something you *love* to do. Instead, stress how you seem to have this uncanny ability to turn yourself into a robot. (If you've been in the armed forces, this shouldn't be a problem. Otherwise, you'll have to come up with your own illustration of how you know this is the way you are.)

And you might say something about how, "Ever since I was a child, I always had this problem with seeing both sides of the story. My family and friends often got annoyed with me, because sometimes I'd almost *insist* on playing devil's advocate. When I was 11, I did something like that when my father's attorney was present. She told me I was 'thinking like a lawyer.' Then she explained to me what that meant. As long as I can't help but do it anyway, I think it's a good idea to try to do it for a living." (Even the North Korean judge will give you a 9.8 for that, as your score in the Creative Program.)

Experience

Remember what chapter 15 had to say about a job interview when you'd had foreign legal study during law school? You emphasize how you found satisfaction in the drudgery amid the delights of the foreign locale. You should do something similar in your law school application essay.

If you've worked in a law office, that should be easy. But even if you haven't, surely you can come up with something in your background where you had to pay attention to detail, and had to keep grinding away at something normal people find dull. Bookkeeping, for example. Or maybe you're a volunteer in a water quality project, where your job is to visit various bodies of water on a regular schedule and take readings of pollutants, using some kind of meter or something. Boring, boring, boring. But, you insist, you find it worthwhile—and even find a quiet and deep sense of satisfaction from constantly repeating such a mundane task, doing a job well and *without recognition* or *thanks*. One more example: Tell them how you were the family member who sorted through all of great-great-grampa's old documents and newspapers in the attic, and catalogued them as part of a project you did for the local historical society.

As long as you don't lay it on too thick, and don't sound as though you're making mock of lawyers, this should count heavily in your favor. (Obviously, if you get the idea, you should be creative enough to come up with your own examples. If five applicants say the same thing about an attic project, the admissions committee will know something's up.)

Son of Affirmative Action

Affirmative action has passed its heyday. However, that doesn't mean it's over—not by a long shot. The courts have begun to withdraw their approval of fixed quotas, explicit racial preferences, etc.. So, schools can't accept applicants from minority groups, simply *because* they're members of minority groups, if their test scores and gpa were lower than those of whites who were rejected. But there are still a lot of law schools (and colleges, for that matter), that want to have a truly diverse student population.

So, the new trend is already clear. The schools are officially moving away from the index number as the major criterion for admitting students. Instead, they're (supposedly) relying more on the application essay. Thus, the admissions criteria are becoming less objective, more subjective. They then decide which counts more, index score or essay. The reason for this is that it enables schools to *tacitly* maintain *informal* quotas for minority groups.*

Recall chapter 20's tip about what to put on your résumé if you're a member of a minority group? Well, when you're preparing your application, be sure to mention your involvement in organizations and activities of the minority group to which you belong.

About Your Undergraduate Major

If you had an artsy-fartsy major in college, chances are it won't count against you. As chapter 23 explained, admissions committees, these days, just look at the index number and possibly the gpa (with the exception as just noted above). However, to be safe, you might want to concoct a story— a true one (of *course*)...but with your own "spin" to it.

---

* By the way, I see nothing wrong with setting up preference quotas for minority group members, as long as all other things are more-or-less equal. If someone "can't cut it," it hurts that person—*and* the person he or she displaced—to accept that person. Otherwise, within reason, variety is the spice. For one thing, if part of a diverse group, you'll be exposed to a wider variety of information and perspectives than otherwise. This will help you as a (future) lawyer. For another, there are all sorts of preference quotas: at

If, for example, you majored in modern dance, there are two ways to handle that: 1) it had *always* been your intention to go to law school after college, so you could become a lawyer with lots of dance troupes among your clientele; or 2) you'd *always* been *torn* between a potential career in modern dance, and one in the Law—and it's only at this late date that you realize your heart is really in the Law. Etc..

If you majored in any of the natural sciences, no problem. Tell them you've turned on to biotechnology patents, or something like that, and want to make your career in "intellectual property" ("I.P.," for short). Etc.

More on Goals

Chapter 20 spoke of how it's important for you to do your research regarding prospective employers. The same is true regarding prospective law schools. For example, if a school you're looking at has a lot of courses in a given area of the Law, and these are offered by *several* professors (instead of just one or two), express an interest in that area. You're always free to "change" your mind, later—as though your mind had really been made up before. You're not offering to sign a contract whereby you pledge you *will* take certain advanced courses and *will* practice in a certain area of law.

Two caveats: 1) Don't choose something that's glamorous or exotic. (Exception: The school is trying to make a name for itself in this area— Space Law, for example.) 2) If it's something that probably requires a particular pre-law background, there better be *something* in your past to make it appear that you know what you're talking about, instead of just taking a shot in the dark.

Examples of things that will fly:

- The school has umpteen courses, taught by umpteen professors, in real estate. Even if you've had no exposure whatsoever to the real estate business, you can safely say you'd really like to make your legal career in it.

- You worked as a tax preparer for H&R Block, three years straight. You say you want to go into Estate Planning. — Even tell them that's how you first got interested in the subject.

some schools, those whose father or mother attended that school get admitted even if their index number is borderline; sometimes those who aren't seeking financial aid get preference over those who are; and there are schools that enroll students from far and wide, even though many applicants from nearby are more qualified than those from distant places. In short, race is just the most recent form of explicit favoritism. (I'm not endorsing these other forms of preferential treatment. But why single out "affirmative action"?)

- The school has several courses in admiralty law. You were on a big boat once, and witnessed a "slip-and-fall" accident that led to a lawsuit. Later the parties took your deposition. That got you interested in Maritime Law, especially Jones Act cases. (Unless one of the professors on the admissions committee is one of the people who teaches one of those courses, he or she will probably have to ask an admiralty law prof what the "Jones Act" is. You knew. You score.)

Above, it was stated that—with certain exceptions—you should not say you want to be a trial lawyer, even if you do. However, it will impress the committee if you say you want to be an *appellate* lawyer—even if you *don't*. They'll be surprised you know the difference. And as long as you make it clear that you *do* know the difference, this will prove you know what you're talking about—and that you've given serious thought to why you want to go to law school.

You might tell the admissions committee that you want to become "Board Certified" in bankruptcy law. Tell them you spoke with several bankruptcy lawyers who are. They said this school was a good place to go for that. Obviously, you *don't* say this if, in fact, the school is unknown when it comes to bankruptcy law. But if it's a powerhouse, express your interest in it.

(The annual ranking of law schools by *U.S. News & World Report* includes a section on schools known to be strong in particular areas of the law. But your research should not stop there.)

(More) Books to Say You've Read

Several chapters mentioned specific books and tapes you should make use of before you ever go to law school. However, for the most part, you do *not* want to tell the admissions committee you've done so. Remember: the faculty is *not* on your side. If you indicate you know how the game is played, and that you won't let them play *you* for a fool, the professors on the admissions committee will be dismayed. (If this sounds strange to you, go back and re-read chapters 3 and 4.) Above all, you do *not* say you've studied materials on examsmanship, or taken a course in it. That would be the kiss of death. (I am dead serious.)

So, what you need to do is to walk a fine line between proving you've made an *informed* choice regarding your desire to go to law school—and to *that* law school—on the one hand, and *hiding your savvy*, on the other.

These books will meet that test: The *Restatements* on Contracts and Torts, and the Moynihan book on Property—all discussed chapter 5. True, by reporting that you've read these, you tip your hand somewhat. However, I do believe the professors (and any students) on the admissions committee will be *astounded* that you're familiar with those works. Such will count heavily in your favor.

Don't bother mentioning any of the books listed in chapter 16, on critical skills. Law schools don't care about these subjects, even though *you* should. Use the length allotted to your essay for more important things.

As long as you don't mention any of the other recommended books, you'll be okay. (And, to repeat: do **NOT** tell them you've read *Planet Law School*. If you can't figure out why, please forget about becoming an attorney.)

There are other books you could add as window-dressing, such as works on American legal history. Chapter 23 mentioned William Burnham's *Introduction to the Law and Legal System of the United States*, and Lawrence M. Fishman's *A History of American Law, 2d ed..* (If you don't take a course related to America's legal system before you start law school, you might want to have actually *read* one of these two. The knowledge might—*might*—come in handy in law school. It will almost certainly be of use once you get out.)

To show that you're high-minded, you might want to say you've read Gerald Gunther's biography of Learned Hand—who was quoted in the addendum to chapter 21. Other good ones for window-dressing are *A History of the Supreme Court* or *Decision: How the Supreme Court Decides Cases,* both by Bernard Schwartz. The last one I'll mention is *Justice Oliver Wendell Holmes: The Law and the Inner Self*, a biography by G. Edward White.

<u>Walking on Eggshells</u>

They who dwell in the Ivory Tower are a *hyper*-sensitive lot. Beware. If you say anything that can even remotely be construed as other than "politically correct," rest assured it *shall* be so construed—and *thou* shalt quite likely suffer for it.

There was a famous incident a few years ago involving an applicant for a teaching position at a very prestigious university. The chair-person of the hiring committee was male, so the applicant addressed her letter to him as "Chairman" What's-his-face. Chairman What's-his-face wrote back and chastised her for addressing him as "Chairman." Seems she should have addressed him merely as "Chair" (not to be confused with the French word *cher*) or "Chairperson."

Something like that could happen to you. *Very* easily. Have others (both liberal *and* conservative) read anything you write to your prospective law schools, before you send it off. The more hypersensitive your readers, the better.

To change the metaphor: you have to walk a tightrope. You don't want to sound bland. But you don't want to offend, either. So, stay away from topics of race, gender, economic inequality, religion, etc...unless you're a member of a favored minority, and your discussion of the subject is directly related to your minority status.

Do *nothing* to indicate you're *aware* of the Law & Economics, Critical Legal Studies, or "New Republicanism" schools of thought. Chances are, each professor on your admissions committee will belong to one of these. Then every one of them will be on the alert for signs that you belong to a *different* school of thought than his or her own. So, for that reason, you do not claim to have read anything by anyone who clearly belongs to one of those schools.

Exception: If you're applying to a school *known* to be a *bastion* of a particular school of thought, go for it. Stress how much you know about it, and how you want to go *there* because it *is* a bastion. I haven't researched this, so I can't give you a listing for the top 20. Besides, at most of them, there's been no clear winner. (Harvard is known to be the stronghold of Critical Legal Studies, but the Crits are still just a—big—minority there...and on their way *out*. And the University of Chicago is the Mecca of Law & Economics. Regarding other schools, be careful.)

And don't refer to specific professors by name—even if they're famous. As has been said, and repeated, law professors can be as petty and as vindictive as you or I. This means, in part, they have petty jealousies and rivalries. If you mention a prof who's an "enemy" of someone who sits on the admissions committee, you've just lost a lot of points. So just let it go, completely.

A Bit of Flattery

Everyone—even a law professor—knows that People Hate Lawyers. Yet, everyone on the admissions committee is committed to the idea that Law (and, by implication, a law school) is a worthwhile endeavor. You might address this point, stating how you reconciled your desire to become an attorney and your awareness that People Hate Lawyers. For example, you could say that you think "society" is using the legal profession as its whipping boy (or, if you prefer, its scapegoat). Maybe play at being a shrink, and explain how you think we always project onto others what we most dislike in ourselves—even when we know that these traits have value in the right circumstances. Sure, you say, you know there are "bad apples." Every barrel has them. But lawyers have gotten a bad rap. Having lots of lawyers is the hallmark of a vigorous democracy: it's only because everyone is equal in the eyes of the Law that everyone has a chance to assert his or her rights through legal redress. And so forth.

If you really have a lot of nerve, *and* have told them you want to go into litigation, you might tell them you want to specialize in defending attorneys who've been sued for legal malpractice. —Most new law school graduates (and a lot of not-so-new graduates) are a walking legal malpractice suit just waiting to happen. Because the law schools themselves are largely responsible for that, they will welcome you as someone who someday will help them to avoid responsibility for their *pedagogical* malpractice (which, of course, they refuse to admit).

Just try to avoid throwing up on your keyboard as you draft this.

Absolutely, Positively the Last Books Mentioned for Your Consideration

I realize that this book has listed a lot of "suggested reading." But hey, if you're not interested in doing a lot of reading, you better forget about law school. Most of what you'll get there is *boring*, and often a complete waste of time. At least what's suggested here is interesting (I think), and worthwhile.

You're trying to decide what to do with the rest of your life. You're thinking about making a commitment that will mark you, for good or ill, for life—and which will take a chunk *out* of your life. So, don't you think maybe you owe it to yourself (and to those whose *money* you'll be using for all this) to try to make sure you know what you're doing—and to do it right?

Getting into Law School, 2d ed., is by Thomas H. Martinson and David P. Waldham. It's a 1994 paperback, $12. I haven't read it word-for-word, but did look through it. What I saw was worthwhile. Also, there's *How to Get into the Right Law School, 2d ed.,* 1997, by Paul Lermack; $15. Looked okay to me.

Remember: every little bit helps. If either of those books uncovers an angle you wouldn't've otherwise thought of, it could be worth its price many times over.

Then there's *How to Get into Harvard Law School,* a 1996 paperback by Willie J. Epps. It's $17, and filled with platitudes. But here's what bothers me most about it: Epps isn't exactly a common last name. Yet, coincidentally, a fellow named Archibald Epps has been the Dean of Students at Harvard College for more than a quarter of a century now. Dean Epps and Willie J. Epps are both black. From the dedication in Willie J's book, I saw that Archibald is not Willie's father. Curious, though, I called Harvard and spoke with Dean Epps's assistant. She promised to check it out and to call me back with the answer. When I hadn't heard from her after a few days, I called again—and got another promise…which again wasn't kept. The third time I called, I just got her voice mail, and left a message. No response. It begins to look to me as if this is just too much of a coincidence to be a coincidence; another Jungian synchronicity. Seems to me that if you're black, and some relative of yours is the Dean of Students at Harvard College, you won't have much problem getting into Harvard Law School. So, *if* Willie J. is indeed related to Archibald, it's a bit disingenuous of him to have written that book.*

However, that said, his book does contain 50 essays from successful applicants to HLS. Regardless of *where* you intend to apply to law school, those might be worth looking over.

---

* Neither Archibald nor Willie J. Epps is any relation to Garrett Epps, quoted in the addendum to chapter 21. (He is now a law professor at the University of Oregon.) Nor is any of these three related to JoAnne A. Epps, listed in the addendum to chapter 13 in connection with NITA's *Trial Evidence—Making & Meeting Objections.* (Ms. Epps is now an associate dean at Temple University's law school.)

A Final, General, Suggestion

Chapter 13 mentioned how trial advocacy is an exercise in storytelling. So is a law school application essay. The difference is that you have *thousands* of stories, not just one, competing against yours. The finder of fact will choose dozens of them, not just one. Yours might not be among them. *What* you say is very important. But *how* you say it might be even *more* important.

Two chapters have quoted Herman Hesse's *Magister Ludi*: "Although humble, he was completely at ease." The way you should want and should try to come across in class is also the way you should want and should try to come across in your law school application essay. Don't show off. Don't be unctuous. Don't be arrogant. And don't sound desperate. Also, don't show a sense of humor: Admissions Committees, like Character & Fitness Committees, are usually composed of pinheads who Take Things Very Seriously.

Instead, you want to sound, well, "professional." Calmly, quietly, confidently give them enough for them to realize that there must be even more to you than meets the eye, despite the fact that what meets the eye is already impressive. While you don't want to sound as though you're doing them a favor to even be applying to their school, you certainly want them to think, after reading your essay and looking at your file, "Now *that's* the kind of student I wish we had *more* of around here!"*

---

* Notice the similarity to the reaction you want to get from prospective employers? There's no time like the present to start building a good habit.

ADDENDUM to CHAPTER 24:
HOW to BECOME a LAWYER
WITHOUT a LAW DEGREE

Eight states will allow you to take that state's bar exam without having a law degree: Alaska, California, Maine, New York, Vermont, Virginia, Washington, and Wyoming. Naturally, they have requirements in *lieu* of the J.D.. In most states, this is called the "Law Office Study" program. Generally, you must follow a prescribed program of study that largely tracks what you'd be studying in law school. For that reason, the recommendations in *Planet Law School*—especially regarding independent study materials—are at least as relevant to you as they are to those who engage in the full-time formal study of the law.

You still have to pass the same Character & Fitness Committee screening. If the C&F Committee says you're kosher, and you pass the barzam, you get a law license every bit as good as that a J.D. receives...unless, of course, you want a job (as opposed to hanging out your own shingle).

Here's a summary of each state's program:

Alaska

You have to prove to the powers-that-be that you are a bona fide Alaskan. You have to have a bachelor's degree from a four-year undergrad school. Even though Alaska has no law school, it apparently doesn't like its lawyers to have skipped a formal legal education. For starters, you have to have completed at least one year of *law school.* —But once you've made it through first-year, you might as well do the other two; so Alaska's Law Office Study program is obviously intended to be seldom used.

You have to file an application with the University of Alaska to be officially registered in the Office Study program. It appears that the University of Alaska then prescribes the program of study you will follow, apparently including what textbooks, casebooks, etc., you will use.

The attorney who's going to serve as your mentor has to have been licensed to practice in Alaska for at least five years before commencing to tutor you. If he or she has ever been censured, reprimanded, suspended, or disbarred, he or she is disqualified. And if there's a grievance pending against your supervisor at any time during your study, everything's put on hold. (That can take a *long* time.)

You must *study* at least 35 hours a week. That does not mean working in a law office. That means *studying*. Your tutor must give you personal instruction in the law. At least once a month, you have to take a closed-book written exam, administered by your supervisor.

You have six years in which to complete the prescribed program of study. Evidently there are no extensions.

Note: As of this writing, Alaska is overhauling its Law Office Study program. It appears that Alaska will adopt Washington's (see below).

California

As in other ways, California is simultaneously nearly the most liberal *and* the most conservative state.

There's a basic requirement of at least two years of credits from an accredited four-year college. Once you have that, you have a choice:

1. You can study under a law tutor. You must *study* at least 18 hours a week, at least 48 weeks in any given calendar or fiscal year, for five years. Your tutor can be either an attorney or a judge. If the former, he or she must have been licensed for at least five years prior to the time your instruction begins. The mentor must personally tutor you at least five hours a week, and must administer at least one exam to you each month. Every six months your supervisor must file a report with the state bar. There is a limit of two students per attorney or judge at any given time.

2. You can enroll in a correspondence course to study law. The course of study has to involve at least 16 hours a week of study, and has to last at least four years.

However, you don't have to do one or the other, exclusively. You can combine them—as long as the state bar approves (apparently in advance).

California seems to be unique in that it has a "baby bar exam." This is primarily for those who attend law schools not officially approved by the ABA—of which there are many in California. (Now that the ABA has eased up its accreditation rules, there should be fewer unapproved law schools nationwide.) However, it's also for those doing a Law Office Study program. Such students must take the "First-Year Bar Exam" at the end of their first year of law school at an unaccredited institution or at the end of their first year of Law Office Study or correspondence course. (Those attending accredited schools are exempt from this requirement.)

After you've passed the baby bar, and have completed the other requirements stated above, you can take the regular bar exam—the same one graduates of ABA-approved law schools take.

Maine

Maine's alternate program is something of a hoax, really. As in California, you have to have completed two years' work at an accredited undergraduate school. But you also have to have completed *two* years of *law* school. The information I obtained did not indicate if the law school had to be ABA-approved. However, I'll bet it does. After finishing those two years, you must *immediately* begin 12 months' continuous study of the law under a supervising attorney. And your proposed mentor had to have submitted a proposed program of study for you, which the Maine bar must approve before you begin. At the end of the 12 months, you can sit for the bar exam just like the law school grads do.

As you can see, this supposed alternative to a law degree is pointless. Anyone who's made it through two years of law school would be ill-advised to drop out and then keep studying law for 12 more months. Other than the money you'd save on tuition, plus the money you'd make from working instead of being in school, there's no benefit to doing it this way. Besides, your chances of getting a good job are a lot better if you have the J.D.. Better to hang in there at law school for the third year…which I'm sure is exactly what the Maine bar folks anticipate you'll do.

New York

New York is almost as liberal as California in the way California is liberal. And there's no "baby bar exam." Further, the information I received indicated no requirement for any undergraduate studies whatsoever. In fact, its only pre-law requirement is that you be at least 18 years old before commencing your program. (Perhaps this liberality is why New York's bar exam is the hardest in the country among all the major states.)

I say "almost" as liberal, because—unlike California—New York requires you to have completed at least a year's work at an *accredited* law school. It makes no difference whether you get that year's worth of credits by going full-time or part-time; just get the credits. You can then leave law school altogether and begin a Law Office Study program—but only if you were eligible to *continue* in law school if you'd wanted to.

Because virtually all law schools require at least three years of college (and even then, they usually allow just three years only if the three years are at the same university where you intend to go to law school), New York's waiver of any undergraduate work is evidently in jest. However, now that it's easier for previously-unaccredited law schools to get ABA approval, perhaps you can find one that will let you in straight from high school. Good luck. (It's a safe bet that such a school would be private, not public. So, you'd have to pay a small fortune in tuition and fees. This would probably more than offset what you'd save on the second and third years of law school, even at a state school—and maybe on college tuition, too.)

·Before you can begin your program, you must file a Certificate of Commencement of Law Office Study. You can study under an attorney licensed to practice in New York, who must tutor you in "those subjects that are customarily taught in approved law schools." Presumably, this means subjects other than those you'd already taken in law school before your program began.

In the material I received, there was nothing about how many hours a week you must spend on the study of law, tutoring, etc.. But you apparently have to do it for three years before applying to take the New York bar exam.

Vermont

The basic requirement is that you have completed at least three years' worth of credits toward a bachelor's degree. Then you can enter a Law Office Study program. Your supervising attorney has to have had his or her law license for at least three years before your study begins. You can also have a judge as your mentor.

You have to study law for at least 44 weeks in the 12 months of a calendar or fiscal year. Study shall be for at least 25 hours a week, or 30 hours in any consecutive two weeks. You have to do this for four years. Upon completion to the satisfaction of your supervisor and the state bar, you're eligible to sit for the Vermont bar exam just like the law school graduates do.

<u>Virginia</u>

In Virginia, it's called the "Law Reader" program. Virginia sent me more materials than anyone else—in part because it apparently wants any prospective "Law Reader" to get the message loud and clear: the State Bar goes out of its way to make it difficult for you. For starters, there was a three-page single-spaced memo obviously intended to dissuade anyone from applying. It said that only 30 people in the Law Reader program had passed in the 11 preceding Virginia bar exams. This is less than 22% of barzam candidates who'd been Law Readers. (The overall pass rate was 72%. Because that includes those who were Law Readers, this means the pass rate for non-Law-Readers was even higher than 72%.) The State Bar seems to do its best to minimize your chances:

You have to have a bachelor's degree from an accredited four-year college. You have to pay a $500 fee just to *apply* for permission to become a law reader. Permission is not automatic. The State Bar might require you to take the LSAT. It refuses to provide the names of any supervising attorneys. Yet, you must submit a statement from your proposed supervisor as part of your *application*. Your proposed mentor has to have been a full-time lawyer in Virginia for at least ten of the preceding twelve years. He or she must have had a "general" practice of law, not a specialty. And the State Bar "prefers" that he or she have had teaching experience in a law school or a Continuing Legal Education program for licensed attorneys. Your mentor must also possess what the State Bar regards as an "adequate" law library *on the premises.*

You are not allowed to be your mentor's employee. You are not allowed to be employed by the law firm where your mentor works. You are not even allowed to be employed by a lawyer or law firm that *shares office space* with your mentor. Yet, you must spend at least 25 hours a week studying the law—*in that lawyer's office.* You must be *physically present* there, not just using that as your official study location. He or she must personally tutor you at least three hours a week. And once a year you *and your supervising attorney* must appear before the powers-that-be so they can grill the two of you on the progress of your program. Care to guess how this affects an attorney's willingness to be your tutor?

I could go on, and on, but I believe you get the idea. If you live in Virginia, and want to get a law license without having gone to an accredited law school, you better move to another state. Even though Virginia doesn't have a "baby bar" exam, the hurdles there appear to be worse than anywhere else. *They don't want you.*

Washington

Washington (State) is almost as bad as Virginia. In Washington, you must first have a bachelor's degree. Your supervising attorney must have been continuously practicing law for at least 10 years before becoming your mentor. Each supervising lawyer is allowed to have only one student at any given time. Your mentor must spend at least three hours a week personally tutoring you, and you must spend at least 30 hours a week *studying*, for four years. (However, if you attended law school and then dropped out, the four years can be reduced to some extent.) The supervising attorney must administer monthly written exams to you. Your mentor has to make written reports to the state bar, regularly. Once a year, *you* must appear before a committee of the Washington bar, to be interviewed as to your program of study and your progress in it. At the end of your program, you apply for a law license in the same manner as law school graduates: get vetted by the C&F committee, take the bar exam.

Wyoming

After two letters, one fax, and a phone call—spread out over nearly two months—the Wyoming people responded. What I got was a copy of the "Rules and Procedures Governing Admission to the Practice of Law in Wyoming"— *all* of them—even though I'd specifically been asking only for information on Wyoming's Law Office Study program.

As for that, here's all that the Rules book has to say:

> The Board shall, before admitting an applicant to an examination, be satisfied that the applicant possesses the qualifications as to the periods of study prescribed by law; and the following information shall be submitted by an applicant:
>
> ...
>
> (2) The time of study in the office of a member of the Wyoming State Bar or a judge of this state by a certificate of such members of the Wyoming State Bar or judge, showing the actual period of study, together with a listing and description of the substantive topics of law studied. Evidence of tests taken, as well as written material, may be requested. Prior approval of a course of study is highly recommended by the Board.

That's it. Maybe you'll be able to get more information out of them than I.

* * *

I've not seen any articles or reports on any of these alternatives to a law degree—other than the memo from the Virginia Board of Law Examiners. But I will share some obvious concerns: For one thing, unless the lawyer who will be tutoring you has done this sort of thing before, he or she will be reluctant to take you on as an understudy. However, if you make use of the materials discussed in various chapters and their addenda in *Planet Law School,* you can easily put together an excellent program of law study and submit that for his or her (and the state bar's) approval.

Less pleasant: Seems to me your supervisor could make life hell for you and there would be little you could do about it. The various state bar organizations do not favor non-academic programs. So, if you have a problem with your supervisor, it's quite possible you would get no sympathy. In this, it isn't much different from law school, of course. However, at least law school the tyranny you encounter from any one professor will end with the course—although the course might last two semesters. And each professor has anywhere from dozens to more than a hundred students in each class. As long as you keep a low profile, chances are your professor won't single you out for abuse—or, at least, not for long, what with so many other potential victims at hand. (In a graduate school, in contrast, the relationship with your thesis advisor is 1:1 or close to it. If you get at odds with that person, you won't ever get your Ph.D., no matter how brilliant and conscientious you are. Nor is there any point in transferring to a new school, because you'll be "black-listed" as a result of your earlier bad experience.) At least if things don't work out with your law supervisor, you can always call it quits with him or her...and go to law school. (They won't know about your previous effort to get a law license without getting a law degree...*nor should you tell them.)*

Also, speaking of economic exploitation: It's unclear to me how many states have a policy similar to Virginia's, whereby you're not allowed to be your mentor's employee. But assuming that in most of the other seven states you are allowed to draw a paycheck, then, even if your mentor didn't make life hell for you, he or she might just decide to cut your pay at some point, or threaten to reduce your hours of tutoring to below the minimum required number. He or she would clearly have you over a barrel.

—Last, speaking of "having" you: while at least some professors definitely make sexual advances to at least some of their students, a supervising attorney clearly has a better opportunity to engage in sexual harassment, and more leverage for coercion.

Most attorneys bill their time out at more than $100 an hour. The longer the attorney has been in practice, the higher his or her rate will be. (That's why it's charming that some of these states require your prospective mentor to have been in practice for a *decade.)* Your supervisor is making a big sacrifice to be your supervisor—unless, of course, you're paying his or her going rate. You don't get something for nothing. Just be careful of what your mentor might eventually seek in return.

I strongly suspect that the states with Law Office Study programs have no rules that protect the students and to ensure them fair due process if there's a problem with the supervisor. So, the moral is: If you want to go this route, choose your mentor wisely. See if a *trustworthy* relative or close family friend who's a lawyer would be willing to oblige you. Barring that, make sure you've thought everything through in advance. If your mentor is also your boss, try to work up a contract that covers the terms of your employment as well as the terms of the tutoring. As this book has said several times already, an ounce of prevention is worth a pound of cure.

* * *

The information I got from most of the eight states was quite meager. Before you seriously consider doing a Law Office Study program, contact the powers-that-be in the state in question. See if you can get the names of attorneys who've served as mentors. (If your state is as bad as Virginia, you might have to run an ad in a newspaper for lawyers.) You don't have to ask any of those attorneys to be *your* supervisor, but it behooves you to get the "inside story" from someone who knows from experience how the system works. Perhaps you can also get the names of people who did or are doing non-academic study, and can then get the inside story from them. (If the state won't give you these names, but will give you the names of mentors, then the mentors can easily put you in touch with their previous or current students.) One last time: An ounce of prevention is worth a pound of cure.

Contact the following for information on a "Law Office Study" program in that state:

Alaska
Executive Director
Committee of Law Examiners
Alaska Bar Association
P.O. Box 100279
Anchorage, AK 99510-0279
Tel: (907) 272-7469
Fax: (907) 272-2932

California
Senior Executive, Admissions
The State Bar of California
Office of Admissions
555 Franklin Street
San Francisco, CA 94102
Tel: (415) 561-8383
(No Fax Number Given)

Maine
Maine Board of Bar Examiners
P.O. Box 30
Augusta, ME 04332-0030
Tel: (207) 623-2464
Fax: (207) 623-4175

New York
Bar Admissions Administrator
Executive Secretary
NY State Board of Law Examiners
7 Executive Centre Drive
Albany, NY 12203
Tel: (518) 452-8700
Fax: (518) 452-5729

Virginia*
Secretary-Treasurer
Va. Board of Bar Examiners
Shockoe Center - Suite 225
11 South 12th St.
Richmond, VA 23219
Tel: (804) 786-7490
(No Fax Number Given)

Vermont
Administrative Assistant
Board of Bar Examiners
109 State Street
Montpelier, VT 05609-0702
Tel: (802) 828-3281
Fax: (802) 828-3457

Washington
WSBA Licensing Dept.
Washington State Bar Association
2001 Sixth Ave. - Suite 500
Seattle, WA 98121-2599
Tel: (206) 727-8200
Fax: (206) 727-8320

Wyoming
Executive Secretary
State Board of Law Examiners of
Wyoming
P.O. Box 109
Cheyenne, WY 82003-0109
Tel: (307) 632-9061
Fax: (307) 632-3737

Addendum to the Addendum

An attorney who read this book in manuscript wrote in a brief commentary on this addendum. Here's part of it:

> I don't know why you're even giving this option the slightest hint of approval. If one wants to be a lawyer, one must play the game—the law school game. The exceptions that warrant non-law-school study are rare to the point of nonexistence. It's obvious the Bar doesn't like this option. Neither should your readers.
>
> I'll be even more forceful: If someone doesn't want the irritation of law school, he or she shouldn't be a lawyer. Boring, boring, remember? And if that person can't get into a decent (top 100) school after reading *Planet Law School,* well, I'd find that hard to believe.
>
> I am not implying that I think self-study is less worthy. Quite the opposite. But reality is reality. —And it's the Bad Guys' reality.

I shall not argue the point.

* To get information, send your request for the "Law Reader Package." Enclose a 9x12 envelope addressed to yourself, with postage affixed—stamps, not a meter strip. To find how much postage to affix, call. However, the lines for incoming calls are open only from 10-noon and 2-4, EST. (Don't you just love a monopoly that knows how to act like one?)

Closing
Argument

A Descent into the Maelström

Off the coast of Norway, near an island named Lofoden, there runs a strange current. It's called the Maelström. Under the right circumstances, cross-currents are set up. These in turn generate whirlpools in the ocean. Sometimes, the whirlpools created are sizable. Small boats—including boats made of steel, weighing several tons—have been capsized and sunk in these whirlpools. Small boats made of wood have been torn apart by the stress.

The Maelström became famous in America in the early 1800s, when Edgar Allan Poe (the Stephen King of the day) wrote a short story called "A Descent into the Maelström." In it, he said there was just *one* whirlpool—but he said it was *enormous*. And he said the *whirlpool's* name was the Maelström. (Old Hollywood saying: "Never let the facts get in the way of a good story." Hollywood learned from Poe.) Naturally, in Poe's story, a small wooden boat gets caught in the current near Lofoden Island at the wrong time. It gets swept toward and then into the Maelström. Two men are aboard; brothers. According to Poe, this oceanic maw was so huge that they could look far down into it as their boat was whirled around within it, circling on the surface of the Maelström's "walls."

As their boat disintegrates, one of the brothers lashes himself to a mast. But the other has been more observant. As he'd looked about in terror, he'd retained sufficient presence of mind to notice that many objects caught in the Maelström had obviously gone all the way to its bottom and were now working their way back to the surface. All these objects were more or less short and cylindrical, almost round. Thinking fast, he decided his only hope for survival was to lash himself not to another mast, but to a *barrel*. He tried to shout to his brother, to explain his reasoning. But the roar within the Maelström was overwhelming. In desperation, he used gestures to try to communicate with his sibling. The other either could not comprehend his meaning—or would have none of it. There was but one survivor: he who saw what needed to be done, and did it.

Well, brother (or sister), the choice is yours. There is no background roar, and I have done what I could to warn you. The title of this book is *Planet Law School*. But just as Jupiter has weather systems, and Mars apparently has water (albeit frozen), so this planet called Law School can have its own Maelström, of the Edgar Allan Poe variety. Poe's Maelström was a fiction. The Law School Maelström is real.

You're already caught up in the current. That's why you've read this book. If you enter the Law School Maelström, you do so on your own: I've already been. Unlike the narrator of Poe's short story, I entered willingly, even eagerly. So will you, perhaps. But I hadn't a realistic understanding of what I was getting myself into. Like the survivor of Poe's short story, I have indeed lived to tell the tale—but not because I was smart and quick-witted, as he was; rather, I was merely lucky.

More than 40,000 people start law school every year. And another 40,000 or so have survived it at the end of three years. Were they lucky, as was I? Yes, but only in the sense that they too survived. For good or ill, they will never be the same. —And for many of them, the experience has permanently warped their soul. It may twist yours as well, for all time. (As for mine: well, the jury's still out.)

You shouldn't have to run such a risk. It shouldn't be that way. It shouldn't have been that way for me—nor for Scott Turow, Richard Kahlenberg, Chris Goodrich, George Roth, Mark McCormack, and hundreds of thousands of others. I have now given you the benefit of my experience, in a way that not even these other authors' books could. It is too late for us. It is not too late for you.

You cannot use what's in this book to *overcome* the Maelström of Law School. Such an effort would be quixotic, even suicidal. But by knowing in advance the nature of the phenomenon, you can keep it from overwhelming *you*. You can not only survive it, you can even *thrive* in it as you plunge deep and then gradually come to the surface again.

This is how the tale of Poe's narrator ends:

> A boat pulled me up—exhausted from fatigue—and (now that the danger was removed) speechless from the memory of its horror. Those who drew me on board were my old mates and daily companions—but they knew me no more than they would have known a traveller from the spirit-land. My hair, which had been raven-black the day before, was as white as you see it now. They say too that the whole expression of my countenance had changed. I told them my story—they did not believe it. I now tell it to *you*—and I scarcely expect you to put more faith in it than the merry fishermen of Lofoden.

"I told you so" is not what I want to be telling you years from now—at least, not under the circumstances in which that statement is usually made. But it's your call. (And by the way: my hair didn't turn white in law school—although my countenance definitely changed. And I did have to start wearing glasses.)

Whether or not you go to law school, I invite you to contact me at any time, via snail mail, in care of the publisher. If you have found particular advice especially worthwhile—or worthless—I'd be grateful if you'd let me know. Likewise if you wish I'd explained something more (or less) fully. The same thing goes for study aids or suggested reading. And if, on your own, you've discovered a new trick to the trade, or a new study aid, good book, etc., please share the news. There might be another edition of *Planet Law School* someday. If so, your input can help others, later: pro bono publico.

I wish you the best, whatever you decide to do. And I hope this book will have been a help to you in your life, whether or not yours is a life in the Law.

I'd like to end by saying something like "Don't let the bastards get you down." But from experience, I can say for certain that they *will* get you down. Just don't let them *keep* you down too long. And when it's all over, let's both hope you come up a winner.

Good luck, and good-bye.

"Atticus Falcon"
Member of the Bar
State of Flux

Appendix

Selected Resources / Vendors

Ace Seminars
(800) 748-6953

Examsmanship course, on-site or on tape, with manual and legal dictionary

American Bar Association
(800) 285-2221

Law Student Division
Young Lawyer Magazine
Lawyer's Guide to the Internet,
by G. Burgess Allison

American Law Institute
(800) 253-6397

Restatements of the Law, especially contracts and torts - *student edition*

The American Lawyer Mag.
(212) 973-2800

Aspen Law & Business
(800) 234-1660

Examples & Explanations series
first year:
Glannon, *The Law of Torts*
Glannon, *Civil Procedure*
May & Ides, *Constitutional Law: National Power and Federalism*
Ides & May, *Constitutional Law: Individual Rights*
Bloom & Brodin, *Crim. Procedure*
Singer & LaFond, *Criminal Law*
Blum, *Contracts*

Other E & E:
Best, *Evidence: E & E*

Essential Concepts series
Reutlinger, *Evidence*
Reutlinger, *Wills, Trusts & Estates*

other books
Knapp & Crystal, *Rules of Contract Law*
Makdisi, *Estates in Land and Future Interests*

Audio Tapes
"Fireside" series for first-year:
Torts (Glannon)

BarBri (Harcourt Brace)
(800) 621-0498

LSAT prep course
Bar Review course

Blond's
(Sulzburger & Graham)
(800) 436-2348

commercial outlines

audio tapes for first-year
Civ Pro (Kloppenberg)
Con Law (Reynolds)
Torts (Reynolds)

Blond's Multistate Questions

Court TV
(212) 973-2882

"Art & Science of Litigation" series
Video Library Service

John Delaney Publications
(201) 836-2543

books by John Delaney:
Learning Legal Reasoning,
How to Do Your Best on Law School
　Exams

Examsmanship course on tape

Emanuel
(800) 362-6835

commercial outlines
Emanuel's (available on CD/ROM),
　Siegel's, and Smith's Review

audio tapes for first-year
　Con Law (Mr. Emanuel)

misc. materials
First-Year Questions & Answers
　(book)

Strategies and Tactics for the MBE,
　book by Kimm Alayne Walton
Finz Multistate Method,
　by Steven Finz

Fleming's Fundamentals
of Law (FFL)

(800) 529-3926 (California only)
(714) 770-7030 (from outside CA)

audio tapes for first-year
Civ Pro, Con Law, Contracts, Crim
Law, Prop, Torts

Examsmanship course, on-site or
　on tape, with manual
Bar Review Course (Cal. only)

Gilbert (Harcourt Brace)
(800) 787-8717

Gilbert Law Summaries commercial outlines (available on disk)

audio tapes for first-year
"Legal Legends"--
Civ Pro (Freer)
Con Law (Nowak)
Contracts (Spak)
Crim. Law (Whitebread)
Prop. (Franzese)
Torts (Conviser)
(all but Con Law available as a First
Year Program" set)
　more "Legal Legends" tapes--
"Future Interests" (Carpenter)
other audio tapes: Evidence

Gilbert Law Summaries:
　Multistate Bar Exam

Stanley H. Kaplan, Inc.
(800) 527-8378

LSAT prep course

Legalines (Harcourt Brace)
(800) 787-8717

commercial outlines

Torts Questions & Answers
Criminal Law Questions & Answers

Lexis
(800) 528-1891

"Student Office" on-line software
Lexis-Nexis for Law Students,
　book by Steven Emanuel

Matthew Bender Co.
(800) 223-1940

first-year student's guide books:
Laurence & Minzer, *A Student's
Guide to Estates in Land and
Future Interests*
Schwartz, *A Student's Guide to the
Rule Against Perpetuities*
Siegel, *A Student's Guide to Ease-
ments, Real Covenants, and
Equitable Servitudes*

Other:
Fishman, *A Student's Guide to
Hearsay*

The Michie Company
(800) 446-3410

Imwinkelreid,
Evidentiary Foundations
Roberts & Schlueter,
Legal Research Guide

MicroMash-Nord
(800) 227-3926

Bar Review course

National Institute for
Trial Advocacy
(800) 225-6482

Aldisert, *Logic for Lawyers*
Bocchino & Sonenshein, *A Practical
Guide to Federal Evidence*
Ball, *Theater Tips and Tactics for
Jury Trials*

The National Jurist, Inc.
(800) 296-9656

National Jurist
magazine for law students

Scoring High on Bar Exam Essays
(book), with *How to Pass the Bar
Exam* (tapes) by Mary Campbell
Gallagher (sold as a set)

Employment Insider (newsletter)
Hiring Directory (periodical)
Judicial Clerkship Insider
(newsletter)

The National Law Journal
(800) 888-8300

newspaper for lawyers

Nolo Publishing
(800) 992-6656

Law on the Net, by James Evans
Legal Research,
by Elias & Levinkind

Numina
(800) 529-1065

CaseBriefs (canned briefs) and
SocraTutor (interactive) software

PMBR
(800) 523-0777

Finals Law School Exam Series -
commercial outlines
audio tapes
bar review tapes sold as first-
year tapes also

The Princeton Review
(800) 273-8439

LSAT prep course
Bar Review course

Siegel's (Emanuel)
(800) 362-6835

commercial outlines

Answers to Essay & Multiple
Choice Questions
(book for each first-year subject)

The Study Group
(800) 239-2349 or 840-6920

Bar Review course

Sulzburger-Graham
(800) 366-7086

The Resume Workbook,
by Carolyn Nutter

Sum & Substance
(800) 876-4457

commercial outlines

"Intensive Exam Writing (Essay)
Seminar - examsmanship
course on audio tapes
"Essay Exam Writing" audio tapes

audio tapes for first-year
Civ Pro (Miller or Blaze)
Con Law (Cheh) - Torts (Finz)
Crim Law (Dressler)
Prop (Juergensmeyer)

more tapes--
"Future Interests"
(Juergensmeyer)
"Winning at Moot Court"
"Interviewing with Law Firms"

Tiger Publishing
(800) 428-0456

audio tapes for first-year
"TextTour" (casebook-specific)
"Incredibly Easy" (generic):
Con Law, Civ Pro, Prop

Wentworth Miller's LEEWS
(800) 765-8246

Examsmanship course,
on-site or on tape - with manual

West Publishing

(800) 328-9352:

"Black Letter Law" commercial
outlines (available on disk)

Moynihan, Cornelius,
Intro. to the Law of Real Property

Trial Advocacy in a Nutshell,
by Paul Bergman
The Common Sense Rules of
Trial Advocacy, by Keith Evans

(800) 850-9378:

"Summer Associate Program" and
"Judicial Clerkship Program" -
training in on-line legal research
using Westlaw

Index

A

ABA *see* American Bar Association
abortion 30
accounting (course/s) 332
Ace Seminars 90-91
ACLJ (American Center for Law
  and Justice) 339
ACLU (American Civil Liberties
  Union) 339
actionable civil wrong 16
activities, extra-curricular 162-166
  see also Mock Trial, Moot Court,
  Client Counseling Competition,
  and Negotiations Exercises
Adachi, Jeff 112, 243
Adaptation to Life (book) 304
addictions (among lawyers) 301
administrative law 198
administrative law judges 258
Advance Placement courses
  (and college) 335
"Advanced Legal Drafting" (seminar)
  219
"Advanced Legal Writing & Editing"
  (seminar) 219
advocacy - oral 22, written 22
affirmative action 30, 360 *see also*
  harassment, racial *and* discrimina-
  tion, racial
Afro-American Students Assoc. 271
Ages of American Law, The (book) 320
agroikos 139, 147
Alaska, law license without law degree
  367
Aldisert, Ruggero J. 111, 200, 333
ALI *see* American Law Institute
ALJs *see* administrative law judges
Allison, G. Burgess 79
ALR *see* American Law Reports
American Law Reports 215
American Bar Association 346 -
  accredited law schools, 6 - "Law
  Day," 9 - Law Students Division
  (ABA/LSD), 175, 270 - law school
  salary survey, 37n. - publications,
  79 - audio tapes, 171
American Law Institute 61, 62
American Lawyer Magazine 40, 260,
  267, 269

American Lawyer Media, Inc. 260
American Standard Law Dictionary
  90
America's Bar Review (company) 249
Anarchy and Elegance (book) *see*
  Goodrich, Chris
"Anglo-American Law" (course) 320
*Answers to Essay and Multiple
  Choice Questions* (book) 93, 112
answers, model *see* exams
appearance, personal 272-273 -
  clothing, 279 *see also* "lookism"
applying to law school (essay for)
  358-366
Arendt, Hanna 208
Ariadne 308
Aristotle 32, 317
Arron, Deborah L. 283, 285, 292, 309
"Art & Science of Litigation" series
  (video) *see* Court TV
Art of Mediation, The (book) 176
Art of War, The (book) 309
Asian-American Students Assoc. 271
Aspen Law & Business - "Examples
  and Explanations" series 55-57, 59,
  167 - "Essential Terms and Concepts" series, 167, 183 - audio tapes,
  63
assault (tort) 85
assistantships, research, *see* research
  assistantships
associates, law firm 266
associates, summer, *see* clerkships,
  summer
Associated Press Style Book 217
Association of Trial Lawyers of
  America 175, 270, 271
"assume the risk" *see* "risk, assumption of"
At the Bar (book) 260
Athena IntelliSystems (software) 77
Athens, Athenians 306-307, 317
ATLA *see* Association of Trial
  Lawyers of America
Attorney General, U.S. 257
attorney-client privilege 327
audio tapes - first-year, 62-69 -
  examsmanship, 89-94 - bar review
  243-244
Authority 196 - "controlling," 196

B

Bachelor of Law (LL.B.) 13
Bachman, Walt 310
Bailey, F. Lee 331, 337n., 340, 353, 355
Ball, David 170
Ballantine's Law Dictionary 73
Bancroft-Whitney (publisher) 25n.
Bankruptcy Court 258
Bar Exam Survival Kit (book) 243
bar examinations (state) - independent study for, 241-243 - New York, 227-229 - California, 228, 229 - Nebraska, 227 - Colorado, 228, 243n. - Indiana, Iowa, Louisiana, Washington, 223
bar prep courses *see* bar review courses
bar review courses 231-233 - cost-sharing, 248 - free course, 248-249 - vendors, 249-250
Barbreaker (book) 243
BarBri (company) 232, 236-238, 249
"barrister" 169n.
Barron's Law Dictionary 73
Barzun, Jacques 217
Basic Concepts in the Law of Evidence with Irving Younger (video) 172
"Battered Wife" Syndrome 123
battery (tort) 85
Battle of Hastings *see* Hastings, Battle of
Baugh, L. Sue 217
Bed of Procrustes *see* Procrustes, Bed of
Bennett, Mark 176
Bergman, Paul 170
Best, Arthur 167
"Big Six" (first-year courses) 14-21
"Black Letter Law" 59, 88, 96-97, 119
Black Letter Law (commercial outlines) 59
Black Students Association 271
Black's Law Dictionary 73
Black's Law Publishing *see* Marino System, The (company)
Blackstone's Commentaries (book) 74
"blaming the victim" 35
Blaze, Doug 66

Bleckley, J. 143
blind grading 133, 155
"Blind Justice" (game) 105
Blond, Niel 63
Blond's - commercial outlines, 59 - audio tapes, 63 - bar materials, 235
Blond's Multistate Questions (book) 235
Bloom, Robert M. 56
Blum, Brian A. 56, 90
"Bobby McGee" (song) 317
Bocchino, Anthony 168
boilerplate 209
bomolokos 139
Boston U. Law School 355
Bottoms, Timothy 121
briefing a point of law 199
briefs, case *see* case briefs
briefs, moot court 163
Brill, Steven 260
Britain *see* United Kingdom
British East India Company 306
"British Rule," The 324
Brodin, Mark S. 56
Broken Contract (book) *see* Kahlenberg, Richard D.
Brook, Sanford A. 171
Brown, John 297
Burger, Warren 35-36, 177-179, 294, 312
Burke, Edmund 288, 313n.
Buckley, William F. 346
Burnham, William 331, 363
Business Organizations (subject) 227
Butterworth Company, The (publisher) 78
Byrd, Robert (Senator) 260

C

California Lawyer, The (newspaper) 267
California, law license, without law degree 368
California, Univ. of - Berkeley 355
California, Univ. of - Los Angeles 355
CALR *see* Computer-Assisted Legal Research

394

J

K

Khayyam, Omar 8, 311
Kierkegaard, Soren 299
Kinder Legal (company) 218
Kinder, Gary 218, 219
King Edward I *see* Edward I, King
King Lear (play) 277
King, Stephen 377
"Kingsfield Syndrome" 122-123, 126,
    129, 286, 343
Kipling, Rudyard 23
Kirkpatrick, Laird 168
Kissam, Philip C. 34n.
KISS-A-MIC 217
Kloppenberg, Lisa Ann 63
Knapp, Charles L. 56
Krevisky, Joseph 339n.
Kroll Associates 193
Kronman, Anthony T. 310, 319
"Ks" 61n.

L

labor law (career) 284
LaFond, John Q. 56
Lamborghini, Lisa 175
Langdell, Christopher 31, 122, 249n.
Latin -course/s, 335 - in the Law, 346-7
Latin for Lawyers (book) 74, 347
Law and Economics (school of thought)
    315-316, 323
"Law Day" 9n.
law dictionaries *see* dictionaries, legal
law firms, "scouting" 265-270
law journal *see* law review
law license without a law degree
    367-369
Law of Torts, The (book) 55
"Law Office" program 367ff.
Law on the Net (book) 79
Law Prose, Inc. (company) 218
"Law Reader" program 370
law review 151-155 - "write-on," 153 -
    outline collection, 155 - social skills,
    154 - and foreign studies, 189-190 -
    footnotes, 152
law school - enrollment, 6 - applicants,
    7 - applications (and decline in), 7 -
    full-time faculty, 40 - deans, 249n. -

(law school - continued)
    tuition rake-off by universities, 178
Law School Admissions Service
    (LSAS) 129
Law School Aptitude Test 334, 353 -
    prep course, 337-338
Law School Data Assembly Service
    334, 337, 357-358
Law Services Report (newsletter) 129
Law v. Life (book) 310, 358
"Law-in-a-Flash" 113, 325
Lawrence, Robert 109
Lawyers Co-op (publisher) 25n.
Lawyers' Guide to the Internet (book)
    79
Lawyer's Weekly (newspaper) 267
Learning Legal Reasoning (book) 57-
    58, 61, 62, 90, 92, 103, 111, 112, 200
LEEWS *see* Miller, Wentworth E.
Legal Analysis (course) *see* Legal
    Writing
legal assistants *see* paralegals
"legal basis of entitlement" 84
legal dictionaries *see* dictionaries,
    legal
Legal Dictionary for Bad Spellers
    339n.
legal encyclopedias 26, 215
Legal Essay Exam Writing System
    see Miller, Wentworth E.
Legal Essay Writing Workshop *see*
    Fleming's Fundamentals of Law
legal information industry 259-260
Legal Job Interview, The (book) 279
"Legal Legends" (Gilbert audio tapes)
Legal Methods (course) *see* Legal
    Writing
legal myths, laypeople's 321-329
legal reasoning *see* reasoning, legal
Legal Research (book) 214
Legal Research (course/s) 13, 22, 41,
    198, real-world: 196-199
Legal Research Guide (book) 215
Legal Writing (book) 217
Legal Writing - law school course, 13,
    22, 41 - in general, 88, 219 - real-
    world, 200-205
    Legalines (commercial outlines) 59,
    112
"legis" 77n.

M

N

T

Tangible Evidence (book) 171
tapes, audio, *see* audio tapes
TAs *see* teaching assistants
Tax Court 258
Tchaikovsky, Peter Ilych 260
teaching (pre-law) 347-348
teaching assistants 41, 42
Teen Court *see* Youth Court
temporary agencies *see* contract work
"Ten Commandments of Cross-
   Examination 172, 173
Tennyson, Alfred 124, 313
tenure 41
Terkel, Studs 260
Terrible Truth about Lawyers, The
   (book) 285, 303, 310 *see also*
   McCormack, Mark
Texas Lawyer (newspaper) 267
Texas, Univ. of, Law School 355 -
   professors' salaries, 37n. - and
   Professor "Perini," 123
"Text Tour" *see* Tiger Publishing Group
"The Lawyers Know Too Much" (poem)
   314
*Theater Tips and Strategies for Jury
   Trials* (book) 170
Theory of Moral Sentiments, A (book)
   316
Theseus 308
"Think/ing Like a Lawyer 33, 81, 83,
   88, 97, 119, 129, 203, 232
Thomas (Clarence) 314
Thomas M. Cooley Law School *see*
   Cooley, Thomas M., Law School
Thomson Corporation 25n.
Thomson, A. J. 217
Tiger Publishing Group 66-67, 169
title, tracing 195
To Be a Trial Lawyer (book) 331
Tolstoy, Leo 314
Tomlin, Lily 313
tort reform 324
Torts (book) 55
Torts (course) 13, 16-17
Torts Questions and Answers (book)
   112
torts, laypeople's myths 323

"tough love" 122
Touro College, Law School 37n.
"transactions" practice 255, 292
TransMedia (company) 173-174
Travolta, John 331
Trial Advocacy (book) 170
Trial Advocacy in a Nutshell (book)
   170
Trial and Practice Skills in a Nutshell
   (book) 170, 279
Trial Evidence (book and audio tape)
   168-169, 171, 174
Tribe, Lawrence 40, 253
Turow, Scott 122n., 128, 129n., 130n.
   One L quoted, 3, 4, 54, 81, 87, 95,
   107, 115, 286, 291, 296, 308 - *One L*
   discussed, 121-127
Twain, Mark 108
typing, typewriters (exams) 108n.,
   346

U

U.S. Supreme Court *see* Supreme
   Court, U.S.
UCLA *see* California, Univ. of - Los
   Angeles
Underhill, Stefan 309
"Understanding the Law" (book series)
   57, 100
"Unintended Consequences," Law of
   196
United Kingdom, legal education 177
"utility maximization" 135 (rape)
   315, 316 (Law and Economics)

V

Vaillant, George 304
van Zyverden, Bill 313
Vermont, law license without a law
   degree 369, 370
vice, in the pursuit victory 292
Video Library Service *see* Court TV
Virginia, law license without a law
   degree 370